ASP.NET Web Development with Macromedia Dreamweaver MX 2004

COSTAS HADJISOTIRIOU WITH
RACHEL ANDREW
AND KEVIN MARSHALL

APress Media, LLC

ASP.NET Web Development with Macromedia Dreamweaver MX 2004
Copyright ©2004 by Costas Hadjisotiriou, Rachel Andrew, and Kevin Marshall
Originally published by Apress 2004

ISBN 978-1-59059-348-6   ISBN 978-1-4302-0674-3 (eBook)
DOI 10.1007/978-1-4302-0674-3

Trademarked names may appear in this book. Rather than use a trademark symbol with every occurrence of a trademarked name, we use the names only in an editorial fashion and to the benefit of the trademark owner, with no intention of infringement of the trademark.

Lead Editor: Chris Mills

Technical Reviewer: Matthieu Nuaud

Editorial Board: Steve Anglin, Dan Appleman, Gary Cornell, James Cox, Tony Davis, John Franklin, Chris Mills, Steve Rycroft, Dominic Shakeshaft, Julian Skinner, Jim Sumser, Karen Watterson, Gavin Wray, John Zukowski

Project Manager: Nate McFadden

Copy Manager: Nicole LeClerc

Copy Editor: Nancy Depper

Production Manager: Kari Brooks

Production Editor: Laura Cheu

Compositor: Kinetic Publishing Services, LLC

Proofreader: Patrick Vincent

Indexer: Brenda Miller

Artist: Kinetic Publishing Services, LLC

Cover Designer: Kurt Krames

Manufacturing Manager: Tom Debolski

To my twin boys, Emilio and Luca, who keep me smiling.

—Costas Hadjisotiriou

Contents at a Glance

Contents

About the Author

Costas Hadjisotiriou earned several engineering degrees before making the switch to web design, databases, and gadgets. He is fascinated with ASP.NET and PDA programming. He balances his various web-programming contracts with trying to be a good family man, and for the last four years, he has been successfully working from his home in Spain, a lifestyle he highly recommends.

Rachel Andrew is an experienced web developer and a director of edgeofmyseat.com, a UK-based web solutions company. Rachel is a member of the Web Standards Project on the Dreamweaver Task Force, and she hopes to encourage best practices in the support and use of W3C standards in Dreamweaver. In addition to coauthoring several books, Rachel writes for various magazines and resource sites, both online and offline. When not writing code or writing about writing code, Rachel spends time with her daughter, tries to encourage people to use Debian GNU/Linux, studies with the Open University, and enjoys a nice pint of beer.

Kevin Marshall lives in Perth, Scotland, and he is a senior programmer with WebXeL.com Ltd. He has been involved in computer programming since 1990, web-based programming using ASP since 1997, and building ASP.NET applications since ASP.NET Beta 2 was released in 2001. He has been an avid Dreamweaver user since version 1 was launched, and with the release of MX, he has moved into developing extensions for ASP.NET and Dreamweaver MX / MX2004. These extensions can be found at `www.webxel-dw.co.uk`. Kevin is also a regular contributor to the Macromedia newsgroups, where he provides ASP.NET-related advice and assistance to other Dreamweaver users.

About the
Technical Reviewer

Matthieu Nuaud discovered computing in the mid-eighties on his brother's Commodore 64. A few years later, after earning his degree in Economics and postgraduate qualification in Information Systems Development, he became involved in various projects relating to project management, database application development, and information security. Now living in Spain, he is currently focused on developing web applications, mainly using ColdFusion, ASP, and ASP.NET.

Introduction

ASP.NET IS NOT ONLY the latest version of Microsoft's Active Server Pages (ASP), it is a whole new programming concept altogether. This incredibly popular server-side scripting language is based on the .NET Framework, and it combines unrivalled developer productivity with performance and reliability.

Dreamweaver MX 2004 is the newest version of the popular integrated web site design tool. It enables quick and efficient web site design and programming and comes with built-in support for ASP.NET and XML web services.

Whether you are an experienced ASP.NET developer and Dreamweaver user or a beginner, this book guides you through the web-development process at the right level. It shows you how to rapidly develop ASP.NET web applications with a minimum of effort. You learn about the .NET Framework, how ASP.NET fits in and interacts with other components, and how to master the ASP.NET controls via Dreamweaver MX 2004.

In summary, this book covers:

- The .NET Framework

- Using and extending the Dreamweaver MX 2004 interface

- ASP.NET programming in VB .NET

- Using and expanding ASP.NET controls

- Interacting with databases

- Using server behaviors in Dreamweaver MX 2004

- Creating data-driven ASP.NET applications

- Incorporating XML web services

- Coding with best practice principles

Let's get started with an introduction to the new Dreamweaver MX 2004.

CHAPTER 1

Introducing Dreamweaver

IN THIS CHAPTER, we give you a brief overview of the Dreamweaver MX and Dreamweaver MX 2004 workspace including the locations of all the common elements in the program. By the end of this chapter, you will be familiar enough with the Dreamweaver workspace to work your way though this book's subsequent chapters.

The Dreamweaver workspace has four main sections. The numbers listed with each section correspond with the numbers shown in Figure 1-1, although your display layout may vary slightly because Dreamweaver allows you to rearrange all the elements by dragging and dropping the panels within the workspace.

- Document window (1)

- Insert bar (2)

- Property inspector (3)

- Grouped panels (4)

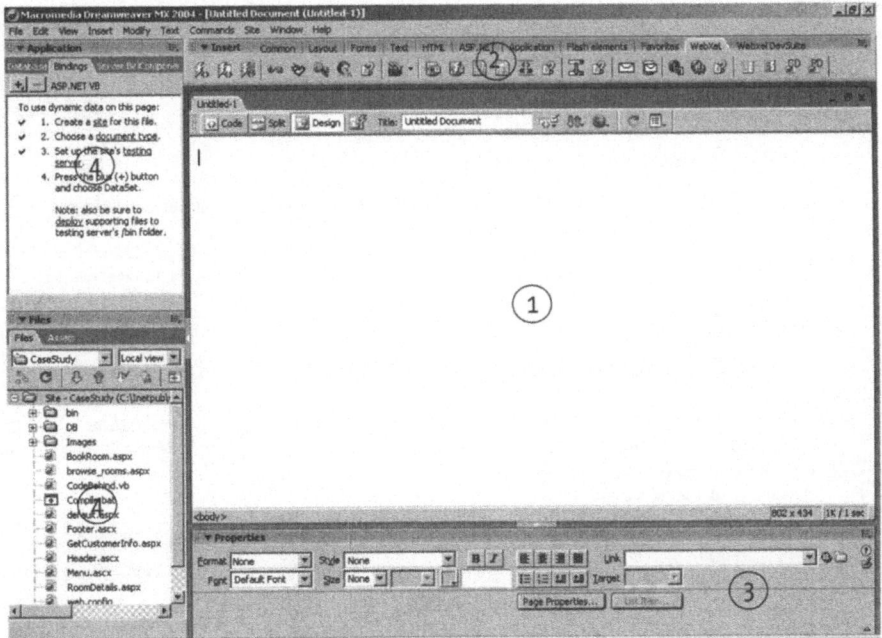

Figure 1-1. The Dreamweaver workspace

Document Window

The document window is the design surface of your document; it is where all the elements that make up your document are inserted. The document window can display the content of your document in three possible views.

- **Design view:** The document window displays your document as it will look when displayed in a web browser.

- **Code view:** The document window displays the HTML markup and any server-side code that makes up your document.

- **Split view:** The document window displays Design view and Code view as two panes with a horizontal resize handle to adjust the size of each pane, as shown in Figure 1-2. This is the most useful view when developing ASP.NET applications.

Another useful feature of the document window is Live Data view, which simulates roughly how the page will look when previewed in a web browser. Although not an exact representation of what a browser will render, Live Data view will show an approximate representation within the Dreamweaver document window.

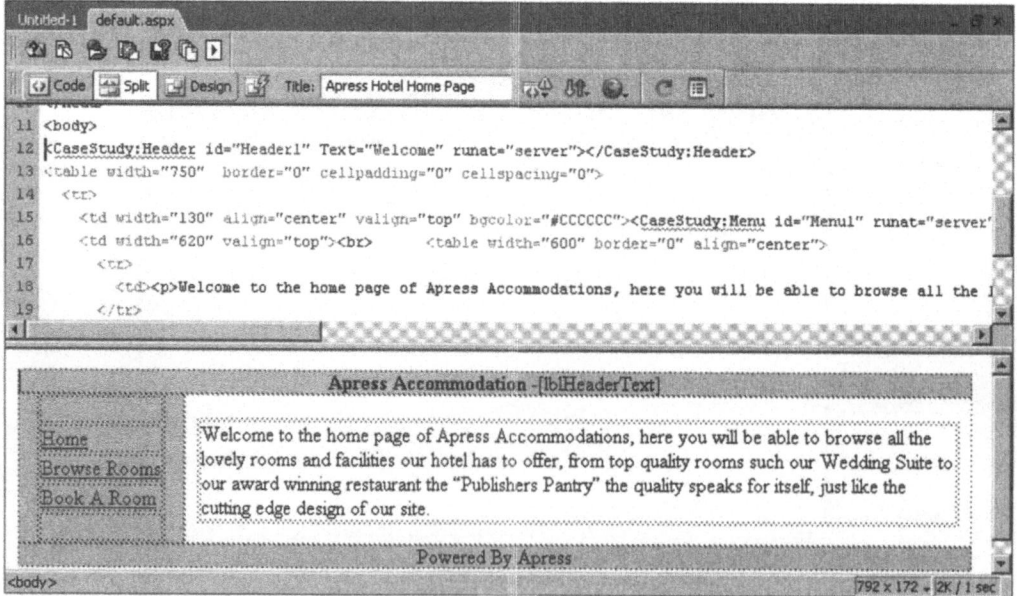

Figure 1-2. Split view

Property Inspector

The Property inspector is a very handy tool that allows you to change attributes on most HTML tags in a very efficient manner. It constantly changes its contents to suit the currently selected element in your document. If you select a block of text, the Property inspector will display fields and buttons that allow you to change the attributes of the selected element such as color, font, and other attributes, as shown in Figure 1-3. If you select a table, the Property inspector will display fields that directly relate to the <table> tag such as cell spacing and cell padding, as shown in Figure 1-4. You will quickly discover that the Property inspector is probably the most useful element of the Dreamweaver interface.

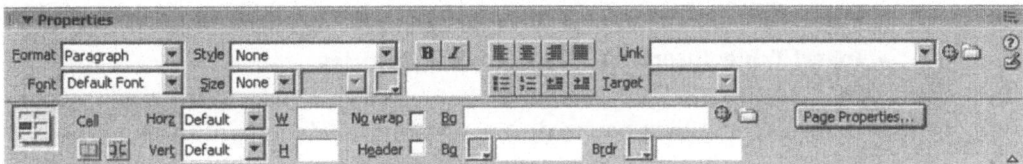

Figure 1-3. The Property inspector when text is selected

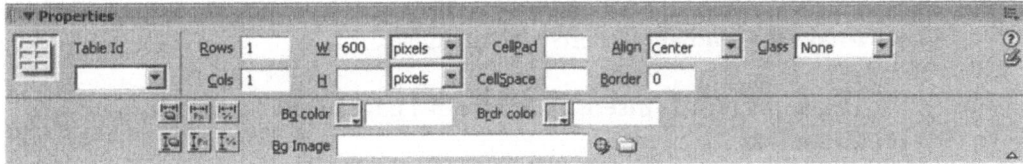

Figure 1-4. The Property inspector when a table is selected

Insert Bar

The Insert bar is used to insert elements into your document. It contains categorized tabs, each containing a collection of icons relevant to the tab's category. By positioning the mouse pointer at a specific location on the document's design surface and clicking an icon in the Insert bar, the associated element can be easily inserted into the document at that location.

The Common Tab

The Common tab of the Insert bar (shown in Figure 1-5) contains icons that can be used to insert many commonly used elements.

Figure 1-5. The Insert bar: Common tab

Icons from left to right are

- **Hyperlink**: Inserts a link to another page.

- **Email Link**: Inserts a `mailto:` link.

- **Named Anchor**: Inserts an anchor link.

- **Insert Table**: Inserts an HTML table `<table>` tag.

- **Draw Layer**: Allows you to draw a layer on the document surface. The end result is an absolutely positioned `<div>` tag with the width and height corresponding to what you drew.

- **Image**: Inserts an image `<img>` tag.

- **Image Placeholder**: Inserts a blank image.

- **Fireworks HTML**: Inserts HTML from a page created with Macromedia Fireworks.

- **Flash**: Allows you to insert Flash elements into a web page.

- **Rollover Image**: Inserts the code to create an image that changes when the mouse pointer moves over it.

- **Navigation Bar**: Inserts a navigation menu.

- **Horizontal Rule**: Inserts an `<hr>` tag.

- **Date**: Inserts the current date.

- **Tabular Data**: Inserts tabular data from external files.

- **Comments**: Inserts an HTML comment.

- **Tag Chooser**: Opens the Tag Chooser to allow selection of tags not present in the Insert bar.

The ASP.NET Tab

The ASP.NET tab of the Insert bar (shown in Figure 1-6) contains icons that can be used to insert many commonly used ASP.NET elements.

Figure 1-6. The Insert bar: ASP.NET tab

Icons from left to right are

- **Register Custom Tag**: Inserts a `Register TagPrefix` line

- **Import Namespace**: Inserts an `Import Namespace` line

- **Trimmed Form Element**: Inserts code for a trimmed `Form` element

- **Trimmed QueryString Element**: Inserts code for a trimmed `QueryString` element

- **Runat Server**: Inserts `runat="server"`

- **Bound Data**: Inserts Bound Data tags (`<%# %>`)

- **Page_Load**: Inserts code for the `Page_Load` procedure

- **Button**: Inserts HTML from a page created with Macromedia Fireworks

- **asp:CheckBox**: Inserts an `<asp:CheckBox>` tag

- **asp:CheckBoxList**: Inserts an `<asp:CheckBoxList>` tag

- **asp:DropDownList**: Inserts an `<asp:DropDownList>` tag

- **asp:ImageButton**: Inserts an `<asp:ImageButton>` tag

- **asp:Label**: Inserts an `<asp:Label>` tag

- **asp:ListBox**: Inserts an `<asp:ListBox>` tag

- **asp:RadioButton**: Inserts an `<asp:RadioButton>` tag

- **asp:RadioButtonList**: Inserts an `<asp:RadioButtonList>` tag

- **asp:TextBox**: Inserts an `<asp:TextBox>` tag

- **More Tags**: Opens the Tag Chooser to allow selection of tags not present in the Insert bar

Grouped Panels

The grouped panels contain many different panels categorized for specific tasks. The following list of panel groups outlines some of the commonly used panels for working on an ASP.NET application. If you can't see any of the grouped panels, display them by selecting the panels you want to see from the Windows menu.

- **Design**: This panel contains tabs to manage CSS Styles. It's worth noting that the HTML Styles tab has been removed in Dreamweaver MX 2004.

- **Application**: This panel is where most of the ASP.NET functionality is located. You can define database connections and insert server behaviors from this panel.

- **Files**: This panel is where all the files that make up your application are managed. You can create, organize, and delete files using this panel; it also has built-in functionality for managing the files on a remote server as well as publishing and synchronizing local and remote files.

Figure 1-7 shows the Files panel with the contents of the case study application from Chapter 11.

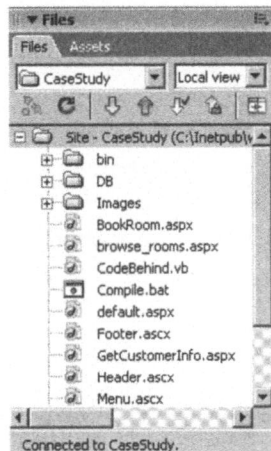

Figure 1-7. The Files panel

Figure 1-8 shows the Application panel's Databases tab containing a defined database connection.

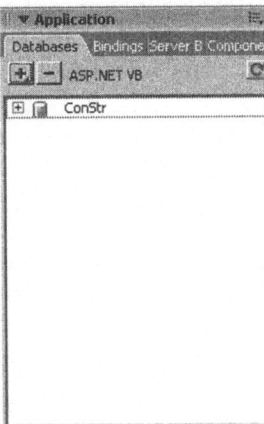

Figure 1-8. The Application panel: Databases tab

Figure 1-9 shows the Application panel's Bindings tab containing the field list for a dataset.

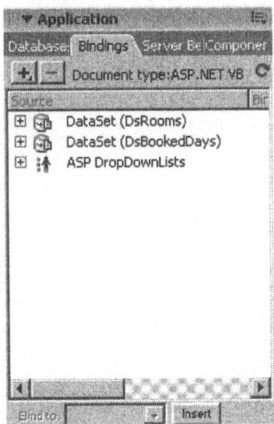

Figure 1-9. The Application panel: Bindings tab

Figure 1-10 shows the Application panel's Server Behaviors tab containing some server behaviors.

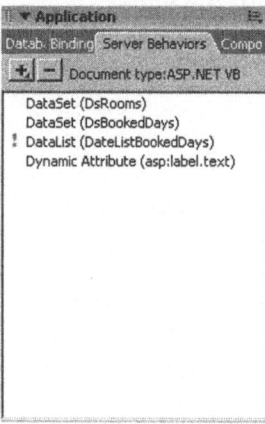

Figure 1-10. The Application panel: Server Behaviors tab

Creating a New Page

To create a new ASP.NET page in Dreamweaver MX and MX 2004, select
File ➤ New, as shown in Figure 1-11.

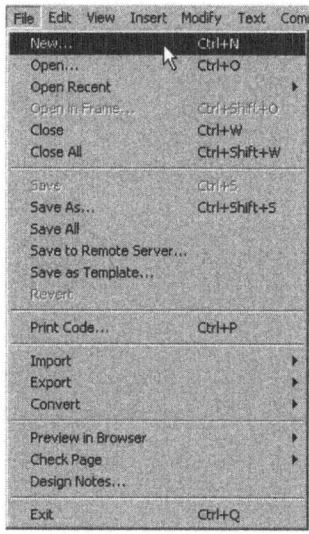

Figure 1-11. The File menu

Upon selecting this menu option, the New Document dialog box will appear.
To create an ASP.NET VB page, select the options shown in Figure 1-12.

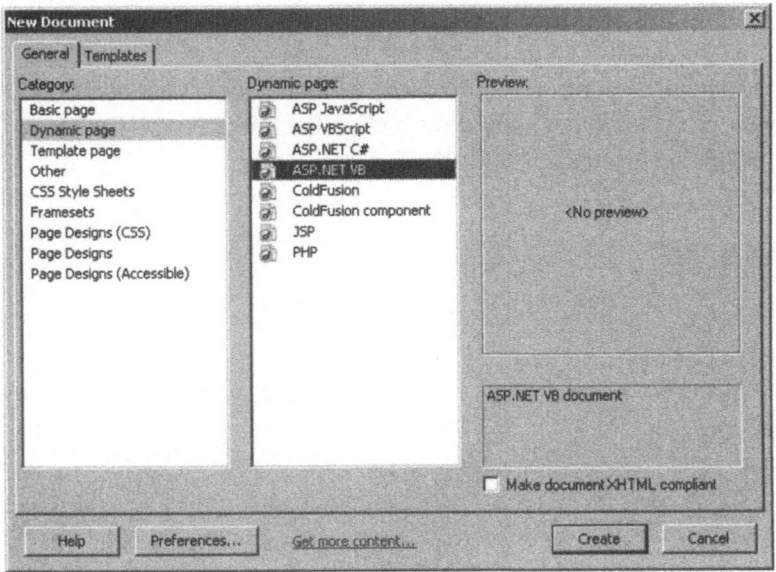

Figure 1-12. The New Document dialog box

You can also create a new page simply by right-clicking the Site panel and selecting New File from the context menu, as shown in Figure 1-13.

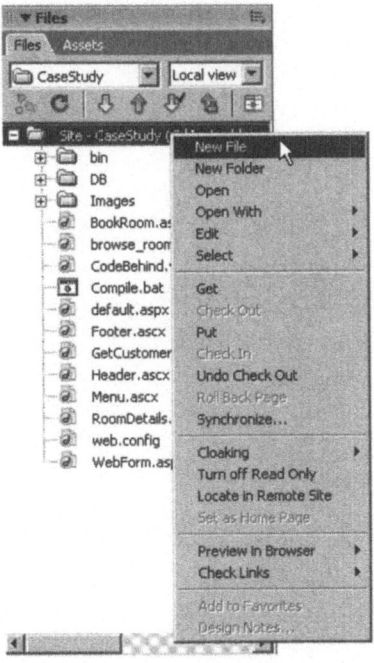

Figure 1-13. Creating a file using the Site context menu

Summary

This chapter gave you a brief introduction to the workspace in Dreamweaver MX and Dreamweaver MX 2004. You should now be familiar enough with the interface to work through the exercises in this book.

CHAPTER 2

Web Standards in Dreamweaver

With the launch of Dreamweaver MX 2004, Macromedia moves further toward web standards support and incorporates more features that enable web designers to put best practices to work when developing web sites. Using clean, standard markup and separating content from presentation by way of Cascading Style Sheets (CSS) can make your job as an application developer far easier. For example, if you are creating an application that allows clients to update their own pages, CSS controls how that content is formatted so it is more likely to fit the look and feel of the whole site.

In this chapter, we will focus on the use of XHTML and CSS when working in Dreamweaver. You will discover why developing in XHTML instead of HTML is a good idea, how to start working in valid XHTML Transitional, how to use CSS within Dreamweaver, and how to create a tables-based layout in Dreamweaver using XHTML Transitional. You will also learn how to convert that layout to XHTML Strict using CSS to replace elements that are not allowed in a document with a Strict DOCTYPE, how to create a site with a CSS layout in Dreamweaver, and how to handle older browsers.

Authoring Valid XHTML

This chapter assumes that you are working in XHTML; however, most of the following is equally valid if you are working in HTML because Dreamweaver will add the correct markup. The DOCTYPE specifies which version of (X)HTML you are using.

If you haven't made the change to XHTML yet, here are some reasons why you might want to make that move:

- **Cleaner markup:** The flexibility that current desktop browsers allow can lead to untidy, sloppy markup. A valid XHTML document can easily be read by traditional browsers as well as other devices (such as PDAs and other mobile devices) that lack the processing power needed to interpret sloppy markup.

- **Greater platform independence**: XHTML's insistence on clean, structured markup makes it far easier to port documents to different environments. XHTML's strict nature means it is far more likely to be displayed correctly on all devices.

- **Accessibility**: XHTML's adherence to strict rules makes it easier for alternative devices such as Braille readers, screen readers, and other assistive technologies to interpret the content and present it to the user in a useful and navigable manner. A valid XHTML document leaves no room for non-standard markup, which eliminates the chance of anything in the document interfering with its accessibility. Making your document accessible to alternate devices also makes it more accessible to search engine spiders. Clean, correct markup is far easier for a robot to index.

- **Forward compatibility**: There will be no future version of HTML. Browser manufacturers are looking toward the future with new releases, and although it is unlikely that support for HTML will be dropped anytime soon, it is always a good idea to work to the newest standards. By doing so, your pages are far less likely to break when the next versions of the major browsers appear on the scene. As you will see later in this chapter, working with the Transitional DOCTYPE enables you to create XHTML documents that will be displayed properly in older browsers but still validate against an XHTML DOCTYPE.

- **Learning the rules of XML**: XML is here to stay. By writing XHTML documents, you are adhering to the strict rules of XML markup, which will stand you in good stead in the future. Getting into the habit of creating well-formed documents will make creating XML documents for different applications in the future second nature to you.

- **Integrating with other XML applications**: XHTML allows the incorporation of tags from other XML definitions, such as Mathematical Markup Language (MathML), Synchronized Multimedia Integration Language (SMIL), and Scalable Vector Graphics (SVG). This might not seem particularly useful to many designers and developers today, but it is likely to become more important as uptake and use of other XML applications grows. Learning XHTML at this relatively early stage will make your résumé and skills very up to date.

- **Page load time**: Valid XHTML documents load faster because the browser does not need to reinterpret bad markup. HTML is lenient about unclosed tags and improperly nested markup, so it leaves more to the interpretation of the browser. Additionally, HTML's inherent flexibility encourages sloppy markup, which in turn can add load time onto the page through increased file size. As you move toward creating XHTML pages that follow the Strict Document Type Declaration (DTD), you need to move style and presentation aspects into CSS, thus trimming your pages down further.

Despite the increasing numbers of people with broadband high-speed connections, page-load time is still an important issue. Although writing valid, well-structured HTML will also enable faster-loading pages, XHTML enforces that strictness and prevents sloppiness from creeping in. Dreamweaver MX 2004 makes it very easy to switch from working in HTML to working in XHTML, and there is no reason why the change should be problematic for you. Sites written in XHTML perform just as well in older browsers as HTML 4 sites, so there are no issues with backward compatibility. If you are about to start work on a new site with the help of this book, why not take the plunge and go XHTML!

The Rules of Writing XHTML

For anyone with a reasonable understanding of HTML, XHTML is not difficult to learn, and of course, Dreamweaver MX will help you all the way. All you need to do is follow a few simple rules that are common to all XML (and therefore XHTML) documents.

Document Type Declaration

An XHTML document must validate against one of the following three XHTML DTDs:

- XHTML Strict

```
<!DOCTYPE html PUBLIC "-//W3C//DTD XHTML 1.0 Strict//EN"
  "http://www.w3.org/TR/xhtml1/DTD/xhtml1-strict.dtd">
```

- XHTML Transitional

```
<!DOCTYPE html PUBLIC "-//W3C//DTD XHTML 1.0 Transitional//EN"
  http://www.w3.org/TR/xhtml1/DTD/xhtml1-transitional.dtd">
```

- XHTML Frameset

```
<!DOCTYPE html PUBLIC "-//W3C//DTD XHTML 1.0 Frameset//EN"
    "http://www.w3.org/TR/xhtml1/DTD/xhtml1-frameset.dtd">
```

As you will see later in this chapter, XHTML Strict does not allow any deprecated elements or framesets, XHTML Transitional supports deprecated elements (those elements that have been flagged for removal in future versions of [X]HTML) but not frames, and XHTML Frameset is the version that supports deprecated elements and frames. There must be a DOCTYPE declaration in the document above the <html> tag, and it must reference one of the XHTML DTDs. Dreamweaver MX inserts the XHTML Transitional DTD by default when you create a document with the Make document XHTML compliant check box selected in the New Document dialog box, as shown in Figure 2-1. However, if you are creating a frameset, it will insert the Frameset DTD.

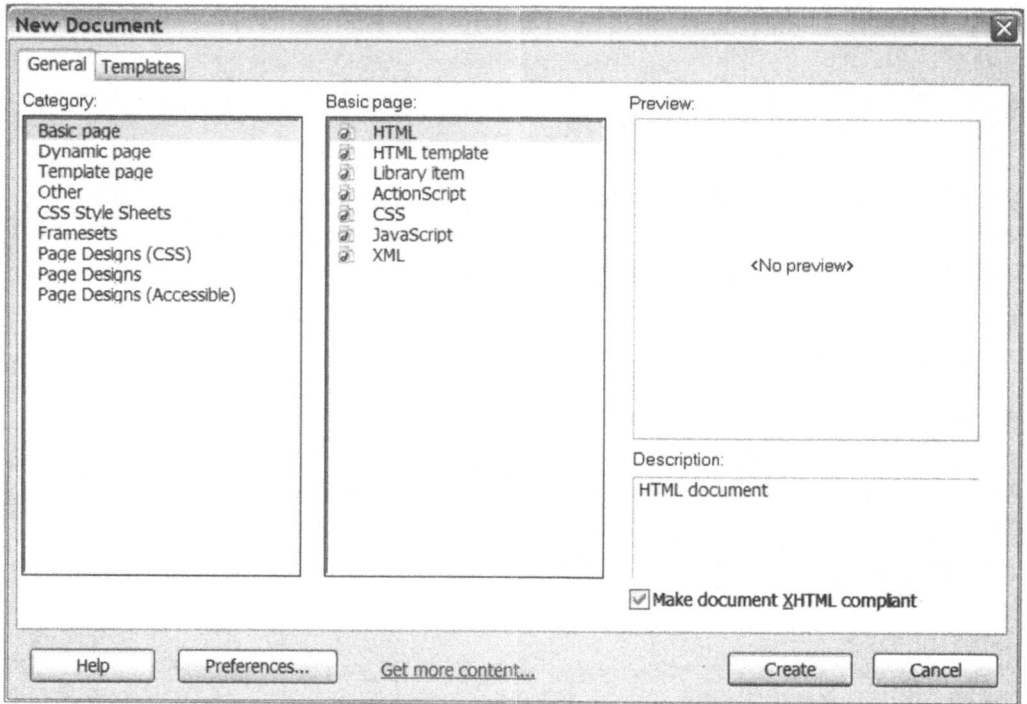

Figure 2-1. The New Document dialog box

Today's web contains a varied mix of web sites; some are written to the new standards of HTML 4.01 or XHTML and others are a mixture of HTML versions utilizing browser-specific tags and quirks for specific effects. In order to handle this, the latest browser releases use the DOCTYPE to decide whether the document's author expects a standards-compliant browser to render the page or whether the page was written for older, non–standards-compliant browsers and might rely on quirky, non-standard behavior. DOCTYPE "sniffing," as it has come to be described, relies on the fact that most of these quirky documents either have no DOCTYPE or use an old DOCTYPE.

Using any of the XHTML examples shown earlier will cause modern browsers to switch into standards-compliant mode and render your pages relatively close to the W3C specifications. Please note that using the XML declaration or prolog

(`<?xml version="1.0" encoding="UTF-8" ?>`) at the top of your document will switch Internet Explorer 6 back into Quirks mode, causing IE 6 to assume that you want to display your pages as they would appear in older versions of browsers, whereas Netscape 6+ and Mozilla will display your pages in a standards-compliant manner. This was added in the previous version of Dreamweaver, so if you want to work to standards-compliant mode, the best advice is to remove it. Your pages will still be valid XHTML documents without it.

If you are still working in HTML, you can also work in standards-compliant mode by using a complete HTML 4.01 DOCTYPE (that contains a URL).

```
<!DOCTYPE HTML PUBLIC "-//W3C//DTD HTML 4.01 ➡
Transitional//EN" "http://www.w3.org/TR/html4/loose.dtd">
```

If you use an incomplete DOCTYPE (like the following one) or no DOCTYPE at all, IE 6, Mozilla, and Netscape 6 will assume that you want your pages to look as they did in older versions of browsers and revert to their Quirks mode.

```
<!DOCTYPE HTML PUBLIC "-//W3C//DTD HTML 4.01 Transitional//EN">
```

Quotation Marks

All attribute values must be enclosed in quotation marks. In the following `<img>` tag, the height and width attributes are incorrectly defined:

```
<img height=100 width=300 alt="my logo" src="logo.gif" />
```

Here is the correct way to do it:

```
<img height="100" width="300" alt="my logo" src="logo.gif" />
```

Although previous versions of Dreamweaver tended to quote attributes correctly, you may find that code snippets that you or other developers on your team use may not be as carefully written. Selecting Commands ➤ Clean up XHTML will add quotation marks where they are needed in your document.

Case Sensitivity

Element and attribute names must be in lowercase. Both of the following lines are incorrect:

```
<IMG HEIGHT="100" WIDTH="300" ALT="my logo" SRC="logo.gif" />
<img HEIGHT="100" WIDTH="300" ALT="my logo" SRC="logo.gif" />
```

15

Here is the correct XHTML:

```
<img height="100" width="300" alt="my logo" src="logo.gif" />
```

If you have always written your HTML tags in uppercase to easily differ-entiate between tags and content, you may find this change difficult at first. JavaScript event handlers such as `onclick` or `onmouseover` must also be written in lowercase.

The following JavaScript is incorrect:

```
onMouseOver="MM_swapImage('img1','','i/button01b.gif',1)"
```

Here is the correct way to do it:

```
onmouseover="MM_swapImage('img1','','i/button01b.gif',1)"
```

When working with an XHTML document, Dreamweaver MX will generate lowercase code, including JavaScript. If you are working in HTML, you can choose whether to use uppercase or lowercase for HTML tags in the Preferences dialog box. However, it is not a bad idea to begin to work in lowercase—even in HTML—because it will be necessary in the future.

Closing Tags for Nonempty Elements

A **nonempty element** is a tag that contains something between the start tag and the end tag. Some HTML elements can be written without the closing tag; for example, the closing `</p>` tag of the paragraph element is optional and therefore omitted by many HTML authors. In XHTML however, all elements must be closed.

The following, although valid in HTML, is incorrect in XHTML:

```
<p>This is some text formatted in a paragraph.
<p> This is the second paragraph.
```

Here is the XHTML way of marking up the same text:

```
<p>This is some text formatted in a paragraph.</p>
<p> This is the second paragraph.</p>
```

Dreamweaver MX closes all nonempty elements whether you are working in HTML or XHTML, and will add closing tags when you run the Clean up HTML command.

Empty Elements

Empty elements are those HTML tags that stand alone and do not include anything between the beginning and end tag, such as ‹br› and ‹hr›. In XHTML, these need to be closed—‹br› and ‹hr› become ‹br /› and ‹hr /›.

 NOTE *There is a space after the tag and before the forward slash. Although it is also correct to close your tags without this additional space, the space will allow those browsers that do not recognize XHTML to display your content correctly.*

Dreamweaver uses the correct syntax for empty tags when generating markup in an XHTML document and also when cleaning up XHTML.

Nesting

An XHTML document must be well formed. This means that all tags must nest correctly—the first tag you open should be the last tag you close. Incorrect nesting is illegal in SGML-based languages but was tolerated by browsers.

Here is an example of badly formed markup:

```
<p><strong>This is bold text.</p></strong>
```

Here is the proper way of nesting the tags:

```
<p><strong>This is bold text.</strong></p>
```

Dreamweaver nests elements correctly and will also correct the nesting of elements when cleaning up XHTML.

Attribute Minimization

Attribute minimization is the practice of writing only the attribute's name without specifying a value. This sets the attribute to its default value. Attributes in valid XHTML documents cannot be minimized. All attributes should be written as name/value pairs even if the value is the same as the name.

This is incorrect in XHTML:

```
<input type="checkbox" name="checkbox" id="checkbox" value="True" checked />
```

Here is the corrected version:

```
<input type="checkbox" name="checkbox" id="checkbox" value="True"
    checked="checked" />
```

When you convert an HTML document into XHTML, Dreamweaver inserts this correct markup and converts minimized attributes to name/value pairs.

Here is an example of an XHTML document that complies with the guidelines:

```
<?xml version="1.0" encoding="iso-8859-1"?>
<!DOCTYPE html PUBLIC "-//W3C//DTD XHTML 1.0 Transitional//EN" ➥
"http://www.w3.org/TR/xhtml1/DTD/xhtml1-transitional.dtd">
<html xmlns="http://www.w3.org/1999/xhtml">
  <head>
    <title>My XHTML Document</title>
  </head>
  <body>
    <p><strong>Hello! World</strong></p>
  </body>
</html>
```

Best Practices for Markup

In the future, we will all need to think more about the various devices that are accessing our web sites. In addition to the devices that enable people with disabilities to access the web, PDAs, phones, and similar devices are now being used. Using HTML tags inappropriately causes enough problems when the content is being accessed with traditional web browsers; the problems are even greater when the content is accessed by devices likely to have a more limited capacity.

Working in a visual-development environment enables rapid development of documents and web sites. However, it can cause us to forget what is actually happening in the code as we move things around the document window, aiming for the right look and feel for our latest project. By structuring a document badly or using tags inappropriately, your document may validate, but it could still cause accessibility problems for those on alternative devices.

Deciding whether your document is structured logically is not something that an automated validator can do easily; however, it is very easy to do yourself. Simply turn off CSS in your browser or remove your stylesheet link and see if the content in your document is still logically presented once it defaults to the browser's standard way of styling the elements.

In addition to checking that your document looks sensible and well structured, consider the following points.

Do Not Use Font Tags for Styling and Sizing Text

Today's widely used browsers can all use CSS for styling text. Although you may be reluctant to move to CSS for page layout, there is simply no reason to ignore the benefits of using CSS instead of font tags for text styling. The cleaner markup that results from the removal of font tags leads to faster downloads and easier maintenance and redesign of a site. All standard desktop browsers released in the last 5 years have CSS support for text styling.

Use Heading Tags for Structure

The heading tags (<h1> to <h6>) provided by (X)HTML are designed to give structure to the document; they are not supposed to be an easy way to have different-sized titles. Although you may use CSS to alter the appearance of these tags, make sure that you are using them logically within the document so that any browser or device that does not recognize the CSS can still follow the structure. A related issue is the use of paragraph (<p>) tags with a larger font size used as a heading. If the text is a heading, use a heading tag for it.

Do Not Use Block Quotes for Indentation

For the same reasons that you should not use the heading tags simply for sizing, you should not use block quote tags to indent text. A nontraditional browser may well interpret <blockquote> as a quote; if you want to indent text for appearance only, use CSS to create a custom class for this purpose. For example, to create a custom class in Dreamweaver, create a new CSS class named .indent. Give this class a padding of 40 pixels on the left. To indent any paragraph, simply apply the custom class.

```
<p class="indent">This is my paragraph that I would like to be indented.</p>
```

This gives you far more control over the indentation than simply using block quote tags, and it ensures that your document remains understandable.

Mark Lists As Lists

In HTML 4.01 and XHTML there are three nondeprecated list definitions to choose from: ordered list, unordered list, and definition list. It is important to use the correct type of list when entering your information—do not simply choose one for visual effect. Once again, if you are going for a certain look, use CSS to achieve it.

Ordered Lists

Use ordered lists for a list of items numbered in sequential order, for example, a list of step-by-step instructions or ranked items.

```
<ol>
        <li>list item one</li>
        <li>list item two</li>
</ol>
```

This is displayed in most browsers as shown in Figure 2-2.

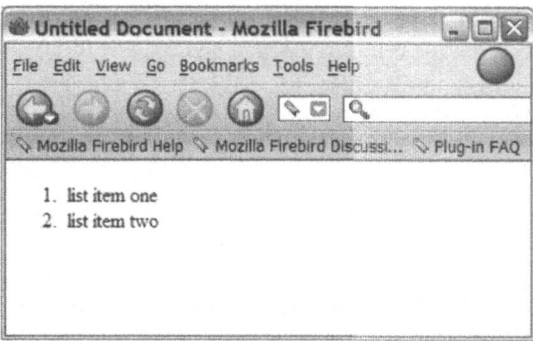

Figure 2-2. Ordered list in a browser

Unordered Lists

Use unordered lists for a list of unordered items, for example, a list of attributes.

```
<ul>
        <li>list item one</li>
        <li>list item two</li>
</ul>
```

This is displayed in most browsers as shown in Figure 2-3.

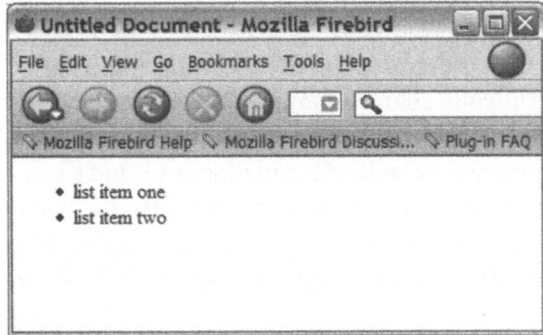

Figure 2-3. Unordered list in a browser

Definition Lists

Use a definition list if you have a list of items and explanations. By using this type of list, you make it clear to someone using an assistive technology such as a screen reader (or other device that can only see the structure of the document) that the list contains items and their definitions.

If you create this kind of list just by altering the presentational aspects of the page, your intentions may not be clear to someone who cannot see that presentation. The definition list includes <dt> tags for terms and <dd> tags for definitions.

```
<dl>
        <dt>the term</dt>
        <dd>the definition</dd>
        <dt>another term</dt>
        <dd>another definition</dd>
</dl>
```

This markup is displayed in most browsers as shown in Figure 2-4.

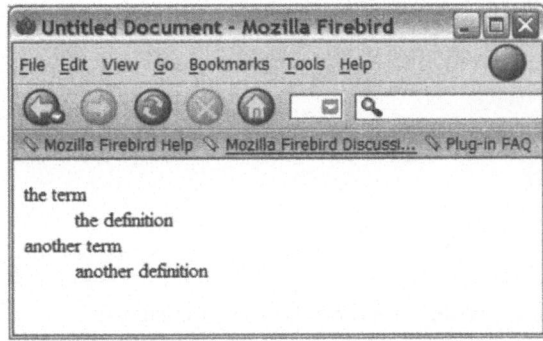

Figure 2-4. Definition list in a browser

Special Characters

When inserting special characters such as brackets (< >) or the ampersand (&),
you should always use the correct Unicode character entities. When you enter
common characters into Design view, Dreamweaver MX enters the correct character code for you, for example, Dreamweaver adds < in place of < and &
in place of &. However, if you are working in Code view or need to insert a character that is not on your keyboard, there are additional characters available from
the Text tab of the Insert toolbar that you can insert into the document. The Text
tab is shown in Figure 2-5.

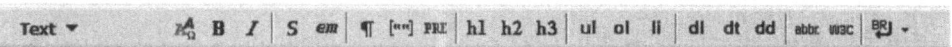

Figure 2-5. Character entities in the Insert toolbar

The more unusual characters can be found by clicking the button on the
right of the Characters tab (or clicking the arrow on the far right and selecting
Other Characters). This opens a panel of characters to choose from and insert
into your document, as shown in Figure 2-6.

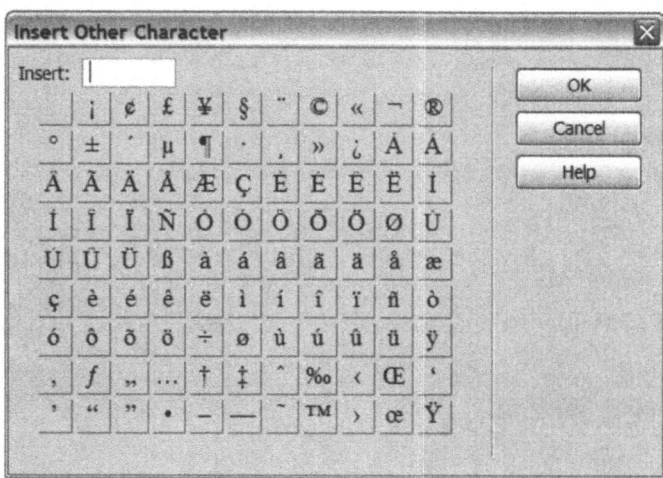

Figure 2-6. More character entities

XHTML in Dreamweaver MX 2004

Whether you are new to XHTML or an experienced developer looking for
a quicker way of working, Dreamweaver MX can help you write valid XHTML
quickly and accurately.

Setting Preferences

Setting your preferences will ensure that Dreamweaver MX is working with you to create valid XHTML or HTML documents right from the outset. To access the Preferences dialog box, select Edit ➤ Preferences.

The General Pane

In the General pane of the Preferences dialog box, make sure that the Use <strong> and <em> instead of <b> and <i> option is checked.

The <b> and <i> tags will not cause your page to be invalid, but from a best practices point of view, it is suggested that you use <strong> and <em> instead. Why? Because <b> for bold text and <i> for italic text are presentational tags designed to tell the browser how something should *look*. The <strong> and <em> tags are logical tags that tell the browser or device that the document author wants a word or statement to have particular *emphasis*. A screen reader, for example, may interpret these tags with an inflection designed to give the person listening to the page the same understanding as someone seeing bold or italic text.

Your page should look exactly the same in a conventional browser whichever choice you make, so this is one place where making a small change can really lift the accessibility of your web site without altering the look of the pages.

While in this pane, make sure that the Allow multiple consecutive spaces check box is well and truly unchecked! If this is checked, pressing the spacebar will insert multiple   into your code, which is really annoying. From a best practices viewpoint, indentation of page elements should be created with CSS, not by adding nonbreaking spaces.

The Accessibility Pane

In the Show Attributes when inserting area of the Accessibility pane, ensure that the Images check box is selected. For your documents to validate against accessibility requirements, they must have alt text. This check box will remind you to add that text each time you insert an image. If you want to create valid and accessible code, you may want to check the Form Objects, Frames, Media, and Tables check boxes as well.

The New Document Pane

If you want to use XHTML for future work, you can set Dreamweaver MX to make new documents XHTML-compliant automatically. To do so, check the Make document XHTML compliant check box in this pane. Alternatively, you can choose to make documents XHTML-compliant each time you create a new document in Dreamweaver MX, although the original default will be HTML.

The Validator Pane

In this pane, you can specify which DTD you want to validate against with the internal validator. Check the DTD that you will most often use—you can always go back and change it if you are working on a site that requires a different DTD.

Authoring Valid CSS

CSS allows the separation of content and structure from the presentation. HTML was originally designed as a language to allow creation of easy-to-read, structured documents. Formatting tags were added by the browser companies (notably Netscape) to extend the capabilities of HTML, and many of these later became part of the official specifications. The CSS1 specification covers basic CSS mainly for text styling. This specification is widely implemented across all the main browsers. The CSS2 specification builds on CSS1 and adds support for positioning elements. Although much of this specification is implemented across browsers, you still need to test thoroughly when using it because it is newer and has been implemented slightly differently between browsers.

Why Use CSS?

If you are working to standards (and especially if you want to validate against a Strict DOCTYPE) you will need to replace presentational tags and attributes in your (X)HTML with CSS. This may sound like a lot of extra work, but it brings many benefits.

Separating Document Structure from Presentation

You will see this phrase a lot wherever stylesheets are discussed. In practice, it means that all information describing how the document *looks* is removed from the HTML and put into stylesheet rules. All information that defines the content and document structure remains in the HTML. Elements such as headings (<h1> through to <h6>), paragraphs (<p>), tables for tabular data (<table>), and so on are used to describe the structure and content of the document. Other elements and attributes are typically used to set text colors and fonts, and to position content.

By replacing these presentational HTML elements and attributes with stylesheets, your pages will become smaller and far easier to read and debug.

Accessibility

CSS allows precise control over layout, obviating tag misuse. Screen readers and other technologies interpret the markup by using the HTML tags that are present on the page. If inappropriate markup is used, a person who is blind will find your page confusing because the structure and meaning of your document is not clear.

Modern browsers allow users to override your styles with a user stylesheet. You might not think this is a good idea at first—why would you want users to replace your carefully crafted stylesheet with theirs? But users with low vision can apply a stylesheet that uses large fonts or high contrast, allowing them to interact with your site much more easily.

By using CSS, you can easily change the font size, colors, and even layout of your site simply by changing the stylesheet. Many sites now offer different themes, for example, providing a high-contrast color scheme or large text in order to assist those who would have difficulty reading your site otherwise. One example of this is http://www.zeldman.com. By displaying different stylesheets, designers are not so restricted in their design choices when attempting to make their sites both visually appealing and accessible to people with disabilities or alternative devices. We will return to the issue of displaying different stylesheets later in this chapter.

More Flexibility in Design

Using HTML tags to lay out and style your pages limits the way you resize and position page elements. Using <font size="xx"> allows resizing, but CSS enables you to specify the spacing between words, letters, and lines of text, and to add or reduce the amount of padding around <h1> and other structural tags. CSS2 goes even further, allowing positioning of page elements outside the grid layout made necessary by using tables as a layout tool.

Smaller File Sizes

Moving to CSS allows you to control the appearance of all the elements in your entire site with one stylesheet. More advanced use of CSS can produce effects that previously would have required an image, such as the layering of page elements.

Browser Support

CSS is very browser friendly. If a browser or device does not support CSS, the browser just ignores the stylesheet and renders the content with its default settings. Apart from certain bugs in traditional web browsers (which we will discuss later), using CSS will not render your pages inaccessible to someone who is using an older browser or device that does not support CSS.

Shortening Development Time

Once you have set up a stylesheet for the common elements across your site, adding new pages that are consistent with the rest of the site is simple because any page that has the stylesheet linked will adopt the same styles for headings, paragraphs, borders, and other elements. Should you want to change the font or the color scheme used throughout the site, you need to alter only one stylesheet and the changes will be reflected across the entire site consistently.

The Basics of CSS

Before you dive into working with CSS within Dreamweaver MX, you should understand some of the basic concepts of CSS design. If you used CSS in the past, this section will serve as a refresher.

Ways to Implement CSS

There are three ways to implement CSS in your web site or document: inline, embedded, or external.

Inline Stylesheets

An **inline** style definition is a one-time style definition placed in your code to style only the element to which it is attached. By using this method, you will lose many of the benefits of CSS because you must style each element individually, which is the same way that you use font tags or other presentational HTML.

```
<h1 style=" font-family: Verdana, Arial, Helvetica, sans-serif; color: #663366;">
```

This markup only affects the particular <h1> tag on that page. If this were the only time that you ever used this style in your site, you might consider using an inline style. If you were going to use this style more than once, however, it would be better to make this into a class and apply it to the <h1> tag because you could reuse the class for other instances of this style. Using an inline style will override anything you defined for this tag in your stylesheet for this instance of the tag, so it can be useful if you want just one <h1> tag to look different from the others. See the "Cascading Style Sheets" section, later in this chapter, for more information.

Embedded Stylesheets

An **embedded** stylesheet controls only the elements on that page, and the CSS code is placed in the head of the document. In the following code example, any <h1> tags in the document will be colored purple. However, this CSS will not be applied to any other pages on the site.

```
<head>
<title>CSS Example</title>
<style type="text/css">
<!--
h1 {
   font-family: Verdana, Arial, Helvetica, sans-serif;
   color: #663366;
}
-->
</style>
</head>
```

If you wanted to use this style on every page of your site and you were using the embedded method, you would need to add this code to every page of the site.

External Stylesheets

An **external** stylesheet is the most useful and flexible way to use CSS. When you link to a single external stylesheet from all pages of your web site, each page uses the definitions from that stylesheet. Changing the purple <h1> tags to orange throughout the site would involve one simple change to the external stylesheet. A simple link to an external stylesheet looks like this:

```
<link href="global.css" rel="stylesheet" type="text/css" />
```

We will discuss the design and implementation of external CSS in more detail later in this chapter.

Cascading Style Sheets

The "cascading" in CSS refers to the fact that styles defined closer to the element will overwrite any other rules. For example, consider the following:

```
h1 {
   font-family: Verdana, Arial, Helvetica, sans-serif;
   color: #663366;
}
```

If you set this in an external stylesheet but decide that on one particular page you want all <h1> tags to be a different color, you could add a style rule in an embedded stylesheet in the head of that document that would override the external stylesheet rule. If you then decided you wanted a single, specific <h1> tag on this particular page to be yet another color, you could use an inline style on that specific tag, and it would take precedence over styles set in the embedded and external stylesheets.

Redefining How HTML Tags Look in the Browser

You have already seen how redefining HTML tags with CSS rules can change the way these structural tags are rendered and preserve the structure of your markup. This method provides a simple way of creating and maintaining a consistent look and feel for your site without bloating the HTML with presentational markup. If you are working with several authors who add content to the site, redefining tags will ensure that their content will fit with the rest of the site because their content will use the formatting defined in your stylesheet.

Creating CSS Classes

CSS classes allow you to create rules for page elements that have classes applied to them. For instance, if in the stylesheet you have the following:

```
.myborder {
  border-width: 1px;
  border-color: #000000;
  border-style: solid;
}
```

then any element, such as the following <img>, with a class of border applied will have a one-pixel-wide black border around it:

```
<img alt="me" height="80" width="40" src="me.jpg" class="myborder" />
```

TIP *Netscape 4 renders this border in a strange way that causes the image to become nonclickable if it is a link. This is just one of the problems that you may encounter while using CSS with Netscape 4. Later in this chapter, we will provide ways to cope with old browsers.*

CSS Tools in Dreamweaver MX 2004

Dreamweaver has a variety of tools that make working with CSS easier.

Setting Preferences

The following preferences will help you get comfortable working with CSS in the Dreamweaver environment.

CSS Styles

Open the Preferences dialog box (shown in Figure 2-7) by selecting Edit ➤ Preferences and selecting the CSS Styles category.

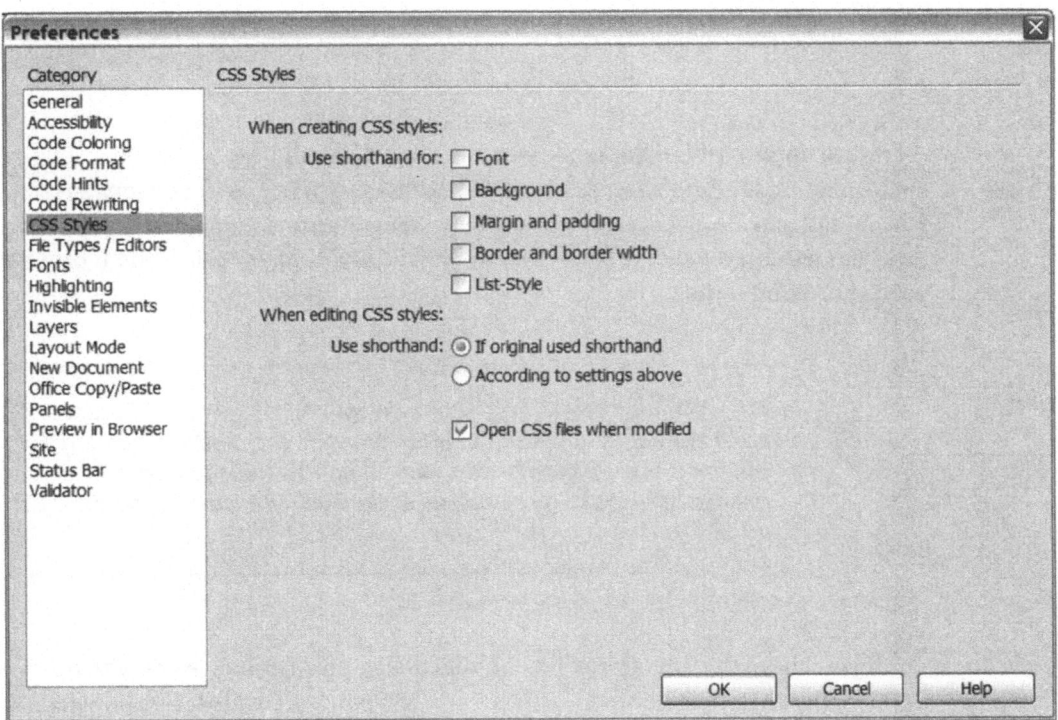

Figure 2-7. The Preferences dialog box

CSS allows shorthand and longhand syntaxes for either brevity or clarity. A snippet of CSS code in longhand syntax looks like this:

```
.longhand {
font-family: Arial, Helvetica, sans-serif;
  font-size: small;
  color: #660066;
  text-decoration: underline;
}
```

In this dialog box, checking the Use shorthand for boxes forces Dreamweaver to use the shorthand syntax. These rules are displayed in exactly the same way in any browser.

```
.shorthand {
  font: small Arial, Helvetica, sans-serif;
  color: #660066;
  text-decoration: underline;
}
```

More important are the radio buttons at the bottom. If you created a stylesheet in another editor such as TopStyle and then make edits in Dreamweaver, you should make sure that any rules Dreamweaver adds are consistent with the style you used in the rest of your stylesheet. In this situation, select the If original used shorthand option.

 TIP *You may find that certain rules work when declared in shorthand but not in longhand in older browsers such as Netscape 4. If you are using the shorthand syntax to handle these problems, it is important to make sure Dreamweaver is set up to assist you with this.*

If you check the final check box on this dialog box, Dreamweaver will open the CSS file when it is modified. This means you can keep a close eye on what the software is adding to your stylesheet.

File Types/Editors

To specify another editor as your default CSS editor, go to Preferences ➤ File Types /Editors, as shown in Figure 2-8.

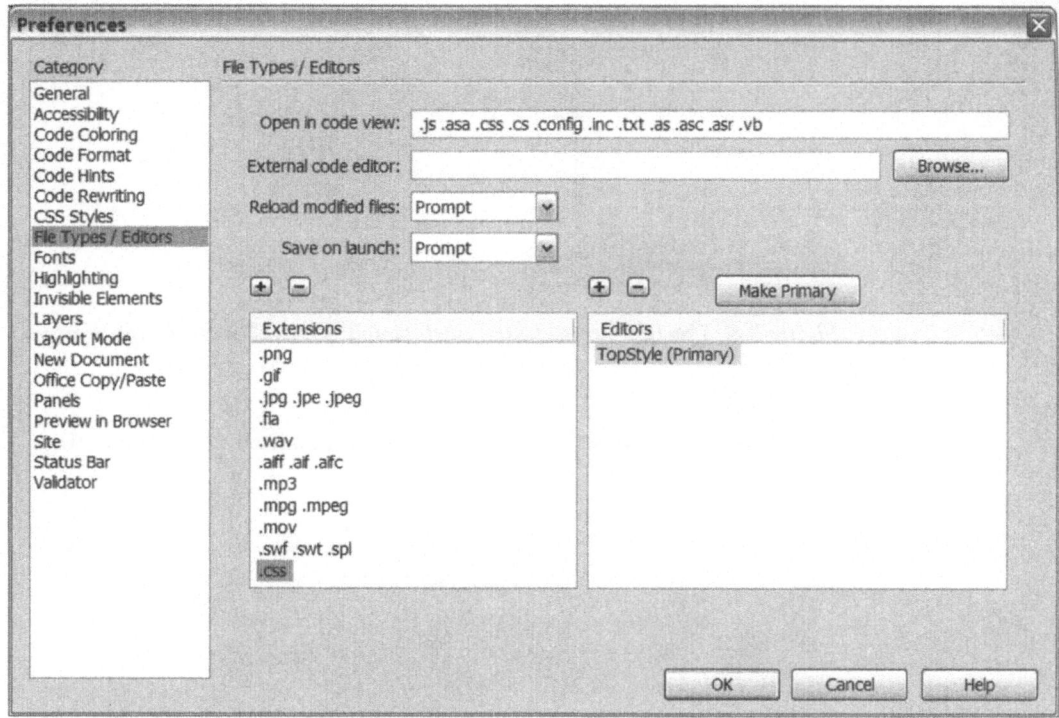

Figure 2-8. File types/editors

We will discuss integrating an external editor later in this chapter.

The CSS Styles Panel

The CSS Styles panel enables you to attach stylesheets to your page, create new styles (either in a new stylesheet, an existing stylesheet, or embedded in your document), and edit styles already created.

Creating a Simple Stylesheet in Dreamweaver

Follow these steps to create a stylesheet.

1. To create a new stylesheet, click the New CSS Style button, which is the second button from the left on the CSS Styles panel, as shown in Figure 2-9.

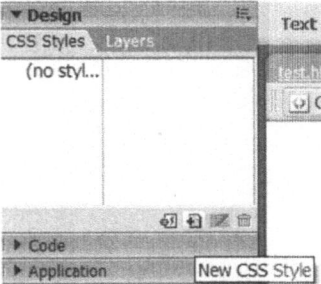

Figure 2-9. The CSS Styles panel with New CSS Style button highlighted

This displays the New CSS Style dialog box, as shown in Figure 2-10.

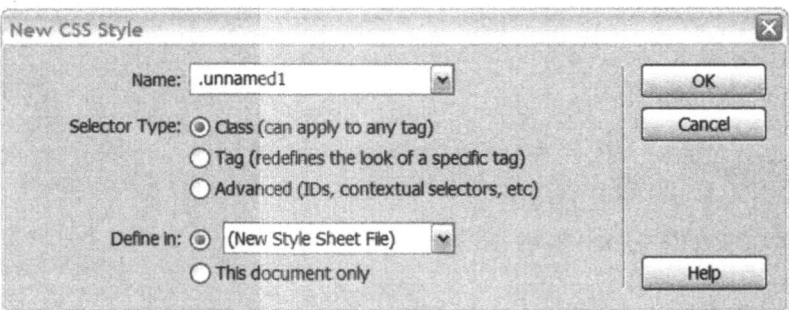

Figure 2-10. The New CSS Style dialog box

2. You will need to create a style definition in order to create a new style-sheet, and a good place to start is with the basic font styles for the body text of the page. Select the Tag (redefines the look of a specific tag) radio button. Next, in the drop-down list at the top of the page, select Body. Select the radio button to define a New Style Sheet File and click OK.

3. Because this is a new stylesheet, a Save As dialog box will appear so that you can save your stylesheet. Make sure that you add the `.css` extension on the end of your stylesheet name (in other words, save as `global.css` and not just `global`). Once you have saved your stylesheet, the dialog box shown in Figure 2-11 appears.

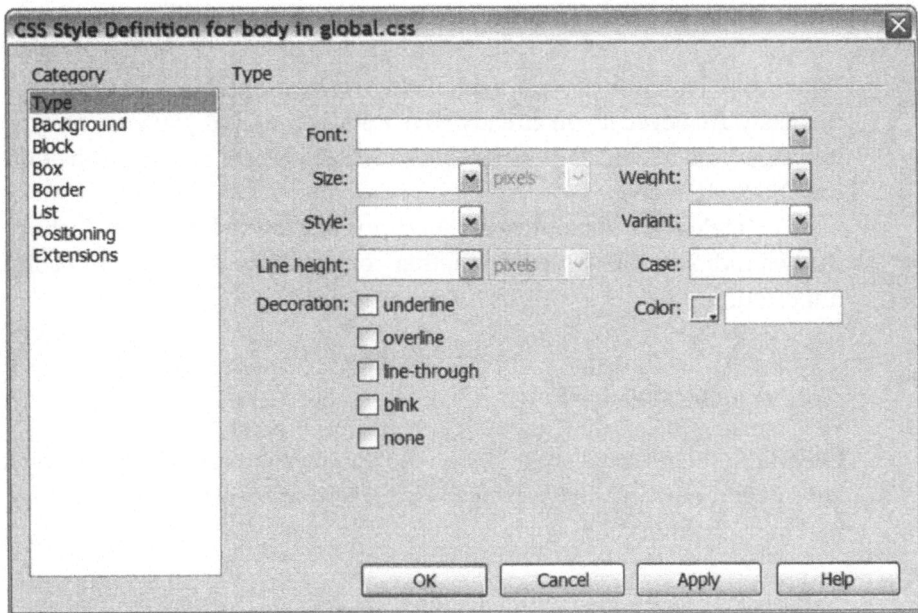

Figure 2-11. The CSS Style Definition dialog box

4. In this CSS Style Definition dialog box, you can set the rules for a tag or class. For the body text, select Type in the Category list; choose a font, size, and color; and then click OK. You can redefine the look of any HTML tags that you want by following these steps.

5. To edit a CSS style, select it in the CSS Styles panel and then click the Edit button (second from the right at the bottom of the panel) to open the CSS Style Definition dialog box. Double-clicking the style in the tree view in the CSS Styles panel opens the stylesheet in Dreamweaver so you can make changes to the stylesheet itself.

Creating Classes

Creating classes in Dreamweaver is as simple as redefining an HTML tag.

1. Open the New CSS Style dialog box once again and select the Class (can apply to any tag) radio button. Next, in the text box at the top of the dialog box, enter a name for your class. It must begin with a period.

2. Click OK and the familiar dialog box will open, allowing you to set the properties for this class. Set the properties you want and click OK. Your new class will appear in the CSS Styles panel.

Attaching a Stylesheet

When you create a new stylesheet, Dreamweaver attaches it to your page automatically. However, if you already have a stylesheet that you want to attach to the page, you can attach it using the Attach Stylesheet button on the bottom of the CSS Styles panel.

The dialog box that appears allows you to browse for your stylesheet. Use the two radio buttons to select whether you want the stylesheet to be linked or imported.

Linking to the Stylesheet

Linking to the external stylesheet is the usual way of attaching a stylesheet to your page. Selecting this option will attach your stylesheet to your page with the following markup:

```
<link href="global.css" rel="stylesheet" type="text/css" />
```

This way of attaching a stylesheet is supported by all CSS-enabled browsers, and it is what you should do if you need to support browsers such as Netscape 4 with your web page.

Importing the Stylesheet

If you choose to import, the stylesheet will be attached with the following markup:

```
<style type="text/css">
  <!--
    @import url("global.css");
  -->
</style>
```

This way of attaching a stylesheet is not recognized by version 4 browsers, but you can use this to your advantage when you have to deal with buggy CSS support in these older browsers. We will return to this subject later.

The Property Inspector

In Dreamweaver MX 2004, the old-style Property inspector that allowed you to add <font> tags to your documents is gone. In its place is the new and improved

Property inspector, shown in Figure 2-12, which allows you to add classes to page elements far more quickly than before.

Figure 2-12. Property inspector

The Format drop-down list lets you add the structural (X)HTML markup to elements. If you select an element in Design view and then choose Heading 1 from this list, the element will become a level 1 heading (<h1>). Other structural markup that you can add using the Property inspector includes the following:

- Click the B button to wrap an element in <strong></strong> tags, making it appear bold in a browser.

- Click the I button to wrap an element in <em></em> tags, making it appear italicized in the browser.

- Click the Unordered List button to turn an element into an unordered list.

- Click the Ordered List button to create an ordered list.

The Text Indent and Text Outdent buttons add and remove <blockquote> elements. You should not use the Text Indent button to indent text; rather, you should use it to mark up a quote. To indent text, you should use a left-padding setting in a CSS class.

The font, size, and color drop-down lists should be used with caution. As already mentioned, the use of <font> tags has been removed from the Property inspector, so if you change the font of an element using this menu, Dreamweaver creates a class in the head of your document and then applies it to the element. You would be better served to create your own classes for text that needs to be specially formatted, or create a special element using these menus and copy the resulting CSS out of the head of your document and into your external stylesheet, where it will be available to any pages that have this stylesheet attached.

The Style drop-down list picks up any classes that you created and gives you an easy way to apply them to page elements. Select an element in Design view and select a class from this drop-down list, and the class will be applied to the element.

The Page Properties Dialog Box

The Page Properties dialog box can be launched from the Property inspector as well as by selecting Modify ➤ Page Properties. This dialog box gives you a quick way to set CSS properties for your document. Once again, these properties will appear in the head of your document, and because you are usually aiming for a unified look and feel throughout your site, you should copy them to your external stylesheet.

Design Files: Premade CSS Stylesheets

Dreamweaver MX ships with a set of ready-made design files, including stylesheets. If CSS seems like a rather abstract concept at this point, or if you just want a way to get started quickly, these files are really useful.

To use a ready-made stylesheet, select File ➤ New, and then select CSS Stylesheets from the New Document dialog box. A list of premade stylesheets is displayed in the center selector box, as shown in Figure 2-13.

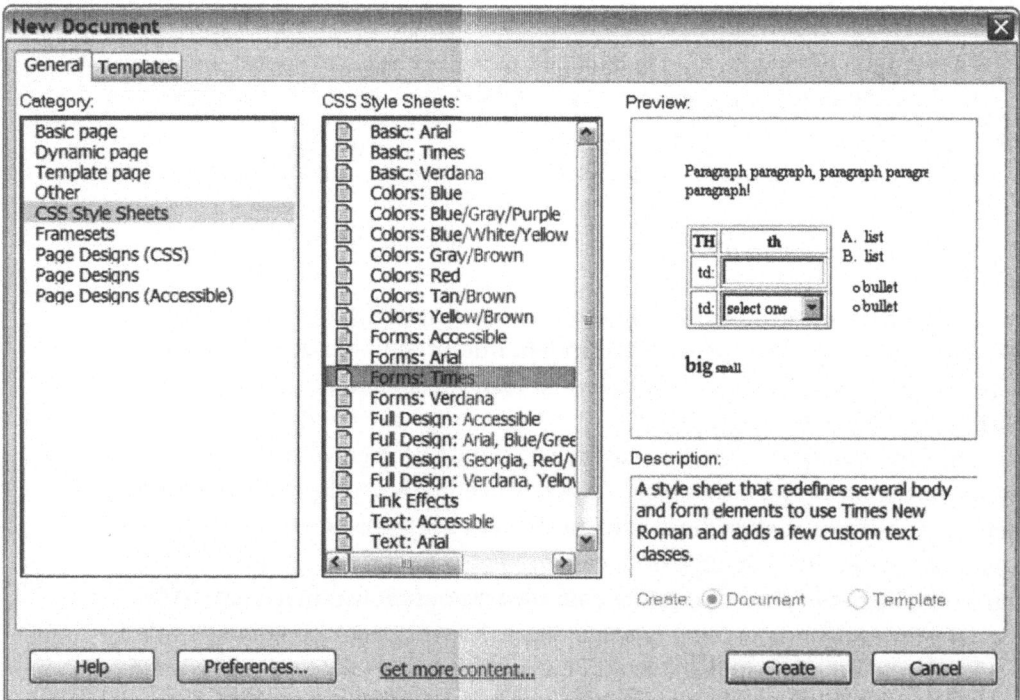

Figure 2-13. Premade stylesheets

Clicking any stylesheet will display some of its elements in the Preview panel. After choosing one that you want, click Create, and the stylesheet is created as a new document in Dreamweaver. You will need to save this stylesheet within your site.

To get started using your stylesheet, attach it to your page. Any redefined tags will adopt the rules set in the stylesheet, and any custom classes defined will be available for your use.

Design Files: Page Designs (CSS)

Dreamweaver also ships with full CSS page designs ready for you to use. These are an excellent way to start using CSS layouts because they give you a starting point from which you can experiment. To use one of these layouts, select File ➤ New ➤ Page Designs (CSS) and pick one of the designs. You can see a preview of the layout in the Preview panel, as shown in Figure 2-14. Click Create, save the HTML document, and copy the CSS file into your site.

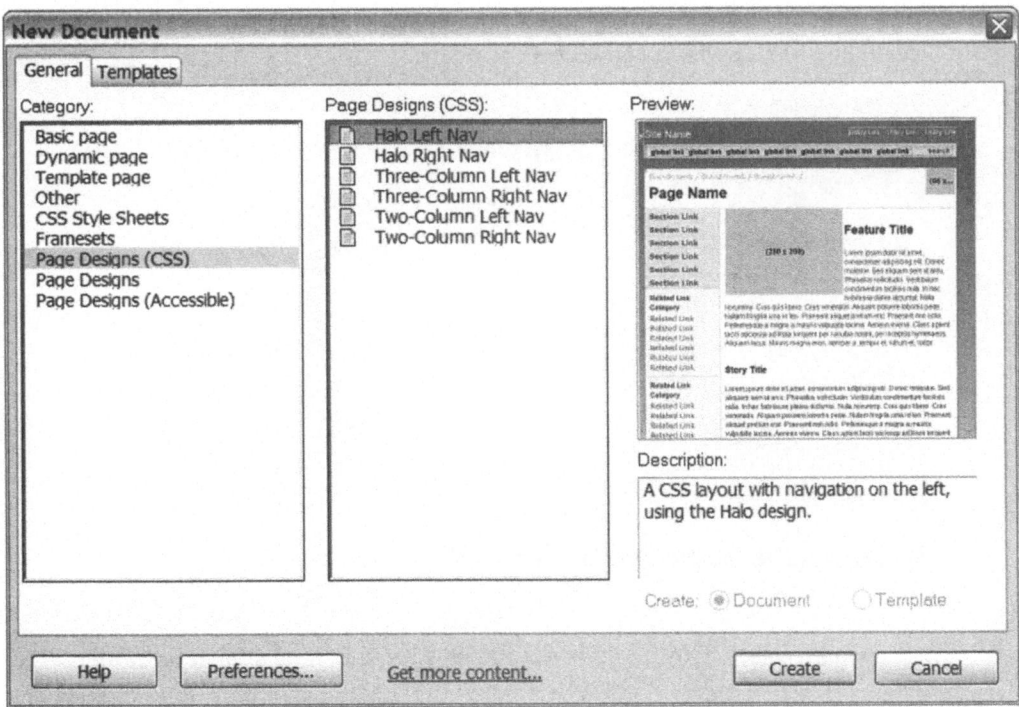

Figure 2-14. Page designs in the Preview panel

The layout will appear in Design view and you can edit the HTML and CSS to your own requirements. Changes made to the CSS file now will not affect the master CSS file that is used to create the layout in the first place, so feel free to experiment as much as you like.

Design-Time Stylesheets

Design-time stylesheets allow you to apply a stylesheet that will not be visible when the site goes live. They are useful when working on a site that has multiple stylesheets, such as sites that use specific stylesheets for different browsers or sites that allow a user to select one of several stylesheets. If you are writing the link to the stylesheet dynamically with ASP.NET, Dreamweaver will not be able to render that stylesheet during the design process. Using a design-time stylesheet allows you to work visually in the Dreamweaver environment.

Working with a Design-Time Stylesheet

You can open the Design Time Style Sheets dialog box by either right-clicking (CMD-clicking on a Mac) the CSS Styles panel and selecting Design Time in the context menu, or by choosing Text ➤ CSS Styles ➤ Design Time Style Sheets. The dialog box shown in Figure 2-15 appears.

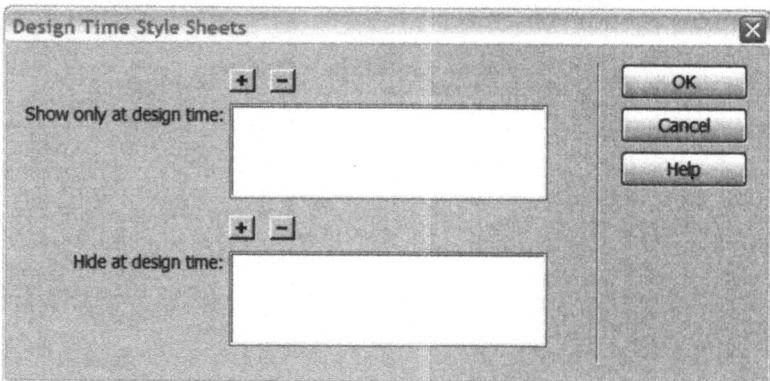

Figure 2-15. The Design Time Style Sheets dialog box

You can select stylesheets saved within your site to be shown or hidden at design time. To display a CSS stylesheet at design time, click the plus sign (+) button above the Show only at design time text box to open a dialog box that will allow you to browse for and select this stylesheet. To hide a CSS stylesheet, click the plus sign (+) button above the Hide at design time text box, and browse for the stylesheet.

You can remove the stylesheet simply by selecting it and clicking the minus sign (–) button.

The CSS Styles panel is updated with the selected stylesheet's name and an indicator (hidden or design) to reflect the stylesheet's status. This only affects the view of the document within Dreamweaver; no changes are made to your code.

Integration with TopStyle CSS Editor

Although you can select any external editor for CSS, Dreamweaver MX has a close integration with the popular TopStyle CSS editor. A trial version of TopStyle is included on the CD with Dreamweaver MX, and it can be downloaded from `http://www.bradsoft.com`. It is a very useful application for anyone working extensively with CSS.

Unfortunately, TopStyle is currently a Windows-only product. There are Mac alternatives (including Style Master, available at `http://www.westciv.com/style_master/index.html`), but it does not currently offer the tight integration with Dreamweaver MX that TopStyle does.

If you are working with TopStyle, changes made to your stylesheet in TopStyle are automatically updated in Dreamweaver's Design view, and new classes that you add are available immediately.

Creating Valid Markup

In this section, we will show you the tools available for laying out web pages. You will create a document using XHTML 1.0 Transitional, tables for layout, basic CSS for text styling, and rollover graphics for navigation.

You will then see how to move this document to XHTML Strict—removing any presentational attributes from your pages. Removing presentational attributes and markup from your pages means that you need to replace them with something, so we will explore replacing them with CSS.

Finally, we will show you more advanced CSS and re-create the layout using CSS positioning, replacing the image rollovers with CSS.

A New XHTML Document

To create a new XHTML documents select File ➤ New to open the New Document dialog box. Select the first two options—Basic page in the Category list and HTML in the Basic page list. Select the Make document XHTML compliant check box at the bottom of the New Document dialog box, as shown in Figure 2-16.

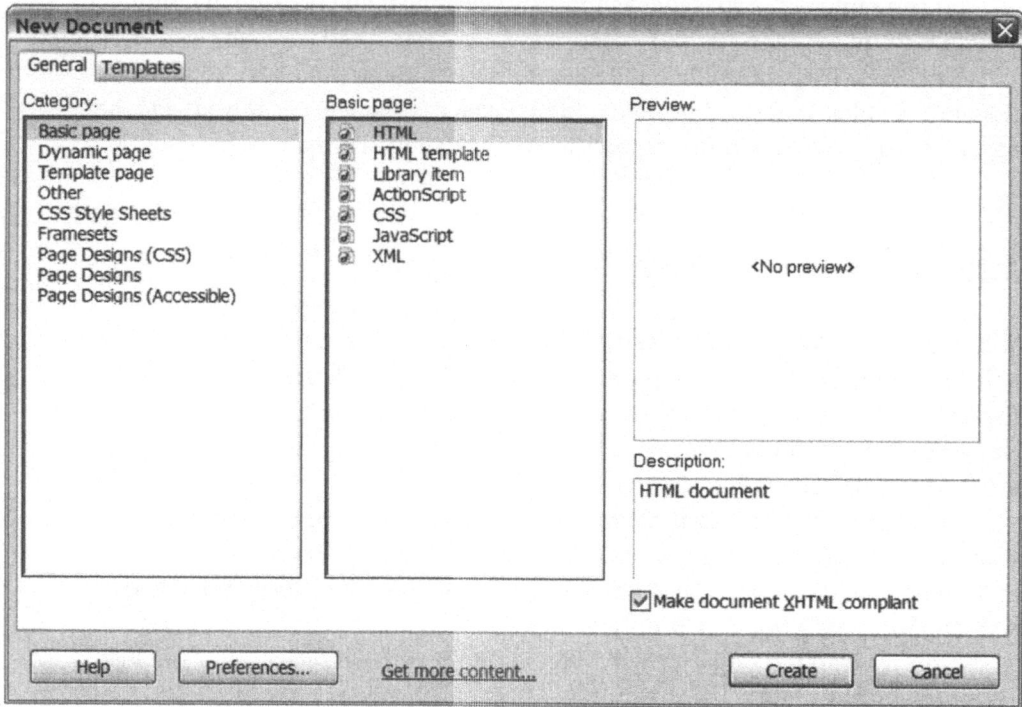

Figure 2-16. Creating a new XHTML document

Laying Out a Page

Follow these steps to create a page layout.

1. To insert a table (in this instance, for layout) into your page, switch the Insert toolbar to the Layout panel, as shown in Figure 2-17.

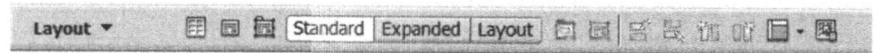

Figure 2-17. The Insert toolbar's Layout panel

2. There are three modes for creating tables-based layouts: Standard, Expanded, and Layout. Layout mode might look like a good idea because you can drag table cells, but it tends to create very messy markup—something you want to avoid! Therefore, start in Standard mode. Click the Table icon on the Insert toolbar to open Table dialog box, as shown in Figure 2-18.

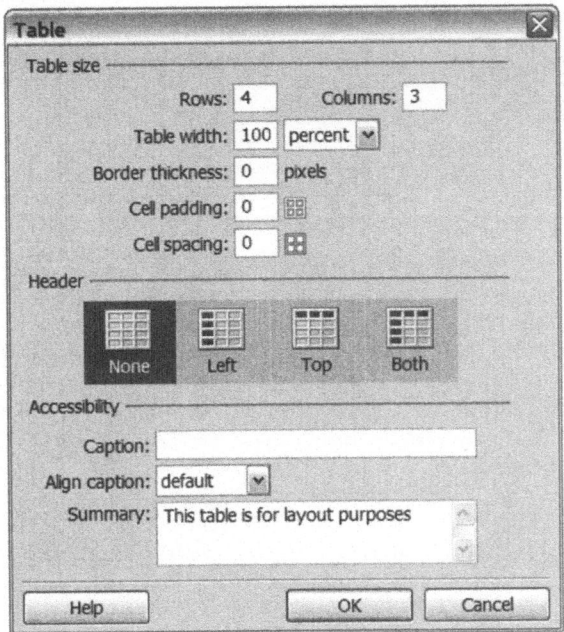

Figure 2-18. The Table dialog box

3. In the Table dialog box, enter the properties of your table as follows:

    *   **Rows:** 4

    *   **Columns** : 3

    *   **Table width:** 100 percent

    *   **Border thickness:** 0 pixels

    *   **Cell padding:** 0

    *   **Cell spacing:** 0

    *   **Header:** None

4. In the Summary text box, type **This table is for layout purposes**.

5. Click OK and your table will appear in Design view, as shown in Figure 2-19.

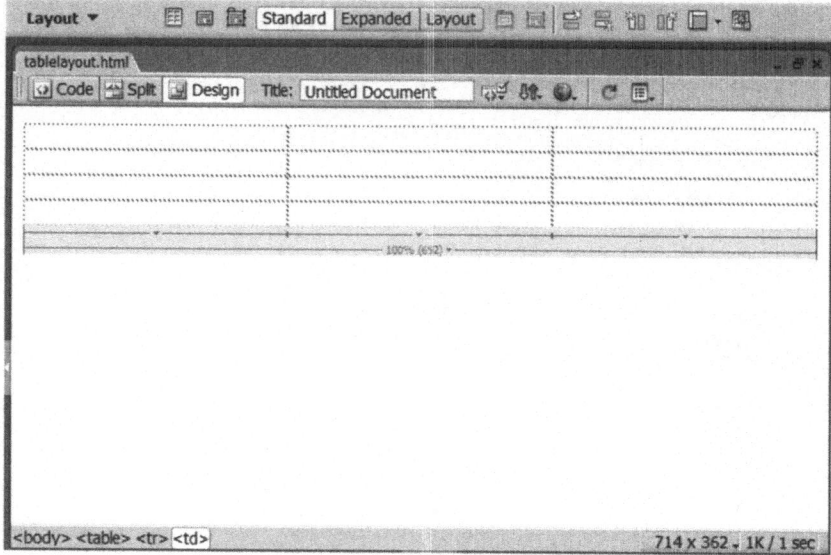

Figure 2-19. Design view after inserting the table

Setting Page Properties

Before continuing, let's set some basic page properties.

1. To open the Page Properties dialog box (shown in Figure 2-20), either click the Page Properties button in the Property inspector or select Modify ➤ Page Properties.

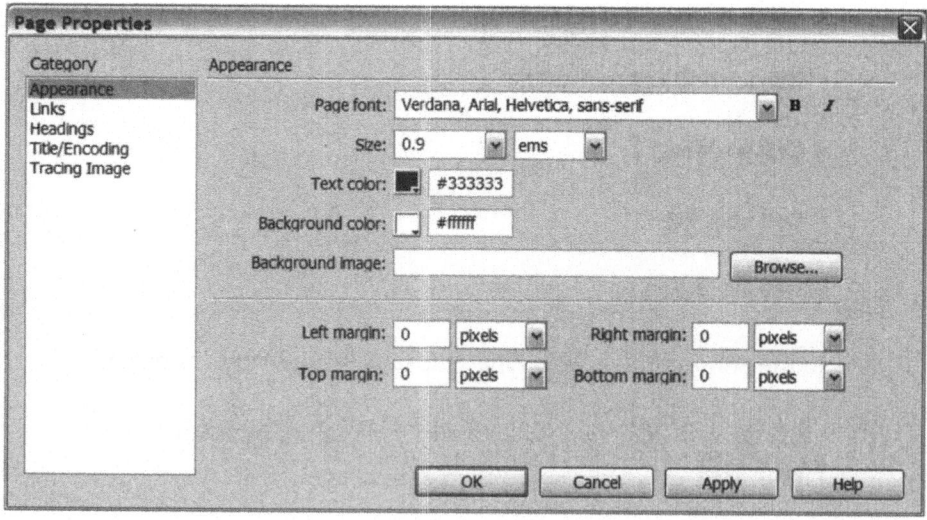

Figure 2-20. The Page Properties dialog box

2. Enter the properties of the page as follows:

- **Page font**: Verdana, Arial, Helvetica, sans serif

- **Size**: .9 ems

- **Text color**: #333333

- **Background color**: #ffffff

- **Left margin**: 0

- **Right margin**: 0

- **Top margin**: 0

- **Bottom margin**: 0

3. Click OK to see the changes in Design view. If you switch to Code view, you will see that these properties have been added with CSS and are in a stylesheet within the head of the document. Because you are likely to want to apply the same properties to multiple pages, it is wise to move these properties to an external stylesheet. To do so, select File ➤ New ➤ Basic Page, and select CSS to open the New Document dialog box, as shown in Figure 2-21.

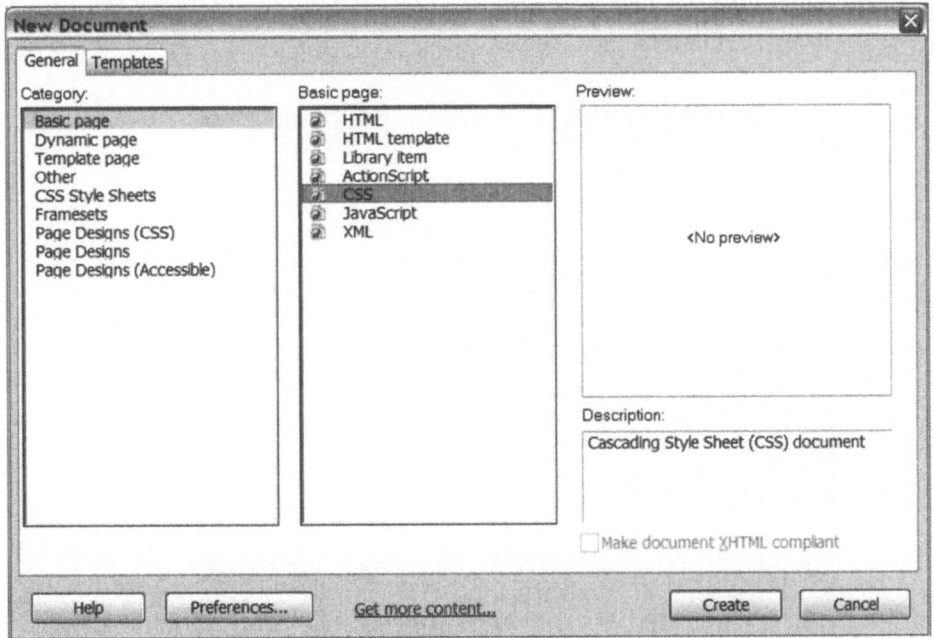

Figure 2-21. Moving properties to an external stylesheet

4. Click Create to open an empty stylesheet in Dreamweaver. Copy the styles from the head of the document (do not copy the `<comment>` or `<style>` tags that enclose them) and paste them into your new stylesheet. Save the stylesheet as `global.css`. Return to your document and delete the `<style></style>` tags and everything inside them. Return to Design view.

5. Now attach your new stylesheet to the page by selecting Attach Stylesheet from the CSS Styles panel and selecting the `global.css` document.

The Layout

You are going to create a layout with a banner at the top of the page and a navigation menu on the left side.

1. To create the banner, select the top row of the table cells and click Merge Cells in the Property inspector.

NOTE *The bottom half of the Property inspector changes to reflect the current selection in Design view.*

2. Repeat this process for the next two rows so your table has three rows containing one cell each, and a fourth row containing three cells, as shown in Figure 2-22.

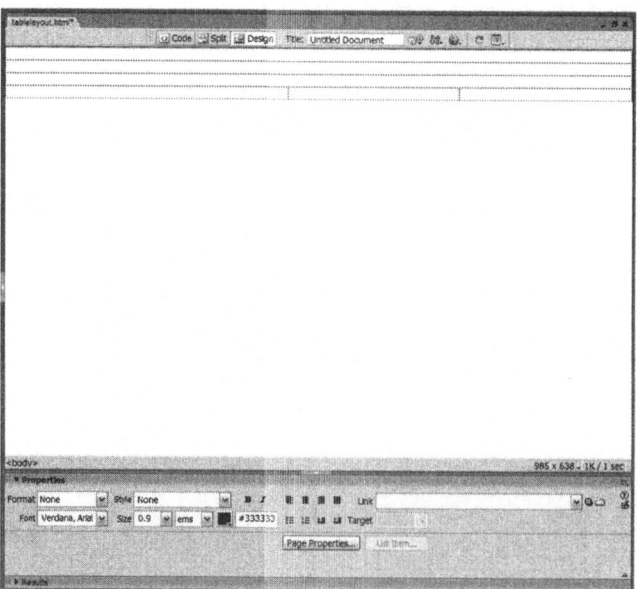

Figure 2-22. Creating a table in the Property inspector

3. Click the left cell of the bottom row. This will be the menu. In the Property inspector, set this cell's width to 200 pixels, as shown in Figure 2-23.

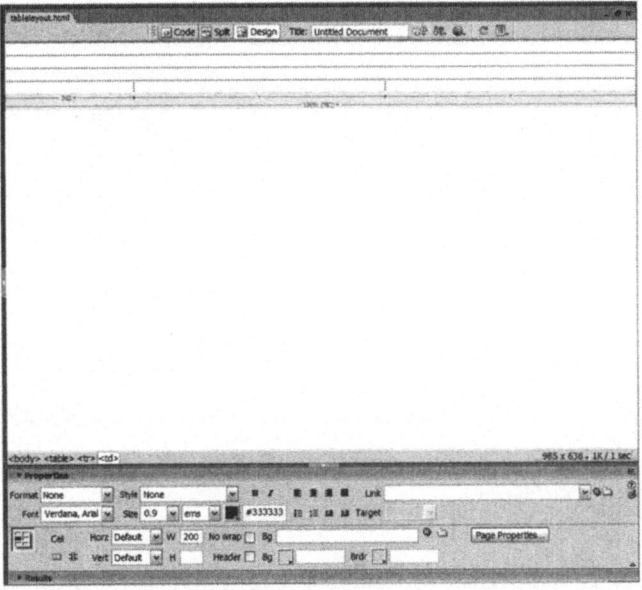

Figure 2-23. Setting table properties in the Property inspector

4. Click the bottom-right cell. Set this cell to 40 pixels wide. The middle cell is where your page content will go.

5. Click the top cell and set it to 20 pixels high. Do the same to the third cell down. Finally, set the middle cell to 80 pixels high.

The Banner

The middle cell will be the banner across the top of the page. You could simply set a background color for the table cell, but it is a better idea to do this using CSS. If you create additional pages from this template page, you can change the color of the banner on every page with one change in the stylesheet.

1. To set the background color using CSS you need to create a class. Create a new class and name it .banner. In the Background category of the CSS Style Definition dialog box, select a color for the banner. Then go to the Border category and give the banner a top and bottom border, as shown in Figure 2-24.

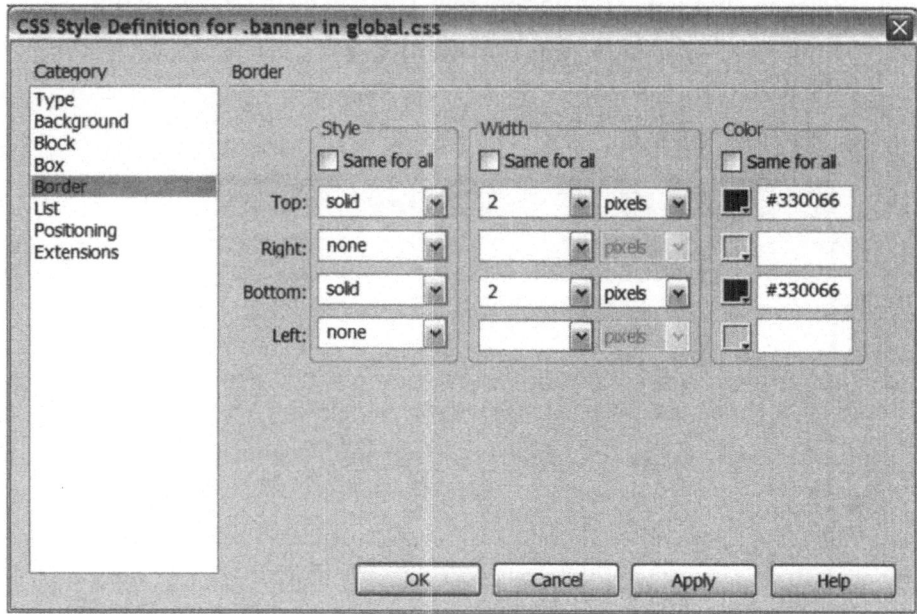

Figure 2-24. The Border category

2. Click OK. Next, using the Property inspector's Style drop-down list, apply the .banner class to the banner table cell.

Adding Page Content

Follow these steps to add page content.

1. In order to see how your content will look, add some dummy content, including a level 1 heading and a level 2 heading, to the main content area of the page (the middle cell of the bottom row).

    The content you add will take on the font of the style you set for page's preferences.

2. You can now set styles for your headings by going to the New CSS Style dialog box, choosing the Tag (redefines the look of a specific tag) radio button, and then choosing the tag you want to style, as shown in Figure 2-25.

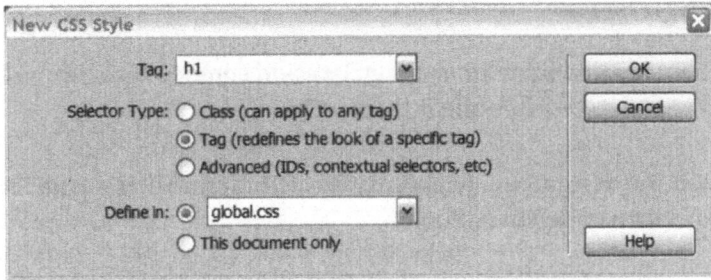

Figure 2-25. Seting styles for headings

The Navigation

Follow these steps to add the table that will contain the navigation.

1. Click the cell on the bottom left. In the Property inspector, select center from the Horz (align) drop-down list, and top from the Vert (valign) drop-down list.

2. Insert a table that contains four rows, one column, and the summary "This table contains the navigation." In Design view, the table looks as shown in Figure 2-26.

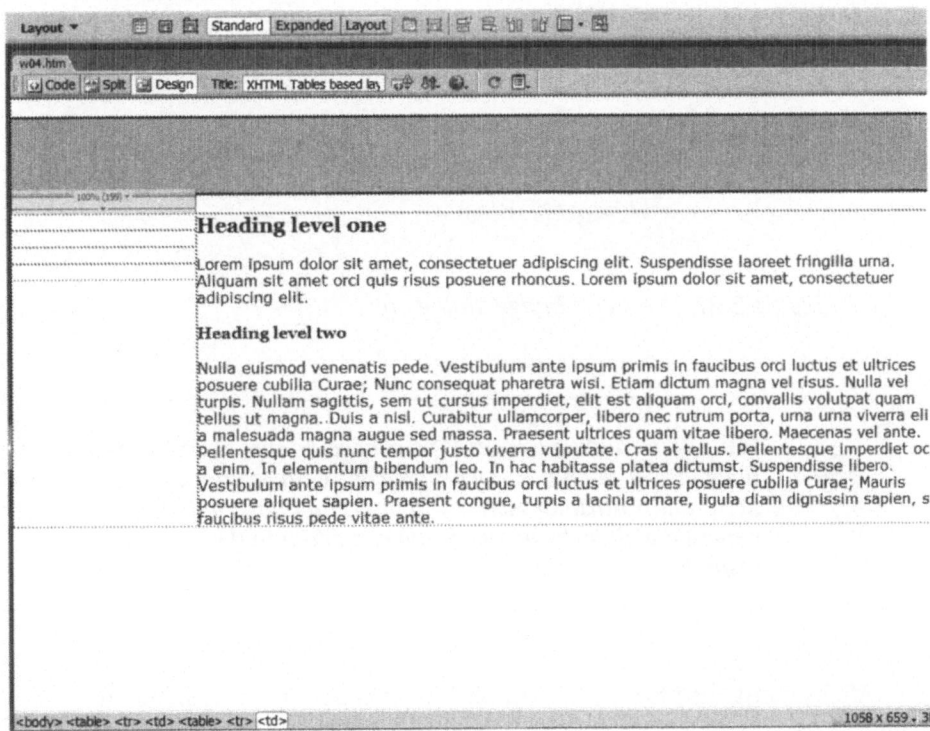

Figure 2-26. The table in Design view

Adding Rollover Images

To make the navigation more interesting, let's add some rollover buttons. Dreamweaver makes it simple to add such effects.

1. Insert the navigation images into the cells. Name them in the Property inspector as you insert them.

2. To add the rollover effect, in the Behaviors panel, click the plus sign (+) button and choose Swap Image.

3. Browse to the image you want and click OK, making sure that the options Preload images (which will load your image as the page loads so there is no delay when the mouse pointer rolls over it) and Restore images onMouseOut (which will roll the image back to its previous state when the mouse pointer is no longer rolling over the button) are both checked, as shown in Figure 2-27.

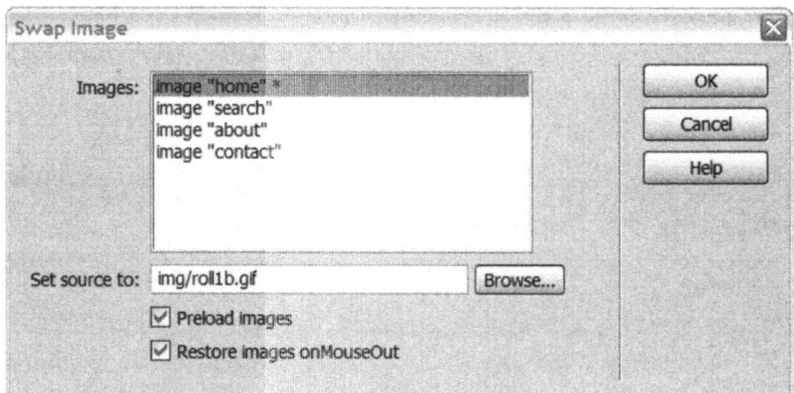

Figure 2-27. The Swap Image dialog box

 TIP *When adding images to your page, be sure to add alt text to the image. If you have set your preferences to prompt you for Accessibility attributes when you insert an image, a dialog box will request the alt text; otherwise, you can add it in the Property inspector.*

After adding the images, this simple layout is complete, as shown in Figure 2-28.

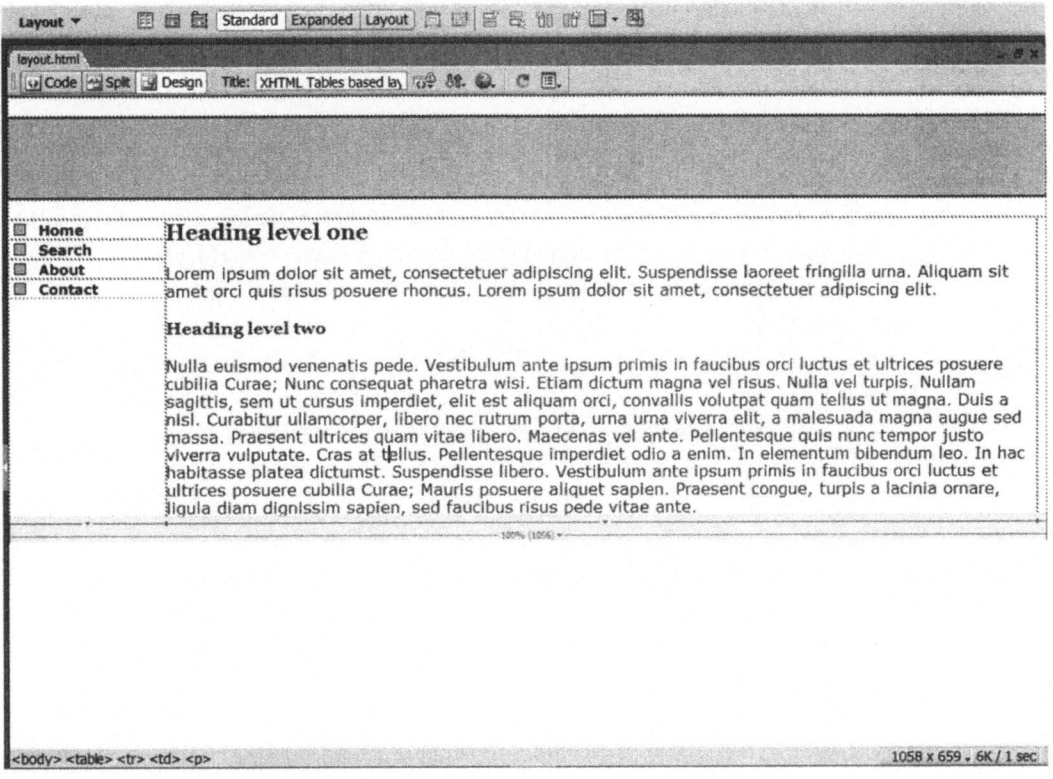

Figure 2-28. The completed layout in Design view

The XHTML markup behind this document looks like this:

```
<!DOCTYPE html PUBLIC "-//W3C//DTD XHTML 1.0 Transitional//EN" ➡
"http://www.w3.org/TR/xhtml1/DTD/xhtml1-transitional.dtd">
<html xmlns="http://www.w3.org/1999/xhtml">
<head>
<title>XHTML Tables based layout</title>
<meta http-equiv="Content-Type" content="text/html; charset=iso-8859-1" />
<link href="global.css" rel="stylesheet" type="text/css" />
<script language="JavaScript" type="text/JavaScript">
<!--
function MM_preloadImages() { //v3.0
  var d=document; if(d.images){ if(!d.MM_p) d.MM_p=new Array();
    var i,j=d.MM_p.length,a=MM_preloadImages.arguments; for(i=0; i<a.length; i++)
    if (a[i].indexOf("#")!=0){ d.MM_p[j]=new Image; d.MM_p[j++].src=a[i];}}
}
```

```
function MM_swapImgRestore() { //v3.0
  var i,x,a=document.MM_sr; for(i=0;a&&i<a.length&&(x=a[i])&&x.oSrc;i++) ➥
x.src=x.oSrc;
}

function MM_findObj(n, d) { //v4.01
  var p,i,x;  if(!d) d=document; if((p=n.indexOf("?"))>0&&parent.frames.length) {
    d=parent.frames[n.substring(p+1)].document; n=n.substring(0,p);}
  if(!(x=d[n])&&d.all) x=d.all[n]; for (i=0;!x&&i<d.forms.length;i++) ➥
x=d.forms[i][n];
  for(i=0;!x&&d.layers&&i<d.layers.length;i++) x=MM_findObj(n,d.layers[i].➥
document);
  if(!x && d.getElementById) x=d.getElementById(n); return x;
}

function MM_swapImage() { //v3.0
  var i,j=0,x,a=MM_swapImage.arguments; document.MM_sr=new Array; ➥
for(i=0;i<(a.length-2);i+=3)
    if ((x=MM_findObj(a[i]))!=null){document.MM_sr[j++]=x; if(!x.oSrc) ➥
x.oSrc=x.src; x.src=a[i+2];}
}
//-->
</script>
</head>

<body onload="MM_preloadImages('img/roll1b.gif', 'img/roll2b.gif',➥
'img/roll3b.gif', 'img/roll4b.gif')">
<table width="100%"  border="0" cellspacing="0" cellpadding="0" ➥
summary="This table is used for layout purposes only">
  <tr>
    <td height="20" colspan="3"> </td>
  </tr>
  <tr>
    <td height="80" colspan="3" class="banner"> </td>
  </tr>
  <tr>
    <td height="20" colspan="3"> </td>
  </tr>
  <tr>
    <td width="200" align="center" valign="top"><table width="100%"  border="0" ➥
cellspacing="0" cellpadding="0" summary="this table contains the navigation">
      <tr>
        <td><a href="javascript:;" onmouseover="MM_swapImage➥
```

```
('home', '', 'img/roll1b.gif',1)" onmouseout="MM_swapImgRestore()"><img ➥
src="img/roll1a.gif" alt="Home" name="home" width="160" height="20" border="0" ➥
id="home" /></a></td>
      </tr>
      <tr>
        <td><a href="javascript:;" onmouseover="MM_swapImage➥
('search', '', 'img/roll2b.gif',1)" onmouseout="MM_swapImgRestore()"><img src=➥
"img/roll2a.gif" alt="Search" name="search" width="160" height="20" border=➥
"0" id="search" /></a></td>
      </tr>
      <tr>
        <td><a href="javascript:;" onmouseover="MM_swapImage➥
('about', '', 'img/roll3b.gif',1)" onmouseout="MM_swapImgRestore()"><img ➥
src="img/roll3a.gif" alt="About" name="about" width="160" ➥
height="20" border="0" ➥
id="about" /></a></td>
      </tr>
      <tr>
        <td><a href="javascript:;" ➥
onmouseover="MM_swapImage('contact', '', 'img/roll4b.gif',1)" ➥
 onmouseout="MM_swapImgRestore()"><img src="img/roll4a.gif" alt="content" ➥
 name="contact" width="160" height="20" border="0" id="contact" /></a></td>➥
      </tr>
    </table></td>
    <td> <h1>Heading level one </h1>
      <p>Content here</p></td>
    <td width="40"> </td>
  </tr>
</table>
</body>
</html>
```

Validating the Document

After creating any layout, particularly if you are going to create multiple pages based on the same layout, it is a good idea to validate it before continuing. Dreamweaver has its own validator to make this easy. Before using the validator, make sure you checked XHTML 1.0 Transitional to validate against in Edit ➤ Preferences ➤ Validator. To run the validator, open the Results panel and click the small green arrow shown in Figure 2-29.

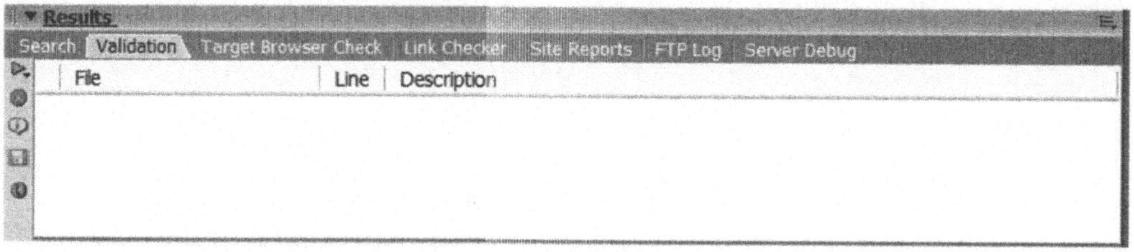

Figure 2-29. Dreamweaver's validator

You can also validate your document by selecting File ➤ Check Page ➤ Validate Markup (for HTML) or File ➤ Check Page ➤ Validate as XML (for XHTML).

You can choose to validate the current document, the entire site, or just selected files in the site. The validator preferences can also be set here. The document should validate as XHTML 1.0 Transitional without needing to be edited by hand.

Using the W3C Validator

Although the internal validator is a useful tool when working on your documents within Dreamweaver, validating at the W3C makes a good final check. The URL for the W3C HTML validator is http://validator.w3.org.

The W3C tool allows you to validate by entering the URL of the page that requires validation or by uploading the document. The easiest way to validate your pages is to FTP them to your web site and then enter the URL into the appropriate box at the validator. If you are using the Dreamweaver validator as you work on your site, you will probably only need to check with the W3C validator as part of your final testing to ensure that all documents, including those that contain dynamic data, are valid.

Moving to XHTML Strict

The XHTML Transitional DTD allows the use of deprecated attributes that will be removed from future versions. The Strict DTD does not allow the use of these deprecated attributes.

To convert your document from the Transitional DTD to the Strict DTD, you must work in Code view. Dreamweaver MX creates XHTML Transitional markup in recognition of the fact that most developers still need to create pages that are backward compatible with older (before version 5) browsers. However, the changes you will need to make are relatively simple.

Change the Document Type Declaration

In Code view, change the DOCTYPE at the top of the page to this:

```
<!DOCTYPE html PUBLIC "-//W3C//DTD XHTML 1.0 Strict//EN"
  "http://www.w3.org/TR/xhtml1/DTD/xhtml1-strict.dtd">
```

Revalidate Your Page in Dreamweaver

In Edit ➤ Preferences ➤ Validator, select the check box to validate against XHTML Strict. Run Validate as XML again. This time you will get a list of errors shown with an exclamation mark inside a red circle, as shown in Figure 2-30.

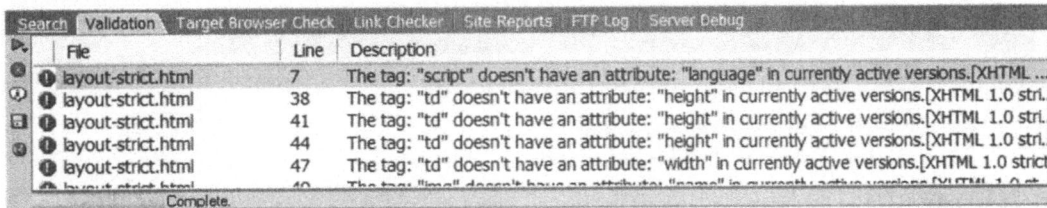

Figure 2-30. Validator showing the errors

TIP   *You can also save this list (right-click on a PC or CMD-click on a Mac and select Save Results) or open the list in a browser (select Open Results in Browser), which is useful if you are validating a large document or entire site because you can use the list as a checklist to ensure that you caught all instances of invalid code.*

The validator at the W3C site gives a similar list of errors, as shown in Figure 2-31.

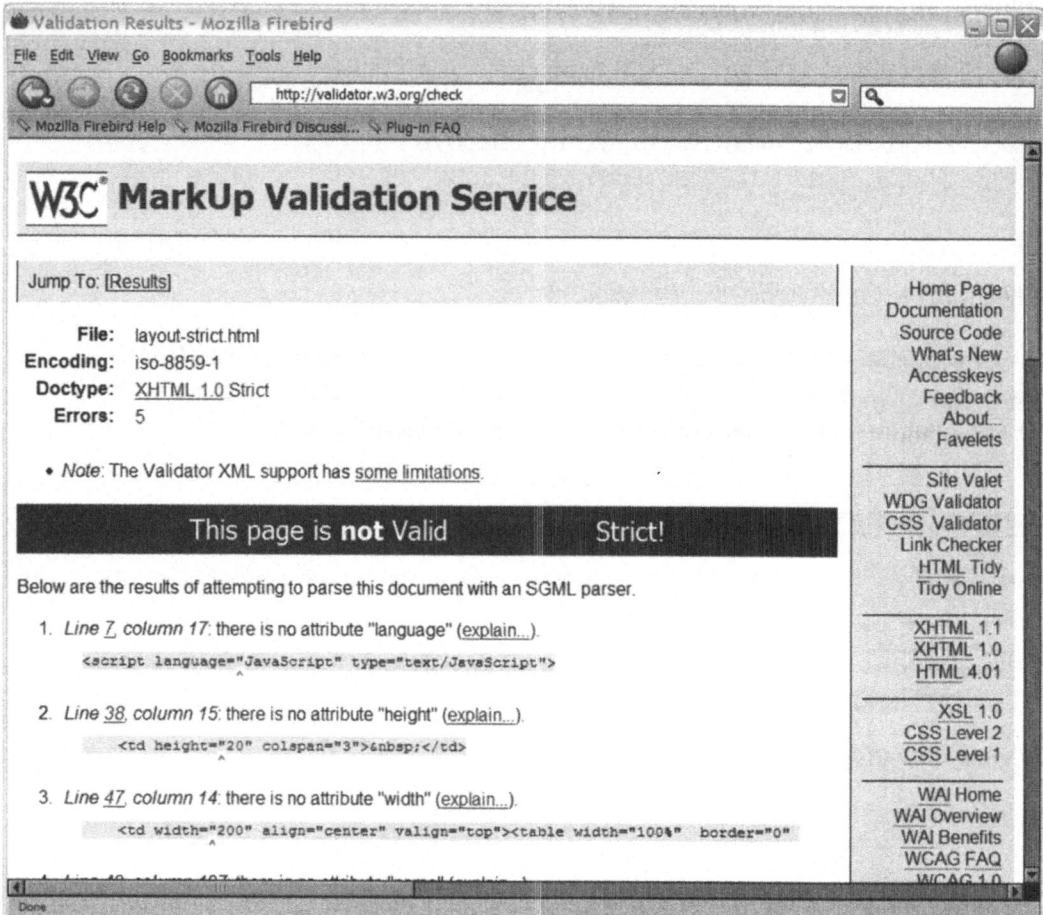

Figure 2-31. W3C validator in a browser showing the errors

These "errors" are simply the tags and attributes that have been removed from the Strict DTD. They are mainly elements that handle how the document looks and therefore should be replaced with CSS. This list is very helpful in making your page validate against the XHTML Strict DTD because it gives you a quick way to see the deprecated elements. (The document validates as XHTML Transitional, so it conforms to the rules of being well formed.)

Table 2-1 shows the errors that the validator flagged and how these are solved.

Table 2-1. Validator Errors and Solutions

Error	Solution
Attribute language is not declared for element script	This refers to `<script language="JavaScript" type="text/JavaScript">`. The language attribute is deprecated and should be removed.
Attribute width is not declared for element td	This refers to `<td width="80">`. The width attribute of the `<td>` tag has been deprecated because it can be replaced by CSS. All width attributes of table cells should be removed.
Attribute border is not declared for element img	This refers to `<img border="0" [...] >`. You might be accustomed to using border="0" to remove the unsightly border around images that are also links. It is possible to use CSS to do this, so border must be removed from all images.
Attribute name is not declared for element img	Dreamweaver MX inserts both a name attribute and an id attribute when you name an image. The name attribute is still used by older browsers and ensures backward compatibility, whereas the id attribute is the attribute in the specification. To use both is valid in XHTML Transitional, but in Strict the deprecated name attribute has to go.

After removing these deprecated attributes you should find that your page validates as XHTML 1.0 Strict, but it looks a bit funny—the banner is shorter and there are big blue borders around the images. You can fix this by replacing the deprecated attributes with CSS.

Remove Borders Around Images

In the days of HTML, you would use border="0" to remove borders from images with links; now you can create the same effect with CSS.

1. Open the New Style dialog box, click the Tag (redefines the look of a specific tag) radio button, and select img in the Tag drop-down list, as shown in Figure 2-32. Then click OK.

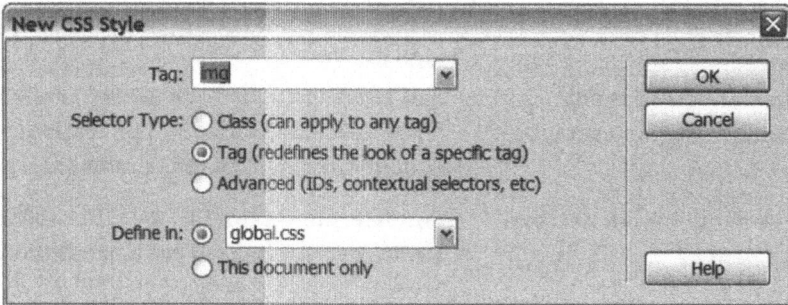

Figure 2-32. Selecting img in the Tag drop-down list

2. Select the Border category in the CSS Style Definition dialog box. In the Style list, select the value none in the Top drop-down list and make sure that Same for all is checked, as shown in Figure 2-33.

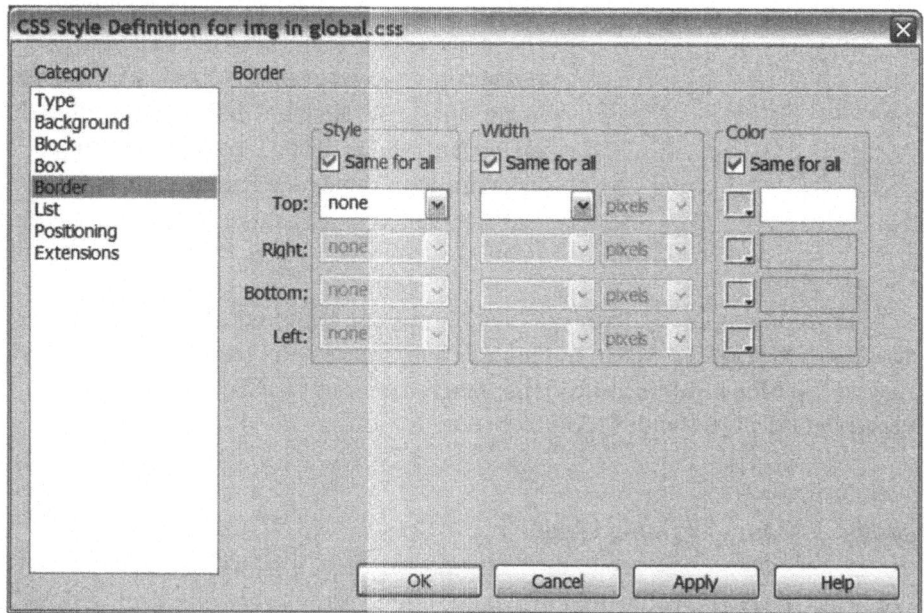

Figure 2-33. CSS definitions for the image

3. Click OK. Your image borders disappear in the Dreamweaver Design view.

TIP *Dreamweaver adds a* border="0" *attribute to any image that is a link. If you need to validate to XHTML Strict or simply do not want this attribute there, you will need to remove it.*

Set Properties of Table Cells

You can use CSS to replace the width and height attributes of table cells. You already have a class for your banner, so you can simply add the height specification to that class.

1. Select the .banner class in the CSS Styles panel and click the Edit Style icon.

2. The dialog box that opens contains the rules that you already set for this class. Go to the Box category, type **80 pixels** in the height box, and click OK. You can create classes for any table cells that you want to change.

Move JavaScript to an External File

Dreamweaver inserts all JavaScript required by its behaviors into the head of your document. This is not ideal. For instance, the JavaScript in the document that enables the rollover effect is 23 lines long. That block of script has to be inserted into every page of the web site and loaded each time.

Moving this JavaScript to a central file that is linked to all pages will trim down the load times of your pages. It also means that search engine spiders will not have to crawl through lines and lines of script to find your content, and pages will be easier to maintain and keep consistent.

1. To move the JavaScript to a central file, simply copy the JavaScript onto the clipboard and open a JavaScript document in Dreamweaver by clicking File ➤ New, selecting Other, and selecting JavaScript. Once you have a JavaScript document, save it as, for example, functions.js, and paste the contents of the clipboard into it. You can now return to the original XHTML document and delete everything between the <script> tags. If you are working in HTML or XHTML Transitional, you should be left with just the following:

   ```
   <script language="JavaScript" type="text/javascript"></script>
   ```

2. If you are working in XHTML Strict, you should be left with just this:

   ```
   <script type="text/javascript"></script>
   ```

   Now add a link within the <script> tags to the source of the JavaScript.

   ```
   <script language="JavaScript" type="text/javascript" src="functions.js"></script>
   ```

If you are using XHTML Strict, that will need to be

```
<script type="text/javascript" src="functions.js"></script>
```

If you add any other behaviors to other page elements, Dreamweaver will continue to add them to your document. However, you can add as many different functions to your external JavaScript file as you like. Just copy and paste them to your file and remember to delete any additional <script> tags that Dreamweaver inserts.

Now when you want to create a new page that utilizes any or all of the functions in your functions.js file, all you need to do is paste the link to the functions file into the head of your document. This is an excellent way to work with templates because you can create your template file with all the JavaScript in the head of your document, move the JavaScript to a functions file, and just keep the link to that file in the head of the template document. When you create new pages from your template, they will automatically contain all the necessary JavaScript.

CSS for Layout

One of the reasons for building and validating an XHTML Transitional and Strict document is to show that you can still work to standards even if you are not ready to go with CSS for layout yet. However, CSS for layout is the way of the future and learning to use CSS in this way is going to be important for the future career of anyone working in this industry. Dreamweaver MX 2004 supports CSS for layout in a far more advanced way than previous versions, making it far easier to get started.

 TIP *You may also hear people talking about layers in Dreamweaver. Layers are simply content structured with inline CSS positioning. They are less useful than an external stylesheet for reasons including reduced code portability and added document size.*

Creating the Banner

Follow these steps to create a banner.

1. To get started building a layout using CSS, create a new XHTML document in Dreamweaver and attach to it the stylesheet that you created for your tables-based layout.

2. You can use the styles you created for your banner table cell. Open your stylesheet in Dreamweaver and change .banner to #banner.

3. To create the banner, add a <div> tag. A <div> tag simply marks an area of the document, which you can then style. To insert a <div> for the banner, select the Layout pane of the Insert toolbar and click the Insert Div Tag icon to display the dialog box shown in Figure 2-34.

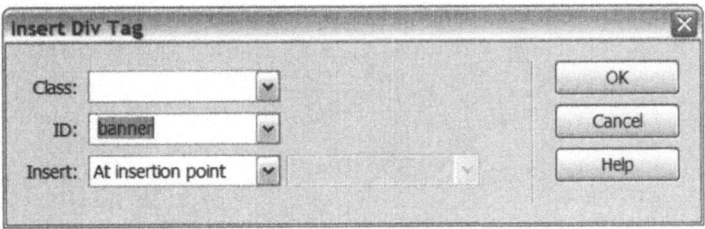

Figure 2-34. The Insert Div Tag dialog box

You will see that the banner shows up as an ID—this is because a pound sign (#) denotes an ID in the stylesheet, whereas a period (.) denotes a class.

4. Select the ID banner and click OK.

TIP *An ID needs to be unique in your document, so it is perfect for use in an area of the page that will occur only once in each document, such as a banner or navigation block. A class can be present multiple times in one document, so you use a class for elements that may appear more than once, such as styles for links, a boxout style to highlight terms, and so on.*

You should see the familiar banner appear in Design view. It contains the text Content for id "banner" Goes Here, as shown in Figure 2-35.

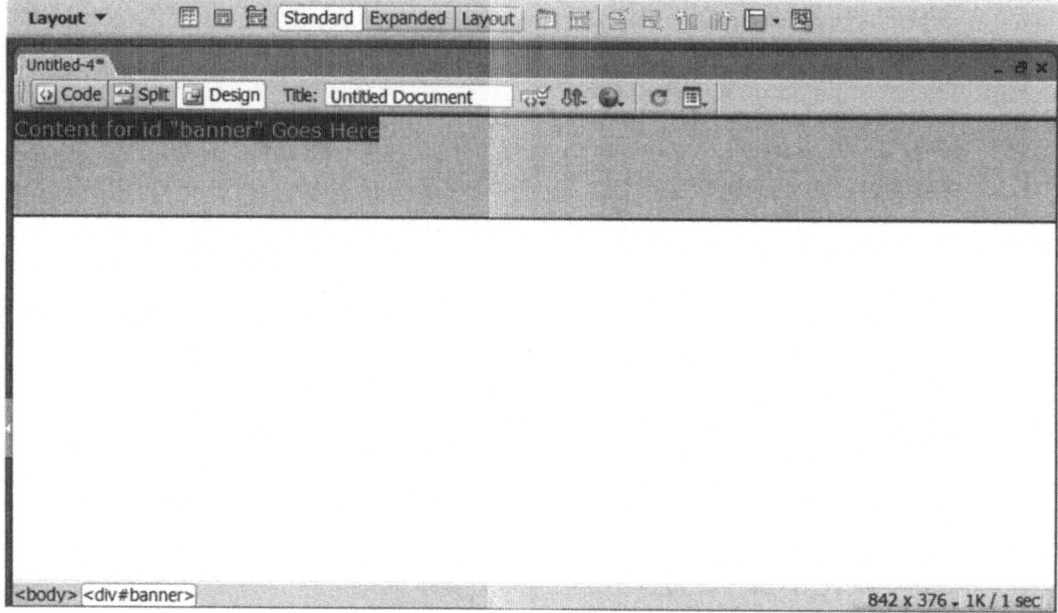

Figure 2-35. A banner in Design view

5. Switch to Code view to see the markup that Dreamweaver added.

```
<div id ="banner">Content for id "banner" Goes here</div>
```

6. Delete the placeholder text. In the tables-based layout, there was some white space above the banner. You can reproduce this with CSS by adding a margin to the top of the banner. Edit the #banner ID again and select the Box category. Uncheck the Same for all check box in the Margin section and then set the following properties, as shown in Figure 2-36:

- **Top**: 20 pixels

- **Right**: 0 pixels

- **Bottom**: 20 pixels

- **Left**: 0 pixels

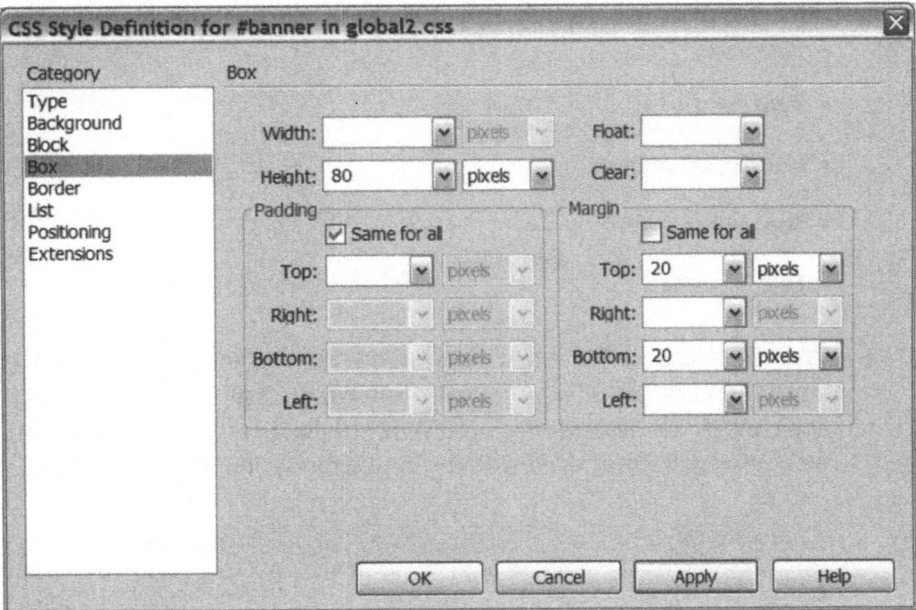

Figure 2-36. The Box category

7. Click OK to see the change in Design view.

Create the Navigation

Follow these steps to create the navigation.

1. Create a new CSS class; this time select the Advanced (IDs, contextual selectors, etc) radio button, and type **#nav** in the Selector text box, as shown in Figure 2-37.

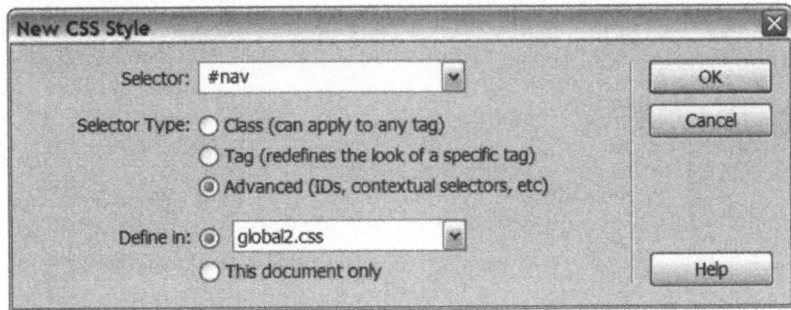

Figure 2-37. Creating an advanced CSS class

2. Click OK. Then select the Positioning category and set the following properties:

   - **Type**: absolute

   - **Width**: 200 pixels

   - **Top**: 140 pixels

   - **Left**: 4 pixels

3. Click OK. Click the Insert Div Tag icon once again, and in the ID drop-down list, click nav. In the Insert drop-down list, select After start of tag, and choose <div id="banner">, as shown in Figure 2-38, to ensure that this <div> tag is created outside the banner and is not nested inside it.

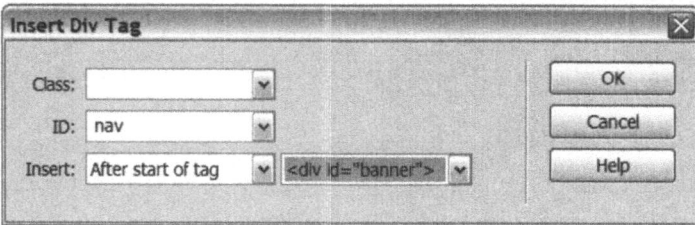

Figure 2-38. The Insert Div Tag dialog box

4. Click OK. The <div> tag will appear underneath the banner on the left, as shown in Figure 2-39.

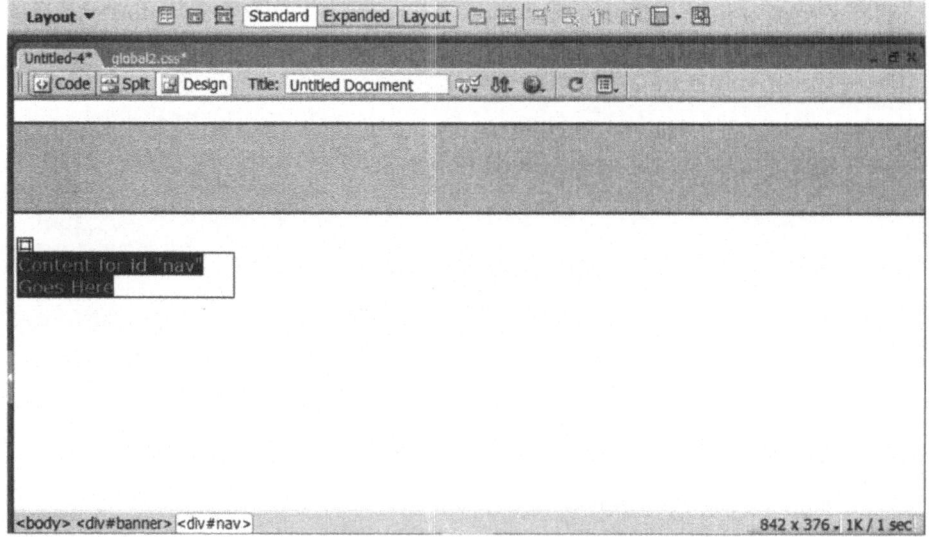

Figure 2-39. The <div> tag Design view

CSS Navigation Buttons

One way to trim down file sizes and improve the accessibility of your document is to use CSS for navigation that would have previously required images. You will use CSS in this way to create your navigation. Your navigation is simply a list of places where the user can go, and as such, using a list to markup the content is a good choice.

1. In the <div#nav> tag, create a list, and make each item a link, as shown in Figure 2-40.

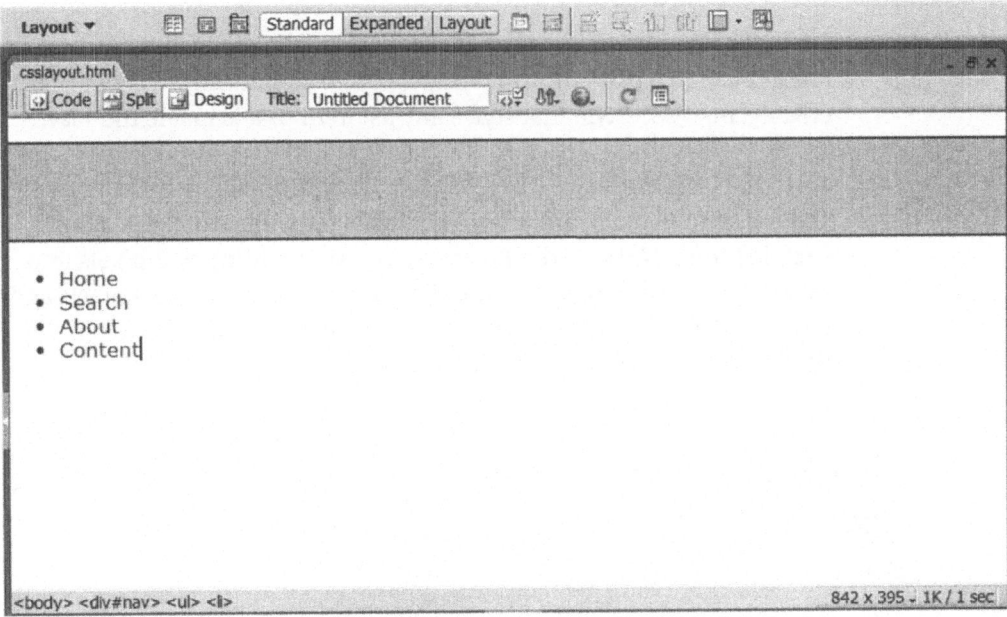

Figure 2-40. Design view showing a list

2. First you will style the list itself. Create a new CSS style, choose Advanced, and in the Selector box, type **#nav ul**, as shown in Figure 2-41.

    Using the selector #nav ul means that you are creating styles for all <ul> tags within the div #nav. Any <ul> tags within that division will be styled in this way, but those not inside this area of the page will retain their default formatting.

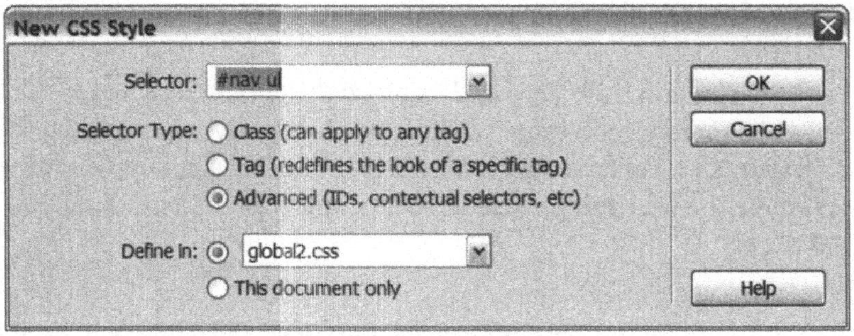

Figure 2-41. Creating styles for all `<ul>` tags

3. Go to the Box category of the CSS Style Definition dialog box and set Margin Left to 0 pixels and Padding Left to 0 pixels. Click OK and then create a new CSS Style that styles any list item that is inside the #nav.

4. Go to the List category of the CSS Style Definition dialog box and under Type, select the none check box to remove the bullet from the start of each list item. Next, in the Box category, set padding to 3 pixels and select the Same for all check box. Set the bottom margin to 4 pixels and clear the Same for all check box. To add a border to each item, use the Border category, as shown in Figure 2-42.

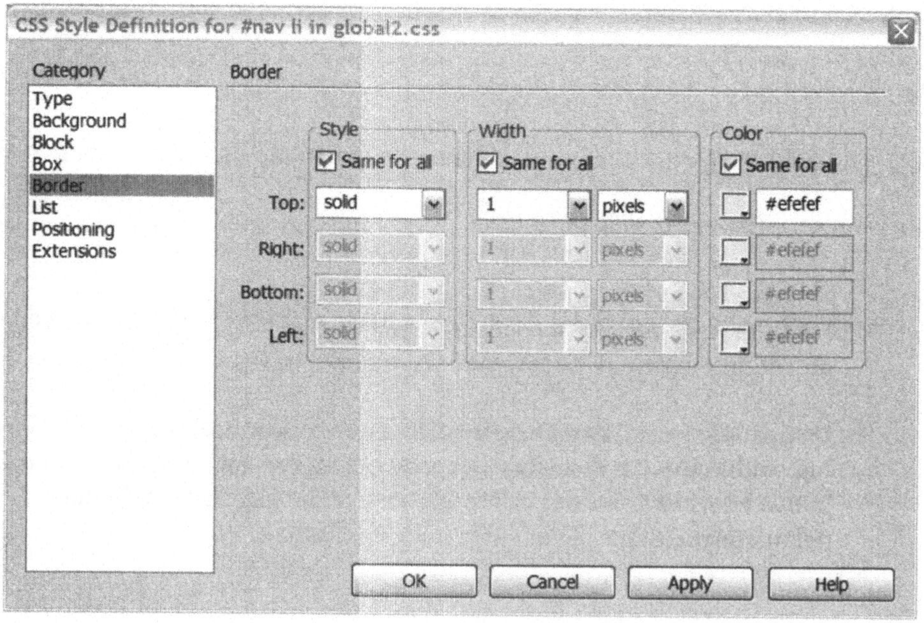

Figure 2-42. Setting border properties

5. You now need to style the anchor tag—the navigation link itself. Create a new CSS class, select the Advanced radio button, and type **#nav a:link**. Using the Type category, style the text of the link and set the color. You can also set the navigation link to have no underline by selecting the none check box, as shown in Figure 2-43.

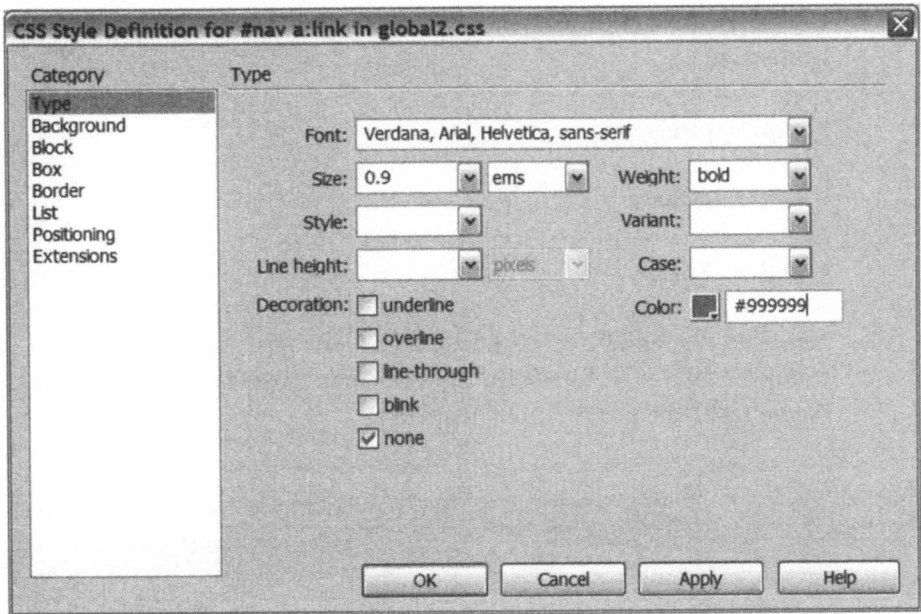

Figure 2-43. Setting text properties

6. After setting up #nav a:link, repeat this process for #nav a:visited, #nav a:hover, and #nav a:active. If you want your navigation to be highlighted when the user holds his or her mouse pointer over the link, set a different color for the #nav a:hover state.

TIP *When setting different properties for the hover state, take care not to change the size of the text. If you do, you will end up with a jiggling effect as the page elements are shifted around by the change in size of the link.*

The Content Area

Finally, for this simple layout, you need to place the content on the page.

1. Create a new CSS style, select the Advanced radio button, and type **#content** into the Selector box. You want your content to be liquid and stretch to fill the user's screen width, so click the Box category, and in the Margin area, clear the Same for all check box and set the following properties:

   - **Top**: 50 pixels

   - **Left**: 260 pixels

   - **Right**: 40 pixels

2. Now click OK, and insert the content after the tag `<div id="nav">`. You should see the `<div>` appear in the main area of the page, as shown in Figure 2-44. Add some dummy content.

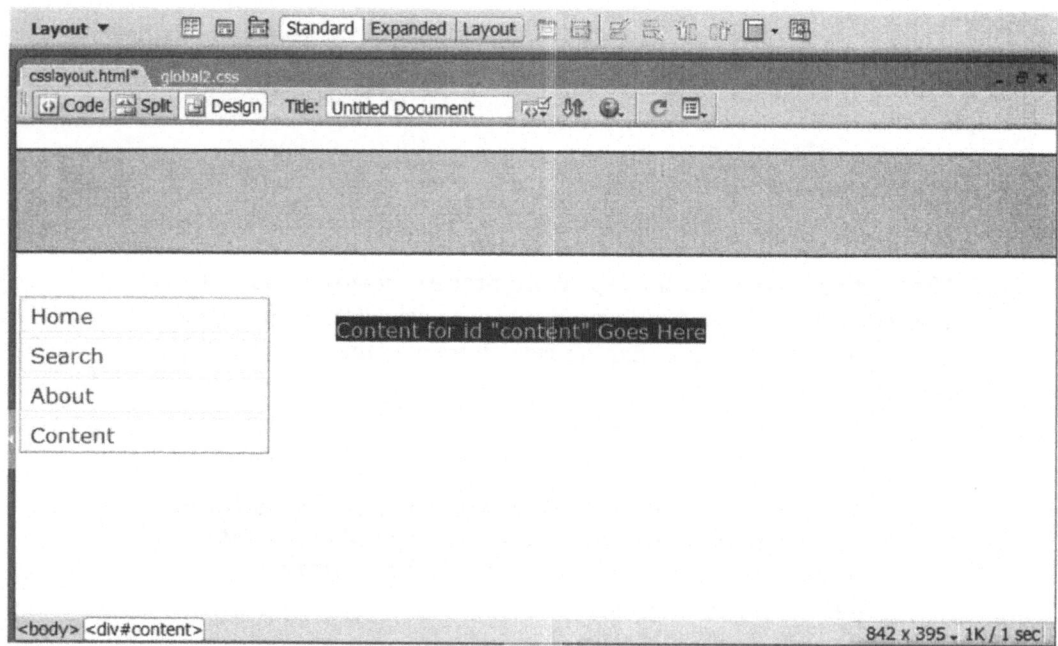

Figure 2-44. The `<div>` tag in the page's main area

As you may have realized, you did not use absolute positioning or anything else to position this content. You simply used a margin to clear it from the navigation, which is absolutely positioned. This works because absolute positioning takes an element out of the flow of the document. The content without any margins applied to it would have simply lain over the top of the navigation as if the navigation was not there.

To display the layout so it is resized with the user's screen size, make sure that the content leaves space for the absolutely positioned navigation.

This is a very simple layout, but hopefully it has given you an idea of the tools that are available in Dreamweaver to work with CSS layouts. If this is your first experience with CSS, you may find the concepts a little tricky, but the best way to become accustomed to any new way of working is simply to experiment and try things out. The "Resources" section at the end of this chapter lists several sites that provide CSS layouts that you can experiment with. There are also the CSS page designs within Dreamweaver that you can use as starting points for your own experiments.

Browser and Device Issues

Browser issues are cited as the main reason that people do not implement CSS on their web sites; however, this excuse is fast becoming outdated. Even so, we will look at how to address these issues in this section.

Although browsers with no support for CSS should render your content in a readable fashion, there are problems with browsers that have partial or buggy support for CSS, and it is these browsers, particularly Netscape 4, that you need to consider.

Versions of Netscape 4 may crash or render your page unusable or just plain ugly when encountering certain valid CSS declarations. Thankfully, there are ways around this problem.

Netscape 4

Earlier, we looked at two ways of attaching a stylesheet to a page: linking it and importing it. Netscape 4 does not recognize the @ Import directive, and you can use this fact to your advantage by attaching two stylesheets to the page: one basic, Netscape 4–friendly stylesheet that you link to your page, and another, more advanced stylesheet that you attach using @ Import, making it invisible to Netscape 4.

1. To attach two stylesheets to your page in this way using Dreamweaver, attach the basic Netscape 4–friendly stylesheet first, using the link method, as shown in Figure 2-45.

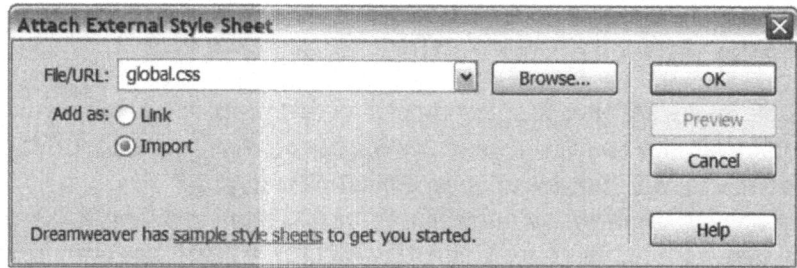

Figure 2-45. The link method

2. Attach the second stylesheet with the declarations for newer browsers using @ Import, as shown in Figure 2-46.

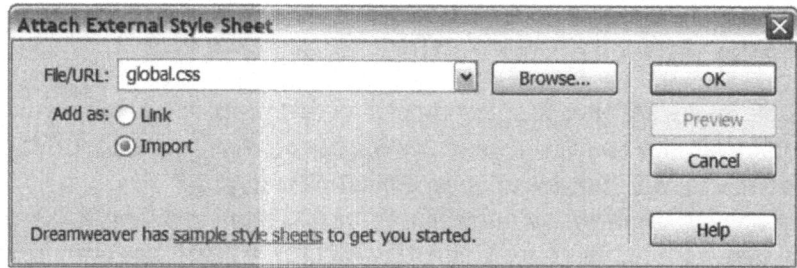

Figure 2-46. The import method

3. Specify the imported stylesheet after the linked stylesheet so that the Netscape 4–friendly CSS is overridden by the second stylesheet. In Code view, the generated code looks like this:

```
<link href="oldbrowsers.css" rel="stylesheet" type="text/css" />
<style type="text/css">
<!--
@import url("newbrowsers.css");
-->
</style>
```

Any CSS that you want to be different for newer browsers must be included in the imported stylesheet. The browser will use the values in the linked stylesheet if no values are found in the imported one for that element.

JavaScript Techniques

It is possible to use JavaScript to detect what browser is being used, and then write an appropriate stylesheet for that browser. This method relies on the user having JavaScript turned on, but it can be very useful if you find that a bug in a particular browser causes a crash or other problem and you need to isolate that browser by attaching a stylesheet designed to be friendly to it.

You can also use JavaScript to detect whether the user is visiting with a newer, more standards-compliant browser or a version of the browser earlier than 5, and display stylesheets accordingly. This method checks to see whether the browser supports the W3C DOM and then writes the appropriate stylesheet into the page:

```
<script language="javascript" type="text/javascript">
if (!document.getElementById) {
document.write('<link rel="stylesheet" href="oldbrowsers.css" type="text/css" />');
}
else
{
document.write('<link rel="stylesheet" href="newbrowsers.css" type="text/css" />');
}
</script>
```

The first stylesheet in the code just shown should be the stylesheet for those older browsers that do not support the W3C DOM; the second stylesheet is for all newer browsers.

Media Descriptors

Media descriptors allow you to specify how a document is presented on different media: monitor screens, paper, screen readers, Braille readers, or other devices. For example, you can specify that one stylesheet is used if a page is being printed and another is used when it is displayed in the browser window. A media descriptor allows a stylesheet designed with speech synthesis rules to be served to screen readers and stylesheets designed with Web TV or PDAs in mind to be served appropriately.

Whether a browser or device understands the media descriptor varies between devices at present, but there is good support for print (the media descriptor you will currently find most useful). Learning to use this method of serving appropriate presentational rules should become more useful in the future as device support grows.

The media descriptors as listed in the CSS2 specification are shown in Table 2-2.

Table 2-2. CSS2 Media Descriptors

Descriptor	Media
all	All devices.
aural	Speech synthesizers (screen readers).
braille	Braille tactile feedback devices.
embossed	Paged Braille printers.
handheld	Handheld devices (small screen, monochrome, limited bandwidth).
print	Documents to be printed.
projection	Projection devices.
screen	Color computer screens—standard web browsers.
tty	Media using a fixed-pitch character grid or portable devices with limited display capabilities. These are typically older mobile devices; most current devices would fall into the handheld category.
tv	Television.

You can use media descriptors either by specifying a separate stylesheet for each type that you want to use or by using @ Import.

Specifying a Separate Stylesheet for Each Media Descriptor

If you already have a stylesheet linked to your page for presenting your document in a browser and you want to add a stylesheet that will only come into play when the document is printed, you can add a second linked stylesheet for print. You will also need to add the media descriptor screen to your existing stylesheet so that the browser knows to use the screen stylesheet in the browser and the print stylesheet when the page is printed.

```
<link rel="stylesheet" type="text/css" media="screen" href="screen.css" />
<link rel="stylesheet" type="text/css" media="print" href="print.css" />
```

Using a print stylesheet allows you to, for instance, hide navigation when a document is printed, change the font from a sans-serif typeface (which is more readable on screen) to a serif typeface (which is more readable in print), and remove a background color or images that would cause the printing to take longer.

Media Descriptors with Imported Stylesheets

The method just outlined means that you need to create a separate stylesheet for each browser. However, by using @ Import, you can specify certain elements within one stylesheet to apply to different types of media. To use the @ Import method, attach your stylesheet to the page.

```
<style type="text/css" media="all">@import "all.css";</style>
```

Within the all.css stylesheet, add attributes for each media descriptor by using @ media.

```
@media print {
  body { font-size: 10pt; }
}

@media screen {
  body { font-size: 12px; }
}

@media screen, print {
  body { color: #000000; }
}
```

The declarations just shown give a font size of 10 points when the page is printed and 12 pixels when the page is viewed in a regular browser. Both screen and print will use #000000 (black) as the color of the body text.

Working with Dynamic Data

Later in this book, you will immerse yourself in developing dynamic ASP.NET sites in Dreamweaver MX 2004. Developing with valid XHTML or HTML should make your life easier when incorporating dynamic data into your page. When data is being pulled from a database, small errors such as unclosed tags and badly nested elements can wreak havoc across your site and become difficult to debug, so starting with a solid framework as you design your layout will save time later on.

A combination of valid (X)HTML and CSS is ideal for a dynamic site, especially those sites that allow users to add information (such as content management systems or client-updateable news pages) because your stylesheets ensure that consistency is maintained across your site.

What to Watch Out For

There are some issues to watch out for when working with dynamic pages.

- When selecting an area to use as a **repeat region** (a dynamic, repeating block of code pulled from a database), ensure that you select the entire block of code that you want to be repeated, and that the tags are properly closed and nested when the page is viewed in a web browser.

- When creating areas of your page that will be displayed conditionally, ensure that all tags are closed correctly when the page is loaded under each possible condition.

- If you are creating pages to which users or authors will add content via an administration section, take extra care in the design of the application so that the authors do not add anything invalid, or add HTML markup where you are working in XHTML.

Validating Dynamic Pages

Dynamic pages should be validated with the online validator at the W3C. If the pages include conditional regions, validate each possible way that the page can be displayed if at all possible. Your server-side code will not cause any validation problems with the validator because by the time it has been parsed by the server, the validator sees only the (X)HTML generated from the server-side code.

If you are maintaining a dynamic site, pages that are frequently modified should be validated occasionally in order to check that you are effectively counteracting invalid items.

Resources

There are many resources available online for those who want to further explore the subjects discussed in this chapter.

- **The Web Standards Project**: http://www.webstandards.org. The WaSP web site provides news and information about web standards and many helpful resources to help you to work with standards in your own projects.

- **NYPL Style Guide**: http://www.nypl.org/styleguide/. This style guide, created for the New York Public Library, is an easy-to-understand explanation of how to use web standards.

- **Macromedia DevNet**: http://www.macromedia.com/devnet/. Keep an eye on this site for tutorials, specifically about using XHTML and CSS with Dreamweaver. There are whole sections devoted to CSS and accessibility.

- **W3Schools**: http://www.w3schools.com. Check out the CSS and XHTML tutorials here. This site has lots of information on many web technologies presented in a clear and easy-to-understand manner.

- **CSS-Discuss**: http://www.css-discuss.org. A mailing list for CSS discussion. Try searching the archives here if you are having a problem with CSS. If you cannot find an answer, posting to the list will get some of the best CSS brains in the world thinking over your problem for you. To get useful help on this mailing list and others like it, it is a good idea to ensure that you have validated your document and CSS file before posting because it makes it easier for people to see whether your problem is an error on your part or perhaps a browser bug for which there is a workaround.

- **CSS Zen Garden**: http://www.csszengarden.com. Inspiration for CSS layouts.

- **Real World Style**: http://realworldstyle.com. CSS layouts, tips, and techniques, many of which work in Netscape 4.

- **CSS Panic Guide**: http://www.thenoodleincident.com/tutorials/css/. A good place to go when it all seems to be going wrong or when you want to find more resources on CSS.

Summary

With Macromedia Dreamweaver MX 2004, creating valid and accessible web sites with HTML and XHTML is within the reach of every designer and developer. In this chapter, we discussed

- How to write valid XHTML in the Dreamweaver environment

- How to create standards-compliant, tables-based layouts in Dreamweaver

- How to use CSS to replace elements that are deprecated in the transitional DOCTYPE and not allowed if you validate to Strict

- How to use CSS for layout

This chapter provided some essential building blocks for good practices in web development that will assist you as you move onward to styling your pages with CSS and adding dynamic data to your web sites. By following best practices, not only will your web sites be more accessible to all web users, but also you will find your working and debugging methods are streamlined and simplified.

CHAPTER 3

Introducing ASP.NET

IN THIS CHAPTER, you will look beyond the three-letter acronyms that form ASP.NET to discover its origins and how it fits in the Internet technologies picture. We will show you the advantages that ASP.NET offers over alternative technologies. We will also compare it to its predecessor, classic ASP. This will ready you for Chapter 4, where we will delve deeper into the technical aspects of ASP.NET and provide you with a basic migration guide from classic ASP.

If you are familiar with ASP.NET and feel ready to get started creating sites in ASP.NET utilizing Dreamweaver's facilities, you can safely skip this chapter, although you may find some of the information presented here useful.

The .NET Framework

To understand why ASP.NET exists at all, you first need to examine the concept of the .NET Framework. The purpose of .NET is quite simple: to create a common framework in which all managed applications will run. For those of you who have worked with Java, this may sound very familiar. In fact, .NET seems to have been inspired by the Java success, but instead of trying to be a common language for different systems, .NET is focused on bringing different programming languages together to operate uniformly on Windows.

As a result, the obvious disadvantage is that .NET applications can only run on Windows systems, whether they act as servers or clients. For web developers interested in ASP.NET, this is probably a nonissue because all the .NET activity is on the server and only HTML reaches the client. The advantages of .NET over its nearest equivalent, Java, include the following:

- Because Java is multiplatform, its scope is limited to the lowest-common denominator of available computers and operating systems. In contrast, .NET programs can take full advantage of any feature of Windows.

- Because Java is the lowest-common denominator, developers often use proprietary classes to access features available to the target platform. This leads to nonportable code that has to be customized for the target platform anyway.

- Because Java Database Connectivity (JDBC) forces round-trips to the database, the .NET application architecture is faster. ADO.NET disconnected data access allows more data functions to be completed in memory.

In this chapter, we explain the basics of how .NET works so that ASP.NET makes sense. Figure 3-1 shows a schematic of the logical layers of the .NET Framework and where ASP.NET fits into it.

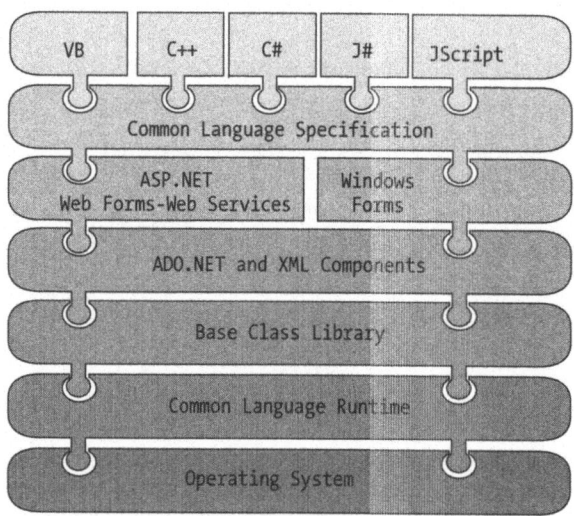

Figure 3-1. The .NET Framework's logical layers

Regardless of which language you use to write your application, it is translated into intermediate code, which is this code that will be executed in real time by the Common Language Runtime (CLR). This intermediate code is generated by the .NET compilers, and it is called Microsoft Intermediate Language (MSIL). It is a CPU-independent set of instructions that can be efficiently converted to CPU-specific code by a just-in-time (JIT) compiler. Because the CLR supplies one or more JIT compilers for each computer architecture it supports, the same set of MSIL can be compiled and run on any supported architecture.

TIP *As you can see from Figure 3-1, ASP.NET is simply another component operating on top of the same architecture as any Windows Forms .NET program. The implication is that any code that handles business logic or other background programming can be easily reused for both desktop and web applications.*

Because of the independence provided by the CLR, developers do not have to worry about missing any features or functionality arising from your language choice.

Another important way .NET affects web developers is it contains features that prevent bad coding practices that create nonreusable components. .NET encourages separation of the logical parts that compose a web page: interface design, business rules, data manipulation functions, custom objects, and so on. More on this in the "Active Server Pages .NET" section of this chapter and of course in subsequent chapters.

Installing the .NET Framework

To install the .NET classes necessary for ASP.NET development, you need to download the Microsoft .NET Framework version 1.1 redistributable from http://msdn.microsoft.com/library/default.asp?url=/downloads/list/netdevframework.asp. It's a 24MB download, but it contains everything you need for ASP.NET web pages or Windows Forms programming. You can also download the .NET software development kit (110MB) from the same page, but it's not essential unless you want to develop XML web services. The redistributable package is available as a stand-alone executable file, Dotnetfx.exe, which you simply double-click after downloading. You need to have administrator privileges to install it.

You can install Dotnetfx.exe on any machine that runs Windows 98 or later; however, ASP.NET is supported only on the following platforms:

- Microsoft Windows 2000 Professional (Service Pack 3 recommended)

- Microsoft Windows 2000 Server (Service Pack 3 recommended)

- Microsoft Windows XP Professional

- Microsoft Windows Server 2003 family

The platforms just listed are the only ones capable of hosting and testing ASP.NET applications. However, you can develop these ASP.NET applications on any computer running Dreamweaver, including the Macintosh.

You also need to have

- Microsoft Data Access Components 2.6; Microsoft Data Access Components 2.7 Service Pack 1 is recommended. This is for applications that use data access.

- Internet Information Services (IIS) version 5.0 or later. To access the features of ASP.NET, IIS with the latest security updates must be installed prior to installing the .NET Framework.

After installation and restarting, you don't need to do anything else. ASP.NET is installed as part of your IIS web server.

ASP.NET-Related Internet Concepts

This section is intended for those of you who are relatively new to web development. You are working with the latest technology available, but you still need some information to understand why ASP.NET is what it is. You may skip this section if you have experience with ASP or other web scripting technologies, but some of the information presented here may be new and interesting to you.

Common Gateway Interface

Sharing information on the Internet is a simple process: A client machine uses a web browser to request a file from a web server, and the web server responds by sending the requested file. Improvements to that model include generating HTML dynamically by using the output of a program, which is executed on behalf of the web client. This is the purpose of the Common Gateway Interface (CGI): to execute a program on behalf of the web server (and by extension, the web client) and merge the output into the response.

ISAPI Filters

The Internet Server Application Programming Interface (ISAPI) model was developed as a higher-performance alternative to CGI. ISAPI provides a number of advantages over CGI, including lower overhead, faster loading, and better scalability.

The chief difference between the CGI and ISAPI programming models is the way processing is handled. With CGI, the system creates a unique process for every request. Each time an HTTP server receives a request, it initiates a new process. Because the operating system must maintain all these processes, CGI is resource intensive. This inherent limitation makes it difficult to develop responsive Internet applications with CGI. With ISAPI, requests do not require a separate process. Threads are used to isolate and synchronize work items, resulting in a more efficient use of system resources.

Because ISAPI applications are compiled code, they are processed faster than ASP files or files that call COM components.

Internet Information Server

On Windows systems, the default software that coordinates all the components of an HTTP request is the IIS server. IIS, along with the HTTP listener (HTTP.sys) handles the following tasks:

- Establishes and maintains HTTP connections

- Populates instances of the ASP and ASP.NET objects with available data from each HTTP request, such as session state information, error information, and client certificate information

- Passes a request body through a chain of possible destinations, as described in Table 3-1

- Populates an instance of the response object as a response is built during the processing of each request

- Modifies HTTP headers in a response according to configuration settings set by the administrator or page-level settings written by the application developer

- Sends HTTP responses back to clients

Table 3-1. Functions Performed by IIS

Request Type	Action Taken by IIS
HTML page	IIS returns the page immediately in HTML format.
ISAPI extension	IIS loads the ISAPI DLL (if it is not already running) and the request is sent to the extension.
File name whose extension is mapped to a particular ISAPI extension	IIS loads the appropriate DLL file and presents the request to the extension. For example, requests for Active Server Pages (*.asp) files are resolved by invoking an ASP-specific extension module named asp.dll. Likewise, requests for ASP.NET resources (for example, *.aspx, *.asmx, *.ashx) are mapped to aspnet_isapi.dll so that all requests for files with those extensions will be directed to aspnet_isapi.dll. The .stm and .shtm extensions are mapped to ssinc.dll.
CGI application	IIS creates a new process. IIS then provides the query string and other parameters that are included with the request through the environment and standard input (STDIN) handle for the process.

Most of the non–Microsoft-related tasks just listed are also performed by many other kinds of web server software. However, we are only concerned with IIS as our Internet enabler. Later, we will take you through the creation of a web site in IIS, and that will put these concepts in perspective.

Layers in Web Request Processing

It's instructive to look at how all the components we've mentioned so far fit together. Today's client/server applications resemble their linearly programmed ancestors so little that they've been given a new name: the **multi-tier application**, also known as **n-tier architecture**. In this model, processing is distributed between the client and the server, and business logic is captured in a middle tier. Most systems perform the following three main tasks, which correspond to three tiers, or layers, of the n-tier model. Table 3-2 describes the three tiers.

Table 3-2. Multi-Tier Architecture Layers

Task	Tier	Description
User interface and navigation	Tier 1	A graphical user interface so that users can interact with the application, input data, and view the results of requests. This layer is also responsible for formatting the data once the client receives it back from the server. In web applications, a browser performs the tasks of this layer.
Business logic	Tier 2	Components that connect the data sources with the presentation application. They are reusable pieces of code that can be changed without the need to change the whole application. Their tasks are logical functions, security checks, calculations, and so on.
Data services	Tier 3	Data services are provided by a structured (databases, XML databases) or unstructured (email programs, directories) data store, which manages and provides access to the data.

Figure 3-2 shows how the Microsoft classic ASP technologies fit in this system architecture.

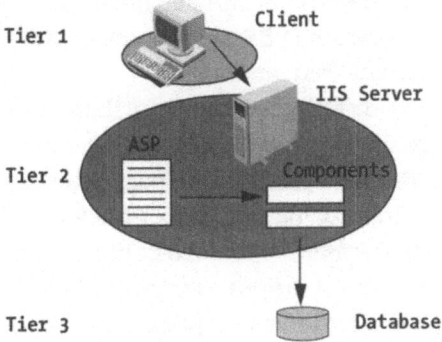

Figure 3-2. Classic ASP and IIS

The three-tier architecture isolates each major piece of ASP and component functionality so that the presentation (user interface) is independent of the processing rules and business logic, which in turn is separate from the data. This model requires much more analysis and design up front, but it greatly reduces maintenance costs and increases functional flexibility in the long run via reuse, easy maintenance, sectional upgrade, and so on. Of course, this is a Windows-based concept, but the principles are platform independent, which is why it has proved popular with most modern web projects. Let's look at how ASP.NET uses the second tier to link the scripts, many more components, and server under one shell.

ASP and Other Web Scripts

Microsoft Active Server Pages can be thought of as a type of ISAPI extension whose code is executed in real time (a script). More specifically, ASP is a server-side scripting environment that you can use to create dynamic and interactive web pages and build powerful web applications. With ASP, you can combine HTML pages, script commands, and COM components to create interactive web pages or powerful web-based applications that are easy to develop and modify.

When the server receives a request for an ASP file, it processes server-side script code contained in the file to build an HTML web page that is sent to the browser. In addition to server-side script code, ASP files can contain HTML (including related client-side scripts) and calls to COM components that perform a variety of tasks, such as connecting to a database or processing business logic.

Unlike conventional CGI applications, ASP was designed to simplify the process of developing web applications. By placing a few ASP tags in the appropriate places, you can add database connectivity or advanced customization features to a static page. ASP uses popular web scripting languages such as

Microsoft JScript (the Microsoft implementation of the ECMA 262 language specification), Microsoft Visual Basic Scripting Edition (VBScript), or any COM-compliant scripting language, including JavaScript, Perl, and others.

This interactivity is valid for most other web scripting technologies. From the web programmer's point of view, ASP may appear to be more intuitive than other scripted technologies by bringing the server execution to an HTML page (others, like PHP, also use the ASP paradigm); however, markup tags get dispersed with programming pieces, which can lead to code that is hard to read. In contrast, languages like Perl use code statements to create the page output, which is clearer but also creates code that looks more like a program than a web page.

Active Server Pages .NET

The easiest way to introduce ASP.NET is to highlight the most fundamental difference from ASP. Even if you have not used ASP before, you will be able to follow the general idea—we simply contrast the concept, not the technicalities.

The Request/Response Model

Recall that in web pages, you send an HTTP request (for example, a URL and the data in a form) to the server and it sends back a response (a web page). Your browser then typically displays that response. When you click various web page elements, such as buttons or links, one of two things can happen. If the web page has client-side script code (downloaded with the web page, typically in JScript or JavaScript), an event handler might handle the event without even talking to the server. Or, depending on the HTML code for the web page element (such as a Submit button), your browser might send an HTTP request to the server.

The programming model for classic ASP is based on the HTTP request/response model. This programming model can be fairly difficult to use because you have to save data across HTTP requests and responses so that you can reconstruct the state of a page at every request. This contrasts with the simpler event-driven forms and controls model that most Windows applications use. For example, if you had a wizard-like series of pages in your web application, you would have to submit all the accumulated data to each page as hidden inputs, whereas a desktop application can simply access the data anytime.

The ASP.NET Forms-Based Model

The programming model in ASP.NET adds forms and controls. The programming model embodied by ASP.NET Web Forms is fairly similar to that of a Windows application, although the mechanisms underneath the programming models are very different.

Conceptually, a pure Web Forms application consists of a set of forms that contain controls and HTML. The controls have properties and methods, and they can generate events. These events are usually handled on the server, although it's possible to handle certain events on the client. This is a much simpler model than the ASP model because you don't have to think about how the browser will reconstruct the state of the page—ASP.NET takes care of that. You only have to create the logic of interaction between the controls of a web page and the logic between web pages.

The abilities of ASP.NET are also augmented by access to a whole new range of components, making it more like a true desktop application. The three-tier schematic then looks as shown in Figure 3-3.

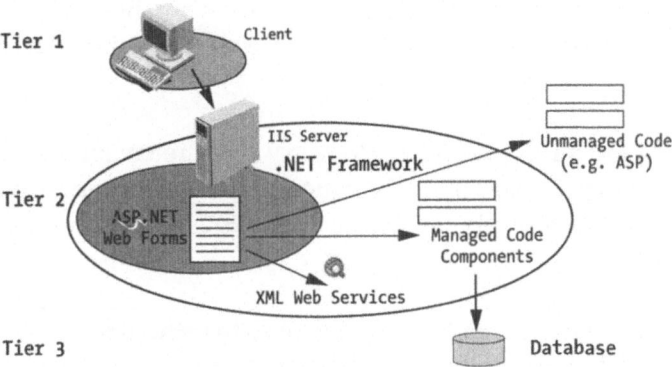

Figure 3-3. The ASP.NET position within the Windows environment

More About ASP.NET

There are many more aspects of ASP.NET that are of interest to web developers.

- **Not just a script**: ASP.NET is not just the ASP version that can run within .NET. As mentioned before, it can be written using up to 20 languages, in addition to the 4 built-in ones: VB .NET, C#, C++, and JScript .NET. A list of ongoing projects on .NET ports of various languages can be found at http://www.cetus-links.org/oo_dotnet.html#oo_dotnet_netlang. ASP.NET also allows you to take full advantage of the features of the CLR, such as type safety, inheritance, language interoperability, and versioning.

- **More built-in controls**: Classic ASP was easy to use and made the creation of dynamic web content easy, but as the complexity of the dynamic content increased, the code necessary to enable complex pages became unmanageable. ASP.NET simplifies the creation of complex pages by providing prebuilt server-side controls and object types that web developers can use much like the drag-and-drop controls that developers use in Windows desktop applications.

- **Real-time configuration**: There's no need to restart the web server any-more. ASP.NET is configured via easy-to-read XML files that are editable with any text editor and that take effect the moment they're saved. The same is true for components that are used in your pages—as soon as the DLL file is copied, the .NET Framework takes care of installation and regis-tration so that it's immediately available for use inside ASP.NET pages.

- **Advanced browser handling**: Because ASP.NET writes the HTML for ASP.NET controls, you don't have to worry about writing different HTML for different browsers. Instead, ASP.NET detects what browser is being used and generates the appropriate HTML. All you do is use the high-level controls and let ASP.NET deal with the details. (This does not, however, get you out of testing your application against all the browsers you intend to support.)

- **Easy programming model**: You don't have to worry about re-creating the state of each control in your page for each request. You can concentrate on writing code for how the controls can interact and ASP.NET handles the presentation to web clients.

- **Rich class framework**: Application features that used to be hard to imple-ment or required a third-party component can now be added in just a few lines of code using the .NET Framework. The .NET Framework offers over 4,500 classes that encapsulate rich functionality like XML, data access, file upload, regular expressions, image generation, performance monitoring and logging, transactions, message queuing, SMTP mail, and so on.

- **Compiled execution**: ASP.NET dynamically compiles your pages and stores the compiled results so they can be reused for subsequent requests. ASP.NET will also automatically detect any changes you make and recompile them in real time. Dynamic compilation ensures that your application is always up to date, and compiled execution makes it fast. Most applications migrated from classic ASP are three to five times faster in pages served.

- **Rich output caching**: ASP.NET output caching can dramatically improve the performance and scalability of your application. When output caching is enabled on a page, ASP.NET executes the page just once and then saves the result in memory, in addition to sending it to the user. When another user requests the same page, ASP.NET serves the cached result from mem-ory without reexecuting the page. Output caching is configurable and can be used to cache individual regions or an entire page.

- **Web farm session state**: ASP.NET session state lets you share session data and user-specific state values across all machines in a cluster of web servers, known as a **web farm**. Users who were once directed to the server holding their session's state now can hit different servers in the web farm over multiple requests and still have full access to their session.

- **Memory leak, deadlock, and crash protection**: ASP.NET automatically detects and recovers from errors like deadlocks and memory leaks to ensure that your application is always available to your users. ASP.NET automatically starts another copy of the ASP.NET worker process if the old one is running an application with memory leak problems, and it directs all new requests to the new process. Once the old process has finished processing its pending requests, it is gracefully disposed of and the leaked memory is released.

- **Easy deployment**: ASP.NET dramatically simplifies installation of your application. With ASP.NET, you can deploy an entire application as easily as an HTML page: Just copy it to the server. No need to run regsvr32 to register any components, and configuration settings are stored in an XML file within the application.

- **Easy migration path:** You don't have to migrate your existing applications to start using ASP.NET. ASP.NET runs on IIS side-by-side with classic ASP on Windows 2000 and Windows XP platforms. Your existing ASP applications continue to be processed by asp.dll, whereas new ASP.NET pages are processed by the new ASP.NET engine. We will show you the details of this in the Appendix.

- **XML web services**: XML web services allow applications to communicate and share data over the Internet, regardless of operating system or programming language. ASP.NET makes exposing and calling XML web services simple. Any class can be converted into an XML web service with just a few lines of code, and any class can be called by any Simple Object Access Protocol (SOAP) client. Likewise, ASP.NET makes it incredibly easy to call XML web services from your application. No knowledge of networking, XML, or SOAP is required.

- **Mobile web device support**: ASP.NET Mobile Controls is a new group of server controls that work at a more abstract level than regular ASP.NET controls. Mobile Controls let you easily target cell phones and PDAs (including over 80 mobile web devices) using ASP.NET. The list of supported devices is also easily updatable via configuration files, and like everything .NET, it is completely extensible to cover any future type of device. You write your application just once and the mobile controls automatically generate WAP/WML, HTML, CHTML, or your custom XML language, as required by the requesting device.

Now that you know where ASP.NET fits into the web developer's radar screen, let's get busy with the details. Next we discuss how an ASP.NET web site is created in Dreamweaver and IIS.

Creating an ASP.NET Web Site

Dreamweaver uses web site information to keep track of changes to files, updates to hyperlinks in documents, file uploads, and so on. What it does *not* do is to act as a web server—that is the role of IIS.

Dreamweaver Setup

Creating an ASP.NET web site is just like creating any other type of site in Dreamweaver. Follow these steps to set up a test site.

1. Go to the Files panel and click Manage Sites, as shown in Figure 3-4.

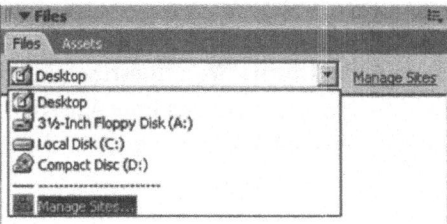

Figure 3-4. Starting the Site Definition Wizard in Dreamweaver

2. The Manage Sites dialog box appears. Click the New button and select Site from the small menu. The Site Definition Wizard appears, in which you can specify your web site's properties.

3. If it is not already selected, click the Basic tab and type a name for your web site—we will use **testASPNETsite** for our example. Select a language, as shown in Figure 3-5.

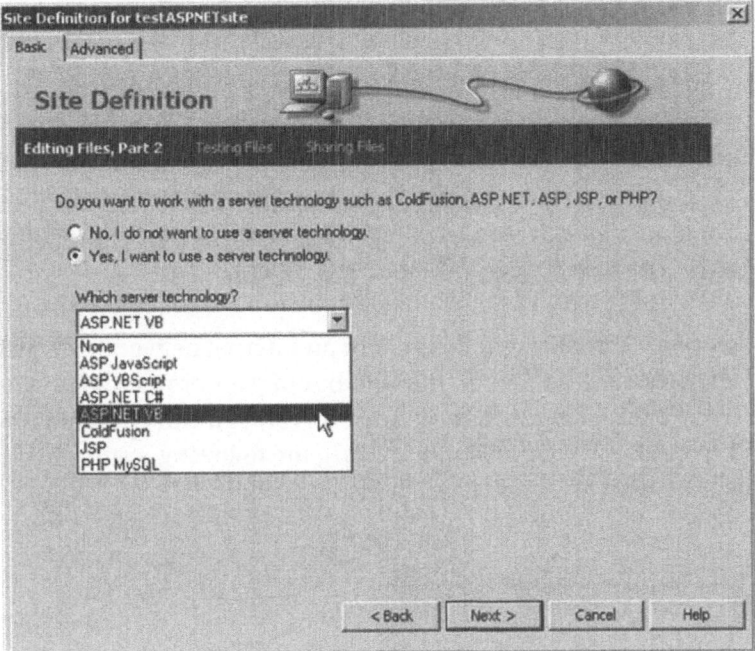

Figure 3-5. Choosing a technology for the new site

4. If you can't see the .NET language you want, select any one. In ASP.NET it's just a matter of changing the @ Page directive's language attribute. We'll show you how to do that in the next chapter.

5. Click Next to define the directory where you want to store your files. Dreamweaver detects the presence of IIS and allows you to use it as the testing server. Dreamweaver's web site definition is only internal—your pages will not be published on the web by merely existing under a Dreamweaver web site. We show you how to set up IIS in the next section. For now, go through the remaining screens of the wizard and specify where the testing server is located, and use the wizard's Advanced tab to customize the site creation. When you are done, your new web site should appear in the Files panel. (Ours is shown in Figure 3-6 with one page. You can use the default.aspx page supplied in the download.)

Figure 3-6. The newly created site, as listed in the Dreamweaver Files panel

6. To set up a page as the default for the web site, right-click it and select Set as Home Page from the menu. This will make it the page that appears if no specific page is requested.

Let's see how a site's contents can be made available to the web.

Internet Information Services Setup

To publish your content (to the Internet or an internal network), you will need to enter the server's IP address in the URL box of your browser. However, if you are just using your local machine as your server, you can enter **localhost** or **127.0.0.1** instead. You eventually want to see the following result when calling your page—we used an imaginary IP address in Figure 3-7.

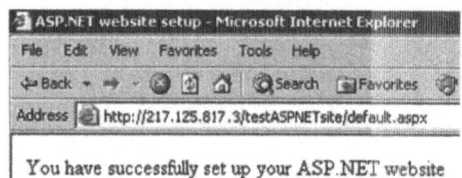

Figure 3-7. The desired result after successfully setting up the web site in IIS

1. Open the IIS interface on your Windows server by clicking Start ➤ Programs ➤ Administrative Tools ➤ Internet Services Manager. A web site is created called Default Web Site. This corresponds to any files you place directly in the C:\inetpub\wwwroot directory. If you are hosting only one web site on your server, you might as well use this predefined site. Otherwise, you can add new ones via the New Web Site Creation Wizard. The Web Site Creation Wizard can be started by selecting Action ➤ New ➤ Web Site, as shown in Figure 3-8.

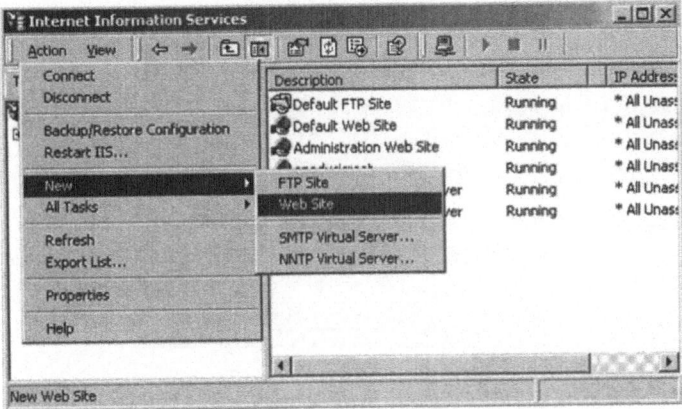

Figure 3-8. Starting the Web Site Creation Wizard in IIS

2. The first screen asks for the web site name, so enter the name you used in Dreamweaver. The next screen asks for your site's IP address. If you don't know it, leave it unspecified. You use the Host Header field (shown in Figure 3-9) when you want to host multiple web sites on the same server. The server needs some way of distinguishing which web site each received request is meant for, so it looks up the value of the HTTP Host Header. If you're hosting only one web site on your server (or if you are using your local machine), leave this field blank.

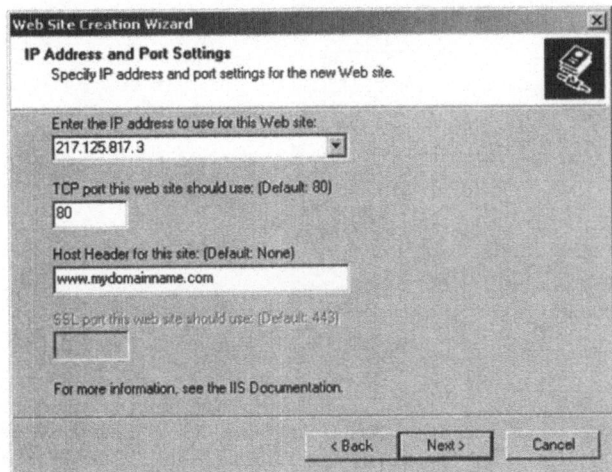

Figure 3-9. Specifying the IP address and the domain of your web site

3. Specify the physical directory where your web site content is stored, just as you did for Dreamweaver, as shown in Figure 3-10.

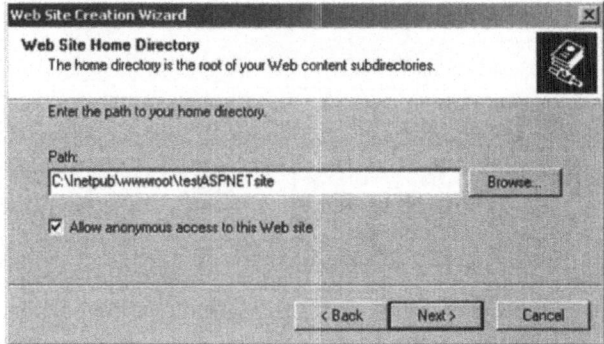

Figure 3-10. Specifying the path to your web site's root

Remember, this can be anywhere on your machine, not just under
C:\Inetpub\wwwroot, as long as web sharing is enabled for that folder.
Let's open a bracket here and quickly see how this is done.

4. Right-click your folder and click Properties. Select the Web Sharing tab
   and choose the Share this folder option, as shown in Figure 3-11. Then
   specify the web site you are sharing it on, if necessary.

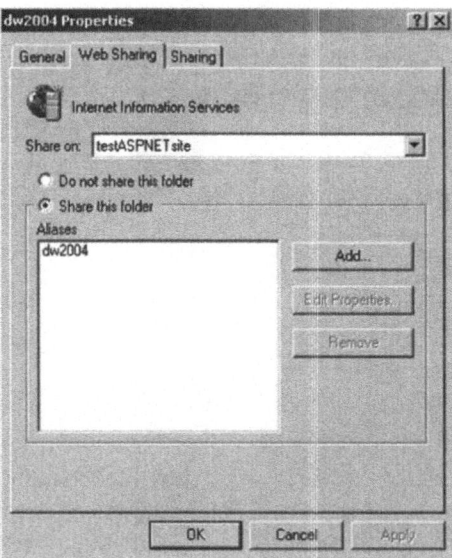

Figure 3-11. Configuring any folder for web access

5. Back to the IIS wizard, accept the defaults in the screen where web site
   permissions are set. The remaining features are advanced settings that
   involve security risks.

6. Click Finish to save the web site setup. Next you'll set your default page. Right-click the newly created web site and click Properties, as shown in Figure 3-12.

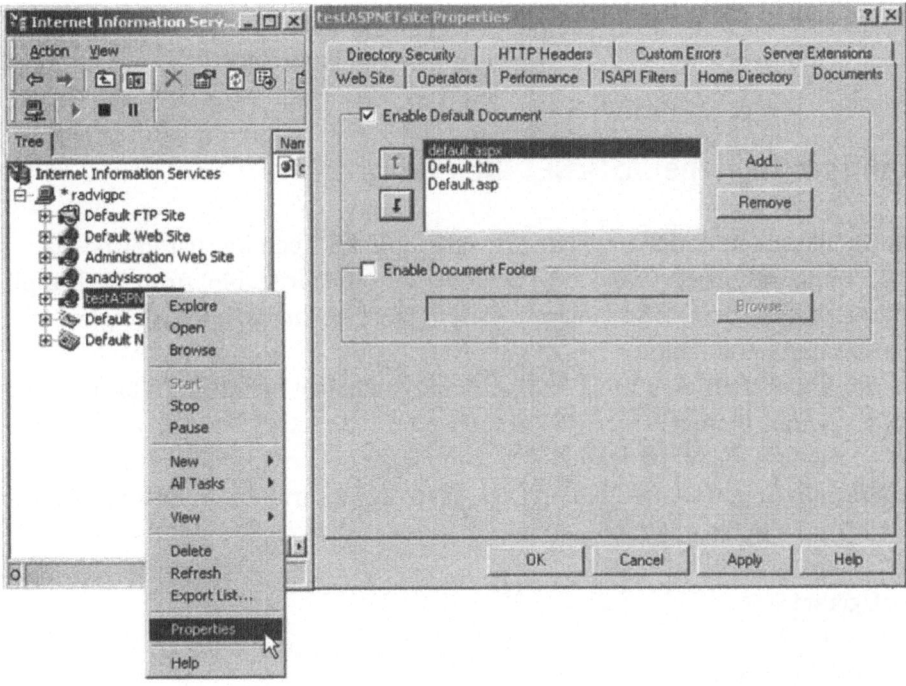

Figure 3-12. Additional web site properties

7. On the Documents tab, you can add the names of the default documents that will be sent to the client browser if none were specified. Let's assume that for your ASP.NET web site, the default is a page called default.aspx, so click Add and type that name. Then use the arrows on the left of the page list to move it up in priority (or remove the other entries).

8. While the Properties dialog box is open, let's check to see if the ASPX pages will be handled properly. Click the Home Directory tab and click the Configuration button. This changes application-related settings for this web site. Click the Mappings tab to display a list of all the ISAPIs that are listening for requests to the page types that they handle. If your installation of the .NET Framework was successful, you will see the extension .aspx in that list and the path to the aspnet_isapi.dll library that processes ASP.NET requests. You don't need to modify anything here, it's just reassuring that the mapping is actually there!

9. Your creation is now viewable to the world! Test your web site by typing the URL and pressing Enter.

```
http://[your IP address or domain name]/testASPNETsite
```

Your page should look as shown earlier in Figure 3-7.

Configuring the ASP.NET Web Site

Almost all aspects of .NET, and by extension ASP.NET, can be customized via XML configuration files. These are readable (but not writeable) from .NET applications, so you can extend their applicability by defining custom configuration sections and parameters.

For an ASP.NET web site, configuration is achieved by placing a file with the correct syntax, named web.config, at the web site directory. You can add more web.config files in child directories that you want to configure more specifically. For example, if you wanted to deny access to only a certain part of your web site, your web.config file might contain

```
<configuration>
    <system.web>
        <authorization>
            <allow roles="Admins"/>
            <deny users="*"/>
        </authorization>
    </system.web>
</configuration>
```

This example allows access to all members of the Admins role and denies access to all other users unless modified by other web.config files.

There are many other sections in a configuration file, and it is more efficient to refer you to the Microsoft documentation at http://msdn.microsoft.com/library/default.asp?url=/library/en-us/cpgenref/html/gngrfaspnetconfigurationsectionschema.asp than try to cover them all here. We will discuss only the most important section from the point of view of web developers, <browserCaps>.

The <browserCaps> section controls the settings of the browser capabilities class, System.Web.HttpBrowserCapabilities. It is contained directly within the <system.web> section.

```
<configuration>
    <system.web>
        <browserCaps>
```

For example, the following sample web.config demonstrates parsing the USER_AGENT HTTP header for the platform type. It uses a regular expression to match portions of text of the user agent string with known systems. If you have used ASP before, you will recognize that the file specifies name/value pairs in the form of assignment statements, similar to the IIS browscap.ini files. For example, the line platform=WinNT sets the value of the platform field to the string WinNT.

```
<configuration>
<system.web>
<browserCaps>
    <result type="System.Web.HttpBrowserCapabilities, System.Web"/>
    <use var="HTTP_USER_AGENT"/>
        browser=Unknown
        version=0.0
        majorver=0
        minorver=0
        frames=false
        tables=false
    <filter>
      <case match="Windows 98|Win98">
          platform=Win98
      </case>
      <case match="Windows NT|WinNT">
        platform=WinNT
      </case>
    </filter>
</browserCaps>
</system.web>
</configuration>
```

Within the ASP.NET page's code, we could also examine the value of the variables platform, browser, version, and so on, and make decisions regarding the content we display.

```
If Request.Browser.Platform="Win95" Then
Response.Write("Your platform cannot host .NET applications<br>")
End If
```

By this point you might be getting impatient to see more ASP.NET code. The next chapter is full of it!

Summary

We covered a lot of theory and concepts in this chapter. It is time to look at some practical examples of applying ASP.NET technology using Dreamweaver to solve everyday web programming problems. In the meantime, if you would like to see who can start hosting your ASP.NET web sites, take a look at `http://www.asp.net/ Default.aspx?tabindex=8&tabid=40`, where you will also find links to various ASP.NET community sites.

ASP.NET Features and Syntax

IN THIS CHAPTER, we show you the fundamentals of an ASP.NET program inside a web page. We explain the underlying principles of creating an ASP.NET application and make sure you understand how to integrate ASP.NET applications into Dreamweaver MX web pages. We focus only on Visual Basic .NET for our programming because it is the easiest way to show some of the coding principles you need. We explain ASP.NET features by creating ASP.NET pages from scratch, and we finish by showing ASP.NET-specific features of Dreamweaver MX.

To get into gear for true ASP.NET programming, let's kick off with a short introduction to the principles of object-oriented programming.

Object-Oriented Programming

The origins of object-oriented programming (OOP) are in the research area of artificial intelligence. OOP is usually contrasted to linear programming and is often mentioned with terms such as "event model" or "class modules." To help you understand the operation mode of ASP.NET, let's decipher what object-oriented programming means.

Everything around you is or is related to objects and the interactions between them. Your desk, your chair, and you are all "objects" with "properties" that have "methods" of reacting to "events." All the words in quotation marks are terms used in OOP technology—but in that programming context, objects are forms or their controls, and events are clicks or hovers of the mouse. Table 4-1 lists common OOP terms and their definitions.

Table 4-1. Common Object-Oriented Programming Terms

Item	OOP Definition	Real-Life Analogy
Object	A combination of code and data that can be treated as a unit. An object can be a piece of an application, like a control or a form. An entire application can also be an object.	An apple tree in your garden is an example of an object.

Table 4-1. Common Object-Oriented Programming Terms (continued)

Item	OOP Definition	Real-Life Analogy
Class	A descriptor of the fields, properties, methods, and events of an object. Each object in OOP is defined by a class. Objects are instances of classes; you can create as many objects as you need once you have created a class, and they will all be of the same format. Classes that are derived from more fundamental classes have a hierarchical relationship. Class hierarchies are useful when describing items that are a subtype of a more general class. Derived classes inherit members from the class they are based on, allowing you to add complexity as you progress in a class hierarchy.	The collection of the attributes that make up an apple tree is a class. The apple tree in your garden is a specific instance of the class "apple tree." A class can be a subclass of another—if your apple tree is of the Valencia variety, "Valencia apple tree" is a subclass of "apple tree."
Property	An attribute of an object that defines one of the object's characteristics, such as size, color, screen location, or an aspect of its behavior, such as whether it is enabled or visible.	An attribute of an object that defines one of the object's characteristics, such as size, color, location, and so on.
Method	An action that an object can perform. For example, the `DataBind` method attaches a data source to an `asp:TextBox` control in an ASP.NET page.	A method is an action that a tree can perform, for example, "grow."
Event	An action recognized by an object, such as clicking the mouse or pressing a key, and for which you can write code to respond.	An event is an action that the object will react to, for example "cutting the trunk."

When you create an application in any object-oriented .NET language, you can use objects provided by the language, such as controls, forms, and data access objects, or you can use control objects from other applications within your application. You can even create your own objects and define additional properties and methods for them. Objects act like prefabricated building blocks for programs—they let you write a piece of code once and reuse it over and over.

Inheritance

Code reuse is achieved via **inheritance**, that is, the ability to define classes that serve as the basis for derived classes. Derived classes inherit and can extend the properties, methods, and events of the base class. For a complete description of inheritance concepts, visit http://msdn.microsoft.com/library/default.asp?url=/library/en-us/vbcn7/html/vaconinheritanceforbasiclanguage.asp. Next we will explain inheritance in an ASP.NET context.

The ASP.NET Context

Say you have a page that inherits from the base class System.Web.UI.Page, which in turn inherits from System.Web.UI.TemplateControl, which is a special form of System.Web.UI.Control, which is again a derived class of System.Object. As you can see, a great deal of coding efficiency is achieved by inheriting in this way because instead of having to redefine common properties and methods for your object, you can just declare that it inherits, say, System.Web.UI.Control, and then add or modify any of the inherited properties and methods. This example is a long chain to follow, but it allows many ASP.NET objects derived from System.Web.UI.Control to be efficiently created.

- System.Web.UI.BasePartialCachingControl

- System.Web.UI.DataBoundLiteralControl

- System.Web.UI.HtmlControls.HtmlControl

- System.Web.UI.LiteralControl

- System.Web.UI.TemplateControl

- System.Web.UI.WebControls.Literal

- System.Web.UI.WebControls.PlaceHolder

- System.Web.UI.WebControls.Repeater

- System.Web.UI.WebControls.RepeaterItem

- System.Web.UI.WebControls.WebControl

- System.Web.UI.WebControls.Xml

A specific ASP.NET page is also an object; that is, it's an instance of the class `System.Web.UI.Page`. When you create a page in Dreamweaver, the top line is the following @ Page directive:

```
<%@Page Language="VB" ContentType="text/html" ResponseEncoding="iso-8859-1" %>
```

This declares that the page inherits all the methods and attributes of the `System.Web.UI.Page` class. If you want your page to inherit from a different class, you use the `inherits` attribute to specify the class you want—we will show you how later in this chapter.

Other ASP.NET directives can be used to import whole groups of classes, called namespaces.

Namespaces

You might already be familiar with **dot notation**. This classification divides classes into logical categories called **namespaces**. The MSDN page http://msdn.microsoft .com/library/en-us/cpref/html/cpref_start.asp explains how the .NET classes are organized into namespaces. The main purpose of namespaces is to make the contained classes available to your code with one statement. For example, if you import `System.Globalization`, you import only the classes relevant to internationalization of your page. You don't have to type the whole series of dot-separated `System.Globalization.[myclass]` every time you want to use [myclass]; you simply type its name.

The most relevant namespaces in ASP.NET programming are explained in the following list. Remember, however, that ASP.NET is just another application running on the .NET Framework, so any class in any namespace is available to your application.

- `System.Web` contains classes and interfaces that enable browser/server communication. `System.Web` also contains classes for managing HTTP output to the client (`HttpResponse`) and reading HTTP requests (`HttpRequest`). Additional classes provide facilities for server-side utilities and processes, cookie manipulation, file transfer, exception information, and output cache control.

- `System.Web.UI` contains classes for creating web form pages, including the `Page` class and other standard classes used to create web user interfaces.

- `System.Web.UI.HtmlControls` contains classes for HTML-specific controls that can be added to web forms to create web user interfaces.

- `System.Web.UI.WebControls` contains classes for creating ASP.NET web sever controls. When added to a web form, these controls render browser-specific HTML and script to create a device-independent web user interface.

- `System.Web.Services` contains classes that enable you to build and use XML web services, which are programmable entities residing on a web server and exposed via standard Internet protocols.

The following namespaces are automatically imported into all ASP.NET pages, so you don't have to explicitly import them:

- `System`

- `System.Collections`

- `System.Collections.Specialized`

- `System.Configuration`

- `System.IO`

- `System.Text`

- `System.Text.RegularExpressions`

- `System.Web`

- `System.Web.Caching`

- `System.Web.Security`

- `System.Web.SessionState`

- `System.Web.UI`

- `System.Web.UI.HtmlControls`

- `System.Web.UI.WebControls`

If you wanted to import a namespace other than the ones just shown, you would need to use the @ Import directive. Let's move on to the ASP.NET page syntax to see how these directives are used.

Directives in ASP.NET

You may be familiar with the classic ASP page directive.

```
<%@ LANGUAGE="VBScript" CODEPAGE="932"%>
```

This directive has been replaced by the ASP.NET @ Page directive, which we showed you earlier.

```
<%@ Page Language="VB" ContentType="text/html" ResponseEncoding="iso-8859-1" %>
```

The @ Page directive can only be included in .aspx files, where it defines page-specific attributes used by the ASP.NET page parser and compiler. One of its attributes, CodeBehind, facilitates the separation of code and design by pointing to the location where the programming code is stored. We will show you a more concrete use of this directive later in this chapter. For a full list of the @ Page directive's attributes, see the MSDN documentation.

Many directives are added to ASP.NET for a variety of different purposes. They are all added before any other code, at the top of a page.

- @ Control defines control-specific attributes used by the ASP.NET page parser and compiler. It can only be included in .ascx files (user controls).

- @ Assembly declaratively links an assembly to the current page or user control.

- @ Implements declaratively indicates that a page or user control implements a specified .NET Framework interface.

- @ OutputCache declaratively controls the output caching policies of a page or user control.

- @ Reference declaratively links a page or user control to the current page or user control.

- @ Register associates aliases with namespaces and class names, which allows user controls and custom server controls to be rendered when included in a requested page or user control.

- @ Import explicitly imports a namespace into a page or user control.

In addition to the @ Page directive, the directives that you will see most often while using Dreamweaver are @ Register and @ Import, found under the Insert ➤ ASP.NET Objects menu.

@ Register is used to utilize namespaces that are not built into .NET. It is used extensively by Dreamweaver to register the custom ASP.NET tags created by Macromedia. These tags have the prefix MM: instead of the standard asp: and they are found in the ASP.NET panel under More Tags. They are also automatically typed if you insert server behaviors in your page. For example, if you attach a dataset via the Application toolbar (more about datasets in Chapter 5), the following will appear near the top of the page:

```
<%@ Register TagPrefix="MM" Namespace="DreamweaverCtrls"
Assembly="DreamweaverCtrls,version=1.0.0.0,publicKeyToken=836f606ede05d46a,
culture=neutral" %>
```

In this way, classes that are contained in the DreamweaverCtrls namespace will not have to be referred to as DreamweaverCtrls.[name of class] every time, and the MM: prefix can be used for the custom controls, for example, the MM:DataSet control inserted further down.

```
<MM:DataSet id="DataSet1" runat="Server" ConnectionString='[some string]'>
</MM:DataSet>
```

The @ Import directive is very similar but is utilized to import namespaces already built into .NET. To continue with the internationalization example, if you wanted to import the relevant classes in your page so that you don't have to refer to them as System.Globalization.[name of class] every time, you would write

```
<%@ Import Namespace="System.Globalization" %>
```

This is a similar structure to the @ Registers directive, with attributes that specify similar properties, but a prefix is not required (it is known to be asp:), and the assembly attribute is unnecessary because .NET knows where to find its own DLL files.

There's one last section to talk about before you assemble all the features into one working page: how the ASP.NET page is processed at execution.

Web Forms Code Model

As you saw in the last chapter, ASP.NET is a server-centric technology—all event processing happens at the server. In the ASP.NET Page class model, the entire web forms page is, in effect, an executable program that generates output to be sent back to the browser or client device. This program is compiled when the page is requested for the first time, and it remains in memory handling requests until it times out or its source is changed. To enable the posting back of events to the server so that they can be handled, you need to designate the controls that need to be processed on the server by placing them within a web form that is run at the server.

```
<form runat="server" ></form>
```

Every change that occurs in a control contained within this form can cause what is called a **postback**—a submission of the form back to itself. That is why there is no need to type in the action attribute; ASP.NET automatically adds the name of the page unless you explicitly specify another action page. Then ASP.NET takes care of any code that needs to be executed as a result of that change and sends back the reconstructed page, while keeping track of what has occurred. Of course, you can choose not to cause a postback and write client-side script that handles these events if you are confident that you can detect the Document Object Model (DOM) and each client browser's abilities. ASP.NET's purpose, however, is to prevent you from having to think about the client's abilities at all.

Event Handlers

How do you write code that handles these events? Every ASP.NET object can have a subroutine assigned as a specific event handler. In the special case of the Page object, ASP.NET provides automatic recognition of five subroutine names. They are Page_Init, Page_Load, Page_DataBind, Page_PreRender, and Page_Unload, one for each of the Page's events. For the code that you want processed whenever your Page is requested, you can create a subroutine called Page_Load that contains instructions to be executed every time. For example, the following code sets the color of a calendar control to red whenever the page is called:

```
<script runat="server" >
sub Page_Load()
Calendar1.DayStyle.BackColor = System.Drawing.Color.Red
end sub
</script>
```

Objects other than Page need to have their event handlers explicitly assigned to them. For example, for an asp:DropDownList control, you could write code to handle the event of changing the selected item. You could then assign that code to the event in one of two methods.

- Assign a subroutine (assume it's called "CarChanged") for the event from within the control's syntax.

  ```
  <asp:DropDownList id="CarList" AutoPostBack="True"
  OnSelectedIndexChanged="CarChanged" runat="server"></asp:DropDownList>
  ```

- Assign a subroutine for the event via explicit statements—in VB this is via the AddHandler keyword, as shown in the following code. This method allows the web designer to concentrate on the page design and the web programmer to do all the coding.

```
<%@ Page Language="VB" ContentType="text/html" ➥
ResponseEncoding="iso-8859-1" %>
<html><head>
<script runat="server" >
sub Page_Load()
    AddHandler CarList.SelectedIndexChanged, AddressOf Me.CarChanged
end sub
sub CarChanged(sender As Object, e As EventArgs)
    Response.Write("You have selected: " & CarList.SelectedItem.Value)
end sub
</script></head><body>
<form method="post" runat="server">
    <asp:DropDownList AutoPostBack="true" ID="CarList" runat="server">
        <asp:ListItem Selected="True" Value="Nissan">Nissan</asp:ListItem>
        <asp:ListItem Value="Fiat">Fiat</asp:ListItem>
        <asp:ListItem Value="VW">VW</asp:ListItem>
        <asp:ListItem Value="Honda">Honda</asp:ListItem>
    </asp:DropDownList>
</form></body></html>
```

For your reference, other events applicable to the asp:DropDownList control and most other ASP.NET objects are listed in Table 4-2.

Table 4-2. Common ASP.NET Control Events

Event	Occurs When	Method Used to Call Event Handler
DataBinding	The asp:DropDownList control binds to a data source.	OnDataBinding
Disposed	The asp:DropDownList control is released from memory, which is the last stage of the life cycle when an ASP.NET page is requested.	OnDisposed
Init	The asp:DropDownList control is initialized, which is the first step in its life cycle.	OnInit
Load	The asp:DropDownList control is loaded into the Page object.	OnLoad
PreRender	The asp:DropDownList control is about to render to its Page object.	OnPreRender
Unload	The asp:DropDownList control is unloaded from memory.	OnUnload

Postback and Viewstate

A postback determines whether a page has been loaded before. This is important if you are building an application that accumulates information or allows filtering of information on the page. For example, you might have an ASP.NET page that asks the user for the state or province in which he or she lives, followed by an event that triggers a handler that creates a list of the cities in that state or province. If postbacks are not used, the form could be cleared again, and the user's selection would be lost. A postback is a way of checking if the page has already been displayed to the same user, and if so, not overwriting everything.

Postbacks can be detected in code via a page property called `IsPostBack`. If `IsPostBack` is true, the page has been loaded before. Naturally, if `IsPostBack` is false, the page is being loaded for the first time.

The purpose of gathering all the page action around the server is to keep control of the state of the page. This is called **viewstate**. It is a way of including information within each response to a client that enables the server to reconstruct the page's state when the client resubmits (performs a postback).

Viewstate is enabled within the @ Page directive by default; you can disable it by setting the attribute `EnableViewState="False"`. The result of the enabled viewstate is the inclusion of a hidden form field in every reply of this form.

```
<input type="hidden" name="__VIEWSTATE" value="dDw2NTE1NTg4ODk7dDw7bDxpP...
```

The value of the field has been truncated here. When the form is posted back, the server can deduce the state of the page via this value, so a busy page will produce a larger string.

Inline Render Blocks

ASP.NET allows the use of inline code (called **inline render blocks**), that is, programming statements inserted within the page's design. You'd be right to wonder why this is allowed after all the discussion about separation of code and design. Often, you'll want to have the ASP.NET routines running at different points in a web page, and it's also a simple matter of migration—there are lots of ASP applications that use inline render blocks. Inline render blocks can be placed in the proper execution location of a web page and they'll be executed when the web server parser reads them, in order, from the top of the page to the bottom. There are three types of code render blocks.

- Inline code (contains statements to be executed): `<% ... %>`

- Inline expressions (a shortcut for the `Response.Write` statement): `<%= ... %>`

- Data-binding expressions (you can save coding effort by directly assigning a data-bound value to a control): `<%# ... %>`

This simple page is an example of an inline code block.

```
<%@ page language="VB" %>
<html><body>
    <%
      Dim s as String
      s = "This code is enclosed between &lt;% and %&gt; delimiters"
      Response.Write(s)
    %></body></html>
```

The output source HTML from the page just shown is

```
<html><body>This code is enclosed between &lt;% and %&gt;
delimiters</body></html>
```

The same output can be achieved via the second type of block.

```
<%@ page language="VB" %>
<html><body>
    <%="This code is enclosed between &lt;% and %&gt; delimiters"
%></body></html>
```

We will show you more of the third type in Chapter 6, when we introduce the asp:Repeater ASP.NET control.

You are now ready to put your knowledge into a working page that you will generate from scratch.

Writing an ASP.NET Web Form

Follow these steps to create an ASP.NET Web Form.

1. Open Dreamweaver MX 2004 and create a new ASP.NET VB page. The page will automatically be populated with this code in Code view.

    ```
    <%@ Page Language="VB" ContentType="text/html" ➥
    ResponseEncoding="iso-8859-1" %>
    <!DOCTYPE HTML PUBLIC "-//W3C//DTD HTML 4.01 Transitional//EN"
    "http://www.w3.org/TR/html4/loose.dtd">
    <html>
    <head>
    <title>Untitled Document</title>
    <meta http-equiv="Content-Type" content="text/html; charset=iso-8859-1">
    </head>
    ```

```
<body>
</body>
</html>
```

2. The @ Page directive is already inserted. Remember that many name-
    spaces are automatically imported into the page, so you may not need
    the @ Import directive. Also, you won't see custom tags until Chapter 6,
    so you won't see the @ Register directive either. Instead, start by insert-
    ing your first ASP.NET control, right after the <body> tag. Click the
    asp:DropDownList button on the ASP.NET panel, as shown in Figure 4-1.

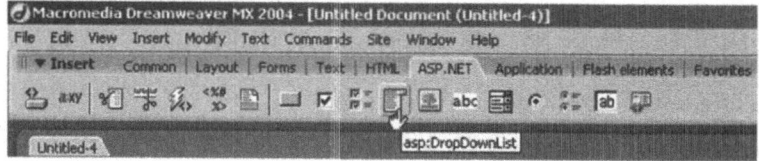

Figure 4-1. Inserting the `asp:DropDownList` *control via the ASP.NET panel*

3. In the screen that appears, type the ID as **ColorList** and make sure that
    the Auto postback check box is enabled, as shown in Figure 4-2.

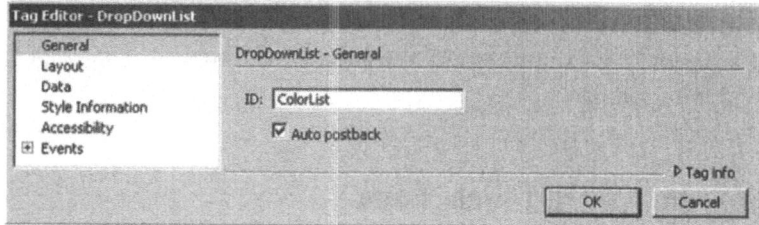

Figure 4-2. The Tag Editor's interface

The following code is added:

```
<asp:DropDownList AutoPostBack="true" ID="ColorList" runat="server">
</asp:DropDownList>
```

The runat="server" attribute determines where the control should be
processed. If it is absent, the control is not processed at the server; it is
sent to the client as is.

CAUTION *Always check that the* runat="server" *is present in the
controls that you want to run on the server.*

Now the drop-down list needs to be populated with data. You aren't allowed to use databases yet—we don't cover them until Chapter 5! So you'll use another method.

4. Place your mouse pointer before the `</asp:DropDownList>` closing tag and type the following:

```
<asp:ListItem Selected="True" Value="White">White</asp:ListItem>
<asp:ListItem Value="Red">Red</asp:ListItem>
<asp:ListItem Value="Green">Green</asp:ListItem>
<asp:ListItem Value="Yellow">Yellow</asp:ListItem>
```

5. As you saw before, you need to enclose this control in a form that will be run on the server. Dreamweaver sometimes automatically inserts a form tag with the `runat="server"` attribute for certain controls, but it's not included with `asp:DropDownList`, so type it manually (or use a regular HTML form from the Forms panel and add the `runat` attribute). Then save your page and give the form's `action` attribute the same name as the page (or `action=""`). Here is the ASP.NET web form code so far:

```
<form action="ColorPage.aspx" method="post" runat="server">
<asp:DropDownList AutoPostBack="true" ID="ColorList" runat="server">
    <asp:ListItem Selected="True" Value="White">White</asp:ListItem>
    <asp:ListItem Value="Red">Red</asp:ListItem>
    <asp:ListItem Value="Green">Green</asp:ListItem>
    <asp:ListItem Value="Yellow">Yellow</asp:ListItem>
</asp:DropDownList>
</form>
```

The simple page you built, when displayed in a browser, will appear as shown in Figure 4-3.

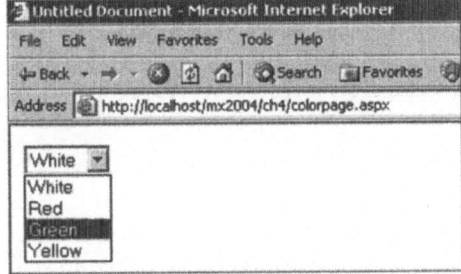

Figure 4-3. A simple ASP.NET page

Postbacks in Practice

If you change the selection in the drop-down list, you will notice that the page posts back to the server and returns with the new selection. Obviously this is not very useful, so let's add some code in a Page_Load subroutine that will perform something exciting with the information posted back. Let's assume that you will display a message with the name of the color that the user has chosen. Insert an asp:Label control with the id="welcomeMessage" right above the drop-down list. Then place your cursor just before the closing </head> tag and click the Page_Load button on the ASP.NET panel, as shown in Figure 4-4.

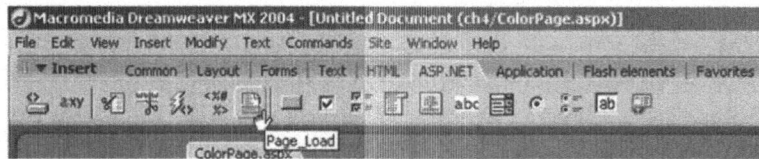

Figure 4-4. Inserting a Page_Load *procedure via the ASP.NET panel*

Dreamweaver automatically inserts the following code:

```
<script runat="server">
Sub Page_Load(Src As Object, E As EventArgs)
If Not IsPostBack Then
DataBind()
End If
End Sub
</script>
```

As it stands, the code doesn't do much. Replace the whole If statement with the following code:

```
If Not IsPostback Then
    welcomeMessage.Text="Select a background color."
Else
    welcomeMessage.Text="You selected " & ColorList.SelectedItem.Value & _
  ". Now select another color."
End If
```

The statement just shown is a direction to display the first message if the page is not posted back (displayed for the first time) or to display the second message, which includes the chosen color for subsequent postings. Call the page in your browser again and do a few postbacks—it should work smoothly. Notice how ASP.NET shields you from worrying about how to retrieve the data from the

URL string by allowing you to program as if the form were wholly contained in the server. The page "knows" that when you refer to

```
ColorList.SelectedItem.Value
```

the reference is to the posted-back value, and the page retrieves it for you. Let's use this value programmatically to modify the rendering of another control on the page. Insert an asp:Calendar control with the following code:

```
<asp:Calendar id="Calendar1" ShowGridLines="True" ShowTitle="True"
runat="server"/>
```

Now add this statement in the Page_Load subroutine, outside the If statement:

```
Calendar1.DayStyle.BackColor = ➡
System.Drawing.Color.FromName(ColorList.SelectedItem.Value)
```

We will talk about web controls such as asp:Calendar later, but for the moment let's focus on the programming logic. Note that the System.Drawing namespace is not automatically imported, so you have to spell out the whole name of the Color class. By running your page now, you can select the color you want as the calendar background and have the choice maintained across clicks, as shown in Figure 4-5.

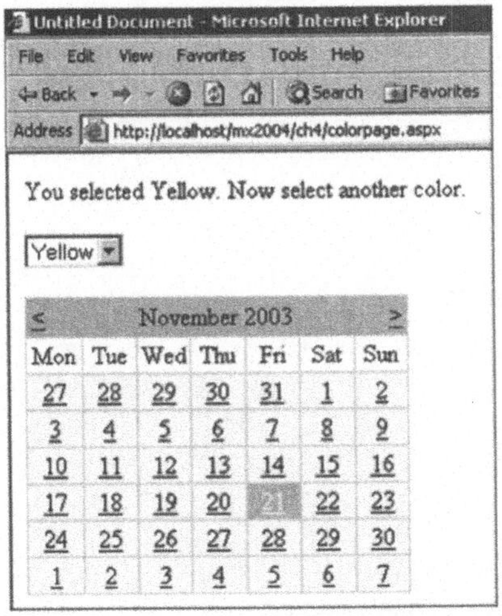

Figure 4-5. Demonstrating how postback operates

Events in Practice

The code works fine, and you could leave it as is. However, imagine a page with many controls that can cause a postback and a long series of commands to be executed for each change. Your code would be concentrated in one subroutine that will be difficult to read and debug, and that might not have been be written by one programmer. It is safer and more flexible to add event handlers for each control and move the relevant commands to those handling subroutines. The following is all of your page's code after being modified by the addition of another drop-down list and separated code (ColorPage.aspx in the code):

```
<%@ Page Language="VB" ContentType="text/html"  ResponseEncoding="iso-8859-1" %>
<!DOCTYPE HTML PUBLIC "-//W3C//DTD HTML 4.01 Transitional//EN"
"http://www.w3.org/TR/html4/loose.dtd">
<html>
<head>
<title>Untitled Document</title>
<meta http-equiv="Content-Type" content="text/html; charset=iso-8859-1">
   <script runat="server" >
sub Page_Load()
    If Not IsPostback Then
          welcomeMessage.Text="Select a background color."
    End If
    AddHandler ColorList.SelectedIndexChanged, AddressOf Me.ColorChanged
    AddHandler ColorList2.SelectedIndexChanged, AddressOf Me.ColorChanged2
end sub
sub ColorChanged(sender As Object, e As EventArgs)
    Calendar1.DayStyle.BackColor = System.Drawing.Color.FromName➥
(sender.SelectedItem.Value)
    welcomeMessage.Text="You last selected " & sender.SelectedItem.Value & ➥
". Now select another color."
end sub
sub ColorChanged2(sender As Object, e As EventArgs)
    Calendar1.WeekendDayStyle.BackColor = ➥
System.Drawing.Color.FromName(sender.SelectedItem.Value)
    welcomeMessage.Text="You last selected " & sender.SelectedItem.Value & ➥
". Now select another color."
end sub
</script></head>
<body>
<form action="ColorPage.aspx" method="post" runat="server">
    <asp:Label id="welcomeMessage" runat="server"></asp:Label>
    <br><br> Day background color:
    <asp:DropDownList AutoPostBack="true" ID="ColorList" runat="server">
        <asp:ListItem Selected="True" Value="White">White</asp:ListItem>
        <asp:ListItem Value="Red">Red</asp:ListItem>
        <asp:ListItem Value="Green">Green</asp:ListItem>
        <asp:ListItem Value="Yellow">Yellow</asp:ListItem>
    </asp:DropDownList>
```

```
      <br><br> Weekend background color:
          <asp:DropDownList AutoPostBack="true" ID="ColorList2" runat="server">
          <asp:ListItem Selected="True" Value="White">White</asp:ListItem>
          <asp:ListItem Value="Red">Red</asp:ListItem>
          <asp:ListItem Value="Green">Green</asp:ListItem>
          <asp:ListItem Value="Yellow">Yellow</asp:ListItem>
          <asp:DropDownList>
      <br><br>
          <asp:Calendar id="Calendar1" ShowGridLines="True" ➥
ShowTitle="True" runat="server"/>
          </form>
</body>
</html>
```

The web page just shown can be called to give output similar to Figure 4-6.

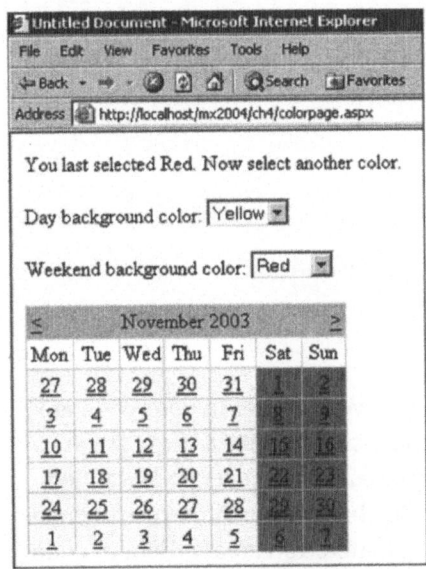

Figure 4-6. Maintaining state across clicks in a calendar

Code Behind in Practice

Now you will put into practice what you've learned about event handling. This structure enables you to treat the page's code like a program and use programming logic techniques. Let's completely liberate your page's design from code by utilizing the Code Behind concept.

1. Make a copy of your current page and name it `ColorPageUI.aspx`. Then copy and paste all the code contained between the `<script>` tags into a new file called `ColorPageUI.vb`. Finally, delete the opening and closing `<script>` tags from the ASPX page. You now have to connect the two files via the @ Page directive—add the two attributes highlighted here:

```
<%@ Page Language="VB" ContentType="text/html" ➥
ResponseEncoding="iso-8859-1" ➥
inherits="ColorPage" src="ColorPageUI.vb"%>
```

The `inherits` attribute specifies which class to inherit from, and the `src` attribute points to where this class definition is to be found. As a result, the page is no longer derived from the `System.Web.UI.Page` class, but instead from a custom one that you will build now.

2. Open the `ColorPageUI.vb` file in Dreamweaver. You need to create a class that inherits the `System.Web.UI.Page` class and adds the modified event handlers that your code contains. Surround the code with the following at the top:

```
Public Class ColorPage
Inherits System.Web.UI.Page
```

3. Surround the code with the following at the bottom:

```
End Class
```

You have your class, but the controls that you refer to in your code are not declared. Remember, with the code inside the ASPX page, the `asp:` controls are created first and then the code within `<script>` is applied. Now your page calls the Code Behind file before any other processing is done, so the page controls are not yet created. You create them in code simply by declaring them as controls.

4. Add the following code just before the `Page_Load` subroutine:

```
Public ColorList As System.Web.UI.WebControls.DropDownList
Public ColorList2 As System.Web.UI.WebControls.DropDownList
Public welcomeMessage As System.Web.UI.WebControls.Label
Public Calendar1 As System.Web.UI.WebControls.Calendar
```

That's it. With a bit of tidying up (importing the namespaces so you don't have to type the full class name), your Code Behind file now looks like this:

```
Imports System
Imports System.Web.UI
Imports System.Web.UI.WebControls
Public Class ColorPage
     Inherits Page
    Public ColorList As DropDownList
    Public ColorList2 As DropDownList
    Public welcomeMessage As Label
    Public Calendar1 As Calendar
    sub Page_Load()
        If Not IsPostback Then
            welcomeMessage.Text="Select a background color."
        End If
        AddHandler ColorList.SelectedIndexChanged, AddressOf Me.ColorChanged
        AddHandler ColorList2.SelectedIndexChanged, AddressOf Me.ColorChanged2
    end sub
    sub ColorChanged(sender As Object, e As EventArgs)
        Calendar1.DayStyle.BackColor = ➥
System.Drawing.Color.FromName(sender.SelectedItem.Value)
        welcomeMessage.Text="You last selected " & sender.SelectedItem.Value & ➥
". Now select another color."
    end sub
    sub ColorChanged2(sender As Object, e As EventArgs)
        Calendar1.WeekendDayStyle.BackColor = ➥
System.Drawing.Color.FromName(sender.SelectedItem.Value)
        welcomeMessage.Text="You last selected " & sender.SelectedItem.Value & ➥
". Now select another color."
    end sub
end Class
```

Call the `ColorPageUI.aspx` page in your browser to see exactly the same functionality but with the full flexibility of a physically separate VB code file. One other advantage of the Code Behind method is that any HTML editor can be used for the HTML pages, whether they support ASP.NET or not. Otherwise, some of the syntax involved in ASP.NET coding would have caused errors in the HTML syntax-checking routines in these HTML editors. Dreamweaver MX allows both inline and Code Behind approaches to writing ASP.NET applications.

You can now concentrate on designing user-friendly and compelling interfaces for your visitors, using the ASP.NET family of controls.

ASP.NET Controls

Classic ASP contained some prebuilt server controls such as asp:AdRotator, asp:Counter, and the like, which were intended to help web designers/programmers perform web site–related tasks. Now, ASP.NET brings with it a plethora of new ready-made controls with the aim of enriching users' experience. They all derive from System.Web.UI.Control but they can be separated into three categories.

- **HTML server controls**: These controls map directly to HTML tags but their state is controlled at the server by adding the runat="server" attribute.

- **Web server controls**: These controls perform various functions, including binding to data, presenting a calendar, and validating input.

- **Mobile server controls**: These controls enable the web form to be displayable in any markup language. There is built-in support for cHTML, WML, and HDML, and the support is extensible and customizable.

Comparing Server Controls

All server controls used by ASP.NET have properties and methods associated with them, and they all handle events through event handlers. The main difference between the three types is the tradeoff between abstractness and flexibility, as shown in Figure 4-7.

- ASP.NET mobile server controls enable any-browser functionality.

- ASP.NET web server controls provide any-HTML-browser functionality.

- ASP.NET HTML server controls provide a single-version level of HTML functionality that you choose to target with your code.

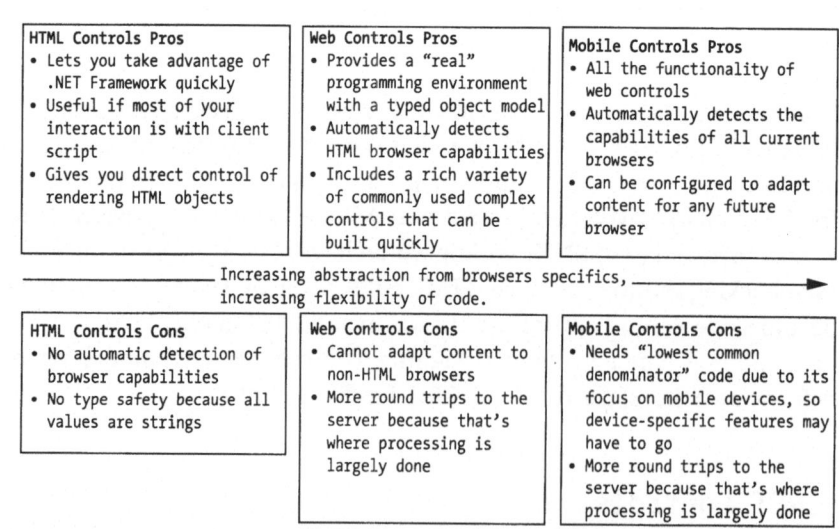

Figure 4-7. Comparison of ASP.NET control categories

Let's examine each group in more detail.

HTML Server Controls

If you know how to program HTML code, you know about HTML elements like buttons, text boxes, and so on. HTML elements always run on the client and are easily created using a line of code like the following:

```
<input type="button" id="Button1" Text="Click" />
```

There is an HTML server control equivalent for every HTML element. HTML server controls are identical in syntax to HTML elements except for the instruction to run at the server instead of the client.

```
<input type="button" id="Button1" Text="Click" runat="server" />
```

The advantage of using HTML server controls is that processing on the server allows all attributes of the element to be customized instead of accepting the default behaviors of HTML elements. This makes them useful for migrating ASP applications to ASP.NET, for example, where you can easily start accessing the controls programmatically by adding the runat="server" attribute.

Web Server Controls

Web server controls have an advantage over HTML server controls because they offer a more consistent interface. For example, the background color for HTML server controls can be managed by using a style attribute in some cases, and by using a property in other cases. Web server controls always expose the background color of the control through the BackColor property. In addition, the web server controls include several other more complex controls that are useful on a web page.

Web server controls are created adding the prefix asp: to an element, like the following:

```
<asp:Label id="TextLabel1" runat="server"/>
```

The web server controls can be further classified into more specific categories, as shown in Figure 4-8.

- **Databound controls**: These controls are bound to a data source that creates their contained subelements.

- **Interface controls**: These controls map to HTML elements with no data binding.

- **Validation controls**: These controls validate user input in a web form.

- **Rich interface controls**: These controls combine a variety of features to provide commonly used functionality.

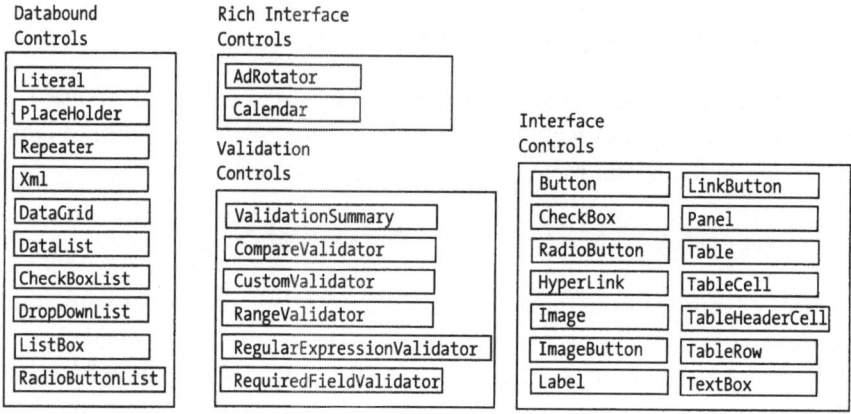

Figure 4-8. Web server control categories

Databound Controls

These controls are created from data sources. They are very powerful because they can generate their own contained elements—you don't have to write the code that loops through the data to construct the HTML elements. Here is a brief description of the most important ones.

- `asp:DataGrid` displays tabular-formatted data in the form of a spreadsheet.

- `asp:DataList` displays a list of formatted data.

- `asp:Repeater` displays text information with repeatable formatting.

- `asp:CheckBoxList` displays a grouping of check boxes.

- `asp:DropDownList` displays a list that can accept text or a selection from a list.

- `asp:ListBox` displays a list of options.

- `asp:RadioButtonList` displays a group of radio buttons.

- `asp:Xml` displays either an unprocessed XML file or an XML file that was modified via an XML Stylesheet Language Transformation (XSLT).

We will go into extensive detail about databound controls in Chapter 6, where we will show you how easily you can assign the data in a database to a control. Here is some sample code in the syntax of the datagrid to demonstrate how easily you can create a data-driven interface in ASP.NET.

Instead of connecting to a database, you start by building an array of values and then assigning that array as the data source of the asp:DataGrid control. The whole page's code is

```
<%@ Page Language="VB" ContentType="text/html" ResponseEncoding="iso-8859-1" %>
<html>
<head>
<script runat="server">
Sub Page_Load(Src As Object, E As EventArgs)
If Not IsPostBack Then
    Dim values As New ArrayList()
    values.Add("Microsoft")
    values.Add("Intel")
    values.Add("Dell")
    simpleDG.DataSource=values
    simpleDG.DataBind()
End If
End Sub
</script></head>
<body><form runat="server">
<asp:DataGrid AutoGenerateColumns="true" ID="simpleDG"  runat="server">
</asp:DataGrid>
</form></body></html>
```

This simplistic page will produce a table with the data in rows. The real power of the datagrid is in its editing abilities and its ability to automatically generate columns and paging controls. Here is a taste of things to come in Chapter 6: Add the EditItemIndex attribute and set it to 2.

```
<asp:DataGrid AutoGenerateColumns="true" ID="simpleDG" EditItemIndex="2"
runat="server"></asp:DataGrid>
```

This will cause the third row (remember, all indexes in .NET are zero-based; that is, they start at 0 instead of 1) to appear as an editable text box that the user can modify, as shown in Figure 4-9.

Item
Microsoft
Intel
Dell

Figure 4-9. Editable datagrid cell

You could also style a selected item in the list. The ASP.NET way of adding styles is via special tags contained within the element to be styled. For example, set the selectedIndex attribute to 1 and the style of the selected row to a red background and a blue font.

```
<asp:DataGrid AutoGenerateColumns="true" ID="simpleDG"
EditItemIndex="2" selectedIndex="1" runat="server">
<selecteditemstyle BackColor="#FF0000" ForeColor="#3300FF"></selecteditemstyle>
</asp:DataGrid>
```

This makes the list look as shown in Figure 4-10. (Because this book is in black and white, the red background and blue font will not be visible.)

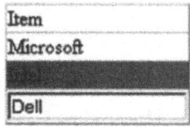

Figure 4-10. Selected datagrid cell

The way user interaction is handled is especially convenient. For example, you could allow a user to select a row and perform actions based on the selected row (perhaps delete it or show details) with the addition of a fairly simple event handler. Let's look at the whole code listing, highlighting the changes in bold (DataGridSimple.aspx).

```
<%@ Page Language="VB" ContentType="text/html" ResponseEncoding="iso-8859-1"
debug="true" %>
<html>
<head>
<script runat="server">
Sub Page_Load(Src As Object, E As EventArgs)
    If Not IsPostBack Then
    Dim values As New ArrayList()
    values.Add("Microsoft")
```

```
        values.Add("Intel")
        values.Add("Dell")
        simpleDG.DataSource=values
        simpleDG.DataBind()
End If
End Sub

Sub ItemsGrid_Command(sender As Object, e As DataGridCommandEventArgs)
Select (CType(e.CommandSource, LinkButton)).CommandName
    Case "Select"
            sender.selectedIndex=e.Item.DataSetIndex
    Case Else
            ' Do nothing.
End Select
End Sub
</script></head><body>
<form runat="server">
<asp:DataGrid AutoGenerateColumns="true" ID="simpleDG"
OnItemCommand="ItemsGrid_Command" EditItemIndex="2" selectedIndex="1"
runat="server">
<selecteditemstyle BackColor="#FF0000" ForeColor="#3300FF"></selecteditemstyle>
    <Columns>
            <asp:ButtonColumn HeaderText="Select item"
ButtonType="LinkButton" Text="Select" CommandName="Select"/>
    </Columns>
</asp:DataGrid>
</form>
</body>
</html>
```

Let's start with the interface. We explicitly added a column to the datagrid to display the link that the user would click to select the row. The <asp:ButtonColumn> tag generates a link in this case because we specified LinkButton as the ButtonType attribute value. If we had specified PushButton instead, we would get a button interface, as shown in Figure 4-11.

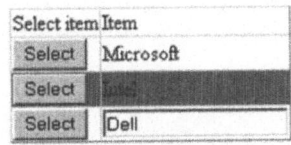

Figure 4-11. Button column in a datagrid

The download code uses simple links—clicking the Select link in the Microsoft row causes the OnItemCommand event to fire. The OnItemCommand attribute of the asp:DataGrid specifies which subroutine to execute. The line that does all the work is

```
sender.selectedIndex=e.Item.DataSetIndex
```

We enclosed it in a case select statement just in case we need to add other buttons. The line is an instruction to make the selected index of the object equal the index of the item row that was clicked. That's it! You don't have to manually check which cell was clicked on the table or rebind the data with another database call. Click away on the rows and you will see the selectedItem style (and presumably any other code that you choose to execute) applied to the clicked row, as shown in Figure 4-12.

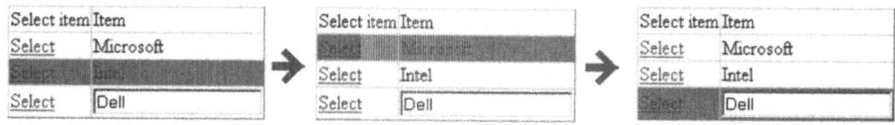

Figure 4-12. The datagrid displays the selected item in the specified format.

Rich Interface Controls

The following two controls make up this group:

- asp:AdRotator accepts a list of images mapped to a specific URL (to display in response to the ad being clicked). The asp:AdRotator control randomly selects an image each time the page is refreshed.

- asp:Calendar displays a fully working calendar in the browser.

You saw the asp:Calendar rich interface control when we covered event handling. Calendar functionality is very common in web applications, and it is a very useful control. Moreover, it requires only the following code:

```
<form runat="server"><asp:Calendar runat="server"></asp:Calendar></form>
```

This code will create a fully functional calendar that can even be automatically converted to other languages, as shown in Figure 4-13.

Figure 4-13. The automatically generated Japanese version of the ASP.NET calendar

The calendar shown in Figure 4-13 is created by simply setting the @ Page directive's Culture attribute to the Japanese code ja-JP. You can get impressive functionality that would have taken tens of lines of code to achieve otherwise with simple code like the following:

```
<%@ Page Language="VB" ContentType="text/html" Culture="ja-JP" %>
<html>
<body><form runat="server"><asp:Calendar runat="server"></asp:Calendar></form>
</body>
</html>
```

The asp:AdRotator control is used to display a randomly selected advertisement banner on the web page. The displayed advertisement can change whenever the page is refreshed. Advertisement information is stored in a separate XML file, which allows you to maintain a list of advertisements and their associated attributes. Attributes include the path to an image to display, the URL to display when the control is clicked, the alternate text to display when the image in not available, a keyword, and the frequency of the advertisement. Here is an example:

```
<asp:AdRotator id="AdRotator1" runat="server" Target="_blank"
KeywordFilter="Topic1"
             AdvertisementFile="adverts.xml"/>
```

In this example, the XML file is of the following form:

```
<Advertisements>
 <Ad>
 <ImageUrl>image1.jpg</ImageUrl>
 <NavigateUrl>http://www.apress.com</NavigateUrl>
 <AlternateText>Apress website</AlternateText>
 <Impressions>10</Impressions>
```

```
<Keyword>Topic1</Keyword>
</Ad>
</Advertisements>
```

The first three XML items are self-explanatory. The `Impressions` attribute is used as a measure of how often the `<Ad>` should be displayed in relation to other `<Ad>` tags within the same file. The keyword item's contents are used as a filter by the `KeywordFilter` property of the `asp:AdRotator` control to enable some basic filtering of `<Ad>` tags from the same XML file. Obviously, the `Impressions` attribute and the `Keyword` property are used only if more than one ad is specified.

Validation Controls

You have probably used some type of user input validation in your HTML forms at some point or another. The ASP.NET controls offer a designer-friendly way of adding validation to your web forms. If ASP.NET detects that the visiting browser is DHTML capable, it automatically inserts client-side JavaScript code to perform validation on the client. Client-side validation enhances the validation process by checking user input before it is sent to the server. This allows errors to be detected on the client before the form is submitted, avoiding the round-trip of information necessary for server-side validation. If client-side validation is not possible, user input is checked on the server without the need for any special coding from the web programmer.

There are five types of controls that perform validation of input.

- **asp:RequiredFieldValidator**: Use this control to ensure that the user does not skip an entry.

- **asp:CompareValidator**: Use this control to compare a user's entry against a constant value or the value of another control.

- **asp:CustomValidator**: Use this control to create custom server and client validation code.

- **asp:RangeValidator**: Use this control to check whether a user's entry is between a specified upper and lower boundary. You can check ranges within pairs of numbers, alphabetic characters, and dates.

- **asp:RegularExpressionValidator**: Use this control to check that the entry matches a pattern defined by a regular expression. This type of validation allows you to check for predictable sequences of characters or sequences of characters.

Here are two examples, one for the asp:RequiredFieldValidator control and one for the asp:RegularExpressionValidator control.

The asp:RequiredFieldValidator control has the following syntax:

```
<asp:RequiredFieldValidator
     id="ProgrammaticID"
     ControlToValidate="ProgrammaticID of control to validate"
     InitialValue="value"
     ErrorMessage="Message to display in ValidationSummary control"
     Text="Message to display in control"
     ForeColor="value"
     BackColor="value" ...
     runat="server" >
</asp:RequiredFieldValidator>
```

You can probably guess the purpose of each attribute. The control is usually placed next to the input field to be validated, and is usually activated via submission of a form or whenever the Page.Validate method is called. The following is an example application (RequiredValidator.aspx):

```
<%@ Page Language="VB" ContentType="text/html" ResponseEncoding="iso-8859-1" %>
<html>
<body>
   <form runat="server">
     Type anything to avoid the error message: <br>
     <asp:TextBox id="Text1" Text="" runat="server"/>
     <asp:RequiredFieldValidator id="RequiredFieldValidator1"
ControlToValidate="Text1"  Text="You have not filled in this required field!"
runat="server"/>
       <br><asp:Button id="Button1" runat="server" Text="Validate"/>
   </form>
</body>
</html>
```

If you click without typing, Figure 4-14 is displayed, either via the DHTML route or with a server round-trip.

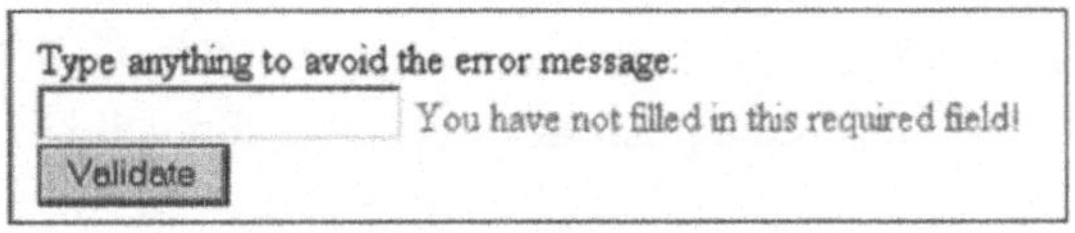

Figure 4-14. Required field validation controls in action

The asp:RegularExpressionValidator can be very powerful and save you lots of coding. To use it, you need to be somewhat familiar with regular expression syntax—for an introduction, visit `http://msdn.microsoft.com/library/en-us/` `jscript7/html/jsreconIntroductionToRegularExpressions.asp`.

You will create a simple page that checks whether a 16-digit credit card number has been entered in an input field. It will also check whether the field has been filled in at all. Note that this requires two separate validation controls, one for each function (`RegExValidator.aspx`).

```
<%@ Page Language="VB" ContentType="text/html" ResponseEncoding="iso-8859-1" %>
<html>
<body>
    <form runat="server">
      Type a 16-digit credit card number to avoid the error message: <br>
      <asp:TextBox id="Text1" runat="server"/>
      <asp:RegularExpressionValidator id="REV1" ControlToValidate="Text1"
ValidationExpression="\d{16}"
ErrorMessage="Credit card numbers must be 16 numeric digits" runat="server"/>
      <asp:RequiredFieldValidator id="RequiredFieldValidator1"
ControlToValidate="Text1"  Text="You have not filled in this required field!"
runat="server"/>
      <br><asp:Button id="Button1" runat="server" Text="Validate"/>
    </form>
</body>
</html>
```

If you attempt to submit this form without any data, you will get the error message shown in the last example. If you type anything with fewer than 16 digits (no spaces), you will see the error message shown in Figure 4-15.

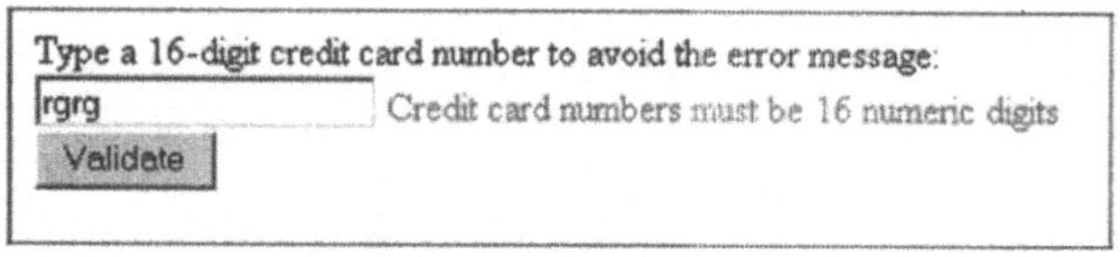

Figure 4-15. Regular expression validator in action

As mentioned earlier, the validation can be performed on the client. There are situations, however, when you might want to force a postback to enable the validation to be performed on the server. Generally, this is done because you want to perform other actions as well. To enable the validation to be performed on the server, use the following attribute within the asp:`RegularExpressionValidator` control:

```
EnableClientScript="false"
```

Interface Controls

The rest of the ASP.NET controls create interface controls similar to HTML controls but with added abilities. Almost all of them can have data assigned to certain properties, and they can all perform a postback, if needed.

- asp:Button displays a button to click to start some process.

- asp:CheckBox displays a box that can be checked or unchecked.

- asp:HyperLink displays a link to a URL.

- asp:Image displays an image.

- asp:ImageButton displays a button with an image on it.

- asp:Label displays noneditable text.

- asp:LinkButton displays a button that looks like a hyperlink.

- asp:Panel displays a borderless division on a form acting as a container for other objects.

- asp:RadioButton displays a single round button that is on or off.

- asp:Table displays a table.

- asp:TableCell displays an individual cell in a table.

- asp:TableRow displays an individual row in a table.

- asp:TextBox displays editable text.

Each of these web server controls has attributes and methods that can be found in Microsoft's ASP.NET documentation. You will see them in action throughout the rest of this book.

Dreamweaver As an ASP.NET Tool

We covered a lot of ground in this chapter. Here now is a summary of where ASP.NET-related features are located in Dreamweaver MX 2004.

When you first start Dreamweaver, you can see the ASP.NET panel at the top of the screen, as shown in Figure 4-16.

Figure 4-16. More ASP.NET tags are available via the ASP.NET panel.

The ASP.NET panel is divided into three parts. The two buttons in the first part are related to page directives. The five buttons in the second part are related to page code. The remaining buttons are ASP.NET controls. You can insert a control in your page by simply clicking the button for the control you want and then filling in the dialog box that appears. The rightmost button on the ASP.NET panel brings up a complete list of all the controls available within Dreamweaver (not just ASP.NET). With this tool, you can insert your own custom controls (more on this in Chapter 8).

You can also use this tool insert the special Macromedia (MM:) controls. Macromedia has encapsulated some commonly used actions into tag controls that allow you to quickly add functionality without coding. Here is the list of these tags and a brief description.

- MM:DataSet eases the burden of retrieving records from databases. In the most basic case, you need to provide only two attributes: the CommandText attribute, which specifies the SELECT statement, and the ConnectionString attribute, which specifies a connection string that points to your database.

- MM:Insert, MM:Update, and MM:Delete inserts, updates, or deletes records, respectively. They require the same attributes as MM:DataSet.

- MM:If allows you to decide whether to use its inner content or not. It is equivalent to typing <% if [test] Then %>...inner content...<% End If %> in a VB .NET page.

- MM:PageBind performs data binding for the page. This control allows you to simply type one tag instead of having to add the following to every page:

```
<script runat="server">
Sub Page_Load(Src As Object, E As EventArgs)
If Not IsPostBack Then
DataBind()
End If
End Sub
</script>
```

Code that you usually have to hand code for standard data processes is now located in these custom MM: controls. The library that contains them is in your application's /bin directory, DreamweaverCtrls.dll. You will see more of these controls in the case study, in Chapter 11.

Dreamweaver MX 2004 saves your site's configuration in the web.config file in the root of your application. This means that your connection parameters and other settings are always available to all pages, and that your web site is easily transportable.

The structure of the web.config file is documented in the Reference tab of the Code panel, which also contains a lot of useful documentation regarding the Page class and the HttpRequest and HttpResponse objects. You may also find that the Microsoft documentation is an essential reference: http://msdn.microsoft.com/library/en-us/netstart/html/cpframeworkref_start.asp.

Next is the Application panel, as shown in Figure 4-17.

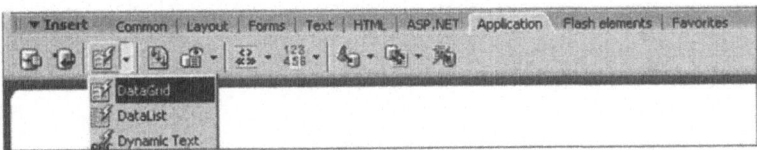

Figure 4-17. Inserting databound controls via the Application panel

The Application panel contains the data-related controls that you commonly need in an application. The shortcuts in this panel are some of the most productive and efficient tools that Dreamweaver offers. Take care when inserting a datagrid, datalist, or dynamic text. This is not the same as inserting an asp:DataGrid control from the More Tags list of the ASP.NET panel. This action inserts a lot more code in your application because it simply drops the item where you specify, which immediately creates a data-connected page. However, the code this inserts is not useful for learning ASP.NET syntax because it uses custom MM: controls for their functions, so the code is precompiled and hidden.

Summary

In this chapter, we covered the basics of ASP.NET, including the .NET Framework, which is critical to your applications. You learned about the development tools available from Microsoft for writing ASP.NET applications, and the requirements for a server to handle ASP.NET applications. Hopefully this information will help you understand the way ASP.NET applications are written, a subject we explore in the next chapter.

You also saw all the elements that go into simple ASP.NET pages and how you can integrate those elements with HTML code. You got a taste of web server controls and how to use them, as well as how to create event handlers. With this basic information under your belt, you can now move on to add new features like database lookups and use XML.

Introducing .NET and Databases

You **have now seen** the wide spectrum of controls that ASP.NET offers. To bring real-time content to these controls, you first need to understand how server-side technologies, particularly ASP.NET, provide the means to access data in an efficient and programming-friendly way.

The first half of this chapter discusses databases and SQL (the language used to query databases) in general. If you are already familiar with these concepts, you may want to jump directly to the section "Data in .NET."

Database Technologies

If static HTML pages are the Internet's bones, data-driven pages are its blood—they supply it with life. By making part of a web page or a group of web pages dynamic, you can keep a web site current with minimal effort. Data can be modified relatively easily so that the content requested by the dynamic pages (images, news text, real-time graphs, and so on) is up to date. In addition, the modified data provides what is effectively a customized page. Depending on the nature of the data requested, users could view information relevant to a current need (for example, a train schedule) or to a particular location (for example, content in their own language). Data can also be an integral building block of a site by keeping track of orders, stock, and shipments, for instance. Nearly all nontrivial web applications deal in some way with complex data.

For all these reasons, a reliable method of storing and retrieving data is essential for a web site, and databases provide just that. Modern databases are almost always **relational databases (RDs)**. The term "relational" means that the data is stored in rows and columns. The columns define the type of data record (the individual pieces of information contained in the records), and a row is the record itself. Rows and columns together make up a table. For example, an RD can keep the details of a customer in one row of a table, the orders placed by this customer in rows of another table, and the products bought in each order in another table, as shown in Figure 5-1.

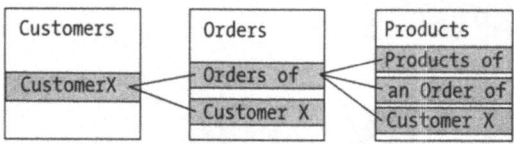

Figure 5-1. Relational database keys

The relationships between tables are controlled via connections between individual columns. The columns that are connected in this way are called **keys**. Keys enable criteria to be enforced (for example, a Customers row must exist before an Orders row can be inserted), efficient row retrieval (the database engine may store related rows of different tables together on the hard disk), and the formation of **views**. Views are like tables that provide an alternative view of combined data.

Each information row in a table contains the same type of information as every other row, and columns cannot be added or removed in any row unless all rows receive the same modification. A piece of information can be located at the intersection of a row and a column, as shown in Figure 5-2; therefore, the order of row storage is not significant for data access.

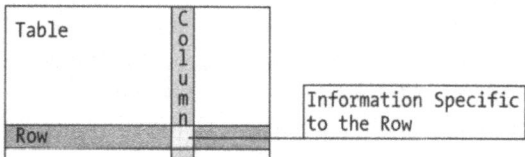

Figure 5-2. Locating information in a relational table

This structure may seem simple and obvious now, but until RDs became the industry norm, other types of databases, like hierarchical or network databases, were prevalent. It could be said that the other types were more flexible in some cases, but they were also less reliable. The consistency of data, commonly known as **data integrity**, was sometimes lost.

RDs are managed via engines called **relational database management systems (RDBMSs)**. These are simply programs that keep the logic behind the structure shown in Figure 5-2. They allow the insertion, modification, and deletion of data, and ensure the maintenance of data integrity. RDBMSs interact with applications to allow data access. Via simple requests or queries that are controlled by the underlying logic of the relational database, the data-driven application can retrieve any combination of information. But it wasn't always that simple.

Structured Query Language

The history of relational databases goes back to E.F. Codd, an IBM researcher who first published an article on the relational database concept in June 1970 (see http://www.acm.org/classics/nov95/toc.html). Codd's article started a flurry of research, including a major project at IBM. Part of this project was a database query language named **SEQUEL** (an acronym for Structured English QUEry Language), subsequently changed to **SQL** (**Structured Query Language**). However, it is still pronounced "Sequel" by some people to this day (although others pronounce it "Es Cue El").

IBM published many articles in technical journals about its SQL database language, and in the late '70s two other companies started to develop similar products; these became Oracle and Ingres. In the late '80s and early '90s, SQL products multiplied and became the de facto standard for database management in medium to large organizations, especially on UNIX systems and mainframes. However, each product came with its own dialect of SQL. As with human languages, the dialects were similar but incompatible in their details, which quickly became a problem.

In 1982, a group of representatives from technical companies, including IBM and Oracle, got together to standardize an interface for RDBMSs. This technical committee on databases was called X3H2 back then, but it is now known as the International Committee for Information Technology Standards (INCITS). Operating under the auspices of the American National Standards Institute (ANSI), this group had the responsibility of standardizing the SQL interface language for storing and retrieving data. Since then, the SQL language has undergone some major revisions and enhancements, as shown by the timeline in Figure 5-3.

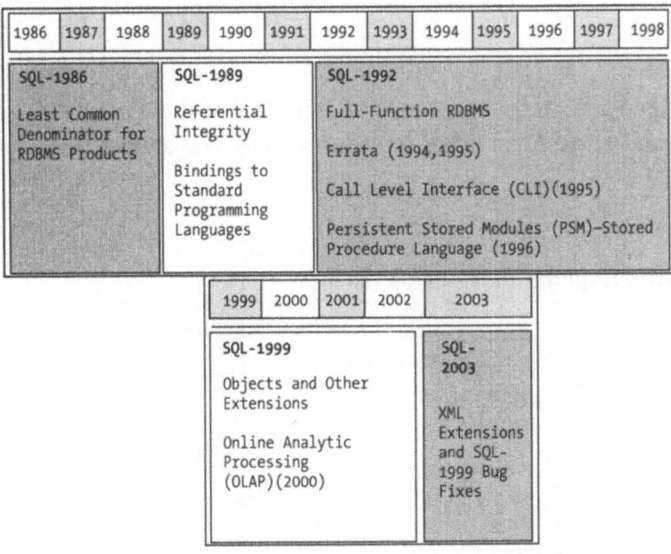

Figure 5-3. The history of revisions to the SQL language

The most commonly used definition is the 1992 version, usually referred to as SQL92. SQL is a database access, nonprocedural language. Users describe what they want done using SQL, and the SQL language compiler automatically generates a procedure to navigate the database and perform the desired task (for example, "retrieve all products with names beginning with the letter L"). The current standard is fairly consistently implemented and it allows web developers to perform certain logical operations on data. These SQL statements can be divided into the following broad categories:

- Data manipulation language (DML) statements

- Data definition language (DDL) statements

- Transaction control statements

Data manipulation language statements allow you to query or manipulate data values in existing data structure objects. This is by far the part of SQL you will use most often. The statements are listed in Table 5-1.

Table 5-1. Data Manipulation Language Statements

Action	Statement
Retrieve data from one or more tables or views	SELECT
Add new rows of data into a table or view	INSERT
Change column values in existing rows of a table or view	UPDATE
Remove rows from a table or view	DELETE

Data definition language statements allow you to define and alter the structure of data objects, as well as perform other structural tasks. The statements are listed in Table 5-2.

Table 5-2. Data Definition Language Statements

Action	Statement
Create, alter, and delete tables and other database structures, including the database itself and database users	CREATE, ALTER, DROP
Change the names of objects	RENAME
Grant and revoke privileges and roles	GRANT, REVOKE

Transaction control statements manage the changes made by DML statements and group DML statements into transactions. These statements are listed
in Table 5-3.

Table 5-3. Transaction Control Statements

Action	Statement
Make a transaction's changes permanent	COMMIT
Undo the changes in a transaction, either since a transaction started or to a save point	ROLLBACK

This is not the whole range of available commands—this chapter is not
intended to cover all SQL syntax. (The formal definition currently stands at 1,800
pages.) However, it is useful to look at a few examples demonstrating how some of
the most common and important SQL commands are used. We will use Microsoft
Access 2000 for the following examples, but you should get similar results from any
SQL-compliant database. Also, bear in mind that other databases may not use the
same SQL implementation, so the syntax may differ slightly.

Using Data Tables and Relationships

To understand how tables are used, we will use an existing Access database—the
download for this chapter contains the file wines.mdb. In it, there are two tables,
tblWines and tblPurchases. The first contains data on various wine brands, and
the second contains a list of wine purchases. For each wine brand, there may be
zero or more purchases of that wine made. This is better explained by looking at
the Access interface. (We use Access 2000, but an Access 97 version is also
included in the download. Rename it to wines.mdb.)

1. Open the wines.mdb database to display the screen shown in Figure 5-4.

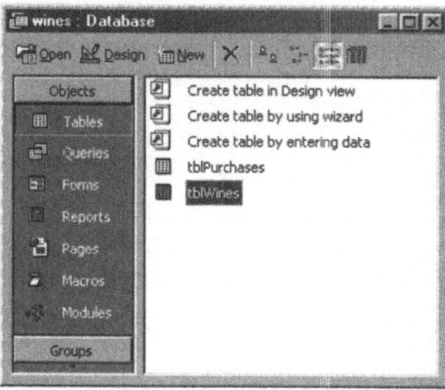

Figure 5-4. The tables in the wines.mdb *database*

2. Select the tblWines table, and then click the Design button.

A screen detailing the columns of the table and their properties will appear, as shown in Figure 5-5.

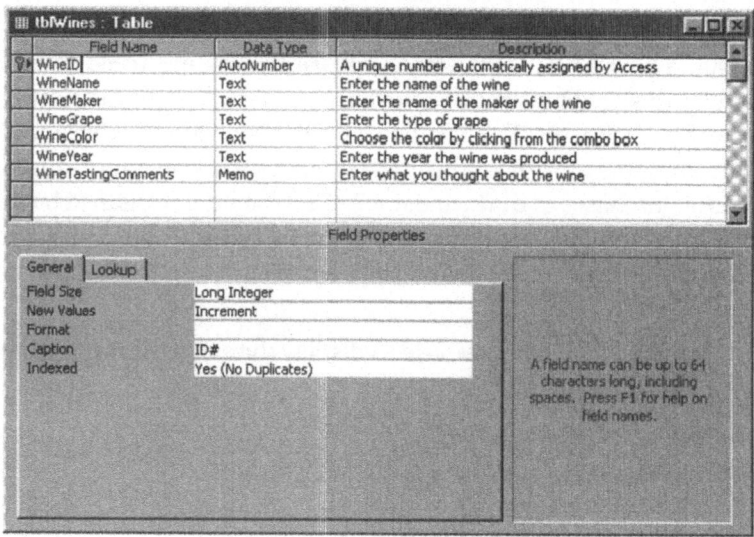

Figure 5-5. The design screen for the tblWines *table*

The screen serves the same purpose as the SQL CREATE TABLE command of the following basic syntax:

```
CREATE TABLE <table name> (<column element> [,
<column element> [,<column constraint> [,
<column constraint>]...]]...)
```

A column element is of this form:

```
<column name> <data type> [DEFAULT <expression>]
```

A column constraint is of this form:

```
NOT NULL | UNIQUE | PRIMARY KEY | FOREIGN KEY
<column name> REFERENCES <Foreign column name>
```

The user-friendly graphical interface of Access allows you to create tables quickly without using SQL. In this particular example, the screen shown in Figure 5-5 is roughly equivalent to the following SQL statement:

```
CREATE TABLE tblWines (
WineID INTEGER,
WineName CHAR (50) ,
WineMaker CHAR (50),
WineGrape CHAR (50),
WineColor CHAR (50),
WineYear CHAR (50),
WineTastingComments CHAR(50),
PRIMARY KEY WineID)
```

Note that the code just shown is the standard SQL version—commercial RDBMS packages such as Oracle and SQL Server differ slightly from the standard in their SQL syntax. For our purposes, the Access-SQL would instead be

```
CREATE TABLE tblWines (
WineID INTEGER PRIMARY KEY,
WineName CHAR (50),
WineMaker CHAR (50),
WineGrape CHAR (50),
WineColor CHAR (50),
WineYear CHAR (50),
WineTastingComments CHAR(50))
```

Strictly speaking, the Access screen also defines other elements, such as an index for the primary key column and a numerical sequence for the values of the primary key, but these are beyond the scope of this book. At the end of this chapter, you will find some useful links that provide details on the SQL language and general database operation and administration. However, the concept of constraints is fundamental to the operation of relational databases.

Constraints are rules that restrict the values that a column can accept.

- The NOT NULL constraint dictates that any rows inserted must contain a value for that column; that is, it cannot be left blank.

- The UNIQUE constraint requires that a value inserted cannot already exist in another row in that column. A primary key column must abide by both the UNIQUE and NOT NULL constraints, which enables any rows in the table to be identifiable via the values of the primary key column.

- The REFERENCES constraint requires that the value inserted needs to already exist in a column of another table.

3. The REFERENCES constraint allows relationships, like the Customer/ Orders/Products example shown earlier, to be built. In the wines.mdb database, click Tools ➤ Relationships to reveal the relationship between the two tables of this database, as shown in Figure 5-6.

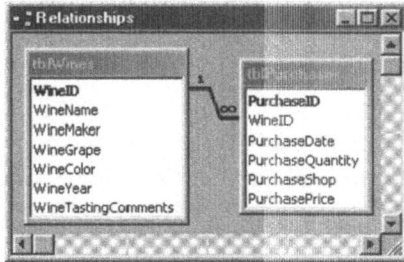

Figure 5-6. The relationship between the tblWines *and* tblPurchases *tables*

Figure 5-6 shows that the WineID column of the tblPurchases table references the WineID column of the tblWines table, which is called its foreign key. The symbols next to the connecting line indicate a **one-to-many** relationship, which means that for each tblWines WineID value there can be many tblPurchases WineID rows containing it.

In less technical terms, purchase records cannot be inserted unless their WineID value already exists in tblWines (that is, it is a valid wine type), but there can be more than one purchase record for the same type of wine. Each wine must have a unique WineID.

4. With the screen shown in Figure 5-6 in focus, click the connecting line and select Relationships ➤ Edit Relationship from the menu bar. The dialog box shown in Figure 5-7 appears.

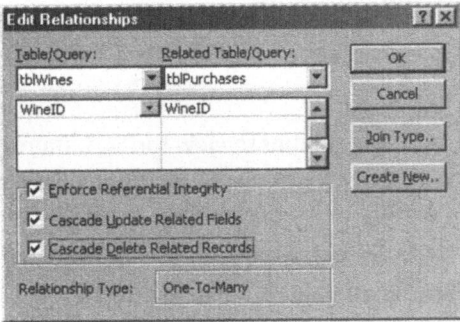

Figure 5-7. Editing relationships in Access

The check boxes specify what action the database should take automatically when records are updated or deleted. By selecting the check boxes, you are instructing Access to delete or update any tblPurchases records with a specific WineID if the record with that same WineID has been deleted or updated in tblWines. This process ensures that the integrity of your data is maintained.

You have seen how tables are the basic building blocks of a database. From a web design perspective, a quick way to access and utilize the data stored in the tables would be very useful.

Data Queries

We will continue using Access for this section because it enables us to easily switch between the SQL and graphical versions of the SELECT, UPDATE, INSERT, and DELETE queries. Note that for high-traffic web sites, Access is not the best solution because it is not optimized to handle many concurrent connections.

1. In the main database window, click the Queries tab of wines.mdb. Select the qryWinesByNameMakerColorYear query, and click the Design button. The graphical query design interface will appear. To include table columns in query results, drag the columns from the interface to the grid shown in Figure 5-8.

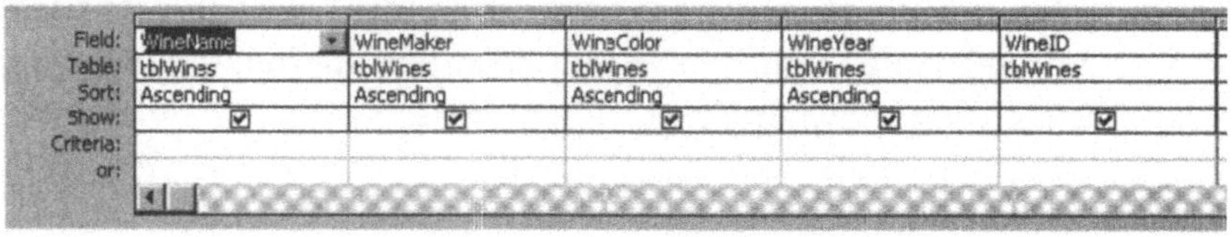

Figure 5-8. The table columns of the database

2. Click View ➤ SQL View on the main toolbar to view the SQL statement that is created. The SQL statement of this particular SELECT query is as follows:

```
SELECT tblWines.WineName, tblWines.WineMaker,
 tblWines.WineColor, tblWines.WineYear, tblWines.WineID
FROM tblWines
ORDER BY tblWines.WineName, tblWines.WineMaker,
 tblWines.WineColor, tblWines.WineYear;
```

The SQL syntax shown here can be used with very few modifications from within your ASP or ASP.NET pages to create queries, execute them, and receive results. We will show you the details of how this is done later, but first let's examine a less straightforward type of query.

3. Open the SQL view of qryInsertNewPurchase.

```
INSERT INTO tblPurchases ( WineID, PurchaseDate,
PurchaseQuantity, PurchaseShop, PurchasePrice ) SELECT 1000 AS
newWineID, #12/12/2000# AS newPurchaseDate, 4 AS newPurchaseQuantity,
"My Wine Shop" AS newPurchaseShop, 12.35 AS newPurchasePrice;
```

If you try to execute the query, you will get an error message telling you that one record was not added due to key violations. This demonstrates that a value of WineID=1000 cannot be used because there is no wine record with that WineID. If you change the value from 1000 to 110, for example, you can execute the query without any problems. This is called an **append query** in Access but the term **insert query** is more widely used.

Note also that this SQL statement deviates somewhat from the standard SQL, which would be

```
INSERT INTO tblPurchases ( WineID, PurchaseDate, PurchaseQuantity,
PurchaseShop, PurchasePrice ) VALUES (1000,#12/12/2000#,4,"Sainsburys",
12.35);
```

However, both of these formats work in ASP/ASP.NET, so you may find it more convenient to design your queries in Access and copy the SQL straight into your pages, if your project's database understands it.

4. To see an example of an UPDATE query, open the SQL view of qryUpdateMalbecToRed.

```
UPDATE tblWines SET tblWines.WineColor = "Red" WHERE
(((tblWines.WineGrape) Like "Malbec*"));
```

This statement changes all values of WineColor to Red if the record value for WineGrape is anything starting with Malbec. The Like operator is just one option of many; other operators include = (equal), > (greater than), <= (less than or equal to), Between <value> And <value>, and In (<range_of_comma_separated_values>). The WHERE clause is not compulsory, but do not forget to include it if necessary, and be sure that you specify the right criteria in it. You can check by switching to Datasheet view and looking at how many records would be affected if you were to execute the query. Checking in Datasheet view is even more important in the next type of query.

The DELETE query is used to remove records from a table with or without qualifying criteria. The qryDeletePiekarz query would delete the one record in which WineMaker equals "Piekarz".

```
DELETE tblWines.WineMaker FROM tblWines WHERE (((tblWines.WineMaker)=
"Piekarz"));
```

A more common form of the DELETE query is

```
"DELETE * FROM <tablename> WHERE ..."
```

In this case, the column names do not have to be explicitly called. The WHERE clause has the same structure as the UPDATE query, but again, make sure you check the potentially affected rows if possible.

Finally, a JOIN query is a slightly more complicated but more useful type of query. With it, you can combine data from more than one table to produce meaningful data reports. The example we will show you is qryWinesMediumPrice.

```
SELECT tblPurchases.PurchaseShop, tblPurchases.PurchaseDate,
 tblWines.WineName, tblPurchases.PurchasePrice
FROM tblWines INNER JOIN tblPurchases ON tblWines.WineID =
```

```
tblPurchases.WineID
WHERE (((tblPurchases.PurchaseShop)="Ye Olde Wine Shoppe") AND
((tblPurchases.PurchasePrice)
Between 5 And 10))
ORDER BY tblPurchases.PurchaseShop,
tblPurchases.PurchaseDate DESC , tblWines.WineName;
```

This SQL statement is somewhat longwinded, so the graphical representation shown in Figure 5-9 might make for an easier explanation.

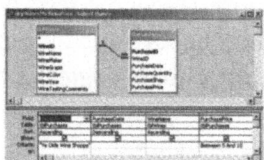

Figure 5-9. The SELECT *query represented graphically*

Here we are selecting the WineID column from the tblWines table, and for each wine, we are joining all the purchase records that exist for it—in other words, we are creating a one-to-many relationship. But we are also restricting the selection to only the purchase records where the point of sale was Ye Olde Wine Shoppe and the price paid was between 5 and 10 currency units. Finally, we are ordering records alphabetically by purchase shop, then by purchase date in descending order, and then by wine name. Figure 5-10 shows what the query returns.

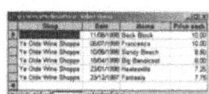

Figure 5-10. The results of the SELECT *query*

That covers the basics of database data manipulation; now you are ready to put your knowledge into action.

Data in .NET

A few words about the structure of **ADO.NET**, the .NET Framework's data access object model, are essential before you look at the way data-driven pages can be programmed. In this section, we explore the components of ADO.NET along with ActiveX Data Objects (ADO), which may aid understanding if you have used classic ADO before.

ADO.NET is a group of object classes (provided by the .NET Framework) that interact with data from data stores. These data stores are usually databases, but they could be spreadsheets, XML files, email servers, and so on. ADO.NET is simply a collection of standardized methods of data access that enable the user to manipulate data without necessarily knowing the details of the data store's operation.

Figure 5-11 is a diagram and description of the ADO 2.5 and ADO.NET object models.

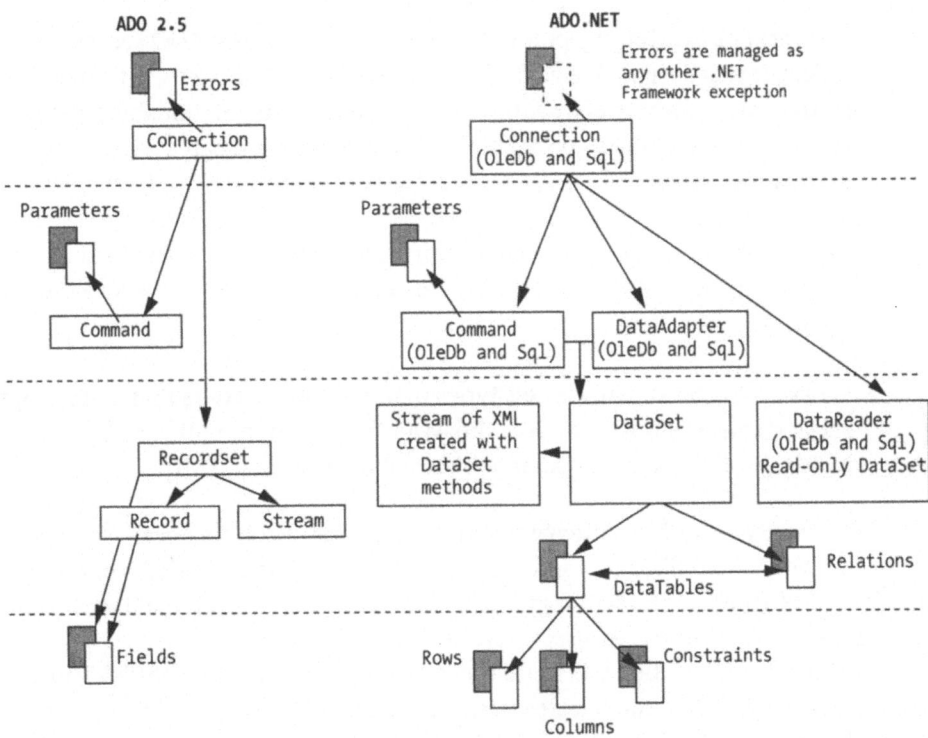

Figure 5-11. A comparison between the ADO 2.5 and ADO.NET data object models

It may look complicated, but you will probably find it to be less so in practice. More flexibility has been added to the new ADO.NET structure, especially when viewed in the overall context of the .NET Framework. Let's look at a few of the items in the diagram.

- **Connection:** A Connection is used to access data in the data store. In classic ADO, any errors were private to ADO, whereas in ADO.NET, they are treated just like any other .NET error. This means that web developers can catch data access errors in the special ASP.NET subroutine Page_Error.

- **DataAdapter:** A DataAdapter is used to populate a disconnectable DataSet object with results from a data store, to read changes made to a DataSet object, and to communicate those changes back to the data store. ADO performs much of this behavior implicitly; however, the explicit design of ADO.NET enables the programmer to fine-tune the interaction with a data store. DataAdapters are mainly used to execute SELECT SQL statements.

- **Command:** The Command object is commonly used to execute stored procedures (or stored queries in Access) or simply to execute SQL statements other than SELECT.

- **DataSet:** The DataSet object is the successor to the classic ADO Recordset object. It was designed specifically for disconnected operation. It can hold results from a variety of dissimilar sources and create relationships between them using data tables and relationships. In essence, it can act like a mini-database in memory.

- **DataReader:** A DataReader is a streamlined, forward-only type of DataSet in which the data is only read; that is, no changes can be sent back to the database.

- **Stream/XML:** The Stream and XML types of objects are readers that can accept serial streams of data. Much of the ADO Stream functionality is absorbed inside the DataSet. It can handle binary data as well as XML.

Let's swiftly move from theory to practice, and use each one of these objects in turn. If you would like more information, Microsoft has compiled a comprehensive data access architecture guide at http://msdn.microsoft.com/library/default.asp?url=/library/en-us/dnbda/html/daag.asp.

The download for the code in this section contains a sample ASP.NET page, dbaccess.aspx, which demonstrates basic data access in ASP.NET. It starts with the following page headers:

```
<%@ Page Language="VB" Debug="true" ContentType="text/html" ➡
ResponseEncoding="iso-8859-1" %>
<%@ Import Namespace="System.Data" %>
<%@ Import Namespace="System.Data.OleDb" %>
```

This defines the code language as VB .NET and turns on debugging messages. By importing the System.Data and System.Data.OLEDB namespaces, you do not have to type the full name of the data objects every time. The first piece of code that is executed in the page is whatever is inside the Page_Load subroutine. You must perform the data manipulation before the rest of the page's controls are processed by the ASP.NET engine.

```
<script runat="server">
Dim filepath As String
Dim strConn As String
Dim conn As OleDbConnection

Sub Page_Load()
' data binding to controls needs to be done before the page is formed

    Dim sqlCommand As OleDbDataAdapter
    Dim dsWines As Dataset

' open the connection
    If (conn Is Nothing) Then
        Call OpenConn()
    End If
```

To open the connection, call the `OpenConn` subroutine.

```
Sub OpenConn()
                filePath = Server.MapPath("wines.mdb")
                strConn = "Provider=Microsoft.Jet.OLEDB.4.0; Data Source=" ➥
& filepath & ";"
                conn = new OleDbConnection(strConn)
                conn.Open
End Sub
```

In the code just shown, you are creating an OLEDB flavor of the DataAdapter (if you were accessing SQL Server, you would code SqlDataAdapter). You then create a DataSet and test for the existence of the database connection. If it has not been created before, the Connection object is created via the specified connection string, strConn. The web site uses an Access database as its data store, so we are using the Jet OLEDB provider connection string. See the "Database Setup" section later in this chapter for more details.

Another way to specify connection strings is via the web.config configuration file shown in earlier chapters. You can add these lines to your web.config:

```
<configuration>
  <appSettings>
    <add key="dbstrconn"
value="Provider=Microsoft.Jet.OLEDB.4.0; Data
Source=C:\Inetpub\wwwroot\mx2004\wines.mdb;" />
  </appSettings>
</configuration>
```

When you add these lines, you can use the following code instead of the bold lines shown earlier (see dbaccessconfig.aspx):

```
strConn = ConfigurationSettings.AppSettings("dbstrconn")
conn = new OleDbConnection(strConn)
conn.Open
```

This imports the key defined in the configuration file. Both methods work, but the second is easier to maintain and modify, especially if many pages utilize the same connection string. More important, it is also the method automatically used by Dreamweaver MX; Dreamweaver adds the keys if a web.config file already exists, otherwise it creates a new configuration file.

Next is the DataSet object. You can use the Access query qryWinesMediumPrice to copy its underlying SQL statement directly into the code. This works because Access is simply a graphic interface to the same data access engine (Jet) defined in your connection string—VB .NET only requires that you replace the single quotes around strings (' ') with double quotes (" "). The following code continues from where OpenConn was called in the Page_Load subroutine:

```
dsWines = new DataSet()
form the SQL command. SQL statement needs to be on one line
sqlCommand = new OleDbDataAdapter("SELECT
tblPurchases.PurchaseShop, tblPurchases.PurchaseDate,
tblWines.WineName, tblPurchases.PurchasePrice FROM tblWines
INNER JOIN tblPurchases ON tblWines.WineID =
tblPurchases.WineID WHERE
(((tblPurchases.PurchaseShop)=""Ye Olde Wine Shoppe"")
AND ((tblPurchases.PurchasePrice) Between 5 And 10)) ORDER BY
tblPurchases.PurchaseShop, tblPurchases.PurchaseDate DESC ,
tblWines.WineName;", conn)
sqlCommand.Fill(dsWines)
```

The Fill method of the DataAdapter object puts the data into your DataSet. That is all you have to do. You can disconnect from the database and do any processing you want with the data now residing in memory. Later, we will bind the contents of the DataSet object to the asp:DataGrid control on the page called YeOldewines, which is simply defined as

```
<asp:datagrid ID="YeOldewines" runat="server"></asp:datagrid>
```

ASP.NET provides an easy way to assign the data to any control, which then creates itself automatically. You will see more details on this in the next chapter—for now, you can see how two lines of code are sufficient to perform the data binding.

```
' bind the dataset to the datalist
  YeOldewines.DataSource = dsWines
  YeOldewines.DataBind()
  dsWines.Dispose()

' close the connection
  Call TidyUp()
  sqlCommand = Nothing
End Sub
```

Finally, the TidyUp subroutine releases memory occupied by the variables.

```
Sub TidyUp()
     filepath=Nothing
     strConn=Nothing
     conn.Close
     conn.Dispose()
     conn=Nothing
End Sub
```

Browse to the dbaccess.aspx page via your browser. The results of your query will appear on the page as shown in Figure 5-12.

Figure 5-12. Your first ASP.NET query results

We brought the data to the page without using too much code. Now let's look into how to set up databases in Dreamweaver.

Database Setup

Our examples assumed that an Access database is holding the data. Table 5-4 lists the different providers that your application may require for different databases.

Table 5-4. Windows Drivers for Various RDBMS Packages

Driver String	Provider
SQLOLEDB	Microsoft OLE DB Provider for SQL Server
MSDAORA	Microsoft OLE DB Provider for Oracle
OraOLEDB.Oracle	Oracle OLE DB Provider for Oracle
Microsoft.Jet.OLEDB.4.0	Microsoft OLE DB Provider for Microsoft Jet
MSDASQL	Microsoft ODBC Provider for MSDE
MSDAIPP.DSO	Microsoft OLE DB Provider for Internet Publishing

To access any other database from within your pages, all you have to do is type in the appropriate driver string in the Provider parameter of the connection string. Dreamweaver provides a friendly interface for setting up some common databases. Before you make the first database connection, the Application panel's Databases tab looks as shown in Figure 5-13.

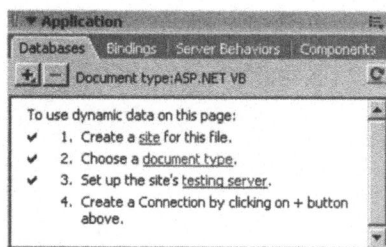

Figure 5-13. The Databases tab of the Application panel

1. As you can see, you need to define a site, choose a web document type (ASP.NET of course, plus either VB or C#), and set up a testing server. Click the plus sign (+) button to display the connection type list, as shown in Figure 5-14.

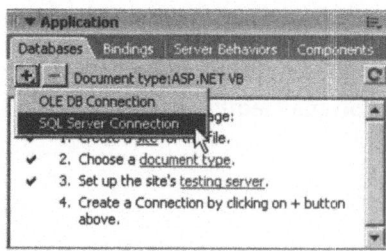

Figure 5-14. The connection types

2. Let's assume that you are trying to connect to a SQL Server database. Click SQL Server Connection to display the dialog box shown in Figure 5-15.

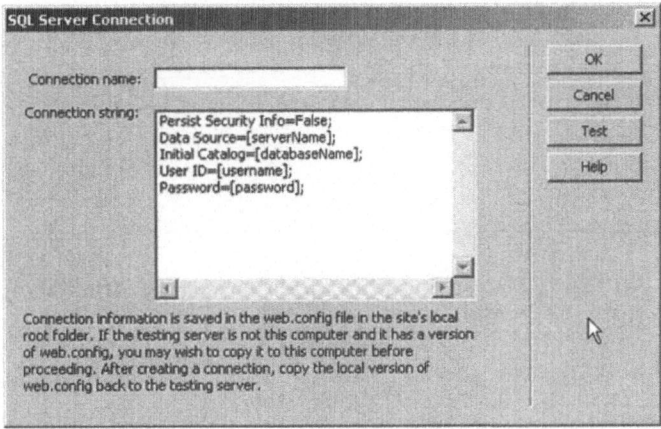

Figure 5-15. The Dreamweaver MX SQL Server Connection dialog box

The connection string is already half-created. All you need to do is replace the bracketed text (including the brackets) with your database's details. Let's assume that your database is called mydb on a networked machine named mypc. Your user name is auname and the password is apwd. This being the case, your connection string would need to be entered as shown in Figure 5-16.

Figure 5-16. An example connection string

3. If you are connecting to an RDBMS other than SQL Server, you need to use the OLE DB providers, so go back and select the OLE DB Connection option. You are then presented with a completely blank connection string, but with a rather helpful button called Templates. Click it to open the Connection String Templates dialog box, as shown in Figure 5-17.

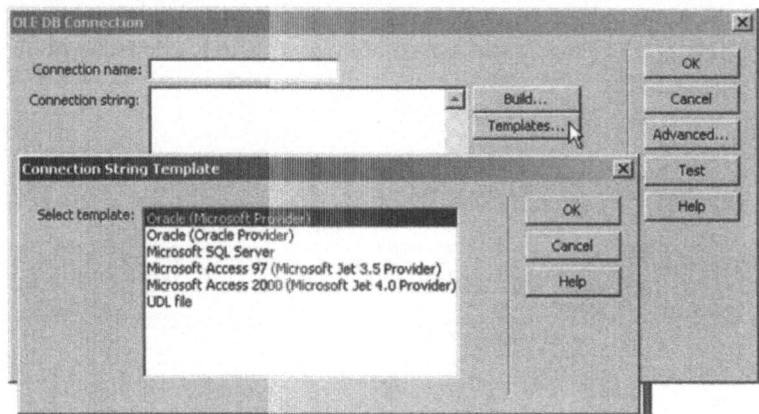

Figure 5-17. The OLE DB Connection and Connection String Template dialog boxes

4. For RDBMSs that are not shown here, choose a **Universal Data Link (UDL)** file. This is a simple text file with a .udl extension—a special Microsoft format for connection string files. If you were trying to connect to the Access 2000 database used for earlier examples, choose Microsoft Access 2000 (Microsoft Jet 4.0 Provider). The template displays the dialog box shown in Figure 5-18.

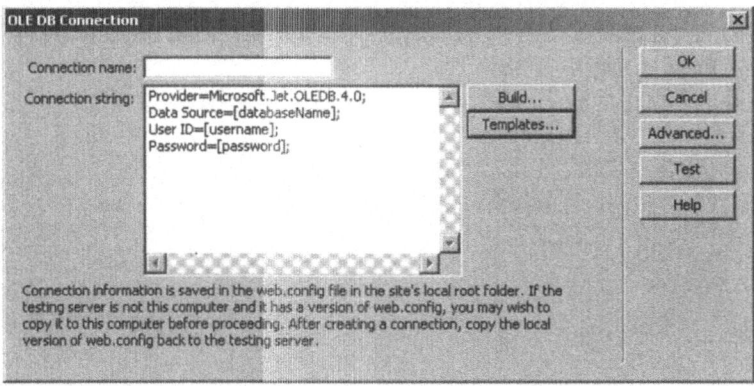

Figure 5-18. A sample template for the OLE DB connection

You can complete the data in square brackets (remove the square brackets) to end up with a connection string similar to the one shown in Figure 5-19 (assuming a user name of myuname and a password of mypwd).

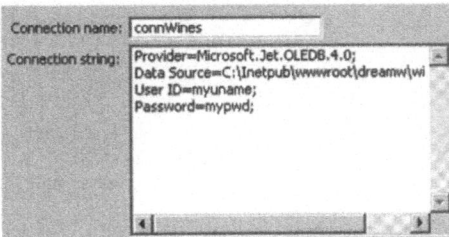

Figure 5-19. The sample template completed

5. You can also build a database connection via the wizard screens that
    are accessed through the Build button. Clicking Build opens a UDL file
    interface—it opens in the SQL Server screen even if you chose to create
    an OLE DB connection. Simply click the Provider tab and select the Jet
    provider, as shown in Figure 5-20.

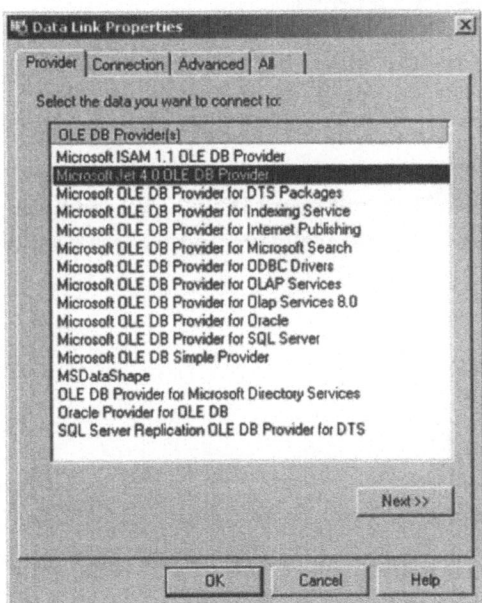

Figure 5-20. The Universal Data Link interface

6. Click Next to display a browse field that you can use to locate your
    database. If you do not have any user-level security configured in your
    Access database, which is the case for our examples in this book, allow
    the default user Admin with a blank password and click OK, as shown
    in Figure 5-21.

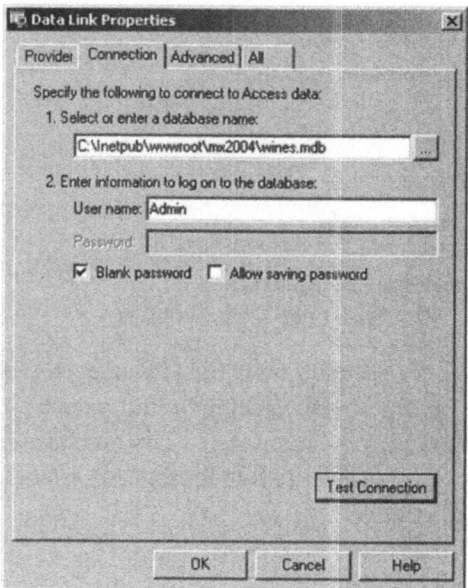

Figure 5-21. The Connection tab of the UDL interface

The connection string is now built for you.

Any databases you connect to in Dreamweaver MX will appear in the Databases tab, which takes its data from the locally created web.config file, as shown in Figure 5-22.

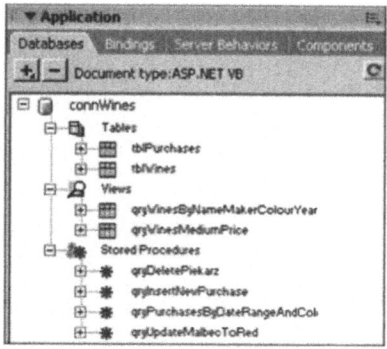

Figure 5-22. Database connections appear in the Databases tab.

You can then refer to the connection whenever you add a databound control or a dataset. Dreamweaver takes care of the connection details behind the scenes, as you will see in the following chapters.

Summary

In this chapter, we showed you the origins of relational databases and the benefits they offer for data access. You used an Access database to learn about how SQL statements provide an interface to the data, and you then used the database in conjunction with ADO.NET technology to create data-driven web pages. In the final section, you saw some Dreamweaver MX specifics on database setup.

The following provide further information on data in .NET:

- **.NET data architecture guide**:
  http://msdn.microsoft.com/library/default.asp?url=/library/en-us/dnbda/html/daag.asp

- **Best practices for using ADO.NET**:
  http://msdn.microsoft.com/library/default.asp?url=/library/en-us/dnadonet/html/adonetbest.asp

- **Oracle .NET data samples**:
  http://otn.oracle.com/sample_code/tech/windows/ole_db/content.html

- **ADO programming**:
  http://www.microsoft.com/accessdev/articles/movs202.htm

- **Connection strings for various databases**:
  http://msdn.microsoft.com/library/default.asp?url=/library/en-us/ado270/htm/pg_ado_providers_1.asp

In the next few chapters, you will see more details of how .NET is used for data binding and how Dreamweaver MX helps with more complicated applications.

Data Applications

IF YOU ARE NEW TO DREAMWEAVER, you are probably getting used to the interface and appreciating how efficient it can be. In this chapter, we will show you one of Dreamweaver's most timesaving and helpful features: databound controls. These controls are also one of the most fundamental strengths of ASP.NET.

In Chapter 4, you learned about the ASP.NET and Application toolbars and their controls, and in Chapter 5, you built a database connection. In this chapter, you will build a data-driven application from scratch.

Creating Datasets

First you will create a dataset. Follow these steps:

1. Click the Bindings tab in the Application panel. You should see the screen shown in Figure 6-1 (if an ASP.NET VB document is open).

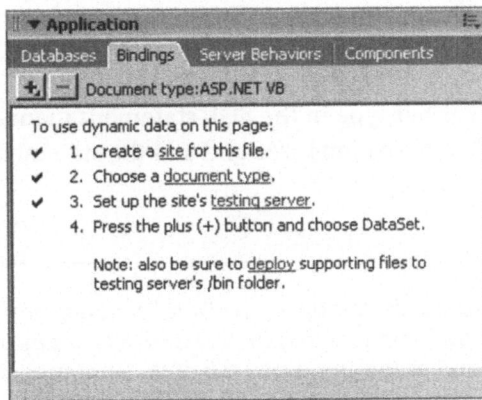

Figure 6-1. The Bindings tab before adding a dataset

2. Click the plus sign (+) button to choose how you want to acquire your data: via a dataset or a stored procedure. There are other possibilities, of course, such as using XML or directory data.

3. For the moment, we will stick with building a dataset. Let's make it a simple one that requests all the data in the tblWines table of the wines.mdb database. Click DataSet on the plus sign button's menu to display the dialog box shown in Figure 6-2. (If your dialog box looks different, click the Advanced button.)

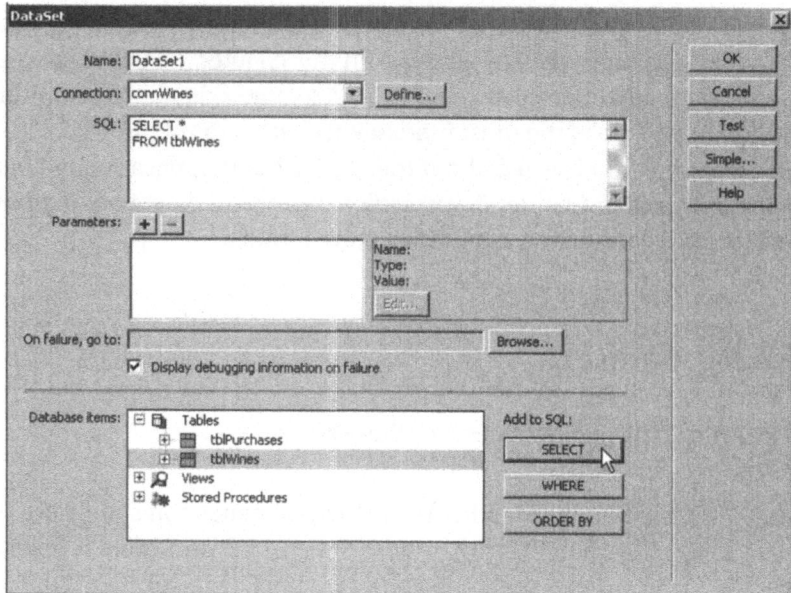

Figure 6-2. The DataSet dialog box

As you can see, you can either type in the SQL statement manually or expand the tree in the Database items area and add the statement parts via the Add to SQL buttons.

 TIP *The Stored Procedures branch of the DataSet dialog box does not display saved action queries in Access (delete or append queries) contrary to what the Databases tab of the Application panel displays.*

---

4. You can ignore the Parameters area of the dialog box for the moment; we will come back to it later in this chapter. Click the Test button to test the connection before confirming the settings.

5. Click OK. You will see a number of things happening in Dreamweaver. First, your dataset appears in the Bindings tab, ready to be used as a data source, as shown in Figure 6-3.

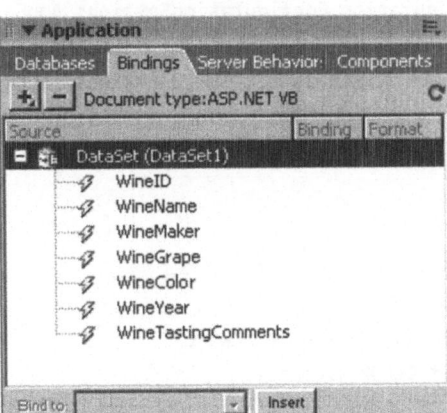

Figure 6-3. The newly created dataset appears in the Bindings tab.

6. Switch to Code view and note that quite a bit of code has been added. Just below the @ Page directive, you will see the following lines:

```
<%@ Register TagPrefix="MM" Namespace="DreamweaverCtrls" ➥
Assembly="DreamweaverCtrls,version=1.0.0.0,publicKeyToken=➥
836f606ede05d46a, ➥
culture=neutral" %>
```

7. As you may recall from Chapter 4, this is how Macromedia's custom MM: controls are registered in your page. At this point, it might be a good idea to check that your /bin directory contains the file DreamweaverCtrls.dll, which is the container for the MM: controls. If it is not there, click the Application panel's Bindings tab, and click the link "Note: also be sure to deploy supporting files on the testing server."

8. Right below the @ Register directive, find the MM:DataSet control.

```
<MM:DataSet id="DataSet1" runat="Server" IsStoredProcedure="false"
ConnectionString='<%#
System.Configuration.ConfigurationSettings.AppSettings
("MM_CONNECTION_STRING_connWines") %>'
DatabaseType='<%# System.Configuration.ConfigurationSettings.AppSettings
("MM_CONNECTION_DATABASETYPE_connWines") %>'
CommandText='<%# "SELECT *  FROM tblWines" %>' Debug="true" >
</MM:DataSet>
```

The code in bold shows the values taken from the `web.config` file of your application. If you did not have one before, Dreamweaver created one for you at the root of the web site, and the values necessary for connecting to the database were saved in it. For example, the `ConnectionString` attribute takes the value `System.Configuration.ConfigurationSettings.AppSettings ("MM_CONNECTION_STRING_connWines")`, which refers to the value of the `web.config` setting named `"MM_CONNECTION_STRING_connWines"`. If you open your `web.config` file, you will see something similar to the following:

```
<configuration>
     <appSettings>
          <add key="MM_CONNECTION_HANDLER_connWines"
value="default_oledb.htm" />
          <add key="MM_CONNECTION_STRING_connWines"
value="Provider=Microsoft.Jet.OLEDB.4.0;Data
Source=C:\Inetpub\wwwroot\mx2004\wines.mdb;Persist Security Info=false" />
          <add key="MM_CONNECTION_DATABASETYPE_connWines"
value="OleDb" />
          <add key="MM_CONNECTION_SCHEMA_connWines" value="" />
          <add key="MM_CONNECTION_CATALOG_connWines" value="" />
     </appSettings>
</configuration>
```

The connection string created in Chapter 5 is shown in bold. You can also see the `databaseType` attribute's value, which for Access is `OleDb`. You may also have other connection information if you created more than one.

The next attribute of the `MM:DataSet` control is `CommandText`, which, interestingly, contains the SQL statement within an inline databinding block rather than in a simple text string.

```
<%# "SELECT *  FROM tblWines" %>
```

This could just as well have been the SQL text without the `<%# %>` tags, but it is evaluated at runtime so you can create it in real time using variables.

If there were stored action queries in your database that you wanted to call, you could just replace the contents of the `CommandText` attribute with the name of the query. This is how you can get around the fact that Dreamweaver cannot "see" stored queries in Access. For example, the `wines.mdb` database contains an append query that inserts a new row (with MX 2004–related values) called `qryInsertNewRow` in the `tblWines` table.

9. Replace the value of CommandText with CreateDataSet="false". In addition, set IsStoredProcedure to true. The MM:DataSet control now looks like the following:

```
<MM:DataSet id="DataSet1" runat="Server" IsStoredProcedure="true"
ConnectionString='<%# System.Configuration.ConfigurationSettings.➥
AppSettings
("MM_CONNECTION_STRING_connWines") %>'
DatabaseType='<%# System.Configuration.ConfigurationSettings.AppSettings
("MM_CONNECTION_DATABASETYPE_connWines") %>'
CommandText='<%# "qryInsertNewRow" %>'
Debug="true" CreateDataSet="false" ></MM:DataSet>
```

10. Execute the page as it stands now (MMDSappend.aspx in the download). For simplicity, the page does not provide any feedback on success, but in a real application, you would specify values for the attributes FailureURL and SuccessURL. Instead, open the database and confirm that your row has been inserted, as shown in Figure 6-4.

	ID#	Name	Maker	Grape	Color	Year	Comments
	110	Modigliani	Blondini Brothers	Cabernet Sauvignon	Red	1996	Fantastic red blah blah
	1001	MX2004	Dreamweaver	MMDataSet	red	2003	Superb!
	(AutoNumber)			Cabernet Sauvignon			

Figure 6-4. A new row is inserted in the database table using the MM:DataSet *control.*

Dreamweaver allows you to see all the attributes of MM:DataSet by presenting a drop-down list while you are typing, but a good reference explaining the control's use can be found at http://www.macromedia.com/support/dreamweaver/building/aspnet_tags/aspnet_tags03.html.

Finally, let's look at the last custom MM: tag inserted in your page, MM:PageBind.

```
<MM:PageBind runat="server" PostBackBind="true" />
```

As you saw in Chapter 4, MM:PageBind simply ensures that all data-related controls on the page are bound when the page is called.

You have the data available in your page, now how do you use it?

Binding Data to Controls

Let's return to the MM:DataSet definition that selects all the data from the tblWines table (DataGridSample.aspx). You have the dataset's definition in the page, so let's look at how to add it to one of the most useful data controls in ASP.NET, asp:DataGrid.

1. Place your cursor inside the body of the page in Code view and click the Application toolbar to select DataGrid from the drop-down list, as shown in Figure 6-5.

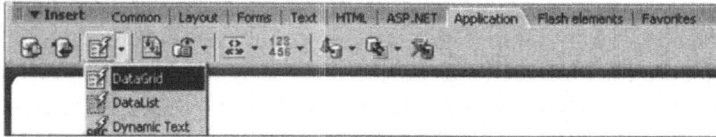

Figure 6-5. Adding a datagrid to a page

2. The DataGrid dialog box appears. Because you already have a dataset in the page, the dialog box includes options to bind the datagrid to that dataset. It also gives you the option of paging through the records or displaying them all at once. You can add special columns to the datagrid via the plus sign (+) button, but save your curiosity for a bit later in this chapter. Finally, you can choose between navigational links.

   Fill in the dialog box as shown in Figure 6-6.

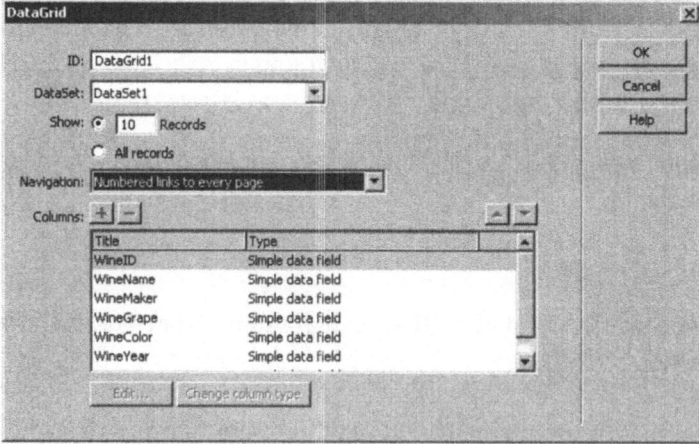

Figure 6-6. The DataGrid dialog box

3.   Click OK. You have successfully built a data-driven page that delivers a friendly interface, as shown in Figure 6-7.

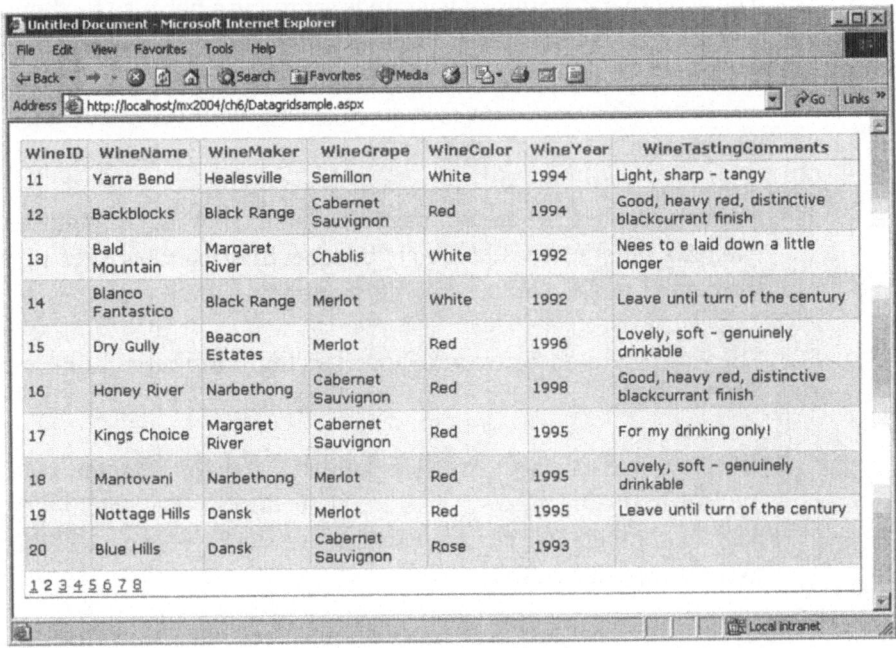

Figure 6-7. The datagrid displayed in the browser

The code contains extensive default formatting that you can easily customize. It is interesting to look at the data-related parts of the datagrid, starting with the tag itself.

```
<asp:DataGrid id="DataGrid1"
runat="server"
AllowSorting="false"
AutoGenerateColumns="false"
CellPadding="3"
CellSpacing="0"
ShowFooter="false"
ShowHeader="true"
DataSource="<%# DataSet1.DefaultView %>"
PagerStyle-Mode="NumericPages"
AllowPaging="true"
AllowCustomPaging="true"
PageSize="<%# DataSet1.PageSize %>"
VirtualItemCount="<%# DataSet1.RecordCount %>"
OnPageIndexChanged="DataSet1.OnDataGridPageIndexChanged" >
```

You will find most of the attributes self-explanatory, but let's look at a few important ones.

- The AutoGenerateColumns attribute is set to false because further down you will see that Dreamweaver has explicitly inserted column-defining tags. Setting the AutoGenerateColumns attribute to true is useful when you do not know which columns exist in your dataset or if the existing columns will change.

- The DataSource attribute points to the default view of the dataset. A dataset can have other views added to it, in effect filtering rows or combining data from other tables. DefaultView returns the unfiltered table.

- The PagerStyle-Mode attribute specifies that numbered links to pages will be used.

- The OnPageIndexChanged attribute points to a custom Macromedia event handler in the DreamweaverCtrls.dll that controls the switching from one page to another. This custom handler sets the current page of the datagrid to the newly clicked index:

```
DataGrid1.CurrentPageIndex = e.NewPageIndex
```

  In this line, e is the event arguments received from the OnPageIndexChanged event. Quite a simple code piece really, shielding the programmer from a much more complicated affair.

There are also attributes that control how the datagrid pages through the data rows. We enable paging, specify that we will perform custom paging, and define a page size and total record count. Note that these attributes are defined by the dataset but they could easily have been integers or some other bound variable.

Further down in the code, you can see the databound columns grouped under the Columns section.

```
<Columns>
<asp:BoundColumn DataField="WineID"
    HeaderText="WineID"
    ReadOnly="true"
    Visible="true"/>
...
</Columns>
```

The attribute ReadOnly can be set to false, which places the value in a text box if the row contains editing command buttons. To edit a row, you can use the datagrid's editing commands.

Editing Data Rows

We will now continue to explore the capabilities of the datagrid by investigating the function of the mysterious plus sign (+) button in the DataGrid dialog box. But to make your dataset a bit more exciting, we will also look at how you can combine data from two tables in the grid.

1. Starting with a new page (DatagridWithActions.aspx), create a dataset from wines.mdb, as shown in Figure 6-8.

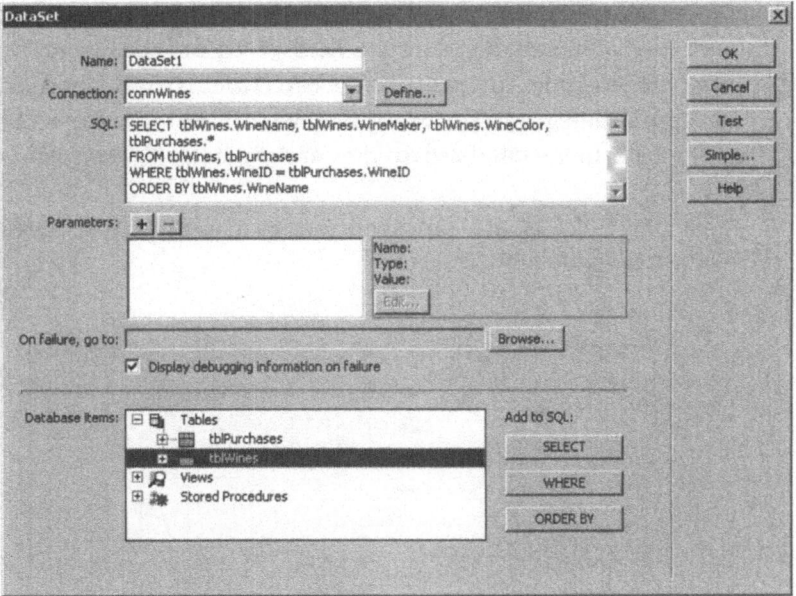

Figure 6-8. Creating a new dataset

2. As you already know from Chapter 5, the SQL statement selects the wine purchases that match each wine in the wines table and displays them as one recordset. You can then create a new datagrid and assign the dataset to it, as you did before. This time, though, click the plus sign (+) button above the Columns list to display a list of special columns that can be added, as shown in Figure 6-9.

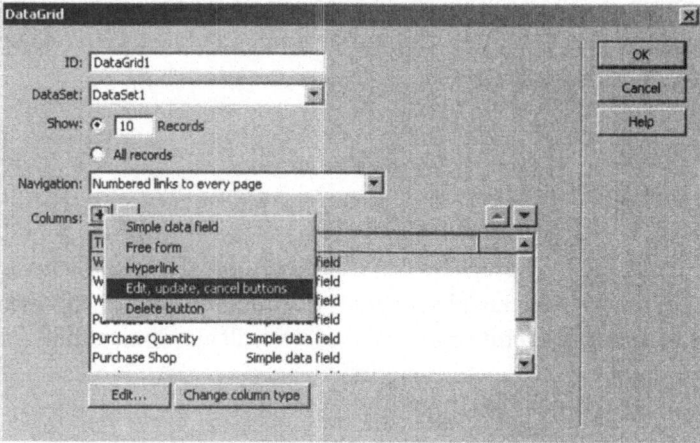

Figure 6-9. Adding action buttons to the datagrid

The choices are pretty much what you would expect: Simple data field adds one of the existing dataset's fields. Free form adds any HTML you want, for example, an image next to each row. Hyperlink adds a link to an appropriate page. The remaining two column types are actions that point back to the database, so they are of greater interest right now.

3. Select the Edit, update, cancel buttons item to display the dialog box shown in Figure 6-10.

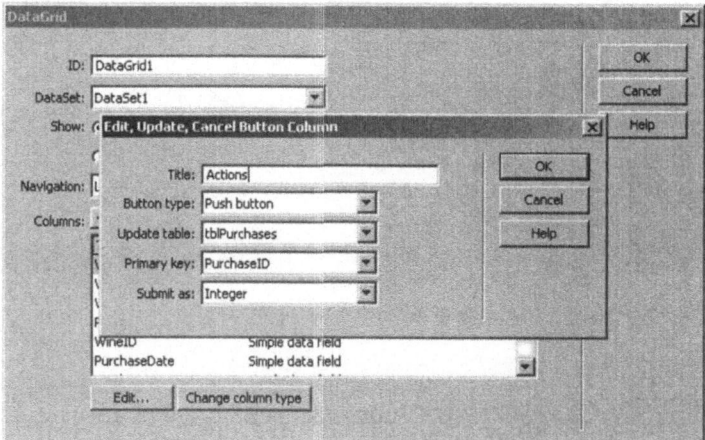

Figure 6-10. The action buttons definition screen

4. The column you are creating will include an Edit button that will allow you to edit data in any columns marked with ReadOnly="false". Note that you can edit columns from only one table at a time, so specify

a table in the Edit, Update, Cancel Button Column dialog box. Next, type a title for the column and choose whether you want a button or a link for the Edit command. Then use the other drop-down lists to specify which table contains the row to be updated, which column contains its primary key, and the primary key's datatype.

5. Click OK. Now you need to specify which columns will be read-only—this can be done in code or from this dialog box. Select the column you want to modify, for example, PurchasePrice, and click Edit to display the dialog box shown in Figure 6-11.

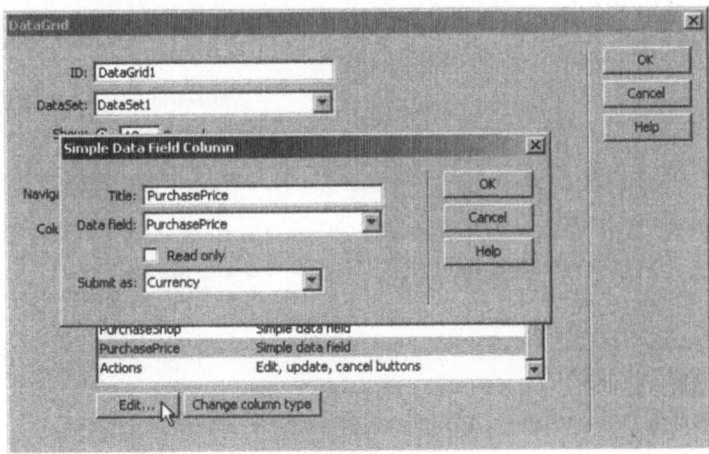

Figure 6-11. Making a datagrid's field editable

6. Make sure the Read only check box is unmarked, and click OK. Then repeat step 5 for any other columns you want to be able to edit. Finally, click OK to create the dataset.

7. Run your page in a browser. It should look as shown in Figure 6-12.

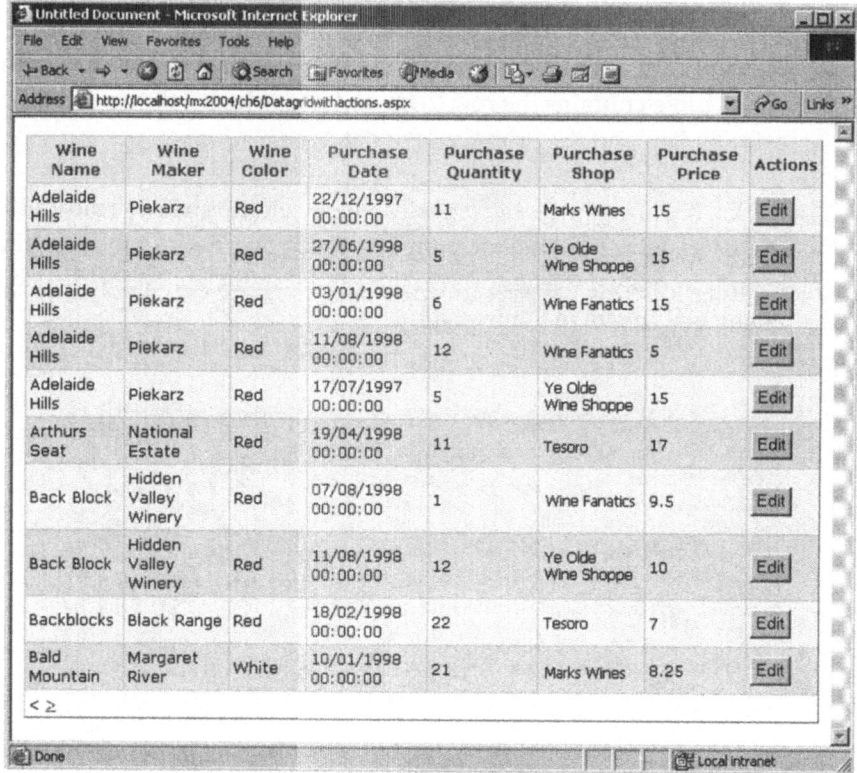

Figure 6-12. The editable datagrid displayed in the browser

8. Choose a row to edit by clicking its Edit button. The page posts back and returns with the editable values in text boxes, as shown in Figure 6-13.

Figure 6-13. Updating the values of editable fields in a datagrid

9. Type **8** for the purchase quantity and click Update. The screen returns the same page with the changes saved in the database, as shown in Figure 6-14.

Wine Color	Purchase Date	Purchase Quantity	Purchase Shop	Purchase Price	Actions
Red	22/12/1997 00:00:00	11	Marks Wines	15	Edit
Red	27/06/1998 00:00:00	8	Ye Olde Wine Shoppe	15	Edit
Red	03/01/1998 00:00:00	6	Le Palate	15	Edit

Figure 6-14. The datagrid displays the updated values.

10. Remember that even after you have created the datagrid, you can edit column properties by selecting a column in Design view and using the Property inspector, as shown in Figure 6-15. Use this method now to add a Delete button for each row.

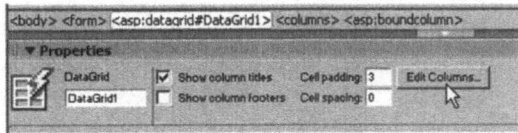

Figure 6-15. Amending the datagrid's properties via the Property inspector

11. Click Edit Columns to display the Edit, Update, Cancel Button Column dialog box. Now you can add the Delete column with a couple of clicks. Your interface then magically appears with a Delete button next to each row, as shown in Figure 6-16.

Wine Color	Purchase Date	Purchase Quantity	Purchase Shop	Purchase Price	Actions	Delete
Red	22/12/1997 00:00:00	11	Marks Wines	15	Edit	Delete
Red	27/06/1998 00:00:00	8	Ye Olde Wine Shoppe	15	Edit	Delete
Red	03/01/1998 00:00:00	6	Le Palate	15	Edit	Delete

Figure 6-16. Adding a Delete button to the datagrid

Inserting these action columns added some new elements to the code. First, the dataset definition changed via the addition of some contained tags.

```
<EditOps>
    <EditOpsTable Name="tblPurchases" />
    <Parameter Name="PurchaseQuantity" Type="Integer" />
    <Parameter Name="PurchasePrice" Type="Currency" />
    <Parameter Name="PurchaseID" Type="Integer" IsPrimary="true" />
</EditOps>
```

These tags are again custom Macromedia tags that correspond to the choices made earlier. In addition, a lot more event handling is now available in the datagrid definition, pointing to additional custom Macromedia event-handling subroutines.

```
...
onUpdateCommand="DataSet1.OnDataGridUpdate"
onEditCommand="DataSet1.OnDataGridEdit"
onCancelCommand="DataSet1.OnDataGridCancel"
onDeleteCommand="DataSet1.OnDataGridDelete"
...
```

Using Parameters

So far you have used relatively simple datasets in the sense that you did not filter any data. Now you will use a URL parameter to narrow the selected rows.

1. Create a dataset from scratch or open an existing page and double-click DataSet on the Server Behaviors tab, as shown in Figure 6-17.

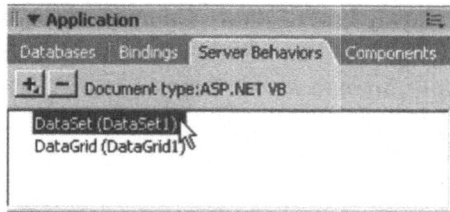

Figure 6-17. The Server Behaviors tab displaying the newly created dataset and datagrid

2. In the DataSet dialog box, click the Parameters plus sign (+) button to display the parameter definition screen in which you can enter the name and value origins of the parameter. Alternatively, you can click the Build button to display the Build Value dialog box, as shown in Figure 6-18.

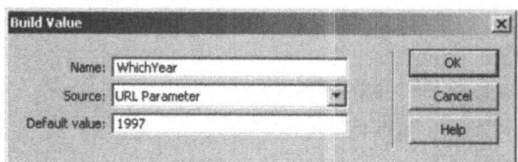

Figure 6-18. Building a parameter value

The parameter can then be used in the SQL statement that defines the dataset. You can denote parameters via question marks (?) in the SQL statement. The example in Figure 6-18 would create the following code as the dataset definition:

```
<MM:DataSet
id="DataSet1"
runat="Server"
IsStoredProcedure="false"
ConnectionString='<%# System.Configuration.ConfigurationSettings.
AppSettings("MM_CONNECTION_STRING_connWines") %>'
DatabaseType='<%# System.Configuration.ConfigurationSettings.AppSettings
("MM_CONNECTION_DATABASETYPE_connWines") %>'
CommandText='<%# "SELECT *  FROM tblWines  ➡
WHERE tblWines.WineYear>?" %>'
Debug="true" PageSize="10" >
   <Parameters>
      <Parameter  Name="WhichYear"  Value='<%# IIf((Request.QueryString➡
("WhichYear")  ➡
<> Nothing), Request.QueryString("WhichYear"), "1997") %>'  ➡
Type="Integer"   />
   </Parameters>
</MM:DataSet>
```

At runtime, the custom Macromedia MM:DataSet code replaces the question marks with whatever is evaluated as the value attribute of the <Parameters> tag. This gives you the ability to, for example, filter wines that are younger than a certain age. None are returned in the query shown in Figure 6-19.

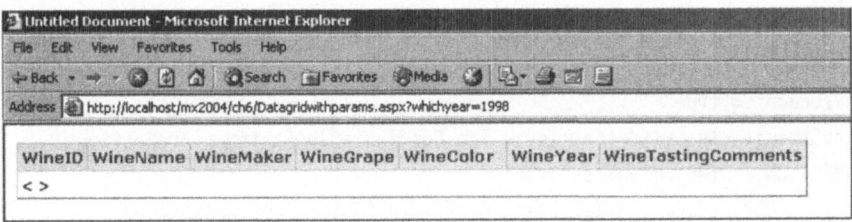

Figure 6-19. Filtering records via DataSet parameters

If there are multiple parameters, Dreamweaver replaces them in the order they appear in the <Parameters> tag. Therefore, you must specify them in the order they appear in your SQL statement text. This is especially important when inserting new values in a table, which we will cover next.

Inserting Rows

We will also take this opportunity to demonstrate the execution of stored procedures via an ASP.NET page. **Stored procedures** are pieces of precompiled SQL statements stored in the database. If you are connected to a SQL Server, stored procedures are visible in the Databases tab of the Application panel. If you are using Access, you will see any saved queries that the database contains, as shown in Figure 6-20.

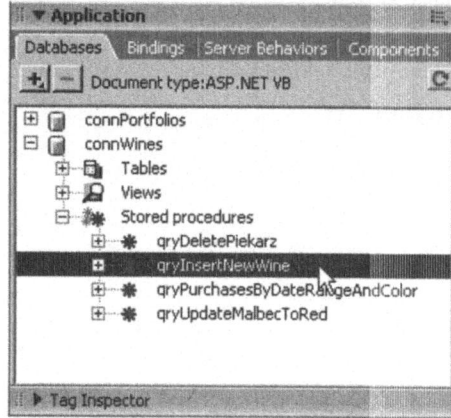

Figure 6-20. Stored procedures in the Databases panel

As you saw earlier, you can execute a stored procedure by typing its name in the dataset's CommandText attribute and setting the IsStoredProcedure attribute to true.

```
<MM:DataSet
id="DataSet2"
runat="Server"
IsStoredProcedure="true"
ConnectionString='<%# System.Configuration.ConfigurationSettings.AppSettings
("MM_CONNECTION_STRING_connWines") %>'
DatabaseType='<%# System.Configuration.ConfigurationSettings.AppSettings
("MM_CONNECTION_DATABASETYPE_connWines") %>'
CommandText='<%# "qryInsertNewRow" %>'
Debug="true" PageSize="10" >
</MM:DataSet>
```

However, you cannot pass any parameters to the stored procedure via the `MM:DataSet` control. You must use the `<MM:Insert>` tag, accessible via the Application toolbar, as shown in Figure 6-21. You can start with a brand-new page, and Dreamweaver will generate everything you need.

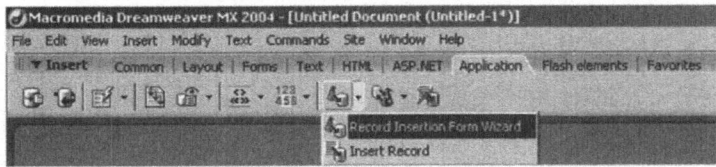

Figure 6-21. Adding an `MM:Insert` *control in an ASP.NET page*

The Record Insertion Form dialog box appears, in which you specify how a new row will be inserted in the tblWines table. Simply specify a connection and a table, and then customize Dreamweaver's guess, if needed, as shown in Figure 6-22.

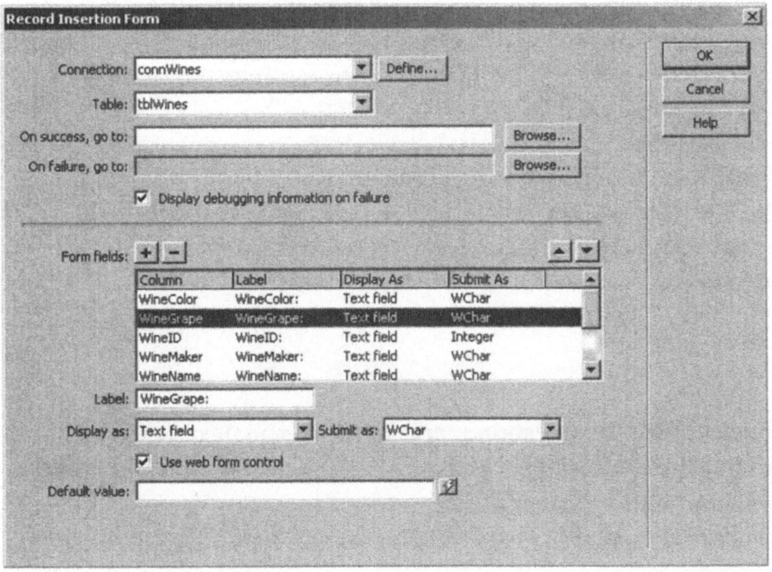

Figure 6-22. The Record Insertion Wizard

Clicking OK generates a web form with the necessary input boxes and inserts an `<MM:Insert>` tag with parameters at the top of the page. The full code of the `<MM:Insert>` tag should be similar to the following:

```
<MM:Insert
runat="server"
CommandText='<%# "INSERT INTO tblWines (WineColor, WineGrape, WineID,
WineMaker, WineName, WineTastingComments, WineYear)
VALUES (?, ?, ?, ?, ?, ?, ?)" %>'
ConnectionString='<%# System.Configuration.ConfigurationSettings.AppSettings
("MM_CONNECTION_STRING_connWines") %>'
DatabaseType='<%# System.Configuration.ConfigurationSettings.AppSettings
("MM_CONNECTION_DATABASETYPE_connWines") %>'
Expression='<%# Request.Form("MM_insert") = "form1" %>'
CreateDataSet="false"
Debug="true" >
  <Parameters>
    <Parameter Name="@WineColor" Value='<%# IIf((Request.Form("WineColor")
 <> Nothing), Request.Form("WineColor"), "") %>' Type="WChar" />
    <Parameter Name="@WineGrape" Value='<%# IIf((Request.Form("WineGrape")
<> Nothing), Request.Form("WineGrape"), "") %>' Type="WChar" />
    <Parameter Name="@WineID" Value='<%# IIf((Request.Form("WineID") <>
Nothing),
Request.Form("WineID"), "") %>' Type="Integer" />
    <Parameter Name="@WineMaker" Value='<%# IIf((Request.Form("WineMaker") <>
Nothing), Request.Form("WineMaker"), "") %>' Type="WChar" />
    <Parameter Name="@WineName" Value='<%# IIf((Request.Form("WineName") <>
Nothing), Request.Form("WineName"), "") %>' Type="WChar" />
    <Parameter Name="@WineTastingComments" Value='<%#
IIf((Request.Form("WineTastingComments") <> Nothing),
Request.Form("WineTastingComments"), "") %>' Type="WChar" />
    <Parameter Name="@WineYear" Value='<%# IIf((Request.Form("WineYear") <>
 Nothing), Request.Form("WineYear"), "") %>' Type="WChar" />
  </Parameters>
</MM:Insert>
```

As mentioned earlier, the question marks in the CommandText attribute are replaced in order by the enclosed parameters. The CommandText attribute is highlighted—we will now modify that slightly.

The advantage of using stored procedures (or saved queries) is that they are precompiled in the database. In contrast, a SQL statement must be parsed every time, which results in delays. To enable the MM:Insert control to use the stored query qryInsertNewWine, set IsStoredProcedure="true" and CommandText="qryInsertNewWine". You also have to make sure the parameters are passed to the query in the right order.

This time you need to open the Access database and look at the query's design. By rearranging the parameters to fit the query's column order, you can ensure that the page runs smoothly (DatagridWithInsert.aspx), as shown in Figure 6-23.

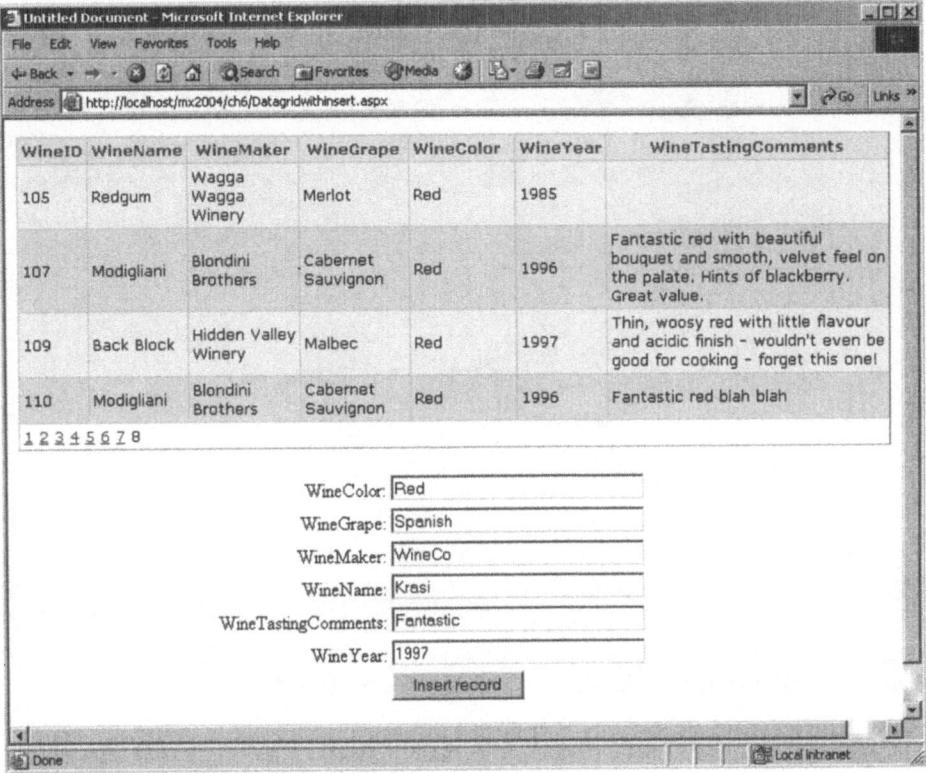

Figure 6-23. Inserting a new record in a table

When you click the Insert record button, the row is inserted and it can be seen in the datagrid of the same page, as shown in Figure 6-24.

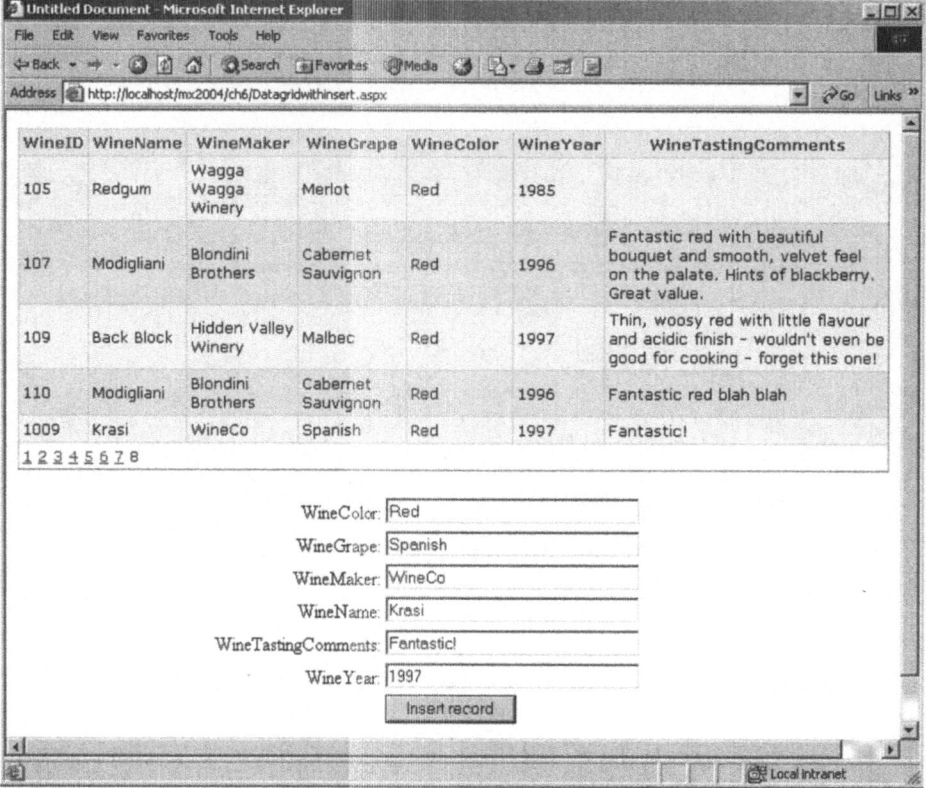

Figure 6-24. The datagrid displays the newly added record.

Other Databound Controls

The principles described so far are valid for most controls available via the Application toolbar. The datagrid is the most flexible of the databound controls, so it enables more data-related actions than the rest. You can easily apply what you have learned about datagrids to the other ASP.NET databound controls.

The `asp:Repeater` control, however, needs special mention because of its particular syntax. Let's use Dreamweaver to create a new ASP.NET VB page with an `MM:DataSet` pointing to the `tblWines` table.

1. Create a simple table with one cell in the body of the page.

```
<table>
  <tr><td>
  </td></tr>
</table>
```

2. Select the row of the table and click the Repeated Region button on the Application toolbar, shown in Figure 6-25.

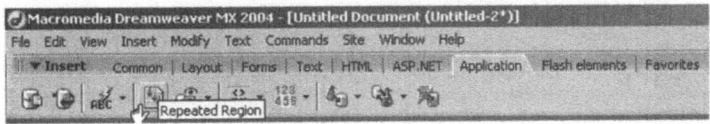

Figure 6-25. Adding a repeater via the Dreamweaver interface

3. In the dialog box that appears, accept the defaults and click OK. Your region is now enclosed in a repeater.

```
    <table border="1">
<ASP:Repeater runat="server" DataSource='<%# DataSet1.DefaultView %>'>
    <ItemTemplate>
        <tr><td>""
        </td></tr>
    </ItemTemplate>
</ASP:Repeater>
    </table>
```

4. However, this merely repeats the table row without displaying anything meaningful. To add an area of dynamic text, on the Application toolbar click Dynamic Text, as shown in Figure 6-26.

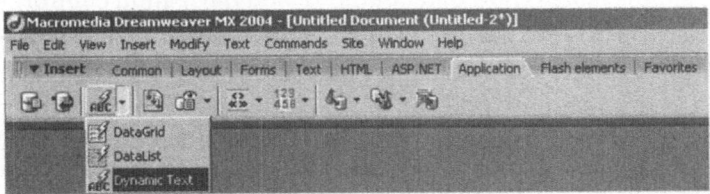

Figure 6-26. Adding dynamic text to the repeater

5. Place your cursor inside the table cell, select which field or fields you want to display, and select the formatting you want, as shown in Figure 6-27.

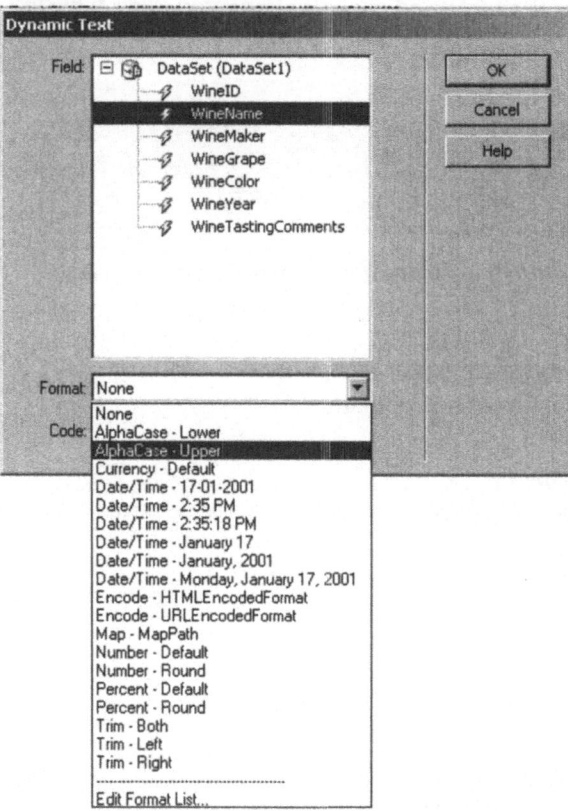

Figure 6-27. Formatting the dynamic text area

6. The simple table is now databound. To add navigation controls via the Dataset Navigation bar on the Application toolbar, specify how many records per page you want, and click OK.

You now have a customized repeated region that you can modify in more ways than any other ASP.NET control (RepeaterSample.aspx). The result is shown in Figure 6-28.

Figure 6-28. The repeater displayed in the browser

Summary

This chapter showed you how powerful the ASP.NET data controls can be. We paid special attention to the datagrid, which has incredible functionality. Dreamweaver made programming these controls extremely easy, so you can create data-driven web sites in no time.

In the next chapter, we will move onto another fundamental area of ASP.NET: XML and XML web services.

Working with XML in ASP.NET

THERE CAN BE LITTLE DOUBT that XML is one of the most important web technologies to come along in the past several years. It has rapidly become the industry standard for data-transfer, interoperability, and storage solutions. The .NET Framework provides robust and integrated support for XML in two main areas: document manipulation and web services. XML includes classes for reading and writing XML data, creating XML documents, and consuming XML web service information. You can use these classes to easily integrate XML functionality into your ASP.NET applications.

This chapter begins with a short overview of XML that will help you understand the rest of the chapter even if you have no prior experience with this technology. If you are already familiar with XML, you can safely skip this first section. We will then explore the ways that XML data can be read and written, and we will introduce some important XML concepts that will be used throughout the chapter. We will explain some of the more advanced concepts involved with using XML in .NET, such as DOM manipulation and type conversions. We will look at XML web services and what they offer web developers, and we close out the chapter by adding a web service to a sample application.

Be forewarned: Dreamweaver MX does not have any XML-related server behaviors. Because of this, most of the code in this chapter must be entered manually. The code snippets provided in this chapter are meant as learning exercises only and will not run on their own. However, we will look at a few larger examples that you can try out for yourself.

What Is XML?

Extensible Markup Language (XML) is a metalanguage—a language for describing other languages—that lets you design your own customized markup languages for many types of documents. It is a subset of **Standard Generalized Markup Language (SGML)**, which is a more generalized form of markup language definition.

Like HTML documents, XML documents consist of elements, attributes, text, comments, and other such constructs. However, you define the names of these constructs for yourself, for example:

```
<?xml version="1.0" ?>
<!-- Price from a fictional real-estate agent  -->
<estate type="PLOT">
  <area>160</area>
  <price>34000</price>
</estate>
```

Even if you are unfamiliar with XML, the code just shown should make a fair amount of sense. XML documents are designed to be readable by humans as well as machines. The code just shown provides area and price information about a land plot.

XML documents have stricter syntax rules than HTML documents.

- All elements must have a closing tag (`<portfolio>` will always be followed at some point by `</portfolio>`) or a closing slash that indicates an empty element (for example, `<portfolio />`).

- All attribute values must be enclosed in either single or double quotation marks (`<stock exchange="NASDAQ">` or `<stock exchange='NASDAQ'>`, but never `<stock exchange=NASDAQ>`).

- All elements must be properly nested (`<stock exchange="NASDAQ">` `<symbol>JOEM</symbol></stock>` is OK, but `<stock exchange="NASDAQ">` `<symbol>JOEM</stock></symbol>` is not).

- All XML documents must contain a single **root element** that contains all other content except the **prolog** and **epilog**. In the example just shown, `<?xml version="1.0"?>` is the prolog, and there is no epilog.

By following these (and a few other) rules, you can make sure that your XML document is well formed. You can also visit `http://www.w3schools.com/xml/xml_syntax.asp` for a good introduction to XML syntax.

When you define your XML language, you define the names of the attributes and elements, the order in which elements appear, and the way elements are nested. These definitions are written in a document called a **Document Type Declaration (DTD)** or an **XML schema**. An XML document that is well formed and follows the rules in the corresponding DTD or XML schema is said to be **valid**.

XML documents are usually read and processed by a **parser**. This may be a piece of software, or, in the case of .NET, a series of classes that are programmed to load, read, and manipulate the XML document.

XML Processing Techniques

The two most common ways of processing XML are the **Simple API for XML (SAX)** and the **Document Object Model (DOM)**. These models process XML in fundamentally different ways, and each has advantages and disadvantages. The SAX model processes an entire document all at once—the application handles the XML content as it goes along. The DOM, on the other hand, loads a document into memory and keeps it around so the application can retrieve and modify information at will.

SAX Processing Fundamentals

SAX uses an event-based mechanism that processes each element in an XML file. The SAX parser reads through the entire document in sequential order and sends the document back to the application for processing at each element. For example, an application can define a function that handles a particular type of XML element. The application then tells the SAX parser to call that function when it encounters that type of element.

As the SAX parser reads an XML element, it notifies the application that there is something to process at three points. These three points are labeled A, B, and C in Figure 7-1.

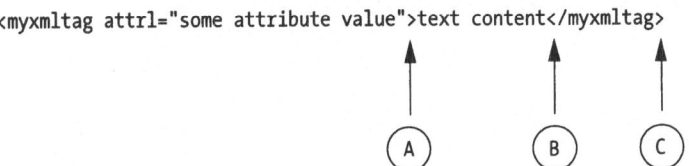

Figure 7-1. The SAX reader notifies the application at three points.

The SAX parser reaches point A when it finishes reading the opening `<myxmltag>` tag and its attributes (in this case, `attr1`). If the application defined a function that handles opening tags and registered that function with the parser, that function will be called. The application will examine the tag's name and its list of attributes, and perform a specified action with that data.

The SAX parser then continues reading until it reaches point B, which is the end of the text content (character data) of the element and the beginning of the closing `</myxmltag>` tag. Again, if the application has a function for handling text content, the parser will call that function.

At point C, the SAX parser has finished reading the closing tag and will call any function defined for handling closing tags. The rest of the document is processed in the same manner.

SAX clearly has some nice advantages. First, it is simple to use because only functions that handle a specific kind of XML data are defined. If an application does not process XML comments, for example, that application does not need to define functions for them. Second, the SAX parser does not require a lot of system resources because the document is not kept in memory. This approach works well for applications that read XML files but do not extract data from them.

Of course, there are disadvantages as well. Because the document is processed only once, the application cannot go back in the XML data to reexamine an element without starting all over again. This also means that the application cannot modify the document. In addition, because the document is not kept in memory, if the application wants to store information contained in the document, it must create separate variables to do so, which involves processing overhead.

DOM Processing

When you use DOM processing, the entire XML document is loaded into a tree structure that matches the hierarchical structure of the document. The DOM provides a set of functions that examine the tree structure and manipulate the document's content.

To see an example of this, consider the following XML document:

```
<node1>
  <node2 />
  <node3>
    <node4 />
    <node5 />
  </node3>
</node1>
```

When this document is loaded via the DOM, it is assembled into a tree structure that corresponds to the document's elements, as shown in Figure 7-2.

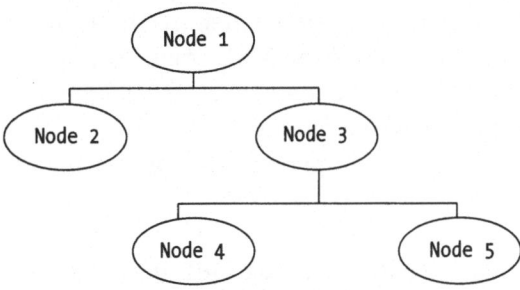

Figure 7-2. The tree structure used by the DOM

The objects in the tree are called **nodes**. These nodes represent the various pieces of the XML file, such as tags, comments, and text.

The DOM is more complicated than SAX, but it has some advantages. First, it keeps the document in memory so the application does not have to build its own internal representation of the document. This allows elements of the document to be read in any order and be modified without having to be stored in memory. Also, because the DOM is a W3C standard, it provides an established, common set of interfaces with which the document can be manipulated. This means you can safely assume that your code will not need to change very much if you want to port it to another platform, and that it will continue to work as your current platform evolves.

However, the DOM requires a lot of system memory resources, especially when the XML documents are large. The DOM can sometimes be too slow for performance-critical applications, and it usually requires more code to perform relatively simple operations.

An interesting open source project is trying to combine the advantages of SAX and DOM. If you are interested in learning more, go to http://www.devsphere.com/xml/saxdomix/.

Using the .NET Processing Model

.NET provides XML-processing classes that combine the advantages of the SAX and DOM models into one system. You can use these classes to parse XML documents with a simple stream-like interface like the SAX model and still work with node objects like the DOM. The base classes for these operations are defined in the System.Xml.XmlReader and System.Xml.XmlWriter namespaces.

The XmlReader class defines an interface for sequential, forward-only processing of XML files. Its subclasses, XmlTextReader, XmlNodeReader, and XmlValidatingReader, provide specific implementations of the XmlReader class that can read XML as text, from a node, or with the added ability to validate against schemas. The XmlWriter class defines an interface for writing information to an XML document. It has one derived class, XmlTextWriter, which writes XML data to a text stream. The XmlDocument class provides support for all DOM operations.

The following list contains some of the more important XML processing–related classes.

- **XmlTextReader:** Reads XML from a text stream in a file, URL, or string.

- **XmlNodeReader:** Processes an XmlDocument class one node at a time as a stream of nodes, starting with a given node. This class is used in conjunction with the XmlDocument class.

- **XmlValidatingReader:** Reads XML from a text stream and validates the document against a DTD or XML schema.

- **XmlTextWriter:** Writes XML data to a text stream.

- **XmlConvert:** Converts XML data into native .NET data types. This class also handles character encoding.

- **XmlNode:** Represents a single node in an XML document and provides a set of DOM-standard methods for accessing information.

- **XmlDocument:** Represents an XML document as a DOM tree and provides DOM-standard methods for navigating the document structure.

For a full list of .NET's XML-related classes, see the MSDN documentation on the System.Xml namespace at http://msdn.microsoft.com/library/en-us/cpref/html/frlrfsystemxml.asp.

Working with Nodes

As mentioned earlier, XML documents are represented as a series of nodes when parsed in the DOM. Each node represents a certain type of content in the document.

Because the Microsoft XML processing classes allow you to work with nodes, you should be aware of the different types of nodes that your code may encounter. The XmlNodeType class provides a set of values that define each type of node. Your application can use these values in conjunction with the NodeType property of the XmlReader classes to examine a node's type. The following list contains the XmlNodeType values. Note that some of these node types are specific to Microsoft's XmlReader and are not standard. These types are marked with an asterisk (*).

- **Attribute**: An attribute on an `Element` node, for example, the attr in `<tag attr="value"/>`

- **CDATA**: The text data enclosed in `<![CDATA[ ... ]]>`

- **Comment**: An XML comment

- **Document**: The root element that represents the entire document

- **DocumentFragment**: A document section

- **DocumentType**: An XML `<!DOCTYPE>` declaration

- **Element**: An entire XML element, for example, `<tag>content</tag>`

- **EndElement***: A closing XML tag (such as `</tag>`)

- **Entity**: A single XML entity declaration

- **EndEntity***: A closing entity declaration

- **EntityReference**: A reference to an entity, such as &

- **None***: The node type returned by the `XmlReader` if a `Read` method has not yet been called

- **Notation**: A notation inside the `<!DOCTYPE>` declaration

- **ProcessingInstruction**: An XML processing instruction

- **SignificantWhitespace***: The white space between markup in a mixed-content model or within the `xml:space="preserve"` scope

- **Text**: The text content of a node

- **Whitespace***: The white space between document markup

- **XmlDeclaration***: The XML declaration of the document: `<?xml version='1.0'?>`

Writing XML with the TextWriter Class

The `XmlTextWriter` class is a concrete implementation of the `XmlWriter` abstract base class, which provides a simple way to write data to an XML file, console, stream, or other output destination. You can use the XmlTextWriter class to easily create XML files.

In addition to providing methods for writing XML data, the XmlTextWriter also helps you to create valid XML. For example, the XmlTextWriter will not let you do things like write an attribute outside a tag. It will also make sure that you write elements in the correct order, such as placing the <?xml version="1.0"?> instruction before the <!DOCTYPE> statement, and so on. Note, however, that the XmlTextWriter will not perform any validation against a DTD or XML schema. To accomplish this, use the XmlTextWriter to write the document to a memory stream and then validate it using an XmlValidatingReader.

The XmlTextWriter will also escape special characters in the output when necessary. For example, it will replace the &, <, and > characters with their corresponding Unicode entities: &, <, and >.

Finally, after you call the Close method to close the document, the XmlTextWriter ensures that the document is well formed; it throws an exception if it finds a problem.

However, XmlTextWriter is not a catchall for plain old bad programming. For example, it does not make sure your code has no duplicate attributes or invalid characters in element or attribute names. For those types of issues, it is your responsibility to make sure you wrote well-formed XML.

Creating a TextWriter

To create an XmlTextWriter object, call the appropriate constructor to create an instance of the XmlTextWriter class. There are three different constructors.

- **XmlTextWriter(TextWriter)**: Creates an XmlTextWriter that uses the specified TextWriter object to write its data.

- **XmlTextWriter(Stream, Encoding)**: Creates an XmlTextWriter that uses the specified Stream object and Encoding type to write XML data. If no Encoding type is given, the writer uses UTF-8 encoding.

- **XmlTextWriter(string, Encoding)**: Creates an XmlTextWriter that uses the specified file path string and Encoding type to write XML data. If no Encoding type is given, the writer uses UTF-8 encoding.

The first two constructors allow you to create an XmlTextWriter that will use an existing TextWriter or Stream object to write the XML data. The third constructor uses a file path: It creates the file if it does not exist or overwrites the existing file. In this chapter, we use this constructor for our examples.

Writing XML Data

The XmlTextWriter provides several methods for writing XML data as well as controlling the formatting of the output. Here are some of the more relevant methods for writing XML content:

- WriteAttributeString(): Writes an attribute containing the passed string value.

- WriteCData(): Writes a <![CDATA ...]]> block with the passed text data.

- WriteChars(): Writes the passed text to a text buffer.

- WriteComment(): Writes an XML comment of the form <!-- --> with the passed text content.

- WriteDocType(): Writes the <!DOCTYPE> instruction.

- WriteElementString(): Writes an element containing the passed string value.

- WriteStartElement(): Writes an opening element, such as <tagname>.

- WriteEndElement(): Closes the previous matching opening element.

- WriteStartAttribute(): Writes the start of an attribute.

- WriteEndAttribute(): Closes the previous matching WriteStartAttribute() attribute.

- WriteStartDocument(): Writes the XML document declaration with the version set to "1.0". Use this method when starting a new document.

- WriteEndDocument(): Closes all open elements and attributes, and returns the writer to the start state.

- WriteRaw(): Writes a raw buffer of content directly to the output. Use with care.

- WriteString(): Writes a passed string to the output.

In addition to writing XML output, you can use the XmlTextWriter object's Formatting, Indentation, and IndentChar properties to control how the XML is formatted. For example, the following code snippet creates an XmlTextWriter, sets the Formatting property to Formatting.Indented, sets the Indentation property to 4, and sets the IndentChar property to 0x20. Thus, the output XML elements will be neatly indented where they are nested inside each other.

```
Dim myWriter As XmlTextWriter = New XmlTextWriter(myFilePath)
myWriter.Formatting = Formatting.Indented
myWriter.Indentation = 4
myWriter.IndentChar = 0x20
```

Valid values for the Formatting property are Formatting.Indented and Formatting.None (the default value). You should also note that the XmlTextWriter will let you specify any character as the indentation character, but in order to make sure that you produce valid XML, you should use a valid white space character such as a tab, space, linefeed, or return (respectively 0x09, 0x20, 0x10, and 0x13).

Starting and Ending a Document

The WriteStartDocument() and WriteEndDocument() functions are used to write the start and end of an XML document.

The WriteStartDocument() function writes the opening <?xml version="1.0"?> statement that all XML documents should contain and takes a Boolean argument that indicates whether the document is a **stand-alone XML document** (all entity declarations required by the XML document are contained within the document). If this argument is true, standalone="yes" is added to the XML declaration.

TIP *The <?xml> declaration is technically optional, but the W3C XML specification recommends that you use it. You can find this specification at* http://www.w3.org/xml.

The WriteEndDocument() function closes any open attribute and element tags. Usually, you do this yourself by closing the elements and attributes as you go, but it is always a good idea to call this function when you get to the end of the document, just to make sure.

Writing Elements

Elements are written using pairs of WriteStartElement() and WriteEndElement() functions or by using the WriteElementString() function. The WriteElementString() function is the simplest, because it allows you to write the name of an element and its content at the same time. The downside is that you cannot write any attributes onto the element when using this function.

For example, to write the XML element <tagname>tag content</tagname>, you would simply use the following code:

```
myWriter.WriteElementString("tagname", "tag content")
```

However, this is not always practical, because often you will want to write an element that contains attributes or other elements. To do this, your code needs to call WriteStartElement() followed by one or more of the other XmlTextWriter methods. For example, the following code snippet writes an element with another element nested inside it:

```
myWriter.WriteStartElement("elem1")
myWriter.WriteElementString("elem2","This is a nested element")
myWriter.WriteEndElement()
```

The XML fragment produced looks like this:

```
<elem1>
  <elem2>This is a nested element</elem2>
</elem1>
```

Writing Attributes

Attributes, like elements, can be written two ways. One way is with the WriteAttributeString() method, which writes an attribute and its value all at once. The other way is to use the WriteStartAttribute() and WriteEndAttribute() methods to add an attribute to an element. For example, the following code snippet uses the second way to add an attribute to an element:

```
myWriter.WriteStartElement("elem1")
myWriter.WriteStartAttribute("attr", String.Empty)
myWriter.WriteString("my attr value")
myWriter.WriteEndAttribute()
myWriter.WriteEndElement()
```

This code produces an XML fragment that looks like this:

```
<elem1 attr="my attr value"/>
```

Writing Other Data

The XmlTextWriter class provides methods for writing other types of XML content to the output.

- The WriteString() method is very useful for writing string content to the XML file. It can be used to write the content of elements and attributes (demonstrated in the code snippet just shown), and it will automatically replace the &, <, and > characters with their corresponding Unicode entities.

- The WriteCData() method will write a CDATA section to the XML file. CDATA sections are used to surround content that you do not want the XML parser to interpret as XML.

- The WriteComment() method will insert an XML comment into the file. XML comments are just like HTML comments: They are surrounded by <!-- and -->.

- The WriteRaw() method can be used to directly insert XML markup into the output. You should use this function with care, because it does not ensure that the markup is balanced or that special characters are converted to their corresponding Unicode entities.

Creating a Document

When creating XML documents, your code usually follows a set sequence for calling each of the XmlTextWriter methods. This sequence typically consists of the following:

1. Create an XmlTextWriter object.

2. Set any optional properties for the XmlTextWriter, such as Indentation.

3. Write the start of the document, including the XML declaration with which every XML document should begin.

4. Write the <!DOCTYPE> declaration (optional).

5. Write the document's content, such as elements, attributes, and comments.

6. Close the document.

The following page (XmlWritingExample.aspx) returns a quote for a land plot XML file from a fictional company by following the sequence just listed:

```
<%@ Page Language="VB" ContentType="text/xml" ResponseEncoding="iso-8859-1" %>
<%@ Import Namespace="System.Xml" %>
<%@ Import Namespace="System.IO" %>
```

```
<%
' Create an XmlTextWriter that outputs to a StringWriter object
Dim sw As StringWriter = New StringWriter()
' Step 1
Dim w As XmlTextWriter = New XmlTextWriter(sw)
' Step 2
w.Formatting = Formatting.Indented
' Step 3
w.WriteStartDocument(true)
' Step 4
w.WriteComment("Price from a fictional real-estate agent")
w.WriteStartElement("estate")
w.WriteStartAttribute("type",String.Empty)
w.WriteString("PLOT")
w.WriteEndAttribute()
w.WriteElementString("area","160")
w.WriteElementString("price","34000")
w.WriteEndElement()
w.WriteEndDocument()
' Step 5
w.Close()
Response.Write(sw.toString())
%>
```

This code produces the output shown in Figure 7-3 in IE 6 (older browsers that have no support for XML may throw errors, and other modern browsers may reveal only the resulting XML if you view the source).

Figure 7-3. The XML document viewed in IE 6

Reading XML with the TextReader Class

The XmlTextReader class provides a fast, forward-only method for accessing XML data in a document by combining the stream-oriented parsing of SAX with the object-oriented node capabilities of DOM. The XML document can originate from a variety of sources, such as a disk file, a string in memory, or a URL.

Reading XML data is a bit trickier than writing it using the XmlTextWriter class, because your application has more work to do keeping track of where it is in the XML data stream and being prepared for unexpected elements. There are two important concepts to remember when using the XmlTextReader to read XML.

- Your code can only read XML in a forward direction. Once the application has read an element from the data, it cannot go back and read it again unless it starts from the beginning of the file.

- When the application calls one of the methods to read XML data, the method reads the element and then *automatically* moves to the next element. This is often a source of great confusion for newcomers to the XmlTextReader, so be aware of it.

Creating a TextReader

To create an XmlTextReader, call the appropriate constructor to create an instance of an XmlTextReader. There are 14 types of constructors for the XmlTextReader class, each of which provide support for reading XML data from a particular input source. The following list contains three of the more common constructors for XmlTextReader:

- **XmlTextReader(string)**: Creates an XmlTextReader that reads XML data from the specified URL string

- **XmlTextReader(Stream)**: Creates an XmlTextReader that reads XML data from the specified Stream object

- **XmlTextReader(TextReader)**: Creates an XmlTextReader that reads XML data from the specified TextReader object

The first example creates an XmlTextReader using a URL to specify an XML data source, such as another web page or a local file. The second example creates an XmlTextReader using an existing Stream object. The last example uses a TextReader object to provide XML data to an XmlTextReader. This should be used in cases when text data has already been read from a source and stored in a TextReader-derived object, such as a StringReader.

Reading XML Data

As mentioned earlier, reading XML data requires a little more effort than writing it. You must create code that can keep track of the kinds of nodes that have been read. You must also ensure that your code can handle unexpected situations, such as encountering unnecessary elements in the XML data.

The XmlTextReader class contains several methods for reading various types of XML document content, including elements, attributes, strings, and large data, such as base64-encoding streams. The following list contains some of the more common methods for reading and navigating data:

- Read(): Reads the next XML node from the document, regardless of node type. Returns false when there are no more nodes to read.

- ReadBase64(): Reads data from the XML document as base64-encoded data.

- ReadBinHex(): Reads data from the XML document as binhex-encoded data.

- ReadChars(): Reads data from the XML document into a character buffer. This method is used for reading large amounts of data.

- ReadElementString(): Reads the content of a text-only node as a text string.

- ReadStartElement(): Reads the opening tag of an element and advances to the next node.

- ReadEndElement(): Checks that the current content node is an end tag and advances the reader to the next node.

- ReadString(): Returns the content of an Element or Text node as a string.

- MoveToAttribute(): Moves to a specified (by index or by name) attribute.

- MoveToContent(): Moves to the next content node in the file, which will be a CDATA, Element, EndElement, EntityReference, or EndEntity node.

- MoveToElement(): Moves to the next Element node.

- MoveToFirstAttribute(): Moves to the first attribute of the Element node.

- MoveToNextAttribute(): Moves to the next attribute on the Element node.

In addition to these methods, the XmlTextReader class exposes properties that provide information about the node currently being examined. The following list contains some of the more useful properties:

- AttributeCount: Indicates the number of attributes on the current element.

- Depth: Indicates the depth of the file of the current node.

- **EOF**: Indicates whether the reader has reached the end of the XML file.

- **HasAttributes**: Indicates whether the current element has attributes.

- **HasValue**: Indicates whether the current node has a value.

- **IsEmptyElement**: Indicates whether the current element is an empty element (such as `<tagname />`).

- **LineNumber**: Indicates the current line number within the XML file. This property is useful for debugging.

- **LinePosition**: Indicates the current line position within the XML file. This property is useful for debugging.

- **LocalName**: Indicates the local name of the current node.

- **NodeType**: Indicates the current node's type. Valid values are defined in `XmlNodeType`.

Reading an XML source requires you to follow a sequence of steps similar to the steps for writing an XML file. The steps are as follows:

1. Create an `XmlTextReader` for the XML source.

2. Begin reading the document. Your code can do this by calling any of the `Read` methods or `MoveToContent()`.

3. Read and process XML content. This usually involves a looping structure that reads the XML content and takes action on it or skips over it. The loop terminates when the end of the XML source is reached or the application has processed all the data it needs.

4. Close the `XmlTextReader` and the XML source, if necessary.

Start Reading a Document

To begin reading an XML document, you can call any of the `Read` methods to extract data from the document. For example, this code snippet uses the `ReadStartElement()` to move to the first element in the document:

```
Dim rd As XmlTextReader = New XmlTextReader(myFileURL)
' skip the XML declaration and go to the first element
rd.ReadStartElement()
```

Alternatively, you can just jump straight to the document content by calling MoveToContent(), which will skip to the next content node if the current node is not a content node. (**Content nodes** are the CDATA, Element, Entity, and EntityReference nodes; see the XML specification for more information.) If positioned on an attribute, the reader will move back to the element that contains the attribute.

```
Dim rd As XmlTextReader = New XmlTextReader(myFileURL)
' skip to the first content node
rd.MoveToContent()
```

In the examples just shown, if myFileURL is the URL of the following file:

```
<?xml version="1.0"?>
<!DOCTYPE stock SYSTEM "abcd">
<!--the price of the stock -->
<stock>
  123.4
</stock>
```

then the code would advance to the <stock> element and skip everything else.

Reading Elements

The Read(), ReadString(), ReadStartElement(), and ReadEndElement() methods can all be used to read Element nodes from the XML source. After reading the element, each method advances to the next node in the document. In comparison, the MoveToElement() method moves to the next Element but does not read it.

The Read() method is the simplest: It reads the next node in the source whether or not it is an Element node. When using this method, you should check the node's name and type to make sure you are processing an appropriate node. For example, the following code uses the Read() method and the NodeType property of the XmlTextReader to read only Comment nodes:

```
Dim rd As XmlTextReader = New XmlTextReader(myFileURL)
' read a node
rd.Read()

Do While NOT rd.EOF
  If rd.NodeType = XmlNodeType.Comment Then
    ' Some code here to process Comments
  End If
  ' read the next node
  rd.Read()
Loop
```

Reading Attributes

Before you attempt to read attributes in an Element node, you should first use the HasAttributes property to make sure that the Element node contains attributes.

Attributes in an Element node can be accessed directly by their name or index. They can also be accessed by the MoveToAttribute(), MoveToFirstAttribute(), and MoveToNextAttribute() methods.

For example, to process an attribute by name, you can call MoveToAttribute() with the name of the attribute.

```
Dim rd As XmlTextReader = New XmlTextReader(myFileURL)
' move to the first element
rd.MoveToElement()
If rd.HasAttributes Then
  rd.MoveToAttribute("attr")
  ' Code to do something with the attribute value, stored in rd.Value
End If
```

Attributes can also be processed by index using MoveToAttribute().

```
Dim rd As XmlTextReader = New XmlTextReader(myFileURL)
' move to the first element
rd.MoveToElement()
If rd.HasAttributes Then
  Dim intCounter As integer
  For intCounter = 0 To rd.AttributeCount-1
    rd.MoveToAttribute(intCounter)
    ' Code to do something with the attribute value, stored in rd.Value
  Next intCounter
  ' Move the reader back to the element node
  rd.MoveToElement()
End If
```

Sometimes, however, you will not know which attributes are in a particular element. The following code processes all the attributes in the first Element node without knowing their names or indexes:

```
Dim rd As XmlTextReader = New XmlTextReader(myFileURL)
' move to the first element
rd.MoveToElement()
```

```
If rd.HasAttributes Then
  Do While rd.MoveToNextAttribute()
    ' process attribute value
    ' Code to do something with the attribute value, stored in rd.Value
  Loop
End If
```

Reading Content and Other Data

Your application can use the ReadString() method to read the content of the current node as a string.

- If the current node is an Element node, ReadString() concatenates all text, significant white space, white space, and CDATA section node types within the Element node and returns the concatenated data as the Element node's content.

- If the current node is a Text node, ReadString() performs the same concatenation on the Text node's end tag as it did on the Element node.

- If the current node is an Attribute node, ReadString() behaves as though the reader were currently positioned on the starting tag of the Element node and returns data as described for Element nodes.

- For all other node types, ReadString() returns an empty string.

Manipulating XML with the Document Class

Although the XmlTextReader and XmlTextWriter classes provide good support for working with XML data, sometimes you need something stronger to get the job done. The XmlTextReader and XmlTextWriter classes are good for processing XML content in only one pass, but for cases when an XML document needs to be loaded, examined, modified, and saved, they are not such a good fit.

The .NET Framework's XmlDocument class is much more suited to this type of task. This class represents an XML document in memory and follows the W3C standard DOM specification for providing methods to access and manipulate the document's content. A full discussion of the intricacies of the W3C DOM is beyond the scope of this chapter, but you can find the full W3C DOM specification on the W3C web site at http://www.w3.org/DOM/.

The Document Class and the DOM

Working with an XmlDocument class is fundamentally different from working with the XmlTextReader and XmlTextWriter classes, though they share some similarities, such as the concept of nodes.

Remember that an XML document has a tree structure under the DOM, and each object in the tree is a node. For example, consider the following sample XML document:

```
<?xml version="1.0"?>
<portfolio>
  <stock exchange="NASDAQ">
    <symbol>ACME</symbol>
    <quote>15.00</quote>
    <quantity>100</quantity>
  </stock>
</portfolio>
```

This document, modeled using the DOM, would be represented as the tree structure shown in Figure 7-4.

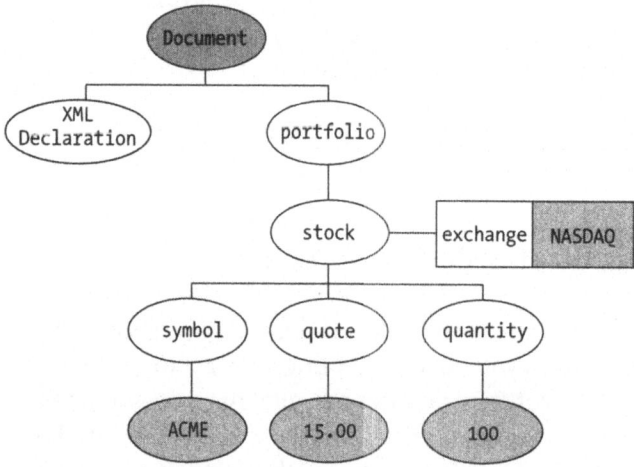

Figure 7-4. The sample document's tree structure in the DOM

Each of the circles in this diagram is a node in the DOM structure. (Note that the exchange attribute on the <stock> tag is also a node, although attributes get special treatment in the DOM and are not actually a part of the document tree.) The class that represents nodes in .NET is XmlNode, and it provides methods for examining and modifying node information. The XmlDocument class, derived from

XmlNode, adds more methods for creating new nodes and adding them to the document.

Each node's relationship to another node in the document is described with the terms **parent**, **child**, and **sibling**. In the example, the <stock> node is a child of the <portfolio> node. The <portfolio> node is a parent of <stock>. The <stock> node has child nodes of its own: <symbol>, <quote>, and <quantity>. These three nodes are siblings.

The XmlDocument class provides methods and properties for manipulating nodes using these terms.

Creating an XmlDocument

To create an XmlDocument, call the following class constructor:

```
Dim myDoc As XmlDocument = New XmlDocument()
```

Once you have an empty XmlDocument, you need to load it with XML data. This is accomplished by calling the Load() method, which reads XML data and populates the document tree structure. There are four different versions of the Load() method, each of which uses a different source to read the data. Here are the various forms of the Load() method:

- **Load(Stream):** Loads the document from a Stream data source

- **Load(string):** Loads the document using the given file name string

- **Load(TextReader):** Loads the document using a TextReader as the data source

- **Load(XmlReader):** Loads the document using the given XmlReader as the data source

In addition to the Load() method, you can also use the LoadXml() method, which loads the document with a string of XML data as its argument. Using the example XML file from earlier in the chapter, this would be written as the following:

```
Dim doc As XmlDocument = New XmlDocument()
doc.LoadXml("<?xml version='1.0'?><portfolio><stock exchange='NASDAQ'>" & _

"<symbol>JOEM</symbol><quote>34.00</quote><quantity>100</quantity>" & _
        "</stock></portfolio>")
```

Navigating a Document Class

After the document is loaded into memory, your application can examine its nodes and retrieve information using the standard DOM methods and properties provided by the XmlDocument class. These methods and properties allow tags to be retrieved by ID, by name, and by using relative node positioning.

Retrieving Specific Nodes

Two of the most common methods for getting nodes within a document are GetElementById() and GetElementsByTagName().

GetElementById() retrieves the node in the document whose id attribute matches the given string passed within the parentheses. Because the id attribute must be unique within the XML document, a single node is returned. (If the id attribute is not unique in the file, the results of the function are undefined.)

GetElementsByTagName() returns an XmlNodeList, which represents a list of elements that have the same name as the given string passed within the parentheses. For example, if the sample XML document contained several <stock> elements, GetElementsByTagName("stock") would return an array of XmlNode objects representing all the <stock> elements.

Using Relative Positioning

In addition to these methods, you can use the FirstChild, LastChild, PreviousSibling, NextSibling, and ParentNode properties of the XmlNode class to move to nodes relative to a given node. The XmlDocument class also includes the DocumentElement property that provides access to the root element of the document.

Using these methods and properties together allows you to access any node in the document. For example, again using the sample XML document, the following code navigates down through the document and back up again:

```
Dim doc As XmlDocument = New XmlDocument()
' assume the string myDocString contains our sample document
doc.LoadXml(myDocString)
' Here we navigate to the "portfolio" tag
Dim myNode As XmlNode = doc.DocumentElement
' Here we navigate down to the "stock" tag
myNode = myNode.FirstChild
' Here we again navigate down to the "symbol" tag
myNode = myNode.FirstChild
' Here we navigate across to the "quote" tag
myNode = myNode.NextSibling
' Here we navigate back up to the "stock" tag
```

```
myNode = myNode.ParentNode
' Finally we navigate up again to the "portfolio" tag
myNode = myNode.ParentNode
```

Modifying Document Class Data

One of the main advantages of using the XmlDocument class over the other XML-processing classes is that you can manipulate and modify the content of the document. You can add, delete, and move nodes, and change the information that they contain. The XmlDocument object provides methods that make these kinds of operations easy.

Adding New Nodes

To add new nodes to the document, you must first use the XmlDocument class's **factory methods** for creating a new node and then add it somewhere in the document. They are called factory methods because they are responsible for creating a new node of a given type. These methods start with Create and end with the node type to create. For example, the method to create a new Text node is named CreateTextNode() and the method to create a new Element node is called CreateElement(). The following list contains all the Create() methods and describes their function:

- **CreateAttribute()**: Creates an Attribute node with the given name

- **CreateCDataSection()**: Creates a CDATA section with the specified content

- **CreateComment()**: Creates a Comment node with the specified content

- **CreateDocumentFragment()**: Creates an empty DocumentFragment node

- **CreateElement()**: Creates an Element node with the given tag name

- **CreateEntityReference()**: Creates an EntityReference node

- **CreateProcessingInstruction()**: Creates a ProcessingInstruction node with the given content

- **CreateTextNode()**: Creates a new Text node with the specified content

For example, suppose we wanted to add another <stock> element to the portfolio document. To do so, we would need to create eight new nodes to hold the information. Each of the four tags is a new node (<stock>, <symbol>, <quote>, and <quantity>), and the text that goes inside the nodes are also nodes. Finally, the exchange attribute on the <stock> tag is a new node.

After each new node is created, it needs to be added to the document. This can be accomplished by using the AppendChild() method of the XmlNode class. This method appends a node to the child nodes of the node being acted upon. Alternatively, we could use the InsertBefore() method, which inserts a new node in front of the node being acted upon.

 TIP *Microsoft also provides the* InsertAfter() *method, which inserts a node after another node, but this method is not part of the standard W3C DOM API.*

For example, to add an entirely new <stock> element to the portfolio, write the following:

```
Dim doc As XmlDocument = New XmlDocument()
' assume the string myDocString contains our sample document
doc.LoadXml(myDocString)

'ADDING NEW NODES
' create the new element nodes
Dim newStock As XmlElement = doc.CreateElement("stock")
Dim symbolName As XmlElement = doc.CreateElement("symbol")
Dim quoteVal As XmlElement = doc.CreateElement("quote")
Dim quantity As XmlElement = doc.CreateElement("quantity")

' add the symbol, quote, and quantity tags to the stock tag
newStock.AppendChild(symbolName)
newStock.AppendChild(quoteVal)
newStock.AppendChild(quantity)

' next create the text values
symbolName.AppendChild(doc.CreateTextNode("ACM"))
quoteVal.AppendChild(doc.CreateTextNode("23.00"))
quantity.AppendChild(doc.CreateTextNode("50"))

' now add the exchange attribute
newStock.SetAttribute("exchange", "NYSE")

' finally, add the whole structure to the document
doc.DocumentElement.AppendChild(newStock)
```

Changing Node Data

Node data can be changed after it has been created. For example, let's suppose that the market has been good lately, so the value of our ACME holdings have gone up. To reflect this in the document, we would need to find the <symbol> node that contains the ACME symbol and update its sibling <quote> node with the new value. The following code shows how to do this using the Value property of the XmlNode class:

```
Dim doc As XmlDocument = New XmlDocument()
' assume the string myDocString contains our sample document
doc.LoadXml(myDocString)


'CHANGING NODE DATA
Dim theNodeList As XmlNodeList = doc.GetElementsByTagName("symbol")
Dim theNode As XmlElement
' now we have a list of all the symbol nodes in the document.
' we need to find the one that contains the ACME stock symbol
Dim intCounter As Integer
For intCounter = 0 to theNodeList.Count-1
  If theNodeList.Item(intCounter).FirstChild.Value = "ACME" Then
    theNode = theNodeList.Item(intCounter)
  End If
Next intCounter
' we now have the symbol node. We need the matching quote tag
Dim quoteTag As XmlElement = theNode.NextSibling
' set the value of the quote text node to 22.00
quoteTag.FirstChild.Value = "22.00"
```

Deleting Nodes

To delete a node, simply remove it from the document. The RemoveChild() method of the XmlNode class accomplishes this. When called on an XmlNode object, the passed child node will be removed from its list of child nodes.

For example, to delete the <stock> node's structure that corresponds to the ACME symbol from the document, use the following code:

```
Dim doc As XmlDocument = New XmlDocument()
' assume the string myDocString contains our sample document
doc.LoadXml(myDocString)

'DELETING NODES
Dim theNodeList2 As XmlNodeList = doc.GetElementsByTagName("symbol")
```

```
Dim theNode2 As XmlElement
' note that the variable intCounter has been declared in the previous code snippet.
' now we have a list of all the symbol nodes in the document.
' we need to find the one that contains the ACME stock symbol
For intCounter = 0 to theNodeList2.Count - 1
  If theNodeList2.Item(intCounter).FirstChild.Value = "ACME" Then
    theNode2 = theNodeList2.Item(intCounter)
  End If
Next intCounter
' Then remove the stock tag from the document
' we're removing the whole structure, so we need to remove the
' parent of the symbol tag we found, which is the stock tag
Dim toRemove As XmlNode = theNode2.ParentNode
toRemove.ParentNode.RemoveChild(toRemove)
```

Saving a Document Class

Of course, this would all be for nothing if there were not some way to save the XmlDocument again after working with it. We can use the Save() method to save the XML content of the document as a given type of output channel.

You can save the XML data to four different types of destinations. The following list explains the four different versions of Save():

- **Save(Stream)**: Saves the document to a Stream data source

- **Save(string)**: Saves the document using the given file name string

- **Save(TextWriter)**: Saves the document to the given TextWriter object

- **Save(XmlWriter)**: Saves the document to the given XmlWriter object

For example, the following code snippet saves the document to a string using a StringWriter object. (The StringWriter class is derived from TextWriter, which writes data to a string.)

```
Dim doc As XmlDocument = New XmlDocument()
Dim sw As StringWriter = New StringWriter()
doc.LoadXml("<?xml version='1.0' ?><portfolio><stock exchange='NASDAQ'>" & _

"<symbol>ACME</symbol><quote>15.00</quote><quantity>100</quantity>" & _
            "</stock></portfolio>")
doc.Save(sw)
' write out the string to the screen
Response.Write(sw.ToString())
```

TIP *Remember that Dreamweaver defaults to ISO-8859-1 encoding for ASP.NET pages (supplied as an HTTP header), whereas XML classes usually default to UTF-8 (declared in the XML root). Although most browsers do not have a problem switching from the HTTP value to the XML root value, some may present errors. It is always better to specify the same encoding value in both locations. More details about XML encoding and potential conflicts are at* http://msdn.microsoft.com/library/default.asp?url=/library/en-us/dnxml/html/xmlencodings.asp.

Converting XML Data to Native .NET Data Types

When working with XML documents, you often want to perform calculations with data from the document. For example, a program that uses a series of stock quotes to calculate the value of a portfolio would need to use the information contained in the <quote> element and the <quantity> element to determine the value of that position. Because XML data is stored as text strings, it must first be converted into a native .NET data type such as an Int16, Single, or native String before you can use .NET methods and operators to manipulate it.

The XmlConvert class provides utility methods for exactly this purpose. Using these methods, you can convert XML data directly into .NET data types.

The utility methods can also be used to encode and decode XML names. Some applications and languages, such as Microsoft Word and Microsoft SQL Server, allow characters that are not legal in XML. In order to use these characters in XML, they must first be encoded using a hexadecimal syntax that can later be decoded. This process is outside the scope of this chapter, but for more on how this works, see the XmlConvert documentation at http://msdn.microsoft.com/library/en-us/cpref/html/frlrfsystemxmlxmlconvertclasstopic.asp.

Most of the methods you will want to use are declared as **static**. This means that you do not have to first create an XmlConvert object in order to use them. The following list contains some of the more useful XmlConvert methods. For the full list, see the XmlConvert class documentation at the URL just listed.

- ToBoolean(): Converts the given string to a Boolean data type

- ToByte(): Converts the given string to a Byte data type

- ToChar(): Converts the given string to a Char data type

- ToDateTime(): Converts the given string to a DateTime data type

- ToDecimal(): Converts the given string to a Decimal data type

- **ToDouble():** Converts the given string to a Double data type

- **ToInt16():** Converts the given string to an Int16 data type

- **ToSingle():** Converts the given string to a Single data type

- **ToString():** Converts strongly typed data to an equivalent string representation

- **ToTimeSpan():** Converts the given string to a TimeSpan data type

For example, the following page (ShoppingExample.aspx) is used to calculate the value of our budding portfolio:

```
<%@ Page Language="VB" ContentType="text/html" ResponseEncoding="iso-8859-1" %>
<%@ Import Namespace="System.Xml" %>
<%@ Import Namespace="System.IO" %>
<html>
<head>
<title>A shopping bill example</title>
<meta http-equiv="Content-Type" content="text/html; charset=iso-8859-1" />
</head>
<body>
The total for your order is: <br />
<%
'CREATING AN XMLDOCUMENT
Dim doc As XmlDocument = New XmlDocument()
doc.LoadXml("<?xml version='1.0'?><shopping><item category='bakery'>" & _
        "<type>Bread rolls</type><price>0.45</price><quantity>6</quantity>" & _
            "</item><item category='fruit'>" & _
            "<type>Pears</type><price>0.70</price><quantity>4</quantity>" & _
            "</item></shopping>")

Dim theShoppingList As XmlNodeList = doc.GetElementsByTagName("item")
Dim itemNode As XmlNode
Dim total As Single = 0.0F
' Now we have a list of all the stock nodes in the document.
' We next add up the value of each holding
Dim intCounter As integer
For intCounter = 0 to theShoppingList.Count-1
  itemNode = theShoppingList.Item(intCounter)
  Dim priceNode As XmlNode = itemNode.FirstChild.NextSibling
  Dim quantityNode As XmlNode = itemNode.LastChild
  ' get the quote value for this item
```

```
   Dim price As Single = XmlConvert.ToSingle(priceNode.FirstChild.Value)
    ' get the quantity value for this item
   Dim numBought As Single = XmlConvert.ToSingle(quantityNode.FirstChild.Value)
    ' calculate the total item value and add it to the total
   total += (price * numBought)
Next intCounter
Response.write(total)
%>
</body>
</html>
```

Web Services

XML web services are the fundamental building block in the move to distributed computing on the Internet. They are components that applications can connect to without concern for how each component is implemented. Experienced programmers might recall previous attempts to achieve this interoperability, namely the Distributed Computing Environment (DCE) and Common Object Request Broker Architecture (CORBA) technologies. However, XML web services are more successful, because they are accessed via web protocols and data formats such as HTTP, XML, and Simple Object Access Protocol (SOAP). These protocols are a lot simpler to program, and they are not proprietary.

All XML web services have the following features:

- Provide useful functionality to web users through a standard web protocol. In most cases, SOAP is the protocol used.

- Provide a way to describe their interfaces in enough detail to allow a user to build a client application that can communicate with the service. This description is usually provided in an XML document called a Web Services Description Language (WSDL) document.

- Registered so that potential users can find them easily. This is done with Universal Discovery Description and Integration (UDDI).

 TIP *We can say that XML web services are software services available on the web through SOAP, described with a WSDL file, and registered in UDDI.*

We will implement a web service in a sample application using Dreamweaver MX 2004. The XML knowledge you have acquired so far will help you understand what is happening behind the scenes, but adding a web service is so simple that you could do it even without understanding XML. Remember, you need to have installed the full .NET Framework SDK from http://www.microsoft.com/downloads/ details.aspx?FamilyId=9B3A2CA6-3647-4070-9F41-A333C6B9181D&displaylang=en before you can create the web service.

Web Service Component Parts

Adding a web service as a component of your application is just like importing any other local component. Figure 7-5 illustrates the analogy between locally available objects and XML web service instances.

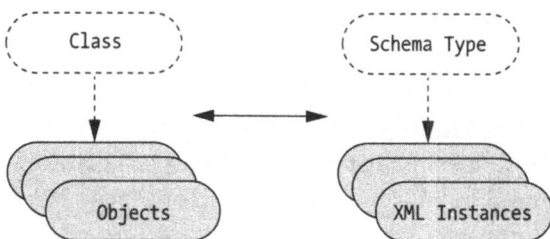

Figure 7-5. XML web services are analogous to locally available objects.

Of course the availability of the network connection between the main application and the component dictates other actions. For starters, the service may not be available while you are compiling your application, so you need a local "pretend" copy of the service with which to compile your page. These local copies are called **proxy classes** and they contain local versions of the service's methods, written in the same language as the rest of your project.

In addition, web services methods must be made asynchronously. That is, your application should call a method and then return immediately rather than wait for a result from that method. The application is notified when the web service's method has finished. If that were not the case, your web site's performance could suffer.

You know that a proxy class needs to have asynchronous methods, but how do you create a proxy class? When you type the URL of an XML web service file (with an .asmx extension), you usually get an HTML interface, a list of the methods you can invoke, and some documentation. If a client issues a GET request for the .asmx endpoint with "?wsdl" in the query string, the .asmx handler generates the WSDL definition instead of the human-readable documentation. Alternatively, the hosts of the web service could supply the WSDL file. In both cases, clients can use the WSDL definition to generate proxy classes that automatically know how to communicate with the web service. In the .NET case, this is done via the wsdl.exe program. The output from the wsdl.exe program can then be compiled with one of the .NET Framework compilers (vbc.exe in our case) and the resulting DLL library is added as a component to our project. Here is a summary of these steps:

1. A client either requests an `.asmx` file with "`?wsdl`" appended on the URL or downloads the prepared WSDL file.

2. A WSDL file is processed by the `wsdl.exe` program and generates a class definition in your preferred coding language.

3. The class code is compiled into a DLL file by one of the .NET compilers.

4. The DLL file is imported to your project as though it were a local reference.

5. The web service's methods can now be used—you have programmed the Internet!

Dreamweaver performs these steps automatically. Let's give it a go.

Adding Web Services in Dreamweaver

First, a warning: This will not work. At the time of this writing, it was not possible to use the Dreamweaver interface successfully to add a web service to a page. Hopefully this glitch will have been sorted by the time you are reading this book, but we will also present a workaround, just in case.

1. Open a blank ASP.NET VB page in Dreamweaver, and click the Components tab of the Application panel. If you have everything installed correctly, you should be able to click the plus sign (+) button, and click Add using WSDL, as shown in Figure 7-6.

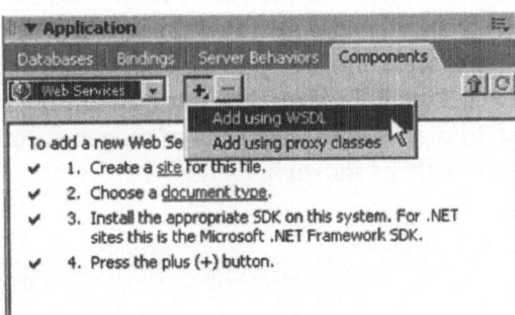

Figure 7-6. Adding a web service in Dreamweaver using WSDL

2. A dialog box appears in which you can enter or browse to a URL of a WSDL file. To browse, click the globe icon and select one of the UDDI locations in the menu. For demonstration purposes, we will use a very useful web service listed in `www.xmethods.net`. It is called `DeadOrAlive` and

it returns details on the life status of famous persons. Enter its WSDL location, http://www.abundanttech.com/webservices/deadoralive/deadoralive.wsdl, as shown in Figure 7-7.

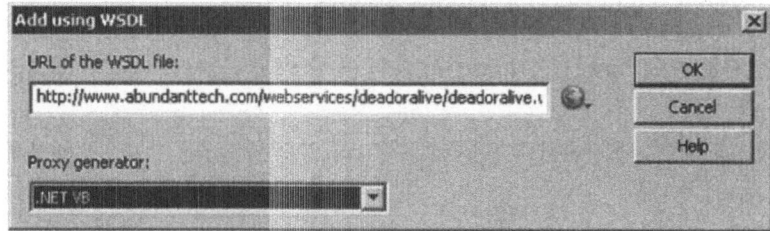

Figure 7-7. Specifying the URL of the web service

The drop-down list shows the applicable proxy generators. For our VB page, the .NET VB treatment would be correct. Unfortunately, clicking OK gives an error, as shown in Figure 7-8.

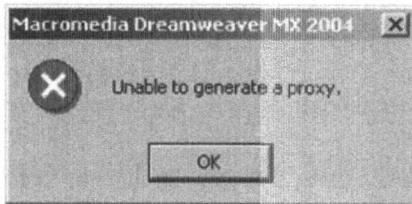

Figure 7-8. Dreamweaver returns an error message.

3. We have hit a dead end, but there is a way out—the old-fashioned manual way. Before we list the series of steps to take, you can take a sneak preview of the commands we will issue by going back to the Add using WSDL dialog box and clicking Edit Proxy Generator list in the Proxy generator drop-down list. In the list of the available proxy generators, .NET VB is the one we want to edit, as shown in Figure 7-9.

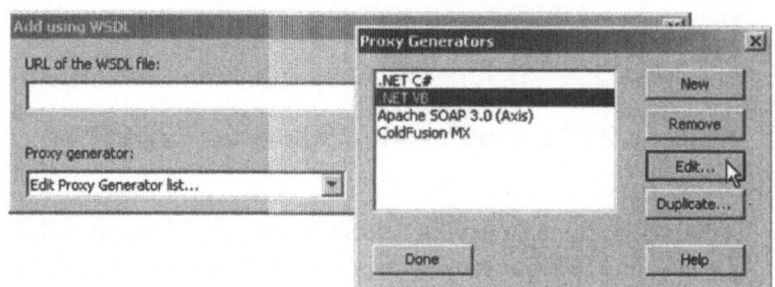

Figure 7-9. Opening the interface to the properties of the .NET VB proxy generator

4. The generator's properties can be seen in the next dialog box. Copy the paths to the wsdl.exe and vbc.exe programs on your system (as shown in Figure 7-10) and keep them handy; you will need them shortly.

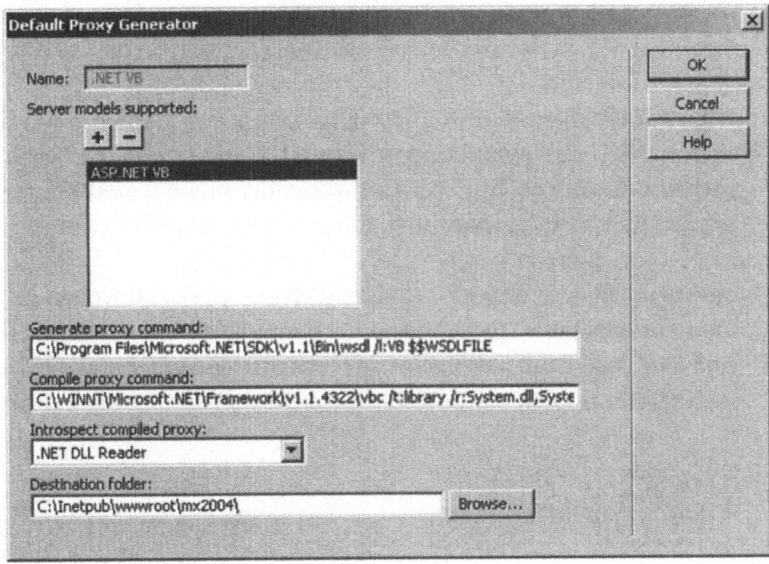

Figure 7-10. Editing the properties of the .NET VB proxy generator

Adding Web Services Manually

To add the Dead Or Alive web service to your project, follow these steps.

1. Navigate to http://www.abundanttech.com/webservices/deadoralive/ deadoralive.wsdl and save that file in any directory (we will refer to that directory as DOAdir).

2. Open a command prompt by clicking Start ➤ Run and typing **cmd**.

3. In the command shell, type **C:\Program Files\Microsoft.NET\SDK\v[your .NET SDK version]\Bin\wsdl.exe /l:VB [DOAdir]\deadoralive.wsdl**.

   This will generate a VB code file and a message on the screen similar to

   ```
   Writing file 'C:\Program Files\Microsoft.NET\SDK\v1.1➥
   \Bin\DeadOrAlive.vb'.
   ```

4. Still in the command shell, type **C:\WINNT\Microsoft.NET\Framework\ v[your .NET Framework version]\vbc.exe /t:library /r:System.dll, System.Data.dll,System.Web.Services.dll,System.XML.dll "C:\Program Files\Microsoft.NET\SDK\v[your .NET SDK version]\bin\deadoralive.vb"**.

This will compile the VB file into `DeadOrAlive.dll` and display a screen message similar to

```
Microsoft (R) Visual Basic .NET Compiler version 7.10.3052.4
for Microsoft (R) .NET Framework version 1.1.4322.573
Copyright (C) Microsoft Corporation 1987-2002. All rights reserved.
```

5. Copy `DeadOrAlive.dll` from C:\WINNT\Microsoft.NET\Framework\ v[your .NET Framework version]\ into the \bin directory of your testing web site directory. This will automatically make it available to your applications if you import it via the `@ Import` page directive.

6. Now you will add the web service reference in Dreamweaver. In the Components tab of the Application panel, click the plus sign (+) button and click Add using proxy classes. Navigate to the DLL and click OK. The web service and its methods should be visible, as shown in Figure 7-11.

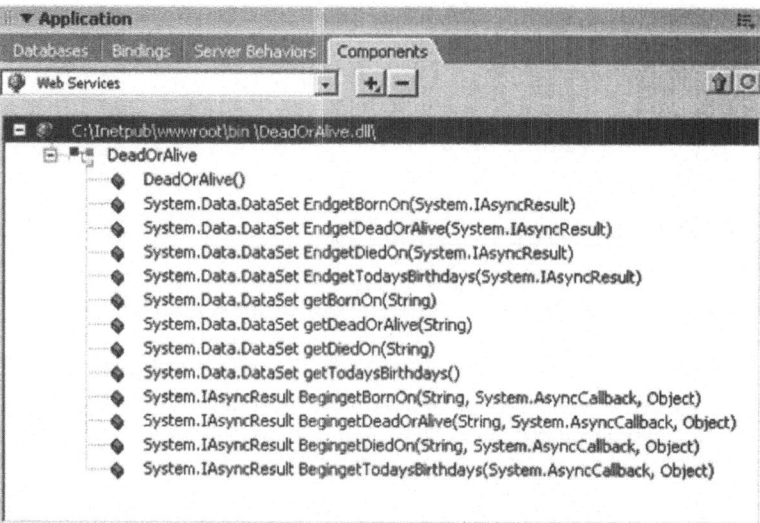

Figure 7-11. The methods of the web service are listed in Dreamweaver.

7. At last we can create a test page. The file `XmlWebService.aspx` contains the code we will be looking at now. Import the `DeadOrAlive` object (or web service proxy; call it what you will) and the relevant web service namespaces.

```
<%@ Page Language="VB" ContentType="text/html"
ResponseEncoding="iso-8859-1" %>
<%@ Import Namespace="DeadOrAlive" %>
```

```
<%@ Import Namespace="System.Web.Services.Protocols"%>
<%@ Import Namespace="System.IO"%>
```

8. Create an instance of the DeadOrAlive class and create a dataset with the results of one of the deadOrAlive methods, namely getDeadOrAlive. We pass the name of a famous person to it and a dataset of results is returned.

```
<script runat="server">
Sub Page_Load()
Dim proxy As New DeadOrAlive()
Dim aDeadOrAlive as System.Data.DataSet = ➥
proxy.getDeadOrAlive("Fred Astaire")
```

9. Assign the dataset as the source for an asp:DataGrid control called **mygrid**.

```
mygrid.Datasource = aDeadOrAlive
mygrid.Databind()
End Sub
</script>
...
<asp:DataGrid id="mygrid" AutoGenerateColumns="true" runat="server">
</asp:DataGrid>
```

That is it! The reward for all your hard work creating a proxy manually is that you have a web-based component as part of your application. Figure 7-12 shows the result for "Fred Astaire."

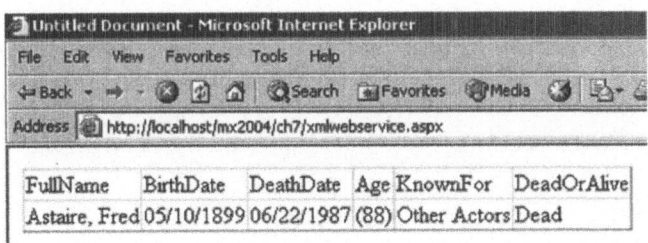

Figure 7-12. The results of a sample use of the web service

As you can see, with distributed components like this, you can build powerful applications by assembling bits of applications that you do not need to host, develop, or know how to implement.

XML Behind the Web Service

We will finish by showing the XML requests sent across the Net to invoke the DeadOrAlive methods. When the Page_Load subroutine of the page was executed we sent the following:

```
<?xml version="1.0" encoding="UTF-8"?>
<soap:Envelope
    xmlns:s0="http://www.abundanttech.com/webservices/deadoralive"
    xmlns:soap="http://schemas.xmlsoap.org/soap/envelope/"
    xmlns:xs="http://www.w3.org/2001/XMLSchema">
  <soap:Body>
    <s0:getDeadOrAlive>
      <s0:sFullName>fred astaire</s0:sFullName>
    </s0:getDeadOrAlive>
  </soap:Body>
</soap:Envelope>
```

This code is the fred astaire string wrapped in the tags of the SOAP protocol. The response from the query is the schema, the data types of the results, and the actual values.

```
<?xml version="1.0" encoding="UTF-8"?>
<soap:Envelope
    xmlns:soap="http://schemas.xmlsoap.org/soap/envelope/"
    xmlns:xsi="http://www.w3.org/2001/XMLSchema-instance"
    xmlns:xsd="http://www.w3.org/2001/XMLSchema">
  <soap:Body>
    <getDeadOrAliveResponse
xmlns="http://www.abundanttech.com/webservices/deadoralive">
      <getDeadOrAliveResult>
        <xs:schema id="NewDataSet"
            xmlns=""
            xmlns:xs="http://www.w3.org/2001/XMLSchema"
            xmlns:msdata="urn:schemas-microsoft-com:xml-msdata">
          <xs:element name="NewDataSet" msdata:IsDataSet="true">
            <xs:complexType>
              <xs:choice maxOccurs="unbounded">
                <xs:element name="Table">
                  <xs:complexType>
                    <xs:sequence>
                      <xs:element name="FullName"
                        type="xs:string" minOccurs="0" />
                      <xs:element name="BirthDate"
```

```
                            type="xs:string" minOccurs="0" />
                        <xs:element name="DeathDate"
                            type="xs:string" minOccurs="0" />
                        <xs:element name="Age"
                            type="xs:string" minOccurs="0" />
                        <xs:element name="KnownFor"
                            type="xs:string" minOccurs="0" />
                        <xs:element name="DeadOrAlive"
                            type="xs:string" minOccurs="0" />
                      </xs:sequence>
                    </xs:complexType>
                  </xs:element>
                </xs:choice>
              </xs:complexType>
            </xs:element>
          </xs:schema>
          <diffgr:diffgram
              xmlns:msdata="urn:schemas-microsoft-com:xml-msdata"
              xmlns:diffgr="urn:schemas-microsoft-com:xml-diffgram-v1">
            <NewDataSet xmlns="">
              <Table diffgr:id="Table1" msdata:rowOrder="0">
                <FullName>Astaire, Fred</FullName>
                <BirthDate>05/10/1899</BirthDate>
                <DeathDate>06/22/1987</DeathDate>
                <Age>(88)</Age>
                <KnownFor>Other Actors</KnownFor>
                <DeadOrAlive>Dead</DeadOrAlive>
              </Table>
            </NewDataSet>
          </diffgr:diffgram>
        </getDeadOrAliveResult>
      </getDeadOrAliveResponse>
    </soap:Body>
</soap:Envelope>
```

Summary

This chapter introduced you to .NET's XML-handling capabilities. The .NET architecture provides the most complete, integrated support platform for XML yet from Microsoft, and it makes many otherwise daunting tasks much easier to accomplish.

We introduced you to the SAX and DOM methods for processing XML, and showed you how the Microsoft approach attempts to marry these two approaches using a model that provides the benefits of both.

You learned how to use the XmlTextWriter class to write XML data files, which greatly reduces the amount of information that an application has to keep track of when writing XML. You learned how to read XML using the XmlTextReader class, and how to use the XmlDocument class to parse and process XML information using the W3C Document Object Model interface. You then learned how to use the XmlConvert utility class to convert XML data into native .NET data types in order to perform calculations on them.

Finally, you learned about the theory and practice of XML web services, and you built a sample ASP.NET page that utilizes a public web service as a component of your application.

Hopefully this chapter gave you the motivation to start writing your own XML applications. XML is clearly going to play a large role in future web development, and learning these skills is essential to the success of any web application developer.

CHAPTER 8

Reusing Code in Dreamweaver and ASP.NET

IF YOU USED PREVIOUS VERSIONS of Dreamweaver, you already know that one of the great things about Dreamweaver MX is its extensibility. The base program is an extremely powerful tool that was itself created by adding extensions to a core engine. In the same way, you can add extra functionality to Dreamweaver by building your own extensions. There is also a growing market for commercial-quality extensions. This means many extensions can be purchased or downloaded, so you don't have to create them yourself.

Some of the more common types of extensions include the following:

- **Snippets**: Pieces of any type of code that you use often and want to avoid having to retype.

- **Objects**: Elements of the Insert bar.

- **Commands**: Code pieces that process your code. You create these with a command recorder in the same way you record macros in Microsoft applications.

- **Tag libraries**: Assemblies of related markup tags.

- **Templates**: Pages that can be used as a base for customized web pages.

- **Panels**: Containers for related functionality.

- **Components**: Services and code that are hosted on remote servers, for example, .NET web services.

- **Behaviors**: Client-side script pieces that perform tasks on the client browser.

- **Server behaviors**: The server-side equivalent of plain behaviors.

In this chapter, we will cover snippets, commands, templates, and tag libraries. We will look at how extensions are built and used, and how they can make your code more efficient.

We will also look at the features in ASP.NET that facilitate code reuse. These features enable the developers in your team to work independently from designers and vice versa, resulting in less risk of accidental modifications and easier version control. This in turn leads to fewer iterations and easier debugging. The following are the two main ways to reuse code to your benefit:

- You can concentrate the programming code in Code Behind files that can be written in the preferred .NET language of the programmer.

- You can add functionality to custom ASP.NET controls (.ascx), which can be imported as though they were HTML or ASP.NET tags.

You saw the principles on which these techniques are based in Chapter 4, and you will apply them in practice in the case study in Chapter 11. In this chapter, we will concentrate on the code-reuse features in Dreamweaver MX 2004.

Let's start with a look at how to create a simple code snippet.

Creating and Using Code Snippets

Snippets can be any combination of server-side code blocks, JavaScript code, and HTML elements. In fact, anything that can legitimately be put into any type of page within Dreamweaver can be converted into a snippet. Most of the time, snippets are created directly from the page itself, so you can work with existing code or code that you just wrote. For example, say you have an asp:Calendar control that you spent a fair amount of time formatting (shown in Figure 8-1), and now you want to insert it into a number of pages (see CalendarSnippet.aspx in the download code).

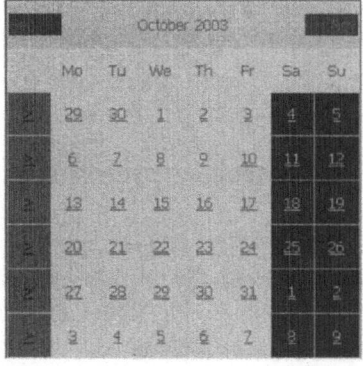

Figure 8-1. A typical asp:Calendar *control*

To create a snippet, follow these steps:

1. To create the folder where you will store your new snippet, right-click the Snippets tab of the Code panel and select New Folder from the context menu, as shown in Figure 8-2.

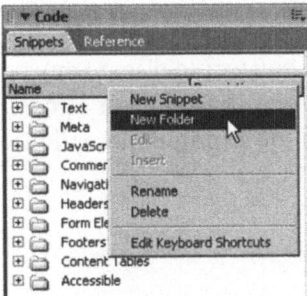

Figure 8-2. Creating a new folder in the Snippets tab

2. Name the new folder **ASPNET** and return to your current document. To turn the calendar code into a snippet, switch to Code view, highlight all the code you want to include in the new snippet, right-click the highlighted code, and click Create New Snippet, as shown in Figure 8-3.

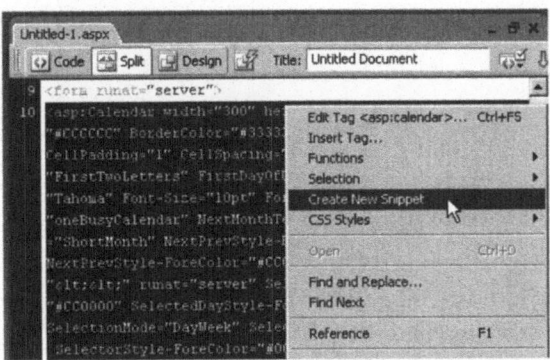

Figure 8-3. Using the Create New Snippet command

In the Snippet editor, when the Snippet type is set to Wrap selection, your code appears in the Insert before box. The Wrap selection option is used if you want to make a snippet out of server-side code that comes before and after an object. For example, to specify that weekend days should be styled the same as whatever else is on the page, you would place your first block of snippet code as follows:

```
<asp:Calendar id="oneBusyCalendar" .... Etc.>
```

The existing code is left unchanged.

```
<WeekendDayStyle BackColor="#CCCCFF"></WeekendDayStyle>
```

The second block of snippet code would be placed after the existing code.

```
</asp:Calendar>
```

To achieve that using the Snippet editor, you would discard any unnecessary sections of code, and break the rest of the code into its two component parts. These parts can then be placed in the appropriate sections within the Snippet editor, as shown in Figure 8-4.

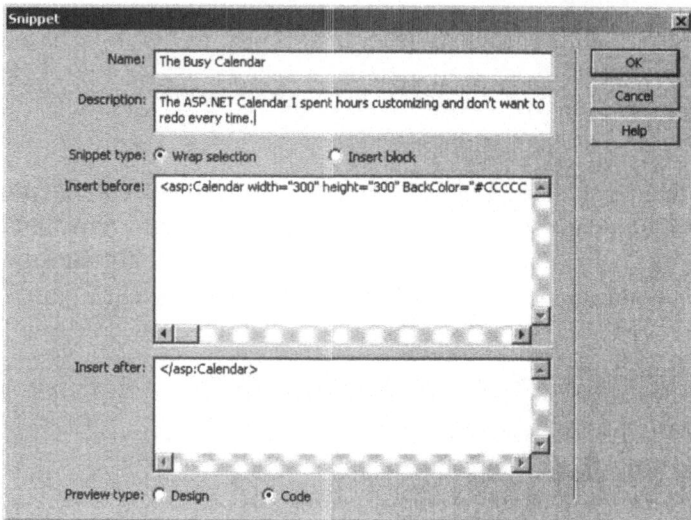

Figure 8-4. The Snippet editor

3. To create a snippet based on one code block or a single HTML element, as we are doing in this exercise, click the Insert block option. This will place all your highlighted code inside one large text area. As you can see in Figure 8-4, there are fields for the name and description of your snippet. It is always a good idea to fill in these fields to help you identify the snippet at a later date.

4. The final option in the Snippet editor is Preview type. This setting affects the Snippets panel, where you can preview the currently highlighted snippet. If the snippet is a representation of an HTML element, you should see the HTML element in WYSIWYG view. Remember, however, this may not work with server-side code that accesses data, because that kind of code is generally not visible if it is out of context. The Preview type can be set to either Design or Code, but Design does not work with the asp:Calendar control, so choose Code.

5. Click OK to insert your new snippet into the specified location. If for some reason the snippet is created in the wrong place, simply drag it to the correct location. Figure 8-5 shows where we saved our snippet.

Figure 8-5. The code snippet is saved in the ASPNET folder.

6. To use the snippet, select it and click the Insert button, or drag it into place. The small buttons on the bottom provide shortcuts for creating a folder and adding, editing, and deleting a snippet.

Snippets are very useful, especially if you regularly use specific functions or .NET controls. If you need to customize a snippet, you must do so by hand, either in Code view if it is a piece of scripted code, or in the relevant Dreamweaver property panel if it is a piece of HTML code. Obviously, any changes you make will not affect code already inserted in a page. If you have a multi-user operating system, you can export your snippets to another system by copying them from your directory, like this:

```
Multi-user OS: [hdd]\[your_user_directory]\Application Data\Macromedia\
Dreamweaver MX 2004\Configuration\Snippets
```

If you have a single-user operating system, export your snippets like this:

```
Single-user OS: [hdd]\Program Files\Macromedia\Dreamweaver MX 2004\
Configuration\Snippets
```

Recording and Using Commands

Commands are the equivalent of macros in Microsoft applications. They are a series of steps grouped together so that a task can be performed in one step. Commands can be created by recording a sequence of actions in Dreamweaver's Design view or by using the History panel (press Shift+F10 if it is not visible). We will look at both methods.

Recording a Command

For our example, we will insert Help image buttons in every page of the web site. We will insert the image button in a table cell, and copy and paste it in another table cell. The same task could be accomplished by inserting a code snippet twice, but by recording the command as one step, you can carry out the task more efficiently.

1. Create a new ASP.NET page, and insert a table with one row of three cells. Imagine that the middle cell contains a page heading that varies from page to page, so you cannot copy the whole row from page to page. Place your cursor in the first cell in Design view, as shown in Figure 8-6.

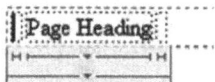

Figure 8-6. The cursor is positioned to record a command.

2. Start recording your steps by clicking Commands ➤ Start Recording, as shown in Figure 8-7.

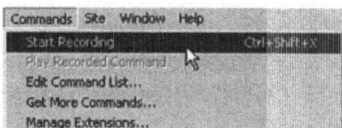

Figure 8-7. Recording a command

3. Your actions will now be recorded and visible in the History panel. Click asp:ImageButton in the ASP.NET control panel, as shown in Figure 8-8.

Figure 8-8. Inserting an `asp:ImageButton` *control*

4. Complete the dialog box with your data (we used `help.gif` from the download code), as shown in Figure 8-9.

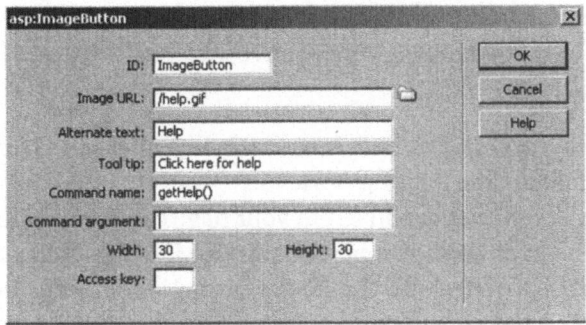

Figure 8-9. The asp:ImageButton dialog box

5. Click OK. Right-click the inserted image button in Design view and select Copy.

6. Mouse movements, clicks, and selections are not recorded, so you need to use the keyboard for the next few steps. Press the right arrow key twice, press the End button (to go to the right end of the middle table cell), and then press the right arrow once more to place your cursor in the right-most cell. Right-click in Design view and select Paste. To stop recording, select Commands ➤ Stop Recording. Figure 8-10 shows the recap as it appears in the History panel.

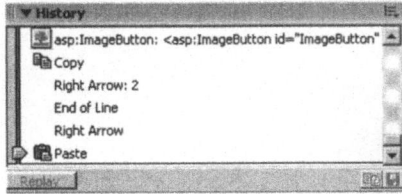

Figure 8-10. The recorded steps appear in the History panel.

All these steps are recorded in one command. If you create another page with a three-celled table and position your cursor in the first cell, you can simply select Commands ➤ Play Recorder Command to automatically perform all the recorded steps and get the result shown in Figure 8-11.

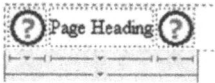

Figure 8-11. The result of replaying the recorded steps

This short and simple example did not save that much effort, but commands can save you lots of valuable time for long tasks.

Unfortunately, not everything you insert in your page can be recorded. For example, if you try to insert an asp:Calendar control via More tags in the ASP.NET panel, the calendar will be inserted, but the History panel will include an entry reading Edit Source with a red cross next to it. This means that the action is not recordable and cannot be replayed. Thankfully, you can get around this problem by creating a code snippet of the asp:Calendar control first, and then recording the action of inserting the snippet.

Storing a Command Permanently

The recorder method of creating a command is very useful, but you can store only one command at a time. To record a second command without losing the first one, store the first one permanently.

1. In the History panel, use the Shift key to select all the steps that you want saved. Then either click the small Save button in the bottom-right corner or right-click and select Save As Command, as shown in Figure 8-12.

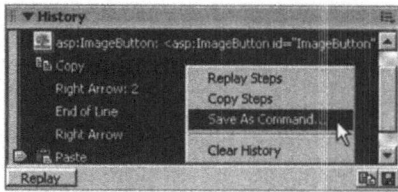

Figure 8-12. Saving steps as a command

2. In the dialog box that appears, type a name for the command. Then whenever you need to replay it, you can go to the Commands menu and select it from the bottom of the list, as shown in Figure 8-13 (we named our command insertHelp).

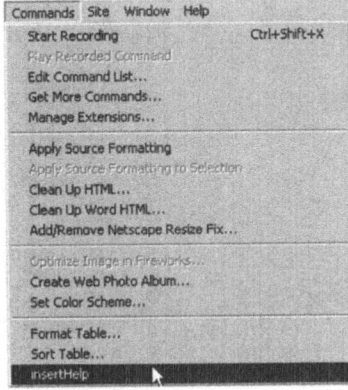

Figure 8-13. The recorded command in the Commands menu

3. The command can also be exported to another system. Simply look in this directory:

```
Multi-user OS: [hdd:]\[you_user_directory]\Application Data\Macromedia\
Dreamweaver MX 2004\Configuration\Commands
```

or in this directory:

```
Single-user OS: [hdd:]\Program Files\Macromedia\Dreamweaver MX 2004\
Configuration\Commands
```

4. To add the command to your system, copy the file insertHelp.htm from the download code.

Creating and Using Templates

Templates help you keep design and content separate. The designer creates a template that defines the look for a page, and authors add appropriate content. Templates offer great flexibility and cost savings, but the real power of templates is that they give you the ability to update multiple pages at once. A document that is created from a template remains connected to that template unless you detach it. That means modifying a template immediately updates all documents based on that template throughout your web site.

As our example, we'll use a template to produce localized versions of a web page.

1. A template can be created in two ways. You can go to File ➤ New, and select Template page in the Category list, as shown in Figure 8-14.

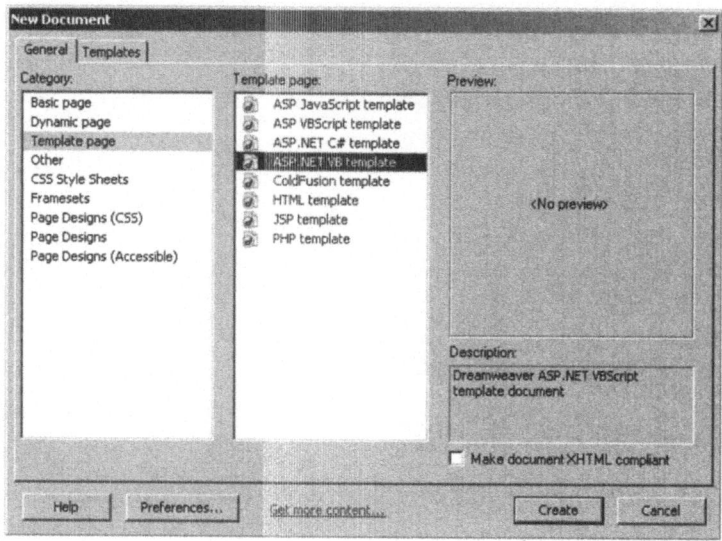

Figure 8-14. Creating a new Template page

You can also go to the Files panel, click the Assets tab, and choose the Templates icon, as shown in Figure 8-15. A list of any existing templates will be shown, as well as a preview of the selected one. You can add a new template by right-clicking and selecting New Template or by clicking the plus sign (+) button at the bottom of the panel.

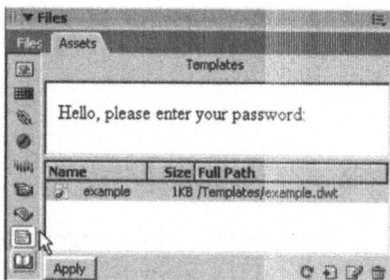

Figure 8-15. Choosing the Templates icon

2. A new VB .NET template is automatically populated with some standard code, but we will work in Design view. Add an ASP.NET form that contains a 2×2 table. Use the left column as headings and include two text boxes in the right column (see sampleTemplate.dwt in the download). To describe the input that the user should enter in each text box, add editable regions in the headings cells. You will customize these areas to create the localized version of the web page. Place your cursor in the top-left table cell and select Insert ➤ Template Objects ➤ Editable Region, as shown in Figure 8-16.

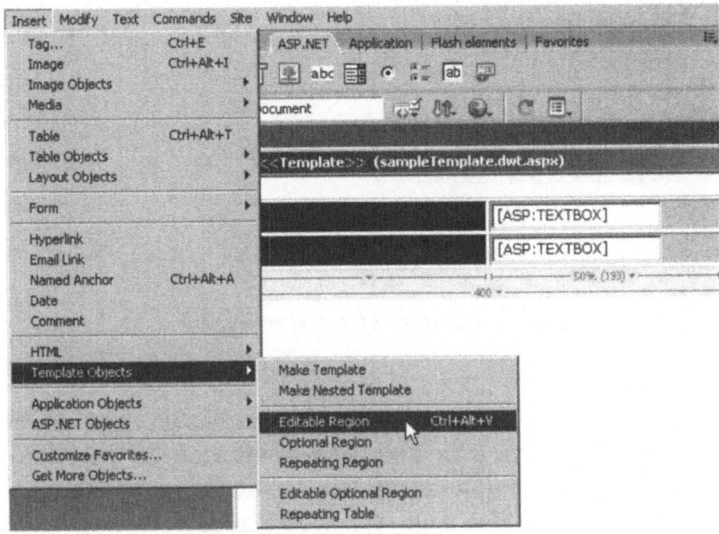

Figure 8-16. Creating an editable region

3. In the dialog box that appears, enter a descriptive region name. Do the same for the bottom-left cell so that your Design view looks something like Figure 8-17.

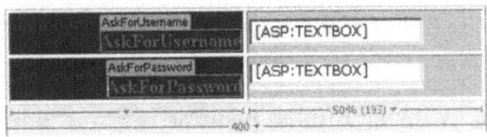

Figure 8-17. Descriptive region names

4. Save and close your template. It should now appear in the Templates list in your Assets panel. It is saved in a folder called Templates, and it has the extension .dwt. To use the template, you (or, for example, the Spanish-language content developer on your team) would go to the Templates list, right-click the template, and create a new page from it, as shown in Figure 8-18.

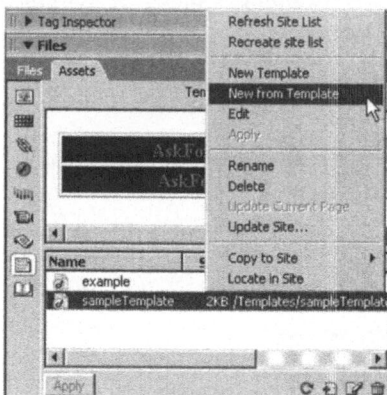

Figure 8-18. Creating a document from a template

The new page looks just like the template in Design view. However, the content developer can only modify the username and password labels to create localized pages. As you can see by the cursor shape in the template-based Spanish page shown in Figure 8-19, everything is locked except the editable regions. (The download also includes a German version.)

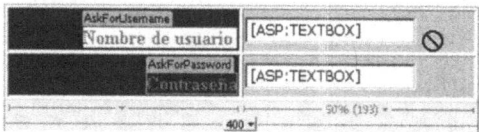

Figure 8-19. The Spanish version of the page, created via the template

5. The biggest benefits of using a template become obvious when you change the original template. Open sampleTemplate.dwt and change the font color of the top-left cell. When you save the template, you will be prompted to update the pages that are based on this template. Our example is shown in Figure 8-20.

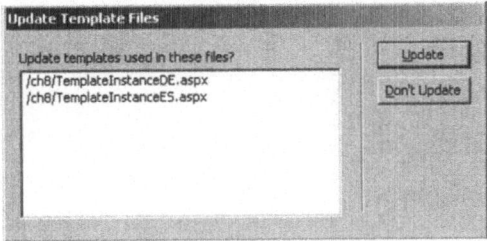

Figure 8-20. Updating dependent documents

With a simple click, you can change the look and feel of your web site. Hopefully, that will keep the accounts manager as happy as the IT chief!

Templates come with many other powerful features in addition to editable areas. For example, you can set an image source to change depending on the value of an expression, which means you do not have to rely on the content developer to decide which image to display.

Using Libraries

We continue with the concept of keeping design and content separate, but this time we will apply a template to the content by way of a **library**. A library is a collection of items that you use throughout the web site. For example, if you have a section of HTML that you want to use on every page of your web site, but you have not finalized that piece of HTML, you can design your pages with a library item in place of the HTML, and then add the finalized HTML when it is complete. Dreamweaver libraries are listed in the Assets panel and stored with the extension .lbi in a library directory in your site's structure.

Unfortunately, Dreamweaver MX 2004 does not supply an interface for inserting ASP.NET items in a library. Instead, you will have to either type the code manually or insert a snippet.

1. Create a new library item that contains the asp:Calendar snippet. In the Assets panel, click the Library icon, right-click the blank area, and select New Library Item. Save the library item as **Calendar for all pages**, as shown in Figure 8-21.

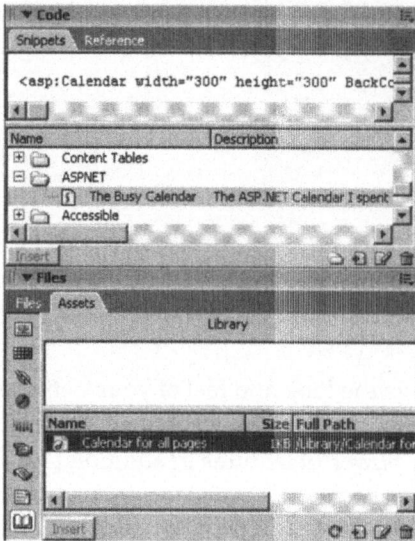

Figure 8-21. Saving a snippet as a library item

2. To insert the new library item, right-click it and click Insert. Dreamweaver automatically uses commented HTML code to mark the region as a library item. In our example, this looks like this:

```
<!-- #BeginLibraryItem "/Library/Calendar%20for%20all%20pages.lbi" -->
...
<!-- #EndLibraryItem -->
```

If you subsequently change the library item, you can instantly update all the pages that use it, which can save you a huge amount of time.

Creating and Modifying Tag Libraries

A **tag library** is a collection of tags and their formatting specifications. Tag libraries provide the information about tags that Dreamweaver uses for code hints, target browser checks, the Tag Chooser, and other coding capabilities.

1. To open the Tag Library Editor, select Edit ➤ Tag Libraries. You can see all the prebuilt tag libraries, such as HTML, ColdFusion, ASP, WML, and so on. Scroll down to the ASP.NET group, expand it, and then click Image, as shown in Figure 8-22.

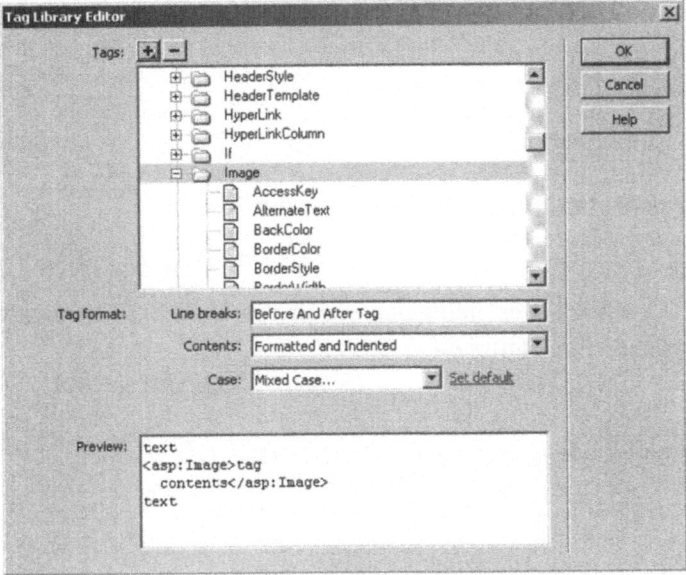

Figure 8-22. The ASP.NET Image tag in the Tag Library Editor

As you can see, Dreamweaver MX 2004 uses this information to format the tag correctly, align it, add its attributes, and so on. This information is also editable and customizable so that when new features are added to ASP.NET's controls, you can keep the tag library up to date. This is what you will do next.

Note that according to the .NET specification 1.1, the <asp:Image> tag contains an attribute in addition to those listed in the Tag Library Editor: UniqueID. The UniqueID attribute is generated automatically when a page request is processed. The difference between the UniqueID and ID attributes is that the UniqueID attribute includes the identifier for the server control's naming container. For example, if you include an asp:Image control within an asp:Repeater control, and the latter is bound to a data source (see Chapter 6) with three rows, the ID attribute will be the same for all three asp:Images controls. UniqueID, in contrast, will be unique, and its value will be a preformatted string of this type:

```
[Container_ID]:ctl[a_number]:[Contained_ID]
```

2. You might want to set the value of UniqueID to a loop or even a data field so that the rest of your script can work. To make this new attribute available, edit the <asp:Image> tag. In the Tag Library Editor, click the plus sign (+) button and choose New Attributes, as shown in Figure 8-23.

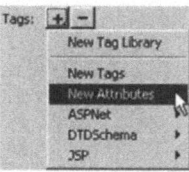

Figure 8-23. Adding new attributes to a tag

3. In the New Attributes dialog box, specify the attribute's name and location, as shown in Figure 8-24.

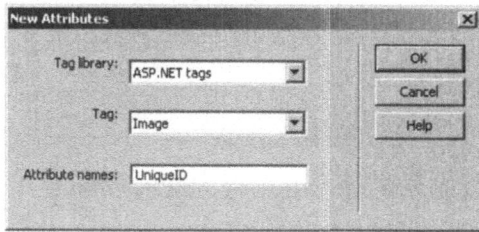

Figure 8-24. The completed New Attributes dialog box

4. Click OK to display Tag Library Editor with the new attribute selected and some additional formatting options available. You can specify whether the attribute is a directory, a class, and so on. In our example, we accepted the defaults. When you next type the `<asp:Image>` tag in your code, the list of suggested attributes will contain `UniqueID`, as shown in Figure 8-25.

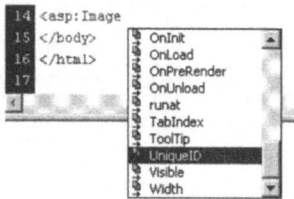

Figure 8-25. The new attribute is visible when you type the `<asp:Image>` tag.

To say this is flexible would be a gross understatement. But there is more for ASP.NET programmers.

Importing Custom Tag Libraries

One way to create a new library is to type it into the Tag Library Editor. First type a new tag group, then type each tag, and then type each tag's attribute. As you saw in Chapter 4, ASP.NET enables you to create custom tags that can be imported into a page with the @ Register directive. These tags point to custom controls (.ascx) or assemblies (.dll) that perform as though they were built-in tags. The Tag Library Editor provides a beautifully efficient way to import these custom tags and controls into a library that can be used and shared within a development group.

1. Click the plus sign (+) button in the Tag Library Editor, and select ASPNet ➤ Import Selected ASPNet Custom Tags, as shown in Figure 8-26.

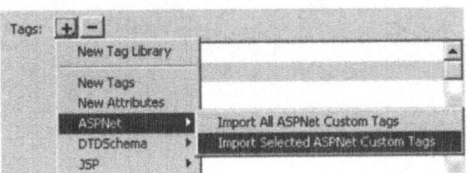

Figure 8-26. Importing custom ASP.NET tags

Dreamweaver scans your testing server for any ASCX files or assemblies, and returns a list of them. The modified asp:Calendar control selected in Figure 8-27 is available in the download code.

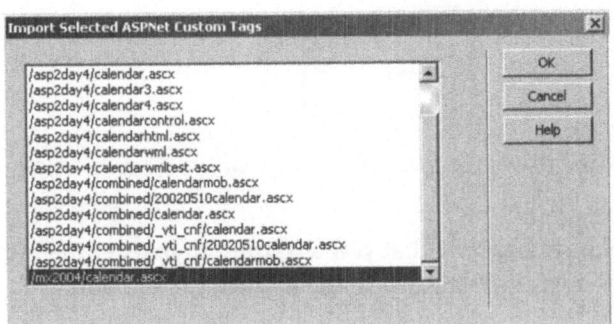

Figure 8-27. The ASP.NET controls found on the web site

2. Click OK to create a new tag library, which will store the ASCX controls you selected. There you can specify the prefix with which to register the controls and the types of pages in which they will be available, as shown in Figure 8-28.

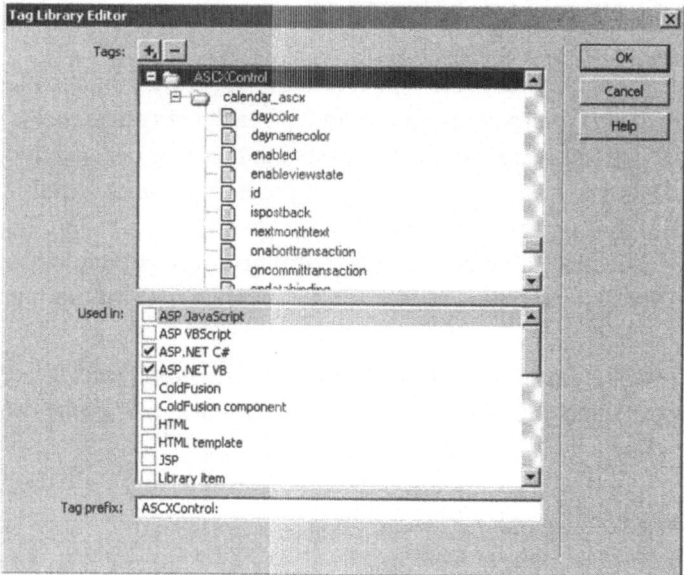

Figure 8-28. Specifying parameters for the imported control

3. To use your new tag library and its items, simply open the Tag Chooser via Insert ➤ Tag and navigate to the custom tag library. After inserting the custom tag, you can see that its attributes are available, as shown in Figure 8-29.

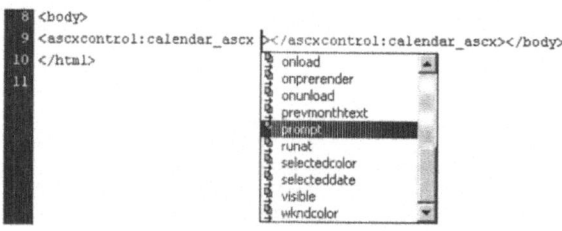

Figure 8-29. The imported control is now available in Code view.

Remember from Chapter 4 that you also need to register the imported control at the top of the page with the following statement:

```
<%@ Register TagPrefix="ascxcontrol" TagName="calendar_ascx"
Src="calendar.ascx" %>
```

For more information about custom ASP.NET controls, read the Microsoft documentation at http://msdn.microsoft.com/library/default.asp?url=/ library/en-us/vbcon/html/vboriwebusercontrols.asp and http:// msdn.microsoft.com/library/default.asp?url=/library/en-us/cpguide/ html/cpconwebformscontroldevelopmentbasics.asp.

The Tag Library Editor has more advanced capabilities, including the ability to import tags defined in XML files or Document Type Definition files (you saw how those are used in Chapter 7). Although this is not directly related to code reuse, it is relevant because it enables the extension of Dreamweaver's coding abilities. For example, if you were defining a new set of tags for your .NET ASCX controls and you wanted to distribute those tags to your team of developers, you could ensure everyone had the same set of tags by forming it as a DTD or in an XML file.

4. The download for this chapter includes the DTD for the Speech Application Language Tags (SALT) language, but any DTD will work. Open the Import DTD dialog box by clicking DTDSchema ➤ Import XML DTD or Schema File, as shown in Figure 8-30.

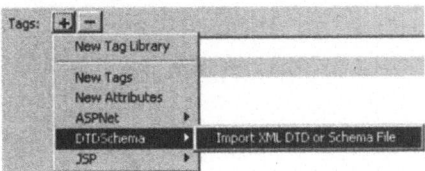

Figure 8-30. Opening the Import DTD dialog box

5. In the dialog box, simply browse to wherever your DTD schema is located and click OK. The new tags are now available within Dreamweaver MX 2004 for use in your code, as shown in Figure 8-31.

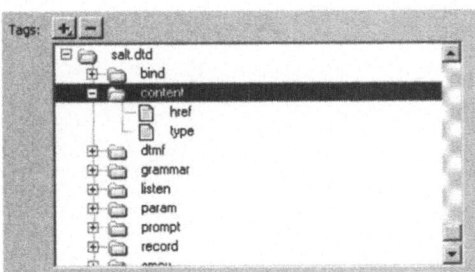

Figure 8-31. The tags defined by the DTD are available for use.

Summary

In this chapter, you saw how code snippets, templates, and libraries can make your coding more efficient. You also learned that Dreamweaver allows you to edit tag libraries and that custom tag libraries are especially useful tools.

In the next chapter, you will continue extending Dreamweaver's reach by creating ASP.NET server behaviors and packaging them for distribution.

Extending Dreamweaver MX

IN THIS CHAPTER, we will look at server behaviors, which are very useful extensions for server-side web development. We will look at how server behaviors are built and how they can be easily integrated inside your code. We will then show you how to build two simple server behaviors. The first will format a currency data field with the appropriate currency symbol, and the second will display either internationalized data or a friendly message redirecting the user.

Note that server behaviors created for earlier versions of Dreamweaver may not work in MX 2004. See the Macromedia web site for further details: http://www.macromedia.com/software/dreamweaver/productinfo/faq/dwmx_extensions.html#1_4.

Building Extensions

Almost all extensions for Dreamweaver are built using HTML and JavaScript documents. Yes, you read that correctly—you can extend the capabilities of Dreamweaver by building HTML pages.

Server Behaviors

Extensions have three component parts. The first part is the code that provides the functionality. The second part is the interface that you use to add the extension to the page. The third part is the code that works behind the scenes to make all the other parts work in the Dreamweaver environment. The average Dreamweaver user will probably never directly encounter the third part of the extension, but it is very important nevertheless.

Dreamweaver MX 2004 includes a special tool called the Server Behavior Builder that automates the process of creating a server behavior from a block of server-side code.

The Currency Formatter

You will begin by creating a server behavior that is useful when you need to format numbers as a currency type other than the default for the development machine.

The Extension Code: Currency Formatter

To create the server behavior, follow these steps:

1. Open a new ASP.NET VB page. Use the Microsoft Access database called Portfolios.mdb in this chapter's download code to create a dataset from the tblMembers table. Save Portfolios.mdb on your server, and create a connection to the database named connPortfolios (see Chapter 5). The Databases tab of the Application panel should look as shown in Figure 9-1.

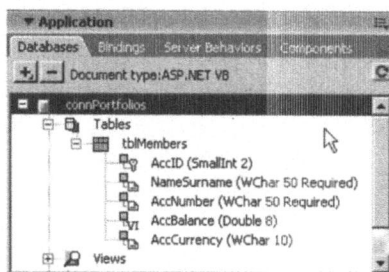

Figure 9-1. The table columns are listed on the Databases tab.

2. Click the Bindings tab, and then click the plus sign (+) button to select DataSet (Query) from the drop-down list, as shown in Figure 9-2.

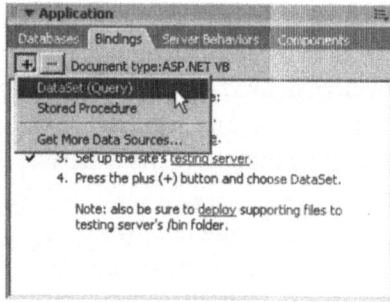

Figure 9-2. Opening the DataSet dialog box from the Bindings tab

3. In the Connection drop-down list, choose connPortfolios and accept the default name DataSet1, as shown in Figure 9-3.

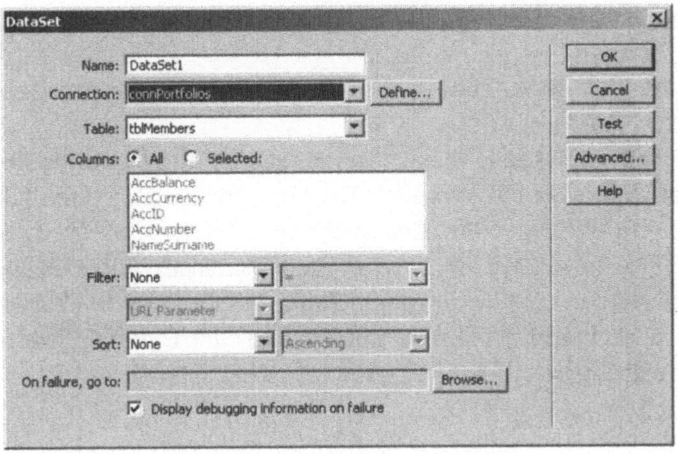

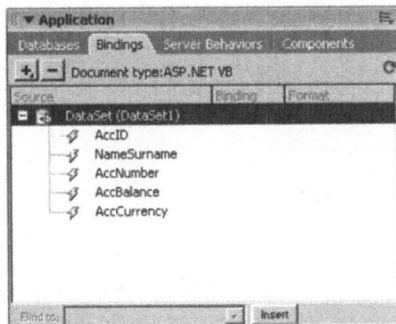

Figure 9-3. The completed DataSet dialog box

When you are done, the Bindings tab of the Application panel should look as shown in Figure 9-4.

Figure 9-4. The new dataset in the Application panel

Your page code should now include the following lines:

```
<MM:DataSet
id="DataSet1"
runat="Server"
IsStoredProcedure="false"
ConnectionString='<%# System.Configuration.ConfigurationSettings.➥
AppSettings("MM_CONNECTION_STRING_connPortfolios") %>'
DatabaseType='<%# System.Configuration.ConfigurationSettings.➥
AppSettings("MM_CONNECTION_DATABASETYPE_connPortfolios") %>'
```

```
CommandText='<%# "SELECT * FROM tblMembers" %>'
Debug="true"
></MM:DataSet> <MM:PageBind runat="server" PostBackBind="true" />
```

4. As you can see in the in the SQL statement, all the rows of the tblMembers table are imported into DataSet1. The table contains account balances in specific currencies, as specified by the value of the AccCurrency column. You want to format the numbers in the AccBalance column as currency with the correct currency symbol. On the Server Behaviors tab, select DataSet1, click the plus sign (+) button, and click Dynamic Text to display the dialog box shown in Figure 9-5.

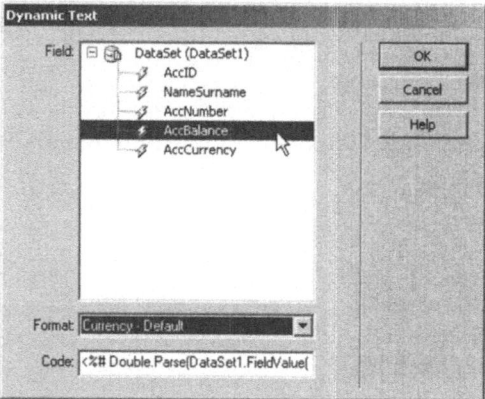

Figure 9-5. Formatting the dataset's fields

5. Select AccBalance, select Currency - Default in the Format drop-down list, and click OK. The following code will appear in Code view:

```
<%# Double.Parse(DataSet1.FieldValue("AccBalance", ⮕
Container)).ToString("C") %>
```

This is a render function that processes the AccBalance field of the containing dataset and derives a double precision number. (The containing dataset is referenced by the keyword "container" in the code. You will add this container shortly.) The function ToString("C") is called with the parameter C (for currency) to convert the number to a string of characters. By adding a few more words, some HTML formatting, and another textual dynamic region for the AccNumber field, you can build a nice row sentence like the one shown in Figure 9-6.

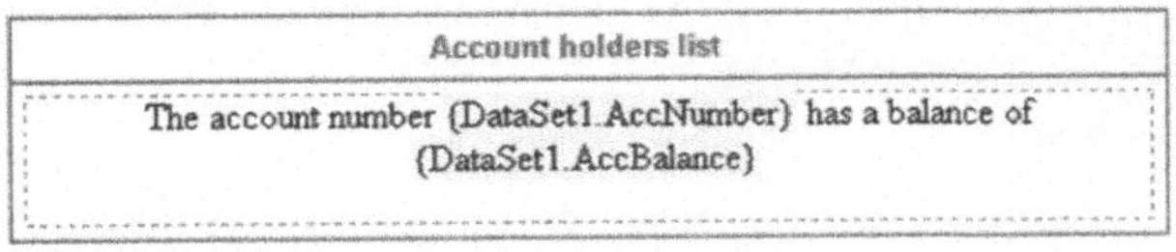

Account holders list
The account number (DataSet1.AccNumber) has a balance of (DataSet1.AccBalance)

Figure 9-6. The page in Design view

Here is the code for the region:

```
<table width="75%" border="1" cellspacing="0" cellpadding="5">
  <tr>
    <td> <div align="center"><font color="#FF0000" size="2"
face="Arial, Helvetica, sans-
serif"><strong>Account holders list</strong></font></div></td>
  </tr>
  <tr>
    <td>
        <div align="center"> The account number
              <%# DataSet1.FieldValue("AccNumber", Container) %>
              has a balance of
              <%# Double.Parse(DataSet1.FieldValue ➡
("AccBalance", Container)).ToString("c")%>
              <br>
        </div>
      </td>
  </tr>
</table>
```

6. The row containing the data is repeated for every row in the associated dataset. To display the data on the page, you will use an asp:Repeater control. Select the row you typed (by clicking the <tr> button at the bottom of the Design view pane), click the plus sign (+) button on the Server Behaviors tab, and then click Repeat Region, as shown in Figure 9-7.

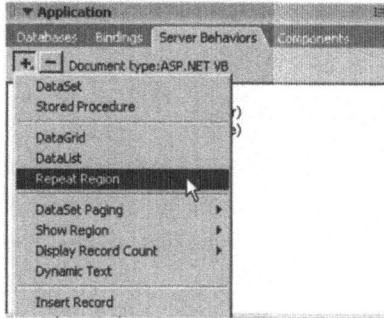

Figure 9-7. Creating a repeat region via the Server Behaviors tab

7. In the Repeat Region dialog box, select the dataset you want to use as the repeater and the number of records to show, as shown in Figure 9-8. Then click OK.

Figure 9-8. Specifying parameters for the repeat region

This will insert an `asp:Repeater` control that is repeated for every table row, producing output like that shown in Figure 9-9. Your numbers are formatted as the default currency on your development machine. If you have localization settings that specify the United Kingdom, Live Data view will reflect your settings.

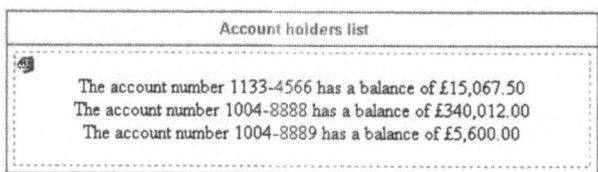

Figure 9-9. The `asp:Repeater` *control's output in Live Data view*

8. The account balances are displayed in units of British currency, but they should be in other currencies. To fix the problem, you can build on the existing dynamic text code. Switch to Code view, and manually change the code snippet that formats the balances to the following (the finished code is in `sb1test.aspx` in the download):

```
<%# DataSet1.FieldValue("AccCurrency", Container) & ➥
Double.Parse(DataSet1.FieldValue("AccBalance", ➥
Container)).ToString("n")  %>
```

9. This adds the currency symbol from the database and formats the balances as numbers. Refresh the page to see the desired result, as shown in Figure 9-10.

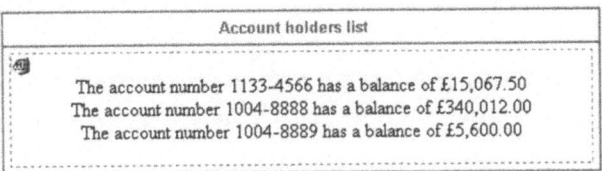

Account holders list
The account number 1133-4566 has a balance of £15,067.50
The account number 1004-8888 has a balance of £340,012.00
The account number 1004-8889 has a balance of £5,600.00

Figure 9-10. The page displaying the correct currency symbols

10. If you had many pages that presented this type of issue, you would want to consider building a custom server behavior to format numbers as the currency specified by a currency symbol field. The code for this server behavior is complete. Select and copy the code shown after step 8, including the <% %> symbols. You will now build the interface.

The Interface: Currency Formatter

To build the interface for your server behavior, follow these steps:

1. Open the Server Behavior Builder by clicking the plus sign (+) button in the Server Behaviors tab and choosing New Server Behavior, as shown in Figure 9-11.

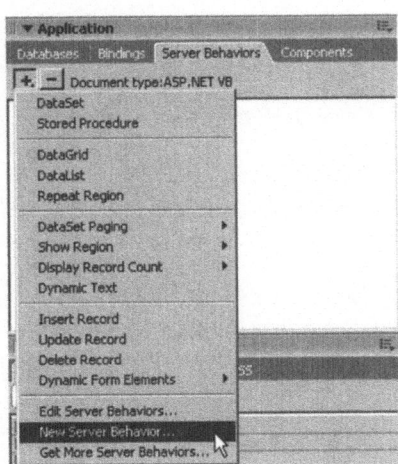

Figure 9-11. Opening the Server Behavior Builder

2. In the New Server Behavior dialog box, select ASP.NET VB as the document type, and type **Set Currency Field** in the Name field, as shown in Figure 9-12.

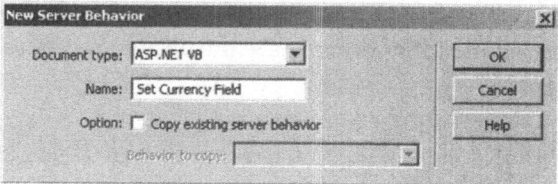

Figure 9-12. Defining basic information for the new server behavior

3. Click OK to continue. In the Server Behavior Builder, click the plus sign (+) button. Then click OK to accept the defaults in the dialog box and add the new block to the Server Behavior Builder. The code corresponding to this block can be added in the (rather cramped) Code block window.

   The following text is already in the Code block window:

   ```
   <% Replace this text with the code to insert when the server
   behavior is applied %>
   ```

4. Delete all the code in the window, and then paste the code that you copied from the original page into the Code block window.

5. The code cannot be reused easily because the names of the datasets and fields are specific to the current page. To replace them with variables that you will define whenever you reuse the server behavior, highlight the word DataSet1 in the code, and click the Insert Parameter in Code Block button, as shown in Figure 9-13.

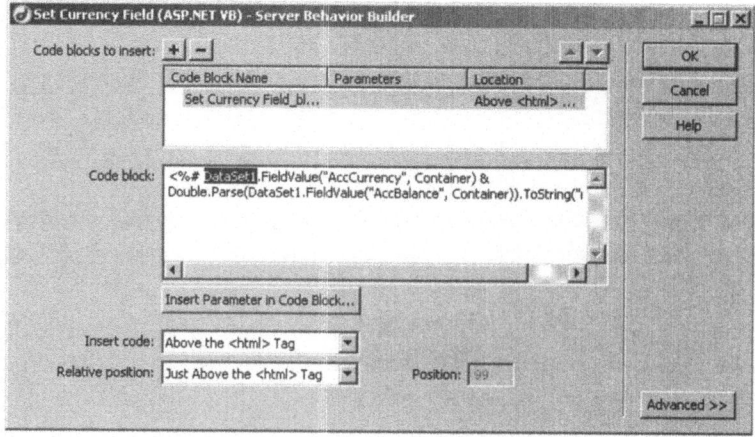

Figure 9-13. Highlighting the code that will be replaced by a parameter

Parameters: Currency Formatter

To add parameters, follow these steps:

1. In the Insert Parameter In Code Block dialog box, type **DataSet Name** in the Parameter name box, as shown in Figure 9-14.

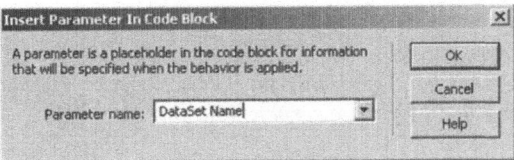

Figure 9-14. Naming a parameter

2. Click OK. Because there are multiple occurrences of DataSet1 in the code, you are prompted to replace all instances of the word—click Yes. Occurrences of DataSet1 now appear as @@DataSet Name@@. The @ symbols tell the Server Behavior Builder that user input is required for this item and that a form element will be created to accommodate this.

3. To enable users to specify which columns in the dataset should be used for the balances and currencies, you must insert two more parameters called Currency Symbol DataField and Numerical DataField. To do this, select the text and click the Insert Parameter in Code Block button.

   The line of code with parameters in place should look like this:

   ```
   <%# @@DataSet Name@@.FieldValue("@@Currency Symbol DataField@@",
   Container) & Double.Parse(@@DataSet Name@@.FieldValue("@@Numerical
   DataField@@", Container)).ToString("n")  %>
   ```

4. In the Server Behavior Builder, set the Insert code and Relative position drop-down lists as shown in Figure 9-15.

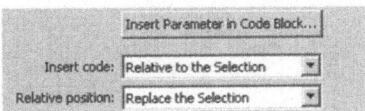

Figure 9-15. Defining the document position of the inserted code

This specifies that the code block is inserted into the document in one piece and that it replaces whatever the user selected. If the user did not make a selection, nothing is replaced on the current page, and the code is inserted at the position of the cursor in the document.

5. Click the Advanced button in the bottom right of the Server Behavior Builder to reveal a few extra items that you need to set, as shown in Figure 9-16.

Figure 9-16. Specifying a title for the server behavior

Selecting the Identifier check box tells Dreamweaver that if this code block is found in the document, the behavior should be displayed in the Server Behaviors panel. For this server behavior, we can leave this check box selected. If you write server behaviors that use multiple code blocks, make sure that only one code block has this check box selected.

By default, the server behavior's title is displayed in the Server Behaviors panel to indicate its presence in the current document.

6. In the Code block to select list, choose Set Currency Field_block1. The Server Behavior Builder should look as shown in Figure 9-17.

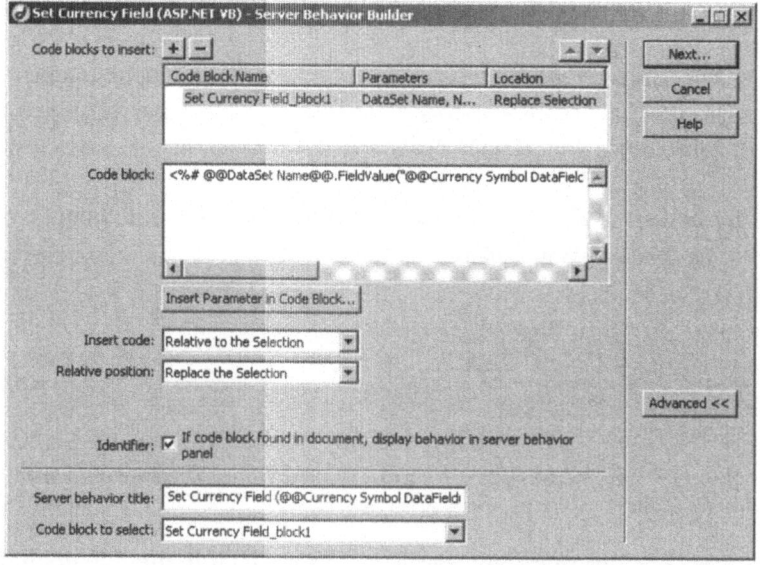

Figure 9-17. The completed Server Behavior Builder

7. Click Next to display the Generate Behavior Dialog Box, in which you specify how the parameters should be defined by the user. When a user wants to apply your server behavior, he or she is presented with a dialog box with form elements to complete. Initially, Dreamweaver suggests the name "Text Field" for each parameter, but you can do better than that. You can create a drop-down list with the names of all available datasets (for the `DataSet Name` parameter) and two drop-down lists with the names of the dataset fields (for selecting `Numerical DataField` and `Currency Symbol DataField`).

8. Highlight the `Currency Symbol Data` parameter, and click the down arrow in the Display As column. Select Recordset Menu for the `DataSet Name` parameter, and select Recordset Field Menu for the other two, as shown in Figure 9-18. These settings will create drop-down lists for datasets and fields.

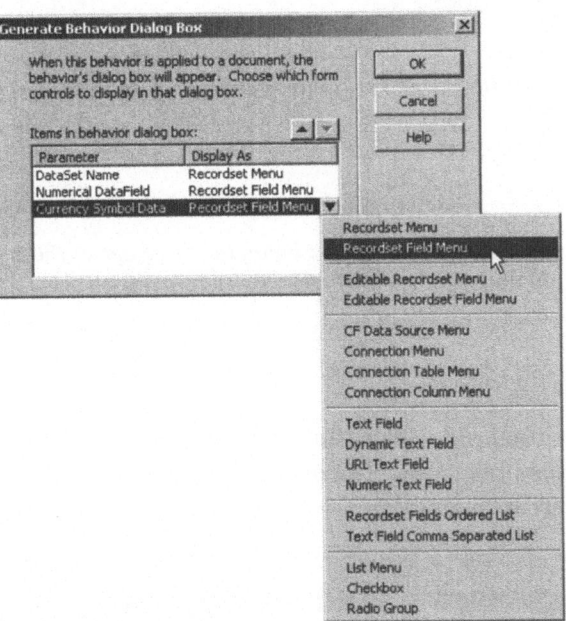

Figure 9-18. Defining the interface elements for the server behavior

9. Put the parameters in the order in which they should appear. To move a parameter up or down, select it and click the up or down arrow. The most logical order is the dataset name first, followed by its fields. This is because the list will be filtered to show only the columns for the selected dataset.

10. Click OK to add the server behavior to the list of behaviors available on the Server Behaviors tab, as shown in Figure 9-19.

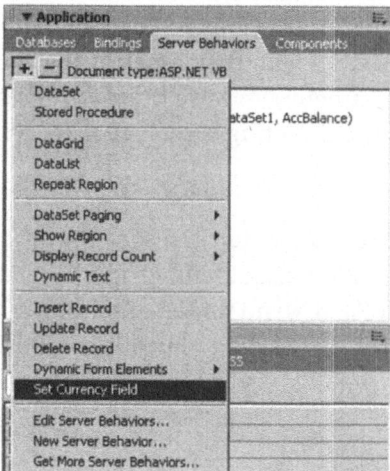

Figure 9-19. The custom server behavior now appears on the Server Behaviors tab.

 TIP   *If you try to apply this server behavior to a page without a dataset, you will get an error message.*

11. To test this server behavior, delete the formatting code and apply the Set Currency Field server behavior. The dialog box that appears should look as shown in Figure 9-20.

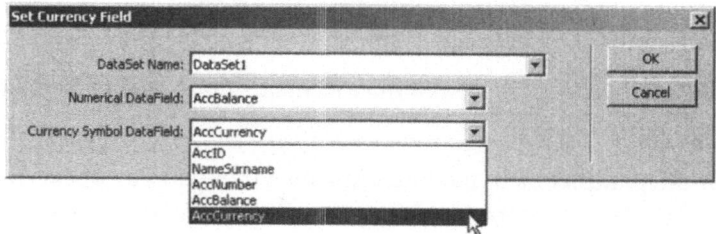

Figure 9-20. The finished server behavior interface

12. Click OK to insert the code in your document.

An Internationalization Extension

The second server behavior extension that you will create is a bit more complex. It will create an ASP.NET culture information object that determines a visitor's language. If your web site has settings specified that can accommodate that visitor (that is, it is in the appropriate language), the rest of the page is displayed. If not, the user is redirected to another page. The aim is to ensure that visitors of an international web site are presented with the content most relevant to them.

The Country Specific Data Server Behavior

You will write the final version of the code, test it, and then use the Server Behavior Builder to add the code. You do it this way because coding space in the Server Behavior Builder is limited and testing is complicated once the parameters are defined.

This server behavior has three parts. Part one imports the .NET namespaces required for internationalization. Part two opens an If statement that checks the user's browser variables, guesses the appropriate language, and then displays the contents of the web page. Part three displays a friendly message referring the user to another page and then finishes the If statement. The relevant code is shown in Figure 9-21.

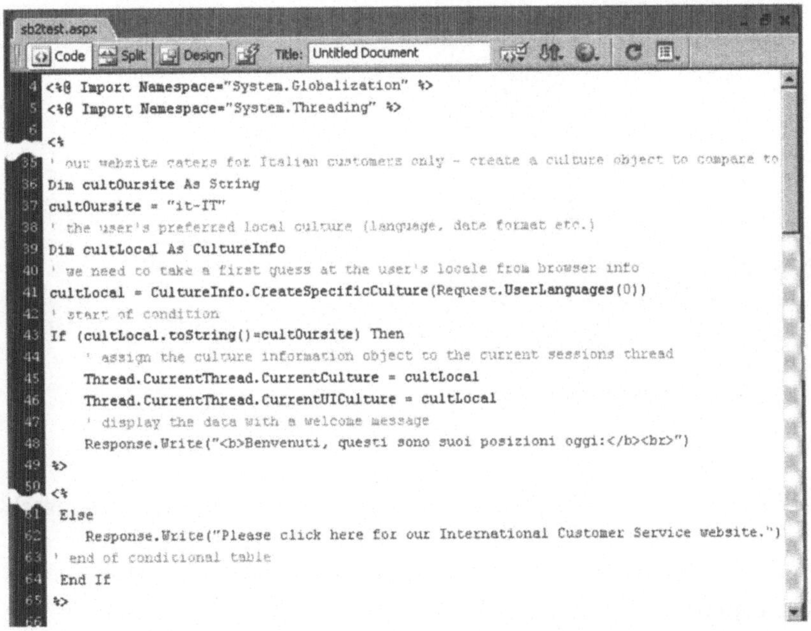

Figure 9-21. The Country Specific Data server behavior in Code view

For convenience, you will use a page similar to the one used in this chapter's first example. You will use the code from the asp:Repeater control (the finished code is in sb2test.aspx in the download).

The namespace tags are placed before the <MM:DataSet> tag, and the two remaining code blocks are placed before and after the asp:Repeater control's opening and closing tags.

In the code shown in Figure 9-21, lines 5 and 6 import the .NET namespaces needed to handle the international content properly. System.Globalization contains culture information classes, and System.Threading enables you to persist a user's preferred culture settings within a session.

Line 35 specifies that the web site caters primarily to Italian-speaking visitors, so the site's culture string is set to the W3C symbol it-IT. To make a first guess as to a web visitor's language, use the Request.UserLanguages(0) environment variable in line 41. This value is customizable in many browsers—in Internet Explorer, it can be found in the Language Preference dialog box (Tools ➤ Internet Options ➤ Languages), as shown in Figure 9-22.

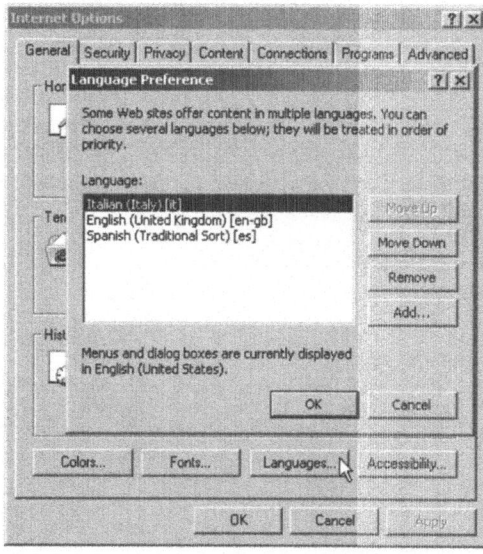

Figure 9-22. Specifying a preferred language in Internet Explorer

Lines 43 to 49 determine whether the user's preferred culture settings match those of the site, and then assign those settings to the current thread's culture properties. When Italian is set as the preferred language, the page shown in Figure 9-23 is displayed (sb2test.aspx).

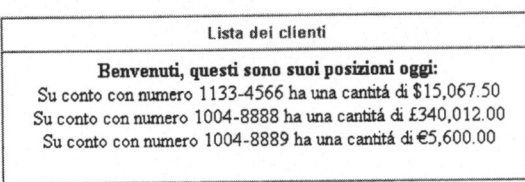

Figure 9-23. The Italian version of the web page

Anyone who does not have Italian settings will see the page shown in Figure 9-24, as specified by code lines 61 to 65.

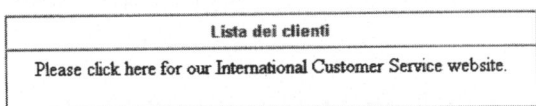

Figure 9-24. Unsupported language preferences cause this message to be displayed.

Interface: Country-Specific Data

You know the procedure by now—let's construct the server behavior interface.

1. The code is ready to go into the Server Behavior Builder, so open the New Server Behavior dialog box. Select ASP.NET VB in the Document type box, enter **Country Specific Data** as the name, as shown in Figure 9-25, and then click OK.

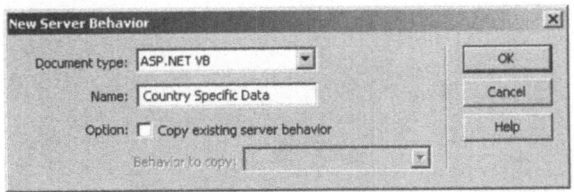

Figure 9-25. Specifying basic data for the Country Specific Data server behavior

2. To add an empty code block, click the Code blocks to insert plus sign (+) button and then click OK. Usually, the next step is to replace the code block with the first part of the server behavior code. However, do not enter the whole first block of code (lines 4 to 6). If you do, Dreamweaver will return an error (a red exclamation mark next to the block's name, as shown in Figure 9-26) because the two import namespaces are not in one common <% %> block.

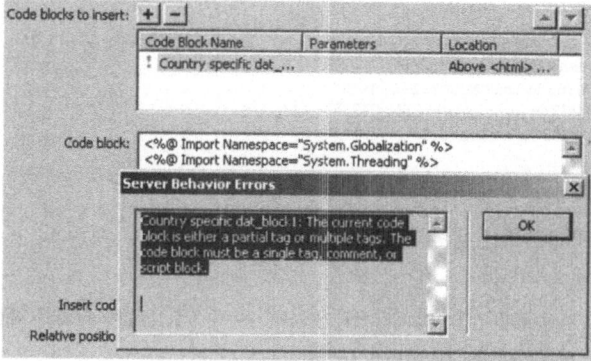

Figure 9-26. Dreamweaver reports an error if multiple code tags are used.

To avoid this problem, you must split the first block of code into two parts, one for each namespace.

3. Create two blocks of code with the following identical settings, as shown in Figure 9-27.

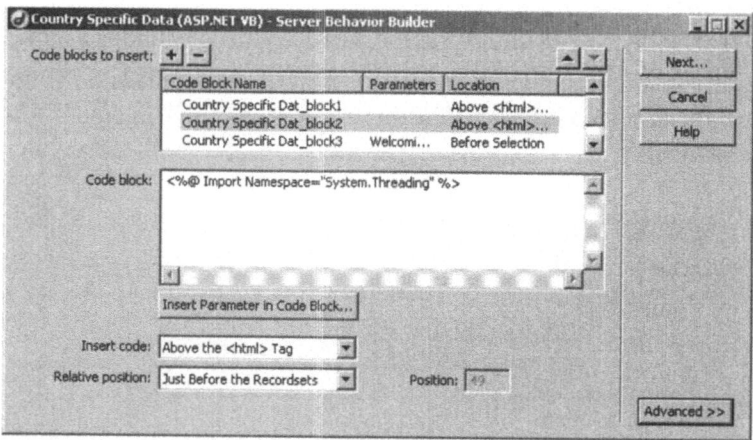

Figure 9-27. The two blocks of code must have identical settings.

Note that you specify that the code is placed above the <html> tag but not at the absolute top of the page (the @ Page directive must come first). The correct position is above any recordsets that may have been defined, which guarantees that the code blocks will be in the top section of the page. No parameters are required for these first two code blocks.

4. The remaining two sections of code will be inserted before and after a user selection. The opening If block (lines 35 to 50) requires that two parameters be defined for data that varies from one site to another. One parameter is the culture string for the web site, and the other is the welcome message. As before, highlight the data that will be requested as input (lines 35 to 50), and click the Insert Parameter in Code Block button. We used the cultOursite variable as an example, and we named it **Culture string**, as shown in Figure 9-28.

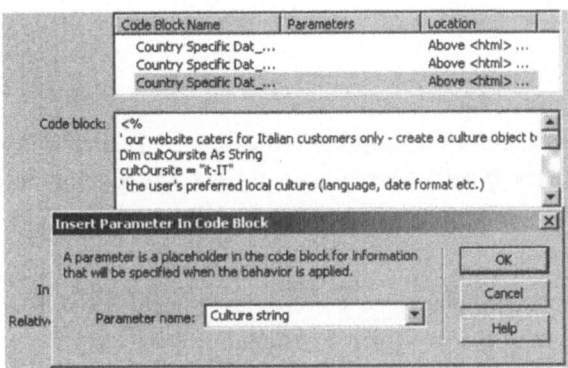

Figure 9-28. Replacing the culture string with a parameter

5. Replace the welcome message (in line 48) with a parameter named Welcoming message. The final code in the Server Behavior dialog box should appear as follows for this block:

```
<%
' our website caters for certain customers only - create a culture
object to compare to user's culture
Dim cultOursite As String
cultOursite = "@@Culture string@@"
' the user's preferred local culture (language, date format etc.)
Dim cultLocal As CultureInfo
' we need to take a first guess at the user's locale from browser info
cultLocal = CultureInfo.CreateSpecificCulture(Request.UserLanguages(0))
' start of condition
If (cultLocal.toString()=cultOursite) Then

' assign the culture information object to the current sessions thread
    Thread.CurrentThread.CurrentCulture = cultLocal
    Thread.CurrentThread.CurrentUICulture = cultLocal
' display the data with a welcome message
    Response.Write("@@Welcoming message@@")
%>
```

6. Position this block by selecting Relative to the Selection in the Insert code box, and Before the Selection in the Relative position box.

   The last block of code contains one parameter, which we will call Redirection message. The resultant code is as follows:

```
<%
 Else
      Response.Write("@@Redirection message@@")
' end of conditional table
 End If
%>
```

7. Define which block should be highlighted when the behavior is selected by choosing Country Specific Dat_block3 in the Code block to select box, as shown in Figure 9-29.

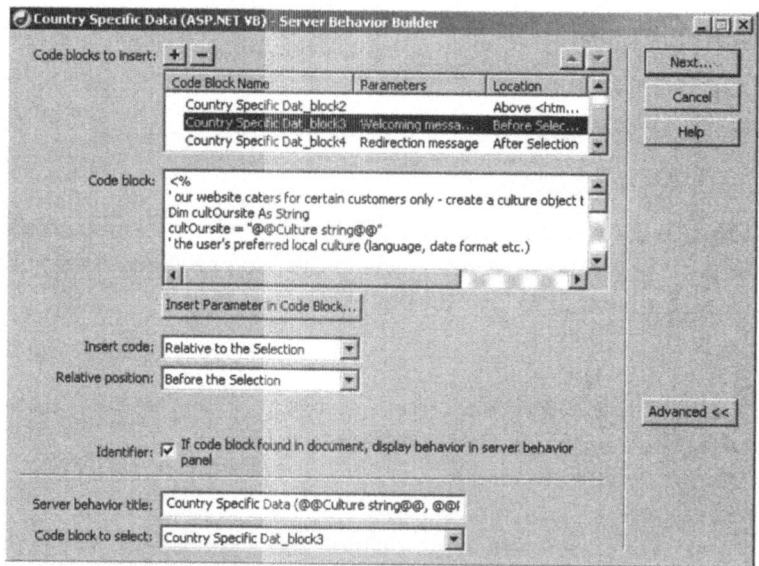

Figure 9-29. Specifying which block should be highlighted

8. Click Next to open the Generate Behavior Dialog Box.

9. Accept the default setting, as shown in Figure 9-30, and click OK to finish the building process.

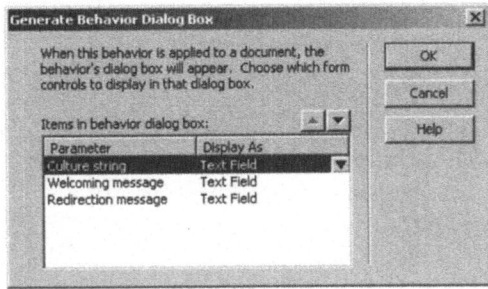

Figure 9-30. The parameters are of the default Text Field type.

The server behavior name appears in the drop-down list and can be tested with any of your pages. For example, if you had a Spanish-language web page, you could include the Country Specific Data server behavior with the data shown in Figure 9-31.

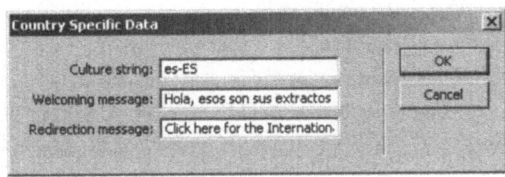

Figure 9-31. The Spanish-language Country Specific Data server behavior

Congratulations—you just extended the abilities of Dreamweaver MX 2004.

Background Helper Code: Country-Specific Data

Now that you know how to program server behavior code and interfaces, let's see what Dreamweaver does behind the scenes.

The files created by the Server Behavior Builder are stored in their specific subfolders in the Configuration folder. We will look at the second server behavior example; its files are located in [DreamweaverMX2004 installation directory]\Configuration\ServerBehaviors\ASP.NET_VB.

If you are not using Windows XP, Windows 2000, Windows NT, or Macintosh OS X, you may not have a Configuration folder separate from the program's Configuration folder. If this is the case, look for the Configuration folder here:

```
[hdd:]Documents and Settings\[your_username]\ Application
Data\Macromedia\Dreamweaver MX 2004\Configuration\ServerBehaviors\ASP.NET_VB
```

In the folder, note that Dreamweaver created the following files:

- Country Specific Data.edml

- Country Specific Dat_block1.edml

- Country Specific Dat_block2.edml

- Country Specific Dat_block3.edml

- Country Specific Dat_block4.edml

- Country Specific Data.htm

The first file, Country Specific Data.edml, is an XML file that identifies the files needed to run this server behavior. Here are the full contents of this file:

```
<group name="Country Specific Data" version="7.0"
serverBehavior="Country Specific Data.htm">
  <TITLE>Country Specific Data (@@Culture__string@@,
@@Redirection__message@@, @@Welcoming__message@@)</TITLE>
<groupParticipants selectParticipant="Country Specific Dat_block3">
  <groupParticipant name="Country Specific Dat_block1" partType="member"/>
  <groupParticipant name="Country Specific Dat_block2" partType="member"/>
  <groupParticipant name="Country Specific Dat_block3" partType="identifier" />
  <groupParticipant name="Country Specific Dat_block4" partType="member"/>
</groupParticipants>
</group>
```

This file points to the interface file and to all other participant files. The following line in this file illustrates the point made earlier about using a single code block as the identifier. If you have multiple code blocks in your server behavior, only one should be marked as the identifier.

```
<groupParticipant name="Country Specific Dat_block3" partType="identifier" />
```

Country Specific Dat_block1.edml contains the first code block to be inserted into the document once the parameters have been set. This file is also an XML file, and part of its code is used to identify the server behavior on the page. It has two methods of doing this: the complete search pattern and the quick search pattern.

```
<participant version="7.0">
  <insertText location="aboveHTML+49"><![CDATA[<%@
Import Namespace="System.Globalization" %>]]></insertText>
  <searchPatterns whereToSearch="directive">
    <searchPattern paramNames="" isOptional="false"
```

```
limitSearch="all"><![CDATA[/<%@ Import
Namespace="System\.Globalization" %>/i]]></searchPattern>
  </searchPatterns>
  <quickSearch>Namespace="System.Globalization"</quickSearch>
</participant>
```

The quick search method looks for the characters `Namespace="System.Globalization"` in the code. The `<searchPattern>` tag defines a regular expression that looks for the whole `<@ Import>` tag.

`Country Specific Data.htm` is an interface file that is used when applying this server behavior to pages. If you open this page in Dreamweaver, you can see that even a simple interface requires fairly complex code.

Next we will look at how to package an extension for distribution.

Distributing Your Extensions

If you plan on joining the thousands of developers who distribute their extensions, you will first need to package your extensions in the correct format so that anyone can install them. The Extension Manager takes care of all the extensions for Macromedia products on your computer.

These files must be formatted as Macromedia eXtension Package (MXP) files. Fortunately, you do not need to know how to build an MXP file—the Extension Manager does that for you. This powerful little program takes care of all the extensions that can be installed into any of the Macromedia products on your computer. It also acts as a packaging tool.

When building extensions, it is a good idea to set up a staging area so you can easily keep track of all the files involved. To this end, open your Configuration folders, locate the parts of the example server behavior, and copy them into your own separate staging area folder. This simply keeps things neat and tidy.

Defining the Extension Components

A Macromedia eXtension Instruction (MXI) file is an XML file that describes all properties of the server behavior, including the following:

- The name and version number of the extension

- The author's name

- A list of the products in which the extension can be installed

- A description of the extension

- The instructions on where to find the extension in the program after installation

- A list of files that are used in the server behavior and where those files should be stored on the user's computer

- Any configuration changes that need to be made to the user's installation of Dreamweaver

You can find sample MXI files here:

```
[Dreamweaver MX 2004 installation dir]\Extension Manager\Samples\Dreamweaver\
```

You can use the sample MXI file as a template by copying and modifying it, or you can use an extension called MXI Doc Type, which adds a blank MXI document type. Once you have the extension installed, you will find the new MXI file type in the Other area of the New File dialog box.

A new, empty MXI file that is ready for a server behavior looks like this:

```
<macromedia-extension
name=""
version=""
type="">

<!-- Describe the author -->
<author name="" />
<!-- List the required/compatible products -->
<products>
<product name="Dreamweaver" version="6" primary="true" />
</products>
<!-- Describe the extension -->
<description>
<![CDATA[
]]>
</description>
<!-- Describe where the extension shows in the UI of the product -->
<ui-access>
<![CDATA[
]]>
</ui-access>
<!-- Describe the files that comprise the extension -->
<files>
<file name="" destination="$dreamweaver/configuration/..." />
</files>
<!-- Describe the changes to the configuration -->
```

```
<configuration-changes>
</configuration-changes>
</macromedia-extension>
```

To build this into a working MXI file that you can use with an extension, make the following additions and alterations:

- Change the `<macromedia-extension>` tag to the extension's name.

- Change the `<author>` tag to the author's name.

- Change the text inside the square brackets of `CDATA[]` in the `<description>` tag to a description of what your extension does.

- Change the text inside the square brackets of `CDATA[]` in the `<ui-access>` tag to an explanation of how the user should access your server behavior.

- Add a `<file>` tag for each file that comprises the extension, completing the source and destination attributes.

- Specify any changed menus or other Dreamweaver components in the `<configuration-changes>` section.

The first four items are descriptive, so we will not go into detail about how to complete them. Your MXI file up to the `<ui-access>` section might look something like this:

```
<macromedia-extension
  name="Country Specific Data"
  version="1.0"
  type="Server Behavior">
    <!-- Describe the author -->
    <author name="Costas Hadjisotiriou" />
    <!-- List the required/compatible products -->
    <products>
      <product name="Dreamweaver" version="6" primary="true" />
    </products>
    <!-- Describe the extension -->
    <description>
      <![CDATA[This is an extension written for Apress.
It displays data if the visitor's browser language preference
matches the website's.
    ]]>
    </description>
    <!-- Describe where the extension shows in the UI of the product -->
```

```
<ui-access>
  <![CDATA[Access by clicking the + button in Server Behaviors tab.
  ]]>
</ui-access>
```

Next you will specify the files to include in the package and their destination when they are installed onto the user's computer. You need the files listed earlier—here they are again:

- Country Specific Data.edml

- Country Specific Dat_block1.edml

- Country Specific Dat_block2.edml

- Country Specific Dat_block3.edml

- Country Specific Dat_block4.edml

- Country Specific Data.htm

Unfortunately, there is a slight problem. To ensure transportability between Apple and PC workstations, Dreamweaver does not allow file names to have more than 31 characters, so the names of the files have been truncated. However, these file names still have 32 characters. The four-letter .edml extension spoiled Dreamweaver's arithmetic, so you must rename the files.

After you have renamed the files, you can complete the <files> section. To define file paths, use the $dreamweaver variable, which points to the correct installation path (whether on a multiuser computer or not). In our example, the <files> section looks like this:

```
<!-- Describe the files that comprise the extension -->
<files>
  <file name="Country Specific Data.edml"
destination="$dreamweaver/configuration/ServerBehaviors/ASP.NET_VB" />
  <file name="Country Specific Da_block1.edml"
destination="$dreamweaver/configuration/ServerBehaviors/ASP.NET_VB" />
  <file name="Country Specific Da_block2.edml"
destination="$dreamweaver/configuration/ServerBehaviors/ASP.NET_VB" />
  <file name="Country Specific Da_block3.edml"
destination="$dreamweaver/configuration/ServerBehaviors/ASP.NET_VB" />
  <file name="Country Specific Da_block4.edml"
destination="$dreamweaver/configuration/ServerBehaviors/ASP.NET_VB" />
  <file name="Country Specific Data.htm"
destination="$dreamweaver/configuration/ServerBehaviors/ASP.NET_VB" />
</files>
```

This instructs Dreamweaver to install each named file into the user's configuration folders at the specified subfolders. If you include images in your server behavior interface or in any documentation that you want to install on the user's system, you need to create a separate file-source line for each image and ensure that it gets installed to the relevant directory in the configuration structure.

The `<configuration-changes>` section can be left blank because you are not modifying any menus. Placing the files in the Configuration/ServerBehaviors/ directory ensures that they will appear in the Server Behavior list. However, if you created a command called newcommand, for example, and you wanted it to appear in the Commands menu and in your own submenu, you would use the following code:

```
<configuration-changes>
  <menu-insert appendTo="DWMenu_Commands">
    <menu name="New Menu Name" id="DWMenu_Commands_Menu_Name">
    </menu>
  </menu-insert>
  <menu-insert appendTo="DWMenu_Commands_Menu_Name">
    <menuitem name="New menu item here" file="newhtmlcommandfile.htm"
              id="A_new_Unique_Identification_String_Here" />
  </menu-insert>
</configuration-changes>
```

The first `<menu-insert>` tag adds a folder to the Commands menu called New Menu Name. The second `<menu-insert>` tag adds a menu item to that folder and references the newhtmlcommandfile.htm file that this particular command uses.

The completed MXI file for the Country Specific Data server behavior should look like this:

```
<macromedia-extension
  name="Country Specific Data"
  version="1.0"
  type="Server Behavior">
  <!-- Describe the author -->
  <author name="Costas Hadjisotiriou" />
  <!-- List the required/compatible products -->
  <products>
    <product name="Dreamweaver" version="6" primary="true" />
  </products>
  <!-- Describe the extension -->
  <description>
    <![CDATA[This is an extension written for Apress.
It displays data if the visitor's browser language preference
matches the website's.
    ]]>
```

```
  </description>
  <!-- Describe where the extension shows in the UI of the product -->
  <ui-access>
    <![CDATA[Access by clicking the + button in Server Behaviors tab.
    ]]>
  </ui-access>
  <!-- Describe the files that comprise the extension -->
  <files>
    <file name="Country Specific Data.edml"
destination="$dreamweaver/configuration/ServerBehaviors/ASP.NET_VB" />
    <file name="Country Specific Da_block1.edml"
destination="$dreamweaver/configuration/ServerBehaviors/ASP.NET_VB" />
    <file name="Country Specific Da_block2.edml"
destination="$dreamweaver/configuration/ServerBehaviors/ASP.NET_VB" />
    <file name="Country Specific Da_block3.edml"
destination="$dreamweaver/configuration/ServerBehaviors/ASP.NET_VB" />
    <file name="Country Specific Da_block4.edml"
destination="$dreamweaver/configuration/ServerBehaviors/ASP.NET_VB" />
    <file name="Country Specific Data.htm"
destination="$dreamweaver/configuration/ServerBehaviors/ASP.NET_VB" />
  </files>
  <!-- Describe the changes to the configuration -->
  <configuration-changes>
  </configuration-changes>
</macromedia-extension>
```

Save the MXI file as Country.mxi. The files stored in your staging area (with their shortened file names) should look as shown in Figure 9-32.

Country Specific Dat_block1.edml
Country Specific Dat_block2.edml
Country Specific Dat_block3.edml
Country Specific Dat_block4.edml
Country Specific Data.edml
Country Specific Data.htm
Country.mxi

Figure 9-32. The extension's component files

You can now begin the relatively simple packaging process, which will create the MXP file.

Assembling the Extension Components

The Extension Manager creates MXP files for you. There are two ways to start the packaging process. The first method is to double-click the MXI file. If your file associations are set up correctly, this opens the Extension Manager and automatically starts the packaging process. To use the second method, follow these steps:

1. Open the Extension Manager. Make sure Dreamweaver MX 2004 is selected in the drop-down list, and then select File ➤ Package Extension, as shown in Figure 9-33.

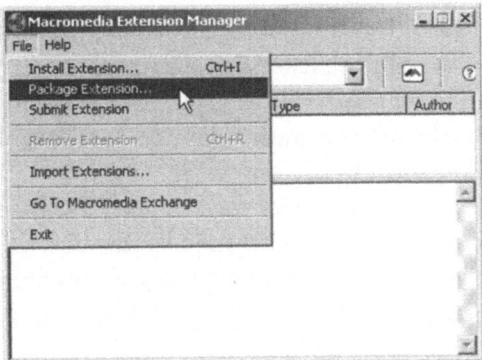

Figure 9-33. Packaging the extension via the Extension Manager

2. Browse to and select Country.mxi. Then select a location in which to save the packaged extension—the current folder is a good choice, so simply click Save. The Extension Manager gives the MXP file the same name as the MXI file by default, as shown in Figure 9-34.

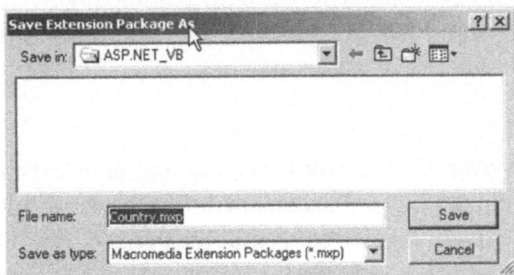

Figure 9-34. Saving the extension as an MXP file

3. Click OK in the dialog box that tells you the extension has been packaged and created successfully.

Your extension has not been installed; it has simply been packaged. The original build of this extension is in your Dreamweaver configuration, which is why you can see and use it in the Server Behaviors panel, but it does not appear in the Extension Manager's list of currently installed extensions.

In the next section, you will test the new MXP file to make sure that it installs everything correctly.

Installing Extensions

Installing extensions is a very straightforward practice. Near the beginning of the MXI file, there is a declaration that tells the Extension Manager which products are compatible with this extension. In the example, you built a Dreamweaver MX 2004 extension, which is denoted by the declaration version="6". This makes it compatible with version 6 and version 7 of Dreamweaver.

You can install server behaviors in one of two ways. If you have the file associations correctly configured on your computer, you can simply double-click an MXP file and the Extension Manager begins the installation process immediately. To use the other method, follow these steps:

1. Open the Extension Manager, and click the Install New Extension button on the toolbar.

2. Select the MXP file, and then click Install to start the process. You will be prompted to accept the disclaimer of liability from Macromedia. Click Accept (if you accept it) and the installation will continue. If you have an older version of the extension already installed, you can update it with the newer version. If you have a newer version already installed, you will be informed of that via a message box.

   You are prompted to overwrite any files that might already exist in your configuration. If you install several extensions from the same author, for example, that author might use the same graphic in his or her user interface. When the installation is complete, the Extension Manager will display a message informing you of the successful installation. The extension will then be listed in the Extension Manager's interface, as shown in Figure 9-35.

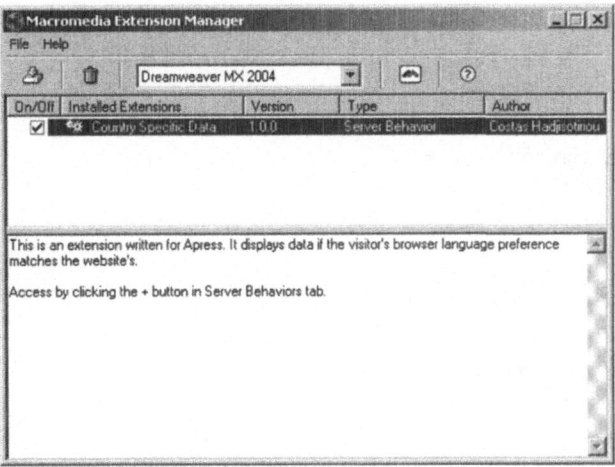

Figure 9-35. The installed extension appears in the Extension Manager.

If Dreamweaver was open while you were installing the extension, you might be prompted to restart Dreamweaver.

The Extension Manager also allows you to quickly "turn off" extensions without having to uninstall them first. You do this by clearing the check box next to the extension in the On/Off column.

Extension Resources

There are hundreds of extensions available at various sites on the Internet. The following list of URLs will provide links to just some of the many Dreamweaver MX 2004 extensions that are not available on the Macromedia Exchange. This list is definitely not exhaustive.

- http://www.macromedia.com/exchange, the official Macromedia extensions exchange

- http://dreamweaverfever.com/

- http://dwmxextensions.com/

- http://dwteam.com/

- http://www.dreamweavermxsupport.com/extensions

- http://www.basic-ultradev.com/

- http://www.fourlevel.com/

- http://www.interakt.ro/

- http://www.kaosweaver.com/

- http://www.massimocorner.com/

- http://www.projectseven.com/

- http://www.thechocolatestore.com/ultradev/

- http://www.dmxzone.com/

- http://www.ultrasuite.com/

- http://www.udzone.com/

- http://www.yaromat.com/dw/

Summary

This chapter focused on extending the server-side capabilities of Dreamweaver by building simple server behaviors that formatted a currency field and displayed internationalized data.

Server behaviors are only one aspect of the extensibility of Dreamweaver MX 2004. There is plenty of room to add behaviors, commands, and objects, too. Unfortunately, there is no mechanism like the Server Behavior Builder to help you build these other types of extensions. Instead you can employ your JavaScript skills and get to work writing them by hand.

For a great learning resource, dive into Dreamweaver's configuration folder and open some of the behaviors, commands, and objects to see how they work.

CHAPTER 10

Debugging and Error Handling

BEFORE YOU CAN FIX an error, you must have a good understanding of its cause and nature, so in this chapter, we begin by looking at some of the errors that can occur in ASP.NET. We then outline some coding practices that reduce the likelihood of errors occurring in the first place. We show you how to debug, correct, and handle ASP.NET errors with the facilities available in Dreamweaver MX. We also provide links to online sources of information throughout the chapter.

Bear in mind that covering ASP.NET errors in detail is beyond the scope of this book. Rather, we will look at general ways to identify coding errors, track down their origins, and correct them.

Types of Errors

To be able to fix errors, you must be able to recognize them. We start, therefore, with a look at the different kinds of coding errors that can occur, how they present themselves, and where and when they appear.

Incorrect Namespaces

If you import the wrong namespaces into your pages, you will get an error telling you that some ASP.NET functions are not defined. To correct such an error, start by checking whether you included the right `<%@ Import %>` statement at the top of your page.

You may want to get in the habit of explicitly writing the fully qualified namespaces by hand instead of importing them—this often removes ambiguities. In the following example, it is unclear which declared namespace the Image declaration came from, so you get a compilation error:

```
<%@ Import Namespace="System.Drawing"%>
<%@ Import Namespace="System.Web.UI.WebControls" %>
<script runat="server" >
Dim ambiguous As Image
</script>
```

To remove the ambiguity, you can simply write the following:

```
Dim ambiguous As System.Drawing.Image
```

For information on importing namespaces (and other page directives), see the MSDN page `http://msdn.microsoft.com/library/default.asp?url=/library/en-us/vbcon/html/vboriDirectivesForASPXPages.asp`.

Syntax Errors

Typos and bad code "grammar" cause most errors. Many code editors provide friendly color coding and predictive typing, but there is always some code that needs to be customized by hand.

Syntax errors are more likely to occur when you are switching between programming languages or when you are copying and combining existing code. The good news is that most editors are good at detecting the exact location of a syntax error. The bad news is that they are not perfect. Nested `If...Then` statements and loops often confuse compilers. Look at the following code snippet:

```
20:  Sub Page_Load()
21:   if (condition) Then
22:     'do one thing
23:   else
24:     'do another
25:     if (condition) Then
26:       'do one thing
27:     else
28:       'do another
29:     'end if
30:     'more lines here
31:   end if
32:   end Sub
```

There is a comment in the `End If` statement in line 29. However, if you run this code, you will get the error message shown in Figure 10-1.

Compiler Error Message: BC30081: 'If' must end with a matching 'End If'.

Source Error:

```
Line 21: if (condition) Then
Line 22: 'do one thing
Line 23: else
Line 24: 'do another
Line 25: if (condition) Then
```

Figure 10-1. Compilers cannot always identify errors in nested If...Then *statements.*

You are directed to line 23 because there is no matching End If for the If statement. However, looking closely at the indentation of the code, you can see that it is in fact the other If statement that has no matching End If. The compiler does not use indentation as a guide, so it matches the first End If it finds (line 31) with the nearest If (line 25).

This example at least gave you a relevant error message. Unfortunately, not all error messages are this straightforward and relevant. SQL statements, especially those that contain variables that will be determined at runtime, often give errors that are very difficult to decipher.

We will use the following OleDbDataAdapter statement and the subsequent dataset creation (assume conn is an existing database connection) as an example:

```
Sub Page_Load()
sqlCommand = new OleDbDataAdapter("SELECT stillfree FROM qryResults ➡
WHERE (Course=""" & Request.Form("course") & """ ➡
AND examDate=#" & Request.Form("examDate") & "#)", conn)

rs = New DataSet()
sqlCommand.Fill(rs)
End Sub
```

As you can see, there are plenty of double quotes and pound signs to confuse you. A mistake in the spelling of the SQL statement will cause an ADO.NET error whose cause will be very difficult to find. For example, if you misspelled the column name stillfree as stllfree, you would get the error shown in Figure 10-2.

No value given for one or more required parameters.

Description: An unhandled exception occurred during the execution of the current web request. Please review the stack trace for more information about the error and where it originated in the code.

Exception Details: System.Data.OleDb.OleDbException: No value given for one or more required parameters.

Source Error:

```
Line 48:
Line 49:     rs = new DataSet()
Line 50:     sqlCommand.Fill(rs)
Line 51:
Line 52: ' display results
```

Figure 10-2. This error is even less helpful than the last one.

 TIP   *To ensure that a SQL statement is correct, store it in a local variable and print it via* Response.Write *statements during design. You can then copy the presented SQL from the page's source, paste it into a query in your database, and test it. This simple trick can save you time and effort.*

If you are working on a large-scale project, it might be safer to transfer all SQL execution into stored procedures that are more easily tested. In addition, Microsoft supplies some SQL debugging tools at http://msdn.microsoft.com/library/default.asp?url=/library/en-us/vsdebug/html/_core_debugging_sql.asp.

Other syntax error types can be caused by variable names that are too similar or that confuse the programmer, or by simple carelessness when specifying data types and the like. For more information, see "Avoiding Coding Errors Through Good Coding Practices" later in this chapter.

Programming errors aside, there can also be problems with your web page's source. Errors in your markup language have traditionally been forgiven by accommodating browsers, but this is changing with XHTML and other markup languages, such as WML and XML. Dreamweaver MX has features that prevent such markup problems, and we will cover them later in this chapter.

Runtime Errors

Let's now assume that you corrected all the misspellings in your code. However, when you try to run your pages, you get runtime error messages if you are lucky and incorrect results if you are not. Let's see what could be causing these errors.

Logical Errors

Logical errors can be separated into two broad types: faulty algorithm design and mistakes in the coding. There is not a lot you can do with the first variety—take care in the design phase. Let's look at where the second type can occur.

Examine the following two ASP.NET subroutines. One calls the other, and the result from the call is assigned to an ASP.NET label. (The code in the example is from debug.aspx in the download code.)

```
Sub Page_Load()
  Dim intSample As Integer
  Dim strSample As String
  intSample=2
  strSample="12"
  Call somesub(intSample, strSample)
End Sub

Sub somesub(password As String, loopnum As Integer)
  Dim i As Integer
  For i = 1 To loopnum
    password &= password
  Next
  message.Text = password
End Sub
...
<asp:Label runat="server" id="message" ></asp:Label>
```

The call to the somesub subroutine passes two parameters, an integer and a string, in that order. The somesub subroutine receives them in the reverse order, which does not cause an error message because there is no loss of data in the type conversion.

The result from the code is a series of 12 "2" characters via 12 loops. However, the Call somesub(intSample, strSample) was supposed to concatenate two "12" characters via two loops. You can imagine how difficult it would be to spot the erroneous results, especially if they were used later in the code.

Some editors can present the programmer with the data type of the parameters expected when a subroutine is called. For example, if the somesub code has already been written, as soon as you type the opening parenthesis after Call somesub, Visual Studio .NET completes it by adding the following:

```
(password As String, loopnum As Integer)
```

Unfortunately, Dreamweaver is not so helpful.

There is no guaranteed way to avoid or detect this type of logical error, but as you will see later, there are some facilities within VB .NET that can help. As a general rule, take great care when transferring parameters between functions and subroutines.

Configuration Errors

The errors that result from configuration settings can also be quite tricky to find. For example, you can detect problems with session state only after you request a session. Let's use the following scenario as an example: Your application is hosted in a multiserver environment. You upload your application (which worked fine on your stand-alone testing server) to the hosted directory, but every page you request gives an error message telling you that it is impossible to set up a session. This is a problem with either the hosting environment or your configuration settings. You might have the following statement in your web.config file:

```
<sessionState mode="InProc"
stateConnectionString="tcpip=127.0.0.1:42424"
cookieless="false" timeout="20" />
```

The parameter mode="InProc", which is the web.config default, tells ASP.NET to store session state in the ASP.NET worker process. Usually, though, this is incompatible with shared-hosted environments because there is more than one machine with an ASP.NET process that can serve a request. The parameter must be changed to mode="StateServer". This value indicates that the state will be maintained by an external process, as specified by the value of stateConnectionString.

Another common web.config-related error is caused by neglecting to change the path to the database once your application is deployed to the live server. For example, if you added a database connection in your project, your web.config file might contain the following entry pointing to the database file:

```
<configuration>
  <appSettings>
...
    <add key="MM_CONNECTION_STRING_myconn"
value="Provider=Microsoft.Jet.OLEDB.4.0;Data
Source=C:\Inetpub\wwwroot\mx2004\mydatabase.mdb;
Persist Security Info=false" />
...
  </appSettings>
</configuration>
```

Your production server, however, will very likely have a different directory structure, so it is important to remember to change it appropriately.

Issues such as these can be quite difficult to unearth until very late in the development, so it is important to perform an early deployment test to iron out these kinds of issues.

Object Interaction

You are programming in an object-oriented environment, so technically, every-thing could count as object interaction, but you are most concerned with external objects. In the following example, the application accesses a Simple Mail Transfer Protocol (SMTP) server called mail-fwd to send an email:

```VB
<%@ Import Namespace="System.Web.Mail" %>
...
  <script language="VB" runat="" server">
    Sub Page_Load(sender As Object, E as EventArgs)
    Try
      Dim Mailer As MailMessage
      Mailer = New MailMessage()

      SmtpMail.SmtpServer = "mail-fwd"
      SmtpMail.Send(Mailer)
        Response.Write("Mail sent successfully")
      Catch ex As Exception
        Response.Write("Your message was not sent: " + ex.Message)
      End Try
    End Sub
  </script>
```

The condition of the mail server is beyond the application's control, so you might get a runtime error if the server is down or too busy. There is clearly no way to completely protect yourself, but you can use the Try...Catch statement (new to VB .NET) to provide a graceful exit.

Client-Side Errors

If you have programmed in JavaScript before, you know that there is no better way to guarantee reliability than by testing your client script on various browsers. Dreamweaver MX has a great JavaScript debugger that catches virtually all errors. But after all the syntax errors have been fixed, there may still be some issues lurking in the code.

Some problems may arise if your JavaScript code is on the top of the page, and if it is executed before the HTML it is accessing is completely loaded. Advanced ASP.NET programmers know that there is a way to register client script so this does not happen. For details, see http://www.fawcette.com/vsm/2002_12/online/hottips/delcogliano.

Finally, client-side errors may simply be a late manifestation of a server-side error. From the moment the ASP.NET page runs on the server, there is no way to programmatically check how the produced script will perform on the client. Web programmers need to think two steps ahead and provide adequate client-side error-trapping code.

Avoiding Coding Errors Through Good Coding Practices

Good coding practices means making sure your code meets the following standards:

- The code is formatted and indented consistently.

- The code uses a logical variable naming convention.

- The variables are declared explicitly.

- The data types are converted explicitly.

- The code is structured properly.

- The code is commented properly.

- The code has been tested thoroughly.

Code Formatting

Earlier in this chapter, you saw that you could quickly detect which If statement was erroneous by looking at the code indentation. Code formatting gives you a quick picture of the logic behind the code, and it is a very efficient way of detecting omissions when dealing with many lines of code.

Variable Naming

Although some programmers find variable naming restrictive, many find that it helps detect data type errors. When naming variables, remember the following rules:

- Be consistent with your naming convention.

- Give your variables meaningful names.

The Hungarian notation adds a prefix to every variable's name to declare its data type. For example, a string variable's name begins with str, an integer variable's name begins with int, and so on. However, if you change a variable's data type, you must remember to change the variable's prefix as well. To see the full list of prefixes in VB, visit http://support.microsoft.com/default.aspx?scid=kb;en-us;173738.

In ASP.NET, it makes no difference in memory whether your variable name is long or short, so assign a descriptive name that gives some insight into what the variable contains. Clearly, the name myVar is not as descriptive as TotalRevenueBeforeTax. On the other hand, though, it is easier to mistype long variable names, so you will need to strike a balance.

You can also capitalize the first letter of each component word of the variable name to enable easier reading. This convention is called **Pascal case**. This convention is particularly helpful in instances when it is easy to confuse two similar characters, for example, the numeral 1 and the lowercase letter L.

Variable Declaration

All versions of VB have traditionally been permissive about variable declaration and initialization; that is, they did not require variables to be declared explicitly. However, declaring variables explicitly is one of the best programming habits you will ever acquire. Declaring variables explicitly entails the following:

- Declaring every variable you use in your code (for example, Dim someVariable)

- Declaring each variable's data type (for example, Dim someVariable As String)

- Initializing each variable's values (for example, follow Dim someVariable As String with someVariable = "InitialValue")

- Destroying each variable after you are finished working with it (for example, someVariable=Nothing)

The last item is often ignored by programmers because of the proliferation of garbage-collection facilities, which automatically set variables to nothing and reclaim the memory they used. Garbage collection affects performance, though, and leaving a variable in memory can prevent effective performance of your applications. For more information, see the related MSDN article at http:// msdn.microsoft.com/msdnmag/issues/1100/GCI/default.aspx.

Data Type Conversions

Although permissive semantics made VB easier to learn, implicit data type casting can let coding errors slip through undetected. **Implicit data type casting** means assigning a value of one type to a variable of a different type, which automatically adjusts the variable type. *Explicit* data type conversion functions, however, make the intention of the programmer clearer and help avoid the accidental loss of data upon conversion.

Structuring Your Code

By dividing your code's tasks into individual functions or subroutines, you make it easier to find errors. Doing this also makes it more likely that you will find any logical errors before deployment.

Commenting Code

Comments make your code easier to understand when you (or your colleagues) revisit it at a later date. For example, at the beginning of each subroutine, include a comment that details that subroutine's purpose and the purpose of its results. Be careful that you do not go overboard (for example, describing every variable)— comment it at an appropriate level for you and your peers.

Testing and Retesting

Test your application intensively. Test it with values that it is likely to receive and also with unpredictable values, such as out-of-bounds variables, variables of the wrong data type, and so on. Make sure some nonprogrammers test it as well. The users of the application can often find errors that you overlooked.

Debugging Your Scripts

Now let's look at how ASP.NET and VB .NET facilitate debugging and error-free coding. If you have worked with ASP before, you may already be familiar with the Microsoft Script Debugger, which is included with Internet Information Services (IIS).

1. To use the Microsoft Script Debugger, click Start ➤ Programs ➤ Administrative Tools ➤ Internet Information Services. Then right-click your web site and click Properties ➤ Home Directory tab ➤ Configuration. The Application Configuration dialog box appears, as shown in Figure 10-3.

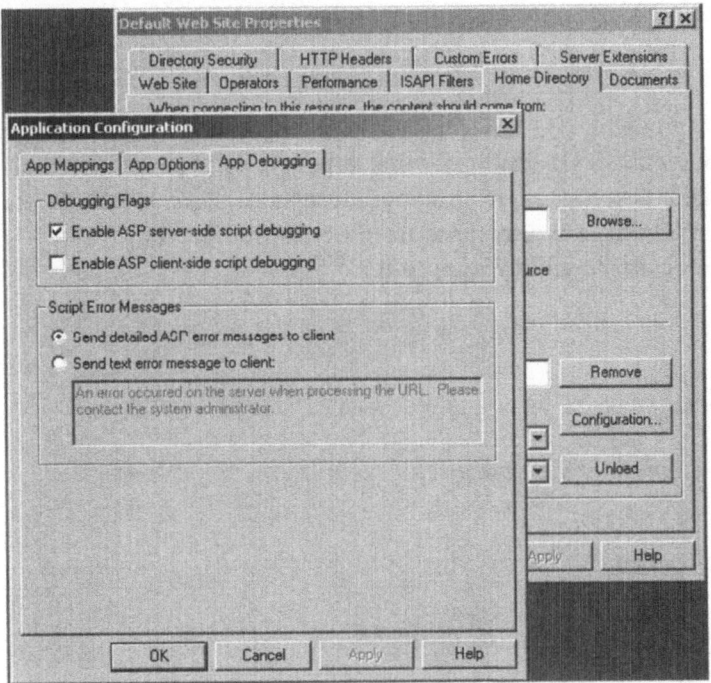

Figure 10-3. The Application Configuration dialog box

2. On the App Debugging tab, select the Enable ASP server-side script debugging check box. This specifies that the Microsoft Script Debugger will appear every time there is an error in an ASP page. Leave the Send detailed ASP error messages to client option selected. In Figure 10-4, the last End If statement is commented out.

```
Microsoft Script Debugger
File  Edit  View  Debug  Window  Help

File  🗋 📂 🔚 | Edit  🔏 📋 📋 ✕ ▣ | Debug 🔚 🔃 🔐 🔳 🔳 🔳 | 🖐 ✋ | 🔳 🔳 🔳

Read only: asp2day2/homeasp.asp

      If Not (rs.EOF And rs.BOF) Then
         Response.Write("There are " & rs("stillfree") & " remaining pla
      If rs("stillfree")>0 Then
         Response.Write("Click <a href=booking.asp>here</a> to book.")
      End If
      Else
         Response.Write("There are 5 places available for your selection
      End If
      rs.Close
      conn.Close
      Set rs = Nothing
      Set conn = Nothing
   'End If
   %>
            <br><FORM name="examform" action="homeasp.asp" method="get">

Ready                                              Ln 123
```

Figure 10-4. The Microsoft Script Debugger interface

A version of the Script Debugger that supports .aspx pages is included with Visual Studio. It can also be downloaded from http://www.microsoft.com/ddk/debugging/default.asp. To debug scripts in Dreamweaver, simply preview them in your browser, as shown in Figure 10-5.

Figure 10-5. Previewing your page

.NET Debugging

Let's look at some debugging issues specific to .NET.

Debugging Unpublished Pages

Setting the Debug="true" parameter of the @ Page directive allows meaningful debugging information to be displayed in your browser. This information is pretty comprehensive, even without the variable watch abilities of the Script Debugger. Obviously, you do not want end users to receive this much detail about your code, so remember to set it back to Debug="false" once you have finished debugging your code.

Tracing is the process of writing information to a file or output page while an application is running. To trace the flow of execution of your pages, use the

Trace.Write method. By default, trace information is presented at the bottom of each page where tracing is enabled. To enable tracing, either add `<%@ Page Trace="true" %>` to the top of the page or add the following in your web.config file:

```
<system.web><trace enabled="true" pageOutput="true" />
</system.web>
```

If you set pageOutput="true", the trace information will be displayed on the client computer at the bottom of each ASP.NET page. If you disable pageOutput, trace information is written to memory instead. It can be viewed in a file called trace.axd, which is stored at the root of the application. To view it, simply open your browser and type its URL in the Address bar.

```
http://localhost/[your application's path]/trace.axd
```

Debugging Published Pages

You can debug pages that have already been uploaded. Say, for example, that you are looking for incorrect flows in an application. To keep track of the flow, you can use the Trace.Write method in every page that you want to debug. To allow users to continue viewing your portal without getting error messages, modify the web.config entry by adding the localOnly attribute.

```
<trace enabled="true" localOnly="true" pageOutput="true" />
```

The localOnly attribute specifies that the trace output will be displayed only to users who access the web application via http://localhost.

Remote Debugging

If you have advanced remote debugging requirements, you must have remote debugging set up on the development machine. You will also need to use the Visual Studio .NET debugger. VS .NET enables remote debugging for native code, managed code, scripts, and even SQL Server. For more information, please refer to http://msdn.microsoft.com/library/default.asp?url=/library/en-us/vsdebug/html/vxtskaspremotedebuggingsetup.asp.

Programming the Debug and Trace Classes

You can add tracing and debugging instrumentation to your .NET application when you develop it, and you can use that instrumentation while developing the application and after deploying it. Trace and debug classes are essentially identical; the only difference is that debug classes are not compiled for final builds, whereas trace classes are. Both can be used to record information about errors and application execution to logs, text files, or other devices for later analysis.

To add debug or tracing code, you must first define a listener. The following is an example of a page with code containing debug instructions:

```
<%@ Page Language="vb" AutoEventWireup="true" Debug="true"  %>
<%@ Import Namespace="System.Diagnostics" %>
<%@ Import Namespace="System.IO" %>
<script runat="server" >

Sub Page_Load()
  Debug.Listeners.Remove("mynewlog")
  Debug.Listeners.Add(new
 TextWriterTraceListener("C:\Inetpub\wwwroot\mx2004\ch10\debugme.log",
"mynewlog"))
  Debug.WriteLine("I am in Sub Page_Load")
  ' some code execution here
  Debug.WriteLine("Everything still fine")
  ' some more risky actions here
  Debug.WriteLine("Continuing... ")
  ' a more direct debugging method
  Response.Write("I am in Sub Page_Load")
  anothersub()
End Sub
Sub anothersub()
  Debug.WriteLine("I am in Sub anothersub")
  Debug.Close
End Sub
</script>
```

You first import the necessary namespaces: System.Diagnostics for the debugging classes and System.IO for writing to a debug file. You then remove and re-create a debug listener. This is a special class to which any subsequent Debug.Write classes will be directed. The listener can write to a file, to the console (the default), or to other media.

In this example, we create a file called debug.log and name it mynewlog. The code is then executed, and the Debug.WriteLine classes send the information to mynewlog. The data is not written to the file until we call Debug.Close. We can then open the file in an editor to analyze the output.

```
I am in Sub Page_Load
Everything still fine
Continuing...
I am in Sub anothersub
```

Remember to set Debug="true" and Trace="true" in your page or in the web.config file, or this will not work.

Tracing and debugging in this way can be very powerful. To learn more, see the MSDN literature at http://msdn.microsoft.com/library/default.asp?url=/library/en-us/vbcon/html/vboriInstrumentationTechniquesDebugTraceForNETFramework.asp.

Error Handling in ASP.NET

Another way to ensure that your application does not fail at runtime is to use error-detection and error-handling methods. Just in case your code is not completely bug free, you can program in a way that hides the disastrous consequences of coding errors from the user.

The .NET Framework treats code errors in ASP.NET pages just like any other .NET errors, whether they occur in configuration, Windows forms, or elsewhere. An ASP.NET page has a specific error-handling subroutine, Page_Error, that is raised when the page encounters an unhandled exception. You can override this subroutine by writing error-handling code that allows the execution of the page to continue. Keep in mind, though, that this is really only a safety net—you should still deal with errors locally, where they occur.

Try, Catch, Finally Statements

We already showed you this structure:

```
Sub TestVBNET()
  Try
    ' Do something in here that
    ' might raise an error.
  Catch
    ' Handle exceptions that occur within
    ' the Try block, here.
  Finally
    ' Perform cleanup code in here.
  End Try
End Sub
```

The first section of the structure is a Try statement. It executes some code that might fail during runtime for reasons beyond the program's control. As a simple example, the following is a piece of code that tries to open a file:

```
Private Sub SimpleException()
  Dim lngSize As Long
  Dim s As FileStream
  Try
' retrieve a user-defined path from TextBox txtFileName and open the file
    s = File.Open(txtFileName.Text, FileMode.Open)
' force the reading of the whole file in memory
    lngSize = s.Length
    s.Close()
  Catch e As Exception
    Response.Write(e.ToString)
  Finally
    Response.Write("this may have worked ... or not")
  End Try
End Sub
```

As you can see, you can use these statements for debugging purposes, too. The Catch e As Exception line enables you to manipulate the Exception object (which is new to VB .NET) to present useful information or take distinct action. Table 10-1 summarizes the members of the Exception object.

Table 10-1. Members of the Exception Object

Member	Description
HelpLink	A link to the help file associated with this exception
InnerException	A reference to the exception instance that caused the current exception
Message	The error message text
StackTrace	The stack trace (as a single string) at the point the error occurred
TargetSite	The name of the method that raised the exception
ToString	A method that converts the exception name, the description, and the current stack dump into a single string

Code that should be unconditionally executed is placed in the Finally block. Note that you can place Finally blocks by themselves without a Catch block. Also, you can nest Try...Catch blocks within Try, Catch, or Finally blocks. This allows you to manage exception handling with as much depth as you require.

On Error Commands

Another way to handle errors in VB .NET is via the On Error commands. You can use these commands to suppress error messages and system actions, handle them appropriately, or clear the error and resume execution. Here is an example of such defensive programming:

```
<%@ Page Language="vb" AutoEventWireup="true" Debug="true"  %>
<script runat="server" >
Sub Page_Load()
    ' Produce division by 0 error
    On Error Resume Next
    Dim zero As Integer = 0
    Dim result As Integer
    result = 8 / zero
    ' error has occurred but we are resuming at this next statement
    Select Case Err.Number
        Case 0
        ' no error
        Case 6, 11
            Response.Write("Some variable must have been 0")
            result = 12
        Case Else
            Response.Write(Err.Description)
            result = 12
    End Select
    ' Err.Clear()
    ' second Err.Description call prints empty strings if above is uncommented
    Response.Write(Err.Description)
End Sub
</script>'''""'
```

This code first creates an error by dividing by zero. Because of the On Error Resume Next statement, the code continues to the next line of code, which is a Select statement that examines the special Err object. This object contains the last error that occurred and its properties. VB errors 6 and 11 represent overflow and the division by zero respectively. By capturing the occurrence of an error, you can present a custom message on your page, let it default to the error's description, or set the variable result to a default value. Finally, the error is cleared by calling the Clear method. For more information, see http://msdn.microsoft.com/library/default.asp?url=/library/en-us/vblr7/html/vaidxErrors.asp?frame=true.

Option Statements

The Option Strict statement determines whether conversions and operations on Object are governed by strict or permissive semantics. To specify that strict semantics should be used, place Option Strict On at the beginning of each Code Behind file, or set <%@ Page Language="vb" strict="true" %> for a single ASPX page. Strict semantics requires the following:

- Narrowing conversions cannot be used without an explicit cast operator. This means conversions in which there is the possibility of loss of data and inaccurate results are not allowed. Note that widening conversions are allowed.

- The As clause cannot be omitted in a declaration.

- Late binding is not allowed. This means you cannot declare a variable as type Object and define the specific type of object during runtime. The following example causes late binding:

```
Dim anObject As Object
anObject= "this now becomes a String variable because this is a string".
```

  The following example causes early binding:

```
Dim anObject As String
```

- Operations on Object other than =, <>, TypeOf...Is, and Is are not allowed.

The Option statement can also be set to Option Explicit Off, which demands only that all variables be declared with the Dim statement before they are used. You may find it easier to program with this setting if you are porting an old application that did not declare variables.

Debugging the script is only part of the story when ensuring your application's success. Dreamweaver can also help you with markup language code.

Coding Assistance in Dreamweaver MX

To see how the Dreamweaver MX interface can help you avoid hand-coding errors, follow these steps:

1. To customize the color scheme, go to Edit ➤ Preferences, and then select Code Coloring in the Category list to display the Preferences panel shown in Figure 10-6.

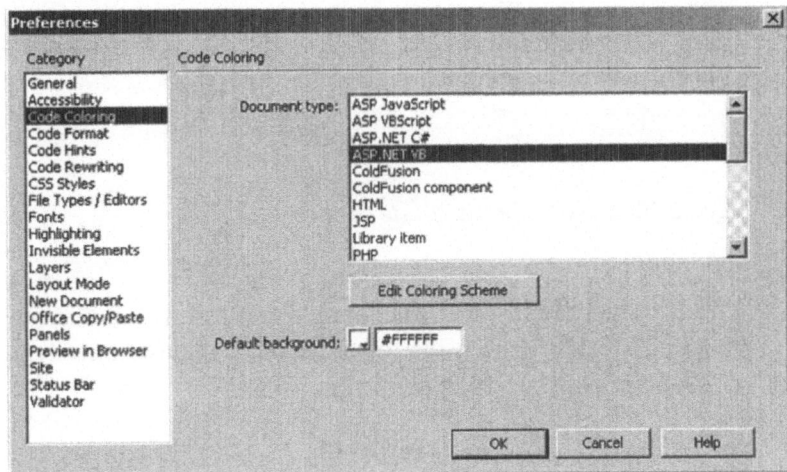

Figure 10-6. Coloring preferences in Dreamweaver MX

2. Select ASP.NET VB in the Document type box, click the Edit Coloring Scheme button, and assign whatever coding color preferences you like.

3. If you are typing your HTML by hand, you will find Dreamweaver's predictive input abilities are very good. Type an opening angle bracket in an ASP.NET VB document to see the list of possible elements shown in Figure 10-7.

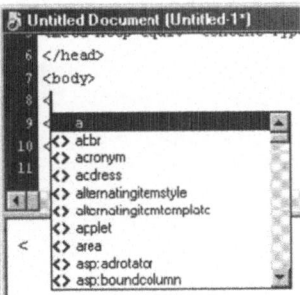

Figure 10-7. Predictive tag input

4. The list includes all the ASP.NET web controls and some custom Macromedia controls. Select one and press the spacebar to see a list of the applicable attributes for that control, as shown in Figure 10-8.

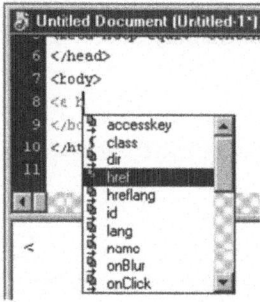

Figure 10-8. Predictive attribute input

The attributes are inserted with double quotes surrounding the value, as required by ASP.NET. Closing the angle bracket automatically inserts the closing tag, as shown in Figure 10-9.

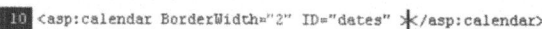

Figure 10-9. Automatic tag closing

This is a great help because ASP.NET syntax requires closing tags. If you have used Dreamweaver before, you already know that the Tag Inspector tab of the Code panel is a great facility for detecting unmatched tags. In MX 2004, the Tag Inspector includes all ASP.NET tags and their attributes, and it has a whole panel of its own, as shown in Figure 10-10 (with an asp:Calendar control selected).

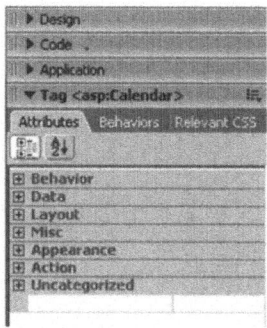

Figure 10-10. The Tag panel

You can use the Tag panel to set the attributes of any ASP.NET control. For example, you can use the Tag panel's Appearance category to select colors for an asp:Calendar control, as shown in Figure 10-11.

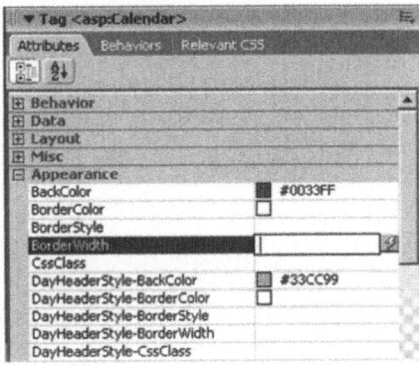

Figure 10-11. The Tag panel's Appearance category

The code reflects your choices, as shown in Figure 10-12.

```
9  <asp:Calendar BackColor="#0033FF" DayHeaderStyle-BackColor="#33CC99" id="dates" ></asp:Calendar>
```

Figure 10-12. The code created via the Tag panel

Dreamweaver MX also provides very comprehensive tag references on the Reference tab of the Code panel. In addition, MSDN has an easy-to-use listing of ASP.NET web controls at http://msdn.microsoft.com/library/default.asp?url=/library/en-us/vbcon/html/vbconSelectingWebFormControl.asp.

Summary

This chapter gave you a look into code debugging in ASP.NET and VB .NET. In particular, you learned how to do the following:

- Identify coding errors, including the most common ones encountered.

- Track down the origin of errors.

- Correct errors.

- Help users take appropriate action.

We showed you ways to minimize the chance that errors will appear in your code in the first place, as well as how to handle them if they do occur. Finally, we explained the various debugging and error-avoidance tools that .NET and Dreamweaver provide. Hopefully, after reading this chapter, you are now armed with resources that will help you get your code right the first time.

Case Study

IN THIS CHAPTER, you will use the techniques you learned in previous chapters to build a hotel booking application. You first build the application with Dreamweaver behaviors, and then you convert the completed application to use CodeBehind and a compiled assembly. Note that this will be a generic online booking system, not a production-ready application.

The Case Study Application

The application will consist of the following pages:

- **Home Page**: This page will be the starting point for all visitors.

- **Browse Rooms**: This page will allow visitors to learn about the rooms and facilities available.

- **Book Room**: This page will allow visitors to check whether a room is available on specific dates and book that room.

Required Software Applications

The following applications and extensions are required to build the case study application:

- **Dreamweaver MX or Dreamweaver MX 2004**: You probably have this software already installed, but if not, you can obtain a 30-day trial version of Dreamweaver MX 2004 from http://www.macromedia.com.

- **Microsoft Access 97, 2000, or 2001 (XP)**: We use Microsoft Access in this chapter because more people have Access than any other database application. You can use a different database, but the steps outlined in this chapter are specific to Access.

- **.NET Framework**: This can be downloaded free from http://www.asp.net. The full SDK version of the .NET Framework is required to complete this chapter.

- **DreamweaverCtrls replacement:** This is a free extension that extends Dreamweaver's interaction with the database.

- **UserControl and Page Directive Suite:** These free extensions add a point-and-click facility for managing user controls and the @ Page directive. Both extensions are included with the code download for this book and are also available from http://www.webxel-dw.co.uk.

Building the Application

Using the procedure for defining an ASP.NET site in Dreamweaver outlined in Chapter 3, create a new site called CaseStudy. You can create all the content from scratch or use the application supplied with the code download. If you decide to use the ready-made application, copy the files from the Inline Code directory to your site folder, and then skip directly to the "Adding Database Content" section of this chapter. To create the content from scratch, follow these steps:

1. Create three new directories—bin, DB, and Images—in the root directory. The bin directory will contain the DreamweaverCtrls assembly, the DB directory will contain the Access database file, and the Images directory will contain the images of the hotel rooms.

 TIP *If you are using an application other than Access, refer to that product's documentation for direction about how to carry out the tasks in this chapter.*

---

2. Open Access and select File ➤ New ➤ Blank Database. Browse to and select the DB directory as the location where the database will be stored, name the database CaseStudy.mdb, and click the Create button, as shown in Figure 11-1.

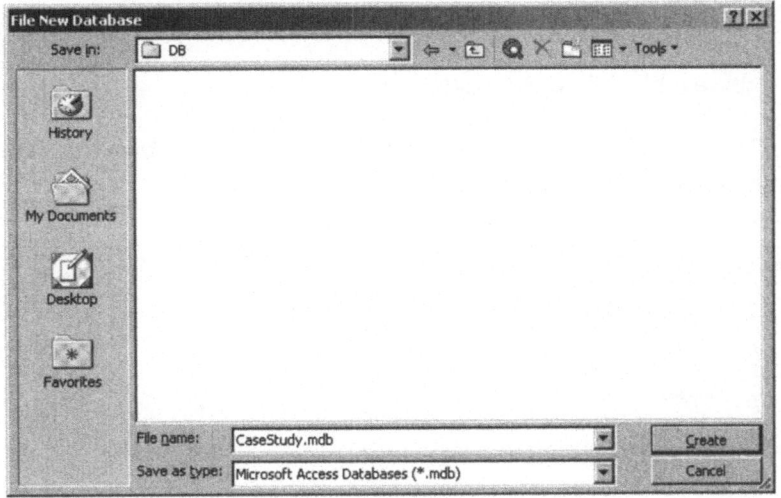

Figure 11-1. The Access File New Database dialog box

Adding Database Content

In this section, we show you how to create the first table, and then you will create all subsequent tables using the same method.

The database will contain the tables and queries shown in Table 11-1.

Table 11-1. Database Contents

Item Name	Item Type
tbl_RoomTypes	Table
tbl_Rooms	Table
tbl_Bookings	Table
tbl_BookedDays	Table
tbl_Customers	Table
qry_BookedDays	Query
qry_Rooms	Query

Creating the First Table

To create a database table, follow these steps:

1. Select Tables on the left menu bar, and then click the New button on the top menu bar, as shown in Figure 11-2.

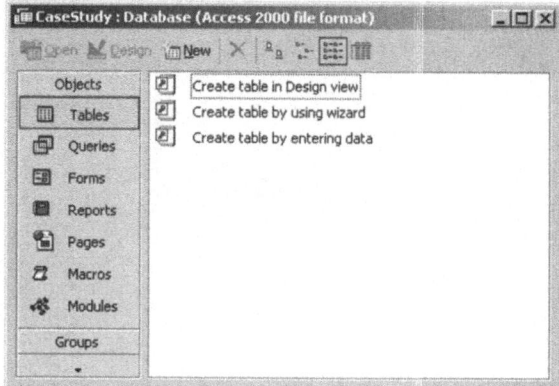

Figure 11-2. Creating a new table

2. In the New Table dialog box (shown in Figure 11-3), select Design View and click OK.

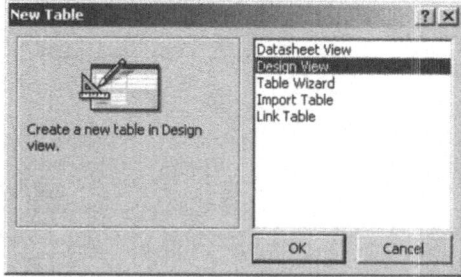

Figure 11-3. The New Table dialog box

3. In the Field Name column, type **RoomTypeID** and then give the field a data type of AutoNumber. This is an automatically incrementing numeric value that will be used to identify individual room types. This type of field is known as an **Identity** field in SQL Server.

4. Create another field, name it RoomTypeText, and give it a data type of Text, which provides a text field that stores the descriptive text shown to users. The table should now look as shown in Figure 11-4.

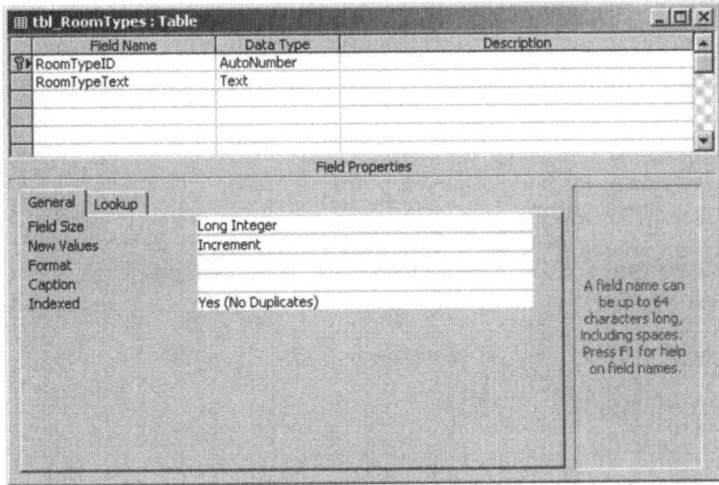

Figure 11-4. The table in Design view

The key icon to the left of the RoomTypeID field indicates that the field is the table's primary key. To set a different field as the primary key, right-click the field and select Primary Key.

5. Save the table as tbl_RoomTypes, as shown in Figure 11-5.

Figure 11-5. The Save As dialog box

6. To add records, open the table and type **Single**, **Double**, and **Family** into the RoomTypeText field, as shown in Figure 11-6.

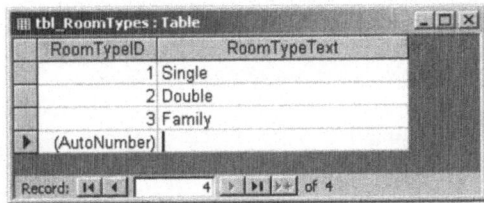

Figure 11-6. The tbl_RoomTypes *table with new records added*

Creating the Other Tables

Create the tbl_BookedDays database table using the information provided in Table 11-2.

Table 11-2. The tbl_BookedDays *Table*

Field Name	Data Type	Field Size	Primary Key
BookedDayID	AutoNumber	Long Integer	Yes
BookingID	Number	Long Integer	
BookedDate	Date/Time	N/A	

Create the tbl_ Bookings database table using the information provided in Table 11-3.

Table 11-3. The tbl_Bookings *Table*

Field Name	Data Type	Field Size	Primary Key
BookingID	AutoNumber	Long Integer	Yes
Customer	Number	Long Integer	
Room	Number	Long Integer	

Create the tbl_ Rooms database table using the information provided in Table 11-4.

Table 11-4. The tbl_Rooms *Table*

Field Name	Data Type	Field Size	Primary Key
RoomID	AutoNumber	Long Integer	Yes
RoomName	Text	50	
EnSuite	Yes/No	N/A	
CostPerNight	Number	Double	
RoomType	Number	Long Integer	
RoomNo	Text	50	
Description	Memo	N/A	

Create the tbl_ Customers database table using the information provided in Table 11-5.

Table 11-5. The tbl_Customers *Table*

Field Name	Data Type	Field Size	Primary Key
CustomerID	AutoNumber	Long Integer	Yes
FirstName	Text	50	
LastName	Text	50	
EmailAddress	Text	50	

Inserting Records

To insert records, follow these steps:

1. Open the tbl_Rooms table, as shown in Figure 11-7.

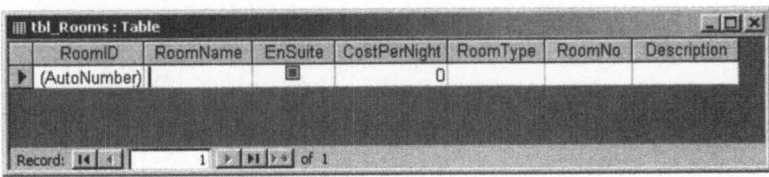

Figure 11-7. The tbl_Rooms *table*

Each field stores the following data:

- **RoomID:** This field identifies individual rooms.

- **RoomName:** This field stores the name of the room.

- **EnSuite:** This field indicates whether the room has en suite facilities.

- **CostPerNight**: This field stores the cost per night.

- **RoomType**: This field indicates the type of room. This value corresponds with the RoomTypeID value of one of the records in the tbl_RoomTypes table.

- **RoomNo**: This field stores the hotel room number.

- **Description**: This field stores a description of the room's features.

Note that the value assigned to the RoomType field corresponds to the tbl_RoomTypes records. This allows you to use small numeric values in the RoomType field rather than retyping text entries. In addition, should you want to change the entry in this field, you need only edit this single instance of it. If you forget the numeric value you associated with each room type, Access includes a Lookup facility that comes to the rescue. Let's take a quick look at the Lookup facility in action.

2. Open the tbl_Rooms table in Design view, select the RoomType field, and click the Lookup tab, as shown in Figure 11-8.

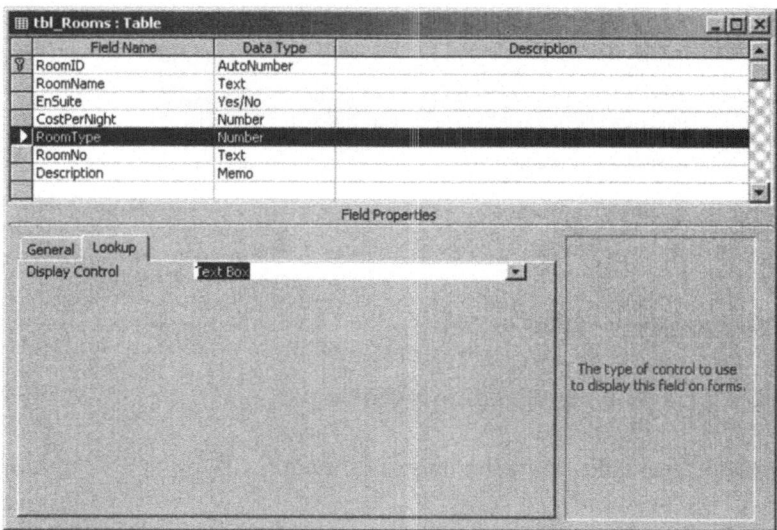

Figure 11-8. The tbl_Rooms *table in Design view*

3. Click the Display Control field, click the down arrow that appears at the right end of the field, and select Combo Box to display more editable fields, as shown in Figure 11-9.

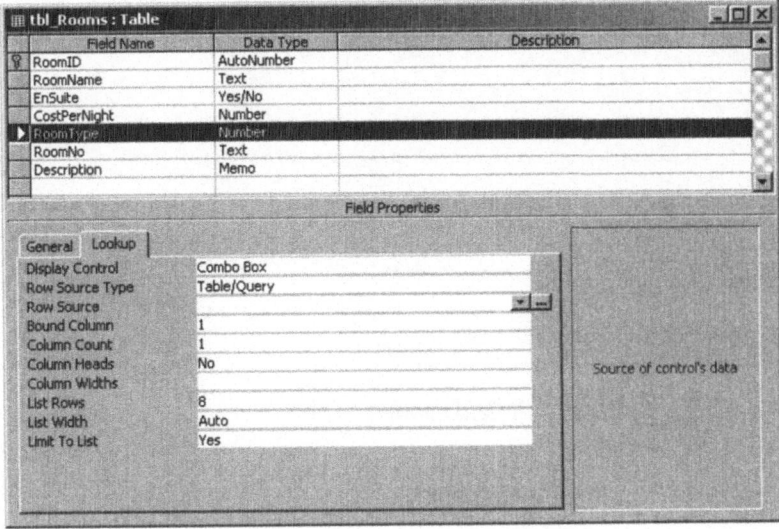

Figure 11-9. The Lookup tab in the tbl_Rooms *table*

4. Click the Row Source field, and click the button with three dots on it to display the Show Table dialog box. In the dialog box, select the tbl_RoomTypes table, click the Add button, and then click the Close button. The Query Builder appears, as shown in Figure 11-10.

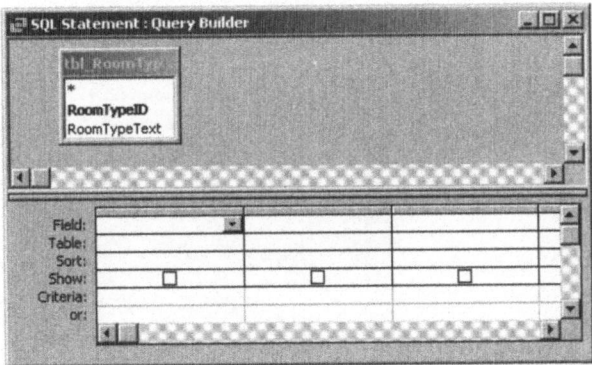

Figure 11-10. The Query Builder

5. Double-click the RoomTypeID field to add it to the Query Builder. Then double-click the RoomTypeText field. The Query Builder should look as shown in Figure 11-11.

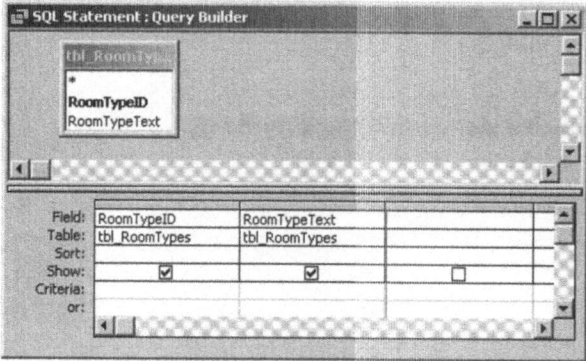

Figure 11-11. The Query Builder with fields added

6. Close the Query Builder, and click Yes when prompted to save the SQL statement and update the property. Next set the value of Column Count to **2** and the value of Column Widths to **0cm;1cm**, as shown in Figure 11-12.

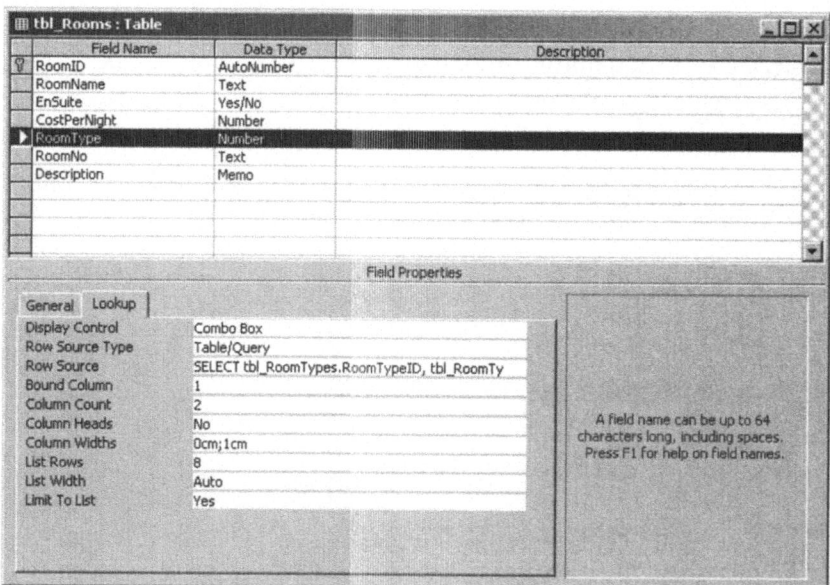

Figure 11-12. The tbl_Rooms *table with specified lookup values*

7. Close Design view and click Yes to save the new lookup information. Now when you open the table and click the RoomType field, you can select textual values from a menu, as shown in Figure 11-13.

Figure 11-13. The tbl_Rooms *table with textual values instead of numeric values*

8. Add the rows shown in Table 11-6. Type anything you like in the Description field.

Table 11-6. The tbl_Rooms *Table*

RoomID	RoomName	EnSuite	CostPer Night	RoomType	RoomNo	Description
1	Bookend Bunk	Yes	40	Single	11b	anything
2	Writers Realm	Yes	60	Family	345a	anything
3	Authors Abode	Yes	60	Double	734c	anything
4	Wedding Suite	Yes	80	Double	24b	anything
5	Skid Row	No	30	Single	145a	anything

Creating the First Query

Next you will create two queries in the database. The first is qry_BookedDays, which will generate a list of currently booked days. The second query, qry_Rooms, will list the details of all the rooms and return data from multiple tables.

1. To create the qry_BookedDays query, navigate to the Queries section of the database and click New, as shown in Figure 11-14.

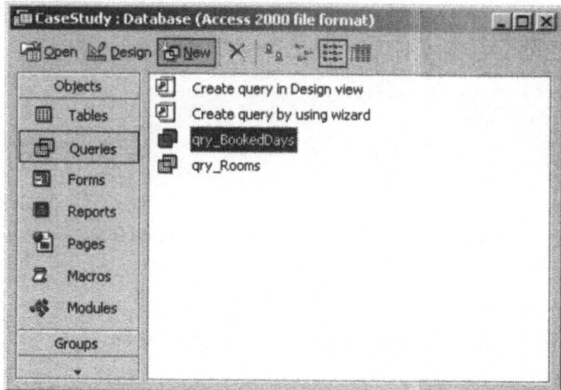

Figure 11-14. The Queries section of the database

2. In the New Query dialog box, select Design View, as shown in Figure 11-15.

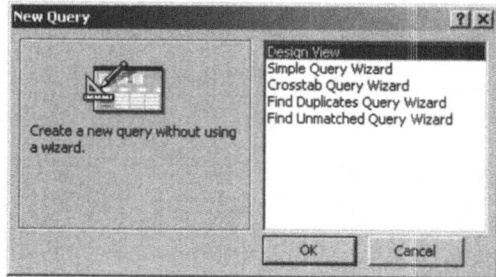

Figure 11-15. Creating a new query

3. Click OK to open the Query Builder. To add the tables to the Query Builder, double-click tbl_Bookings and tbl_BookedDays in the Show Table dialog box, as shown in Figure 11-16, and then click Close.

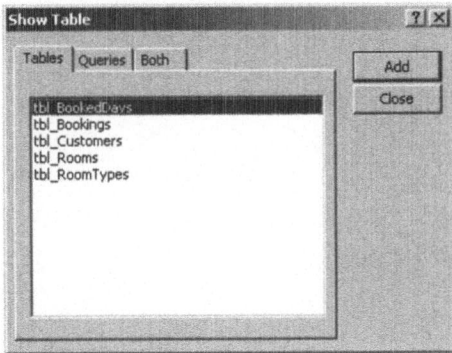

Figure 11-16. The Show Table dialog box

4.   To add a field to the query, double-click the Room field in the tbl_Bookings table. Do the same with the BookedDate field in the tbl_BookedDays table. The query should look as shown in Figure 11-17.

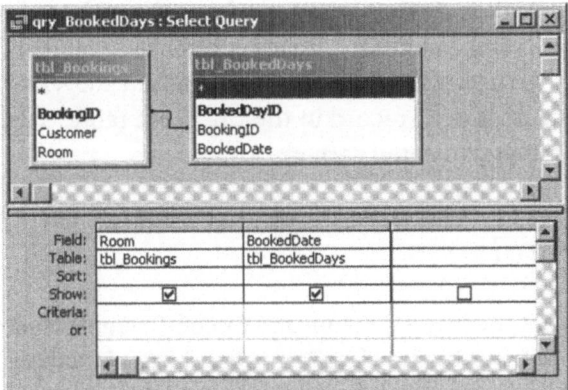

Figure 11-17. The qry_BookedDays *query*

5.   Close the Query Builder, click Yes to save the query, and name it qry_BookedDays.

Creating the Second Query

Create the qry_Rooms query using the procedure just outlined. The qry_Rooms query takes its data from the tbl_Rooms and tbl_RoomTypes tables and should contain the fields listed in Table 11-7.

Table 11-7. The qry_Rooms *Fields*

Field Name	Source Table
RoomID	tbl_Rooms
RoomName	tbl_Rooms
EnSuite	tbl_Rooms
CostPerNight	tbl_Rooms
RoomType	tbl_Rooms
RoomNo	tbl_Rooms
Description	tbl_Rooms
RoomTypeText	tbl_RoomTypes

Creating the Room Images

Your application will include a page that displays photographs of the rooms. The sample files include images of each room, and each image contains the name of the room in text. Each image is saved as a .gif file with dimensions of 200×150, and each file is named according its parent record in the tbl_Rooms table. Save the images in the Images folder that you created earlier.

Creating the User Controls

Now you will create user controls for the header, menu, and footer. To create these controls, you will use features provided by the UserControl and Page Directive Suite extension. When you install the extension, four buttons are added to the Dreamweaver Insert bar, as shown in Figure 11-18.

Figure 11-18. The UserControl and Page Directive Suite Insert bar buttons

From left to right, these buttons are as follows:

- **New UserControl:** Use this button to create new ASCX files.

- **Insert UserControl:** Use this button to insert user controls into a page.

- **Insert/Edit Control Directive:** Use this button to insert and edit @ Control directives.

- **Insert/Edit Page Directive:** Use this button to insert and edit @ Page directives.

1. Click the New UserControl button to open a new document that contains the following content:

```
<%@ Control Language="C#" %>
New UserControl
```

Note that the language attribute of the <Control> directive tag defaults to C#. Because you are working in VB .NET, change it to VB.

```
<%@ Control Language="VB" %>
New UserControl
```

This will be your header control, so it will be placed at the top of each page in your application. It will also have a property that can dynamically change the text of an asp:Label control.

2. Insert an HTML table with one row, one column, and a width of 750 pixels. Set the background color to silver and the cell spacing and cell padding to 0. In the table's cell, type **Apress Accommodation -,** and then insert an asp:Label control. (The button to insert this control is on the ASP.NET tab of the Insert bar, but you may have to save the page before it becomes visible.) Give the label an ID of lblHeaderText, and then align the contents of the table cell to center. The table should look similar to Figure 11-19.

Figure 11-19. The header controls in Design view

3. Let's look at the server-side code for the header control. Type the following code block after the `<Control>` directive tag:

```
<script runat="server">
  Public Property Text() As String
    Get
      Return Me.lblHeaderText.Text
    End Get
    Set(ByVal Value As String)
      Me.lblHeaderText.Text = Value
    End Set
  End Property
</script>
```

4. The first and last lines are the script tags that mark the code as a server-side script block. Next, a public property called Text is defined. This property is mapped to the Text property of the lblHeaderText label. When the Text property of the header control is specified by placing Text="Welcome" in the control's tag, the value is applied to the label within the user control. The text in the header will now read "Apress Accommodation – Welcome." Save this control as Header.ascx.

5. The menu control will provide the site's main navigation link. The navigation will include a table that contains HtmlAnchor controls, which are hyperlink tags with runat="server" attributes applied. HTML elements with this attribute applied are sometimes called HtmlControls, and you can use them to reference the hyperlink from your server-side code. This enables you to unlink the hyperlink associated with the page currently being viewed. Create a new user control, save it as Menu.ascx, and then define its contents as shown in the following code block:

```
<%@ Control Language="VB" %>
<script runat="server">
Sub Page_Load(Src As Object, E As EventArgs)
  Dim Ctl As Control
  For Each Ctl In Me.Controls
    If Ctl.GetType() Is GetType(System.Web.UI.HtmlControls.HtmlAnchor)➠
Then
      Dim TheLink As System.Web.UI.HtmlControls.HtmlAnchor = Ctl
      Dim PageName As String = Request.Path()
      PageName = PageName.Substring(PageName.LastIndexOf("/") + 1)
      Dim LinkPage As String = TheLink.Href
      LinkPage = LinkPage.Substring(LinkPage.LastIndexOf("/") + 1)
      If LinkPage.ToLower().Equals(PageName.ToLower()) Then
```

```
            TheLink.Href = ""
            Exit For
        End If
      End If
    Next
  End Sub
</script>
<table border="0">
  <tr>
    <td align="left"> </td>
  </tr>
  <tr>
    <td align="left"><a href="default.aspx" runat="server">Home</a></td>
  </tr>
  <tr>
    <td align="left">
      <a href="BrowseRooms.aspx" runat="server">Browse Rooms</a>
    </td>
  </tr>
  <tr>
    <td align="left">
      <a href="BookRoom.aspx" runat="server">Book A Room</a>
    </td>
  </tr>
  <tr>
    <td align="left"> </td>
  </tr>
</table>
```

After the code has been inserted into the Menu.ascx control, the menu should look as shown in Figure 11-20.

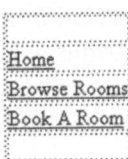

Figure 11-20. The Menu.ascx *control in Design view*

The empty first and last rows space things out a little and help keep the menu links away from the header and footer. The second table row contains a hyperlink with a runat="server" attribute, which turns the hyperlink into an HtmlControl that can be accessed from server-side code. To be precise, the hyperlink is a System.Web.UI.HtmlControls.HtmlAnchor control.

Now let's examine the server-side code. Although users are unlikely to click a link to a page they are currently viewing, you can see how any HTML element can be accessed and manipulated with server-side code. Let's look at this code again.

```vb
Sub Page_Load(Src As Object, E As EventArgs)
    Dim Ctl As Control
    For Each Ctl In Me.Controls
        If Ctl.GetType() Is GetType(System.Web.UI.HtmlControls.HtmlAnchor) ➥
        Then
            Dim TheLink As System.Web.UI.HtmlControls.HtmlAnchor = Ctl
            Dim PageName As String = Request.Path()
            PageName = PageName.Substring(PageName.LastIndexOf("/") + 1)
            Dim LinkPage As String = TheLink.Href
            LinkPage = LinkPage.Substring(LinkPage.LastIndexOf("/") + 1)
            If LinkPage.ToLower().Equals(PageName.ToLower()) Then
                TheLink.Href = ""
                Exit For
            End If
        End If
    Next
End Sub
```

All the code is placed in the Page_Load event procedure. The first line declares an object variable of the type Control. This is where you will store each control as you loop through the page's controls collection. Next is a For loop that works through the controls collection. Within the For loop there is an If block that checks the current control's type. If the control type is System.Web.UI.HtmlControls.HtmlAnchor, the control is one of your hyperlinks so it is stored in an object variable called TheLink. This variable is of the type System.Web.UI.HtmlControls.HtmlAnchor. The code then grabs the full path of the current page and uses the LastIndexOf method to extract the page name. Next the page name is extracted from the Href attribute of the TheLink object. If the name of the current page matches the name defined in the TheLink object's Href attribute, it indicates that the link points to the current page and the link will be removed by setting the Href attribute to an empty string.

6. Create a new user control file, save it as Footer.ascx, and insert the following code:

```
<%@ Control Language="VB" %>
<table width="750"  border="0" cellpadding="0" cellspacing="0">
  <tr bgcolor="#CCCCCC">
```

```
        <td align="center" bgcolor="#CCCCCC">Powered By Apress</td>
    </tr>
</table>
```

The code for the footer control is quite simple. The HTML table contains only a single cell that is 750 pixels wide. The cell contains the text "Powered By Apress" aligned center, as shown in Figure 11-21.

Figure 11-21. The footer control in Design view

Creating the Home Page

To create the home page, follow these steps:

1. Create a new ASP.NET VB page, title it **Apress Hotel Home Page**, and then save it as default.aspx. To insert the header control, click the Insert UserControl button (second from the left). The dialog box shown in Figure 11-22 will appear.

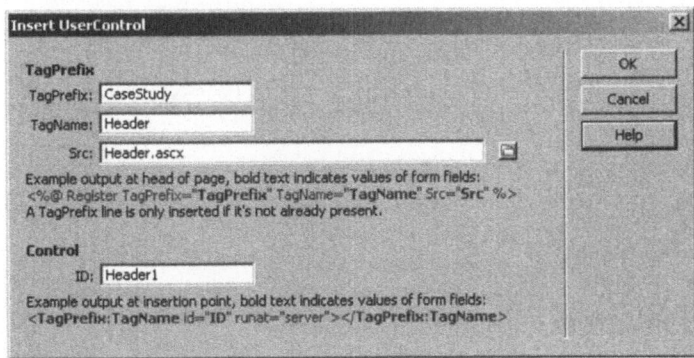

Figure 11-22. The Insert UserControl dialog box

2. Fill in the following values:

   - **TagPrefix:** CaseStudy

   - **TagName:** Header

   - **Src:** Header.ascx

   - **ID:** Header1

3.   Click OK to insert the following code near the top of the document:

```
<%@ Register TagPrefix="CaseStudy" TagName="Header" Src="Header.ascx" %>
```

The following code is inserted at the point where the cursor is located:

```
<CaseStudy:Header id="Header1" runat="server"></CaseStudy:Header>
```

When you created the header control, you defined a property in the control called Text using the following code:

```
<script runat="server">
  Public Property Text() As String
    Get
      Return Me.lblHeaderText.Text
    End Get
    Set(ByVal Value As String)
      Me.lblHeaderText.Text = Value
    End Set
  End Property
</script>
```

4.   Add Text="Welcome" to the control tag. The tag should look similar to the following line of code:

```
<CaseStudy:Header
id="Header1"
Text="Welcome"
runat="server"></CaseStudy:Header>
```

5.   Position the cursor after the header control tag, and insert a table that is 750 pixels wide and has one row and two columns. Set the <td> tag attributes of the left column as follows:

- **Width**: 130

- **Align**: center

- **Valign**: top

- **Bgcolor**: #CCCCCC

6. Set the attributes of the right `<td>` column as follows:

   - **Width**: 620 pixels

   - **Valign**: top

7. Click the left table column and then click the Insert UserControl button to display the Insert UserControl dialog box. This time, define the following values in the dialog box:

   - **TagPrefix**: CaseStudy

   - **TagName**: Menu

   - **Src**: Menu.ascx

   - **ID**: Menu1

8. Click OK to insert the code into the document. Then type some text in the right column of the table—anything will do. To insert the footer control, position the cursor after the table, click the Insert UserControl button again, and then define the following values in the dialog box:

   - **TagPrefix**: CaseStudy

   - **TagName**: Footer

   - **Src**: Footer.ascx

   - **ID**: Footer1

9. Save your changes and test your home page. It should look similar to Figure 11-23.

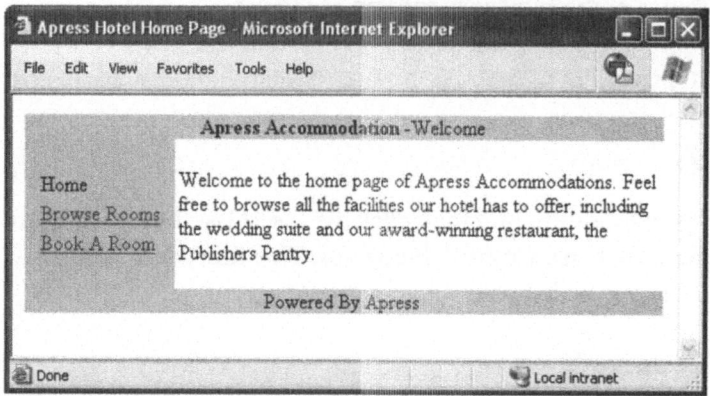

Figure 11-23. The home page displayed in a browser

The following code block shows the source code for the home page.

```
<%@ Page Language="VB" %>
<%@ Register TagPrefix="CaseStudy" TagName="Header" Src="Header.ascx" %>
<%@ Register TagPrefix="CaseStudy" TagName="Menu" Src="Menu.ascx" %>
<%@ Register TagPrefix="CaseStudy" TagName="Footer" Src="Footer.ascx" %>
<html>
<head>
<title>Apress Hotel Home Page</title>
</head>
<body>
<CaseStudy:Header
id="Header1"
Text="Welcome"
runat="server"></CaseStudy:Header>
<table width="750"  border="0" cellpadding="0" cellspacing="0">
  <tr>
    <td width="130" align="center" valign="top" bgcolor="#CCCCCC">
      <CaseStudy:Menu id="Menu1" runat="server"></CaseStudy:Menu>
    </td>
    <td width="620" valign="top">
      <br>
        <table width="600" border="0" align="center">
          <tr>
            <td>
                <p>Welcome to the home page of Apress Accommodations.
Feel free to browse all the facilities our hotel has to offer, including
 the wedding suite and our award-winning restaurant,
the Publishers Pantry.</p>
```

```
            </td>
          </tr>
        </table>
      </td>
    </tr>
  </table>
  <CaseStudy:Footer id="Footer1" runat="server"></CaseStudy:Footer>
  </body>
  </html>
```

Creating the Browse Rooms Page

Now you will create a page that enables users to browse through a list of rooms. Each room has a link to a page that contains more detailed information.

You must have installed the DreamweaverCtrls replacement extension to complete this exercise. Once the extension is installed, deploy DreamweaverCtrls.dll to the site's bin folder by clicking Deploy supporting files on the Site menu. To ensure that you have the correct version of the DLL file, check its file size: The standard DLL is 40k and the DreamweaverCtrls replacement version is 52k.

1. Open default.aspx, delete the contents of the table's right column, and change the header control's Text attribute to Browse Rooms. Then save the page as BrowseRooms.aspx.

2. Next you must define a database connection. On the Databases tab in Dreamweaver's Application panel, click the plus sign (+) button and select OLE DB Connection from the menu, as shown in Figure 11-24.

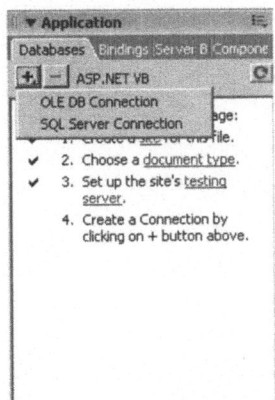

Figure 11-24. Defining a database connection

3. In the OLE DB Connection dialog box, type **ConStr** in the Connection name field, as shown in Figure 11-25, and then click the Build button.

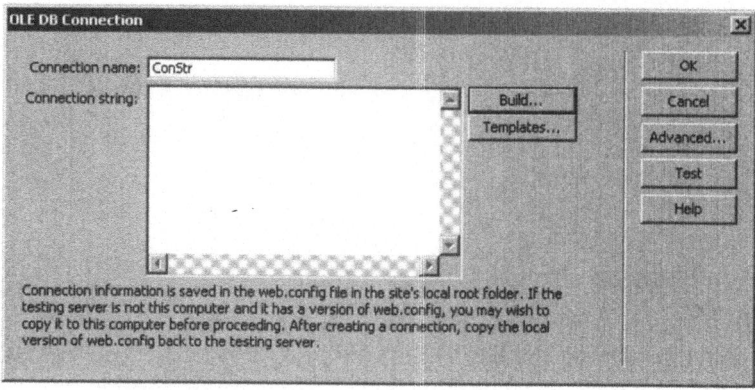

Figure 11-25. The OLE DB Connection dialog box

4. In the Data Link Properties dialog box, click the Provider tab, select Microsoft Jet 4.0 OLE DB Provider, and click the Next button. Then click the Connection tab as shown in Figure 11-26, and click the Browse button.

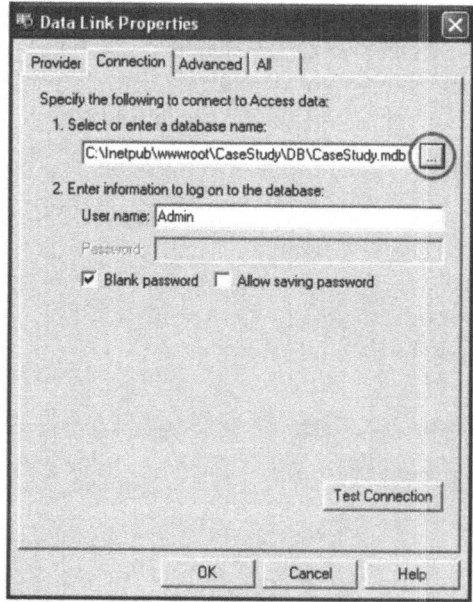

Figure 11-26. The Browse button

5. Select the CaseStudy.mdb database, and then click the Test Connection button. If all is well, you should see the message box shown in Figure 11-27.

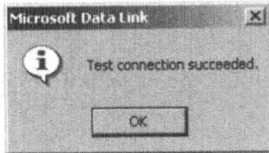

Figure 11-27. The test connection is successfully created.

6. Click OK to return to the OLE DB Connection dialog box, which now contains a connection string, as shown in Figure 11-28.

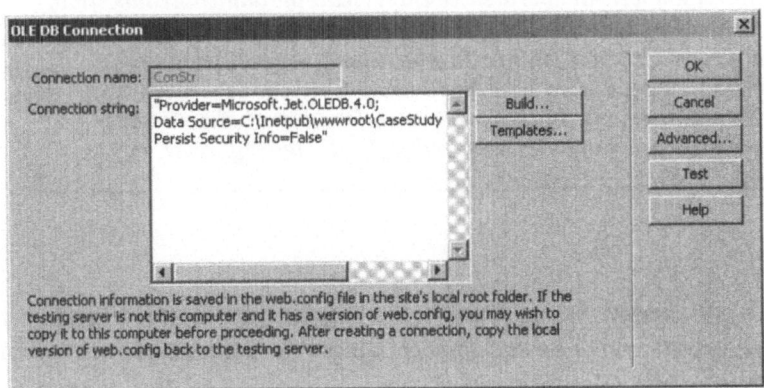

Figure 11-28. The OLE DB Connection dialog box with a connection string

7. Click the Test button. If all is well you will see a message informing you that the connection was made successfully. Click OK, and the new connection will appear in the Databases tab, as shown in Figure 11-29.

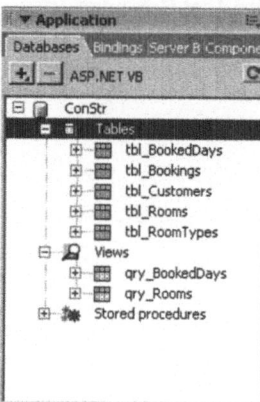

Figure 11-29. The Databases tab with the new connection

 TIP *If you were unable to successfully create the database connection, the problem might be insufficient permissions on the database file or incorrect site definitions. To add database permissions, see* http://support.microsoft.com/default.aspx?scid=kb;en-us; 175168&Product=asp. *To correct site definitions, make sure you selected a valid server model and defined a testing server.*

8. Insert a new dataset into the page by clicking the plus sign (+) button on the Bindings tab and choosing DataSet (Query) from the menu, as shown in Figure 11-30.

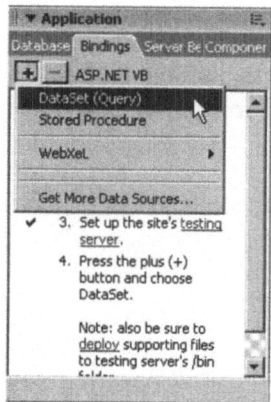

Figure 11-30. Inserting a dataset from the Bindings tab

9. In the DataSet dialog box, fill the values as follows:

    - **Name:** DsRooms

    - **Connection:** ConStr

    - **Table:** qry_Rooms

    Leave all the other options set to the default values. The completed dialog box should look as shown in Figure 11-31.

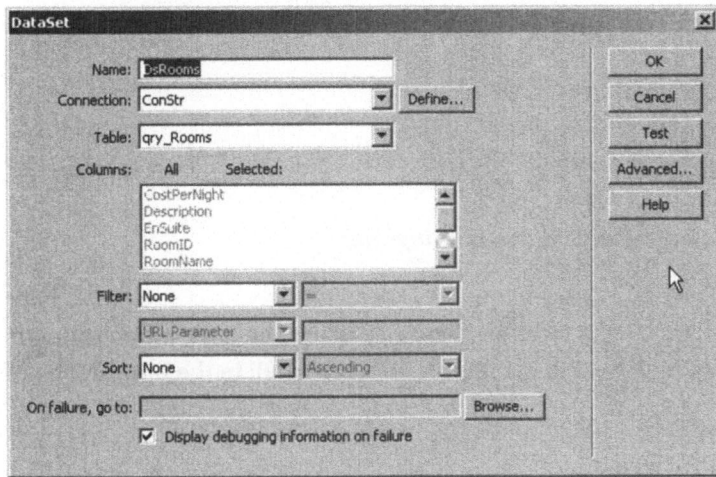

Figure 11-31. The completed DataSet dialog box

10. Click OK to insert the code, or click the Test button to preview the data retrieved from the database.

11. Insert an HTML table containing two rows and six columns. In the top row, type the following column headings from left to right:

    - **RoomNo**

    - **RoomName**

    - **EnSuite**

    - **RoomType**

    - **CostPerNight**

    The last column has no header text.

12. Select all the cells in the top row and make the headings bold. Before you place the dataset values into the bottom row, make sure all the cells in the bottom table row and all the dataset's fields in the Bindings tab are visible, as shown in Figure 11-32.

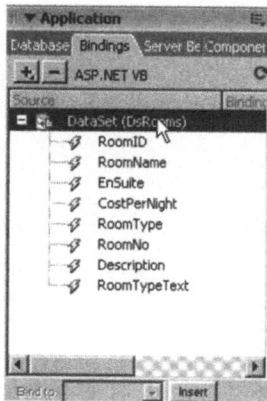

Figure 11-32. The dataset's fields in the Bindings tab

13. To insert a field, drag it from the Bindings tab to the page where it should appear. Drag each field value into its own table cell in the bottom row of the table.

14. Select all the cells of the bottom table row, and then on the Server Behaviors tab, select Repeat Region to display the Repeat Region dialog box shown in Figure 11-33.

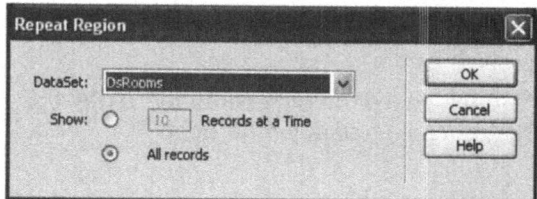

Figure 11-33. The Repeat Region dialog box

15. Select the All records option and click OK. This will place an `<asp:Repeater>` control tag around the table's bottom row. Test the page in a browser to make sure it functions without errors.

TIP *If you test your page after each notable change, any errors will be immediately identifiable as related to the most recent update. This will make it much easier to identify and rectify any problems.*

16. Once the page is running in the browser, you will notice that the CostPerNight field is not formatted very well. In Design view, select the dynamic text item that represents the CostPerNight field. Note that it is selected in the Bindings tab as well, as shown in Figure 11-34.

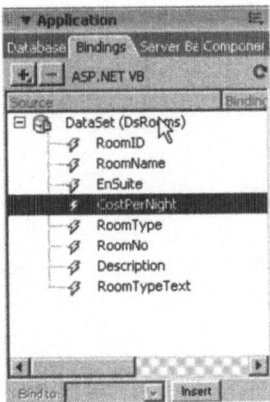

Figure 11-34. The Bindings tab with the CostPerNight *field selected*

17. Adjust the size of columns in the Bindings tab so the Format column is visible. Click the arrow button, and then select Currency ➤ Default, as shown in Figure 11-35.

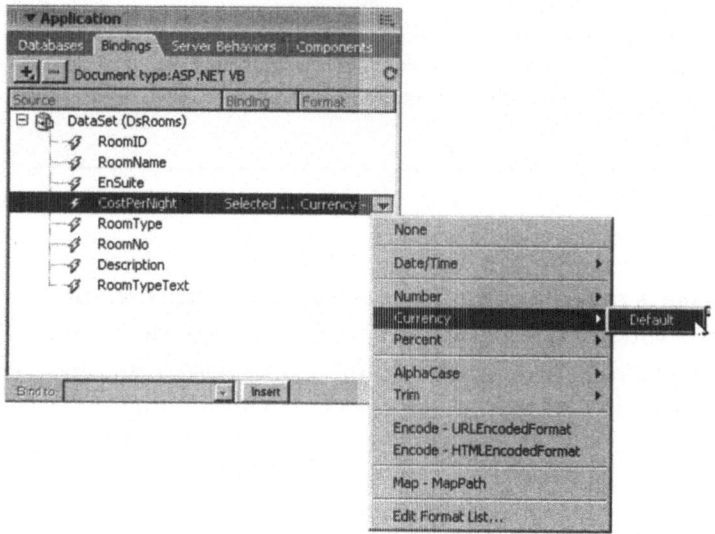

Figure 11-35. Setting the format using the Bindings tab

The code selected in the page will change from this:

```
<%# DsRooms.FieldValue("CostPerNight", Container) %>
```

to the following:

```
<%# Double.Parse(DsRooms.FieldValue("CostPerNight", Container)).↪
ToString("C") %>
```

The CostPerNight field value is now formatted as currency.

18. Next you will change the available selections in the EnSuite field from true and false to yes and no. To do this, simply replace the raw values. The raw value is displayed using the following expression:

```
<%# DsRooms.FieldValue("EnSuite", Container) %>
```

19. Add the following code to the end of the expression:

```
.Replace("True", "Yes").Replace("False","No")
```

The new expression should look like this:

```
<%# DsRooms.FieldValue("EnSuite", Container).Replace("True", "Yes").➥
Replace("False","No") %>
```

Preview the page in the browser to see your changes.

20. Now you will add a hyperlink to a page with more details about the
    selected room. Click the far right column on the bottom row and type
    More.... Then select the text and click the Browse button to the right of
    the Link field to display the Select File dialog box shown in Figure 11-36.

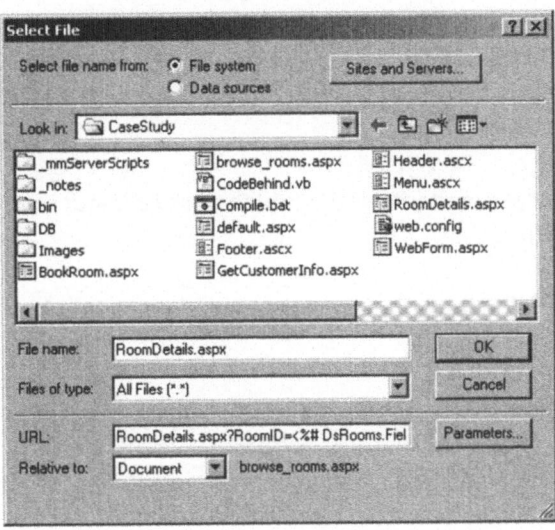

Figure 11-36. The Select File dialog box

21. Type **RoomDetails.aspx** in the File name field, and then click the
    Parameters button to open the Parameters dialog box shown in
    Figure 11-37. This is where you define the URL parameters that will be
    passed to the target page.

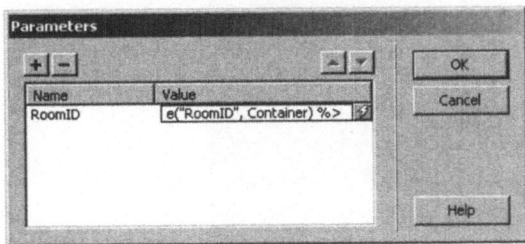

Figure 11-37. The Parameters dialog box

22. Type **RoomID** into the left column, click the lightning bolt icon, select the RoomID field from the DsRooms dataset, and then click OK to close the Parameters and the Select File dialog boxes. Save the page and preview it in the browser. Move the mouse pointer over each link to see its target displayed in the browser's status bar.

```
http://localhost/casestudy/RoomDetails.aspx?RoomID=#
```

The pound sign (#) represents the numeric value of the RoomID field.

Creating the Room Details Page

To create RoomDetails.aspx, follow these steps:

1. Open default.aspx, delete the contents of the table's right cell, and save the page as RoomDetails.aspx.

2. Create a dataset with the following criteria, as shown in Figure 11-38:

   - **Name:** DsRoomDetails

   - **Connection:** ConStr

   - **Table:** qry_Rooms

   - **Filter:** RoomID, =, URL Parameter, RoomID

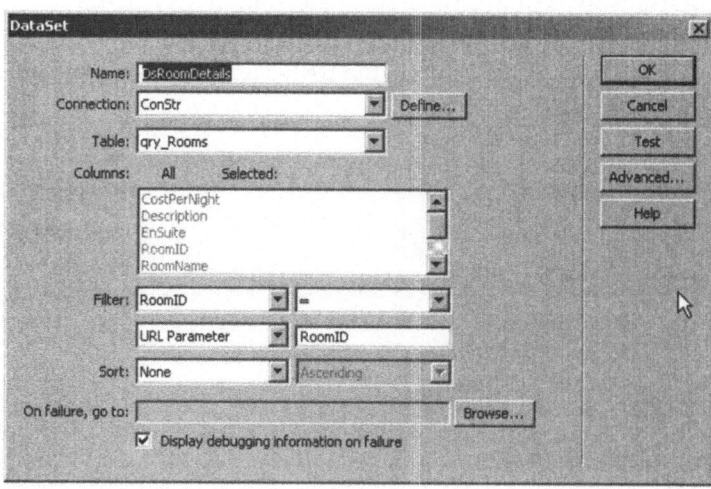

Figure 11-38. The completed DataSet dialog box for the RoomDetails.aspx *page*

The dataset will include a single row containing the details from the selected room. Only database records with a `RoomID` value that matches the passed URL parameter are pulled from the database.

3. Insert an HTML table as shown in Figure 11-39.

RoomNo:	(DsRoomDetails.RoomNo)	
RoomName:	(DsRoomDetails.RoomName)	
EnSuite:	(DsRoomDetails.EnSuite)	
CostPerNight:	(DsRoomDetails.CostPerNight)	
RoomType:	(DsRoomDetails.RoomTypeText)	
Description:	(DsRoomDetails.Description)	
	Book This Room	

Figure 11-39. The HTML table in Design view

To create the large cell, select multiple cells and click the Merge Cells button in the Property inspector.

The `EnSuite` field value should use yes/no instead of true/false values, as demonstrated at the end of the last section.

The image should come from the Images directory. In the HTML source code, the tag should look like this:

```
<img src="Images/<%# DsRoomDetails ➡
.FieldValue("RoomID", Container) %>.gif">
```

Notice that the image name is built with a combination of dynamic values and hard-coded values. There is an image in the directory called `1.gif`, so if the URL parameter that filters the dataset had a value of 1, the return value of

```
<%# DsRoomDetails.FieldValue("RoomID", Container) %>
```

will also be 1. The resulting value that is used as the image's `src` attribute is

```
Images/1.gif
```

When the page is viewed in a browser, the `src` attribute will be changed to a valid image path and the browser will find and display the image file correctly.

Note a problem in the Description field: Access uses line break characters that will not render on an HTML page. Do not be tempted to place <br> tags into the database. Inserting these tags effectively renders the data useful only within the context of a web page.

4. To preserve the structure of the Description field when displaying it in a web page, change this:

```
<%# DsRoomDetails.FieldValue("Description", Container) %>
```

to the following:

```
<%# DsRoomDetails.FieldValue("Description", Container).Replace➡
(VbCrLf, "<br>") %>
```

VbCrLf is an internal constant variable that matches line breaks and carriage returns. The code now includes instructions to replace all line breaks or carriage returns with <br> tags.

The hyperlink at the bottom of the page is set up to pass the RoomID value of the room being viewed. This allows the user to transfer the information on the current page to the BookRoom.aspx page automatically.

```
<a href="BookRoom.aspx?RoomID= ➡
<%# DsRoomDetails.FieldValue("RoomID", Container) %>" ➡
>Book This Room</a>
```

Creating the Main Booking Page

This is the main page in the application. It provides visitors with a user interface (UI) to select the room they want to book, see dates when the selected room is available, and book the room. The page is relatively complex and is made up of a number of elements that interact with one another.

We will first explain how to create the visual elements of the UI and then show you how to create the invisible elements such as datasets and server-side code. We walk you through creating the page in stages: You will complete a stage and then review it before moving to the next.

Creating the Visual Elements

To create the visual elements, follow these steps:

1. Open default.aspx, delete the contents of the table's right cell, and save the page as BookRoom.aspx.

2. Insert a form into the table's right cell, and give this form a runat="server" attribute. Insert an HTML table with two columns and seven rows into the form. Select both cells in the top row of the table, and click the Merge Cells button shown in Figure 11-40.

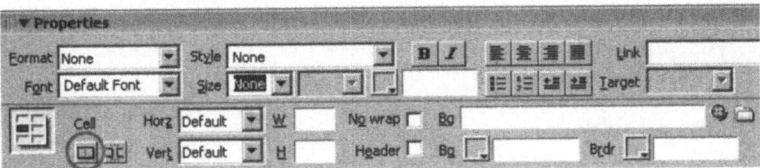

Figure 11-40. The Merge Cells button

3. In the merged cell, type **Select Room:**. Then insert an asp:DropDownList control and give it an ID of drpRooms.

4. In the left cell of the third row, type **Available Dates for:**. Then insert an asp:Label control and give it an ID of lblSelectedRoom.

5. In the left cell of the fourth row, type the following:

   - **Red Text = Room Already Booked**

   - **Green background = Your Selections**

   - **Red background = Your Selections but Room already booked**

6. In the right cell of the fourth row, type the following:

   - **Green text = Date is Available**

   - **Red text = Date is Unavailable**

7. In the left cell of the fifth row, insert an asp:Calendar control. If this control is not listed on the Insert bar, click the More Tags button, and select it from the list. Give the new calendar the following attributes:

- **ID**: CalAvailableDates

- **OnPreRender**: CalAvailableDates_PreRender

- **OnDayRender**: CalAvailableDates_DayRender

8. In the right cell of the fifth row, insert an asp:DataList control and give it the following attributes:

- **ID**: DateListBookedDays

- **RepeatColumns**: 3

- **RepeatDirection**: Horizontal

- **RepeatLayout**: Table

- **CellPadding**: 5

- **OnItemCreated**: DateListBookedDays_ItemCreated

9. To insert an <ItemTemplate> tag in the datalist, click the More Tags button and select ItemTemplate from the list. In the <ItemTemplate> tag, insert an asp:Label control with the following attributes:

- **ID**: lblBookedDate

- **Text**: <%# Container.DataItem.ToShortDateString() %>

The entire <DataList> tag should resemble the following code:

```
<asp:DataList ID="DateListBookedDays" RepeatColumns="3"
RepeatDirection="Horizontal" RepeatLayout="Table" CellPadding="5"
OnItemCreated="DateListBookedDays_ItemCreated" runat="server">
  <itemtemplate>
    <asp:Label
ID="lblBookedDate"
Text="<%# Container.DataItem.ToShortDateString() ¬ %>"
runat="server"></asp:Label>
  </itemtemplate>
</asp:DataList>
```

10. Select both cells of the table's bottom row and click the Merge Cells button. In the newly merged cell, insert an `asp:Button` control with the following attributes:

- **ID**: btnBook

- **Text**: Book Now

- **OnClick**: btnBook_Click

11. In the same cell, insert a second `asp:Button` control with the following attributes:

- **ID**: btnSelectRange

- **Text**: Select Range

- **OnClick**: btnSelectRange_Click

12. In the same cell, insert a third `asp:Button` control with the following attributes:

- **ID**: btnClear

- **Text**: Select None

- **OnClick**: btnClear_Click

13. In the same cell, insert an `asp:Label` control with the following attributes:

- **ID**: lblStatus

- **ForeColor**: #FF0000

In Design view, this page should now look as shown in Figure 11-41.

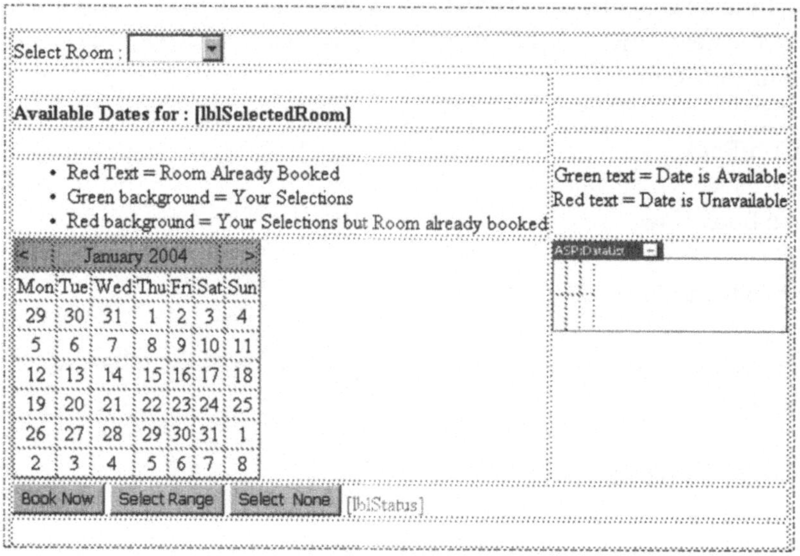

Figure 11-41. The BookRoom.aspx *page in Design view*

On this page, the user selects a room from the drop-down list or by clicking the link on the RoomDetails.aspx page. Once a room has been selected, the calendar shows when the room is available. The user selects dates by clicking the calendar or by using the btnSelectRange button. Available dates appear in green and unavailable dates appear in red. Once the user has selected a room that is available for the desired dates, he or she clicks the btnBook button to continue to the final booking page.

Creating the Invisible Elements

Now you will create the invisible elements of the page such as datasets and server-side code.

To create a dataset, follow these steps:

1. Insert a new dataset with the following attributes:

    *   **Name**: DsRooms

    *   **Connection**: ConStr

    *   **Table**: tbl_Rooms

    *   **Fields**: RoomID and RoomName

Leave all the other options on the DataSet dialog box set to the default values, as shown in Figure 11-42.

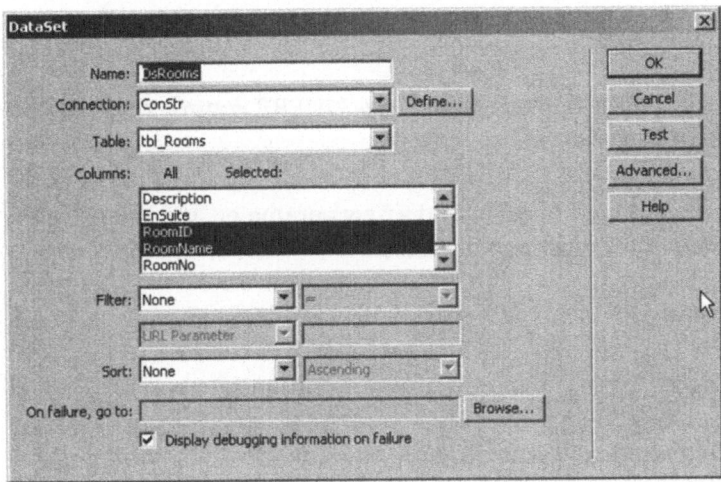

Figure 11-42. The completed DataSet dialog box for the Rooms *dataset*

2. Insert another dataset. In the DataSet dialog box, click the Advanced button to display the advanced options, as shown in Figure 11-43.

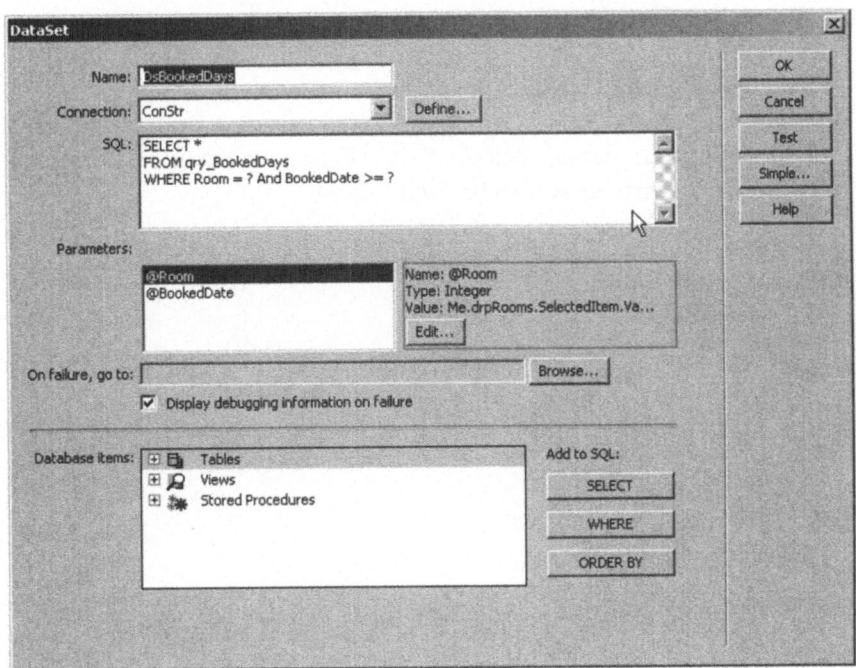

Figure 11-43. The advanced options of the DataSet dialog box

3.   Fill in the following attributes:

   - **Name**: DsBookedDays

   - **Connection**: ConStr

   - **SQL**: SELECT * FROM qry_BookedDays WHERE Room = ? And BookedDate >= ?

4.   Click the plus sign (+) button to add a new parameter, and then give the new parameter the following attributes:

   - **Name**: @Room

   - **Type**: Integer

   - **Value**: Me.drpRooms.SelectedItem.Value

5.   Add a second parameter with the following attributes:

   - **Name**: @BookedDate

   - **Type**: DBDate

   - **Value**: DateTime.Now

6.   Click the OK button to insert the dataset.

7.   In the Application panel, click the Server Behaviors tab and then select DataSet(DsRooms), as shown in Figure 11-44.

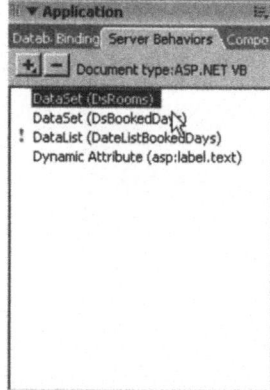

Figure 11-44. Selecting the DataSet(DsRooms) dataset

8.   Click the ManualMode check box in the Property inspector, as shown in
     Figure 11-45. If you do not see this Property inspector, you need to install
     the DreamweaverCtrls replacement extension.

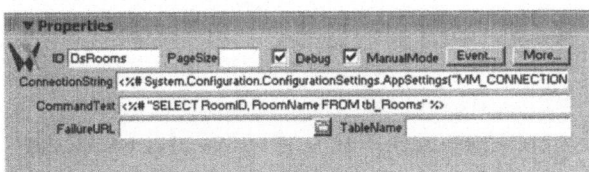

Figure 11-45. The DataSet Property inspector

The following code can be seen in the page. Do not worry if your code is
not identical.

```
<MM:DataSet
id="DsRooms" runat="Server"
IsStoredProcedure="false" manualmode="true"
ConnectionString='<%# System.Configuration.ConfigurationSettings. ➥
AppSettings("MM_CONNECTION_STRING_ConStr") %>'
DatabaseType='<%# System.Configuration.ConfigurationSettings. ➥
AppSettings("MM_CONNECTION_DATABASETYPE_ConStr") %>'
CommandText='<%# "SELECT RoomID, RoomName FROM tbl_Rooms" %>'
Debug="true"
></MM:DataSet>
<MM:DataSet
id="DsBookedDays"
runat="Server"
IsStoredProcedure="false"
ConnectionString='<%# System.Configuration.ConfigurationSettings. ➥
AppSettings("MM_CONNECTION_STRING_ConStr") %>'
DatabaseType='<%# System.Configuration.ConfigurationSettings. ➥
AppSettings("MM_CONNECTION_DATABASETYPE_ConStr") %>'
CommandText='<%# "SELECT *  FROM qry_BookedDays ➥
WHERE Room = ? And BookedDate >= ?" %>'
Debug="true"
><Parameters>
  <Parameter
Name="@Room"
Value='<%# Me.drpRooms.SelectedItem.Value   %>'
Type="Integer"   />
  <Parameter
Name="@BookedDate"
Value='<%# DateTime.Now  %>'
```

```
     Type="DBDate"    />
</Parameters></MM:DataSet>
<mm:pagebind
runat="server"
PostBackBind="true"
Ignore="false"></mm:pagebind>
```

The DsRooms dataset populates the drop-down list with a list of available rooms. The DsBookedDays dataset selects records from the qry_BookedDays query. RoomID corresponds to the room selected in the drop-down list, and BookedDate must be equal to or later than the current date.

Understanding the Server-Side Code

Let's first look at the code and then we will examine each part in greater detail.

```
<script runat="server">

Dim SelectedDates As System.Collections.ArrayList

Sub Page_Init(Src As Object, E As EventArgs)
  Dim i as Integer
  For i = Page.Controls.Count-1 To 0 Step - 1
    If Page.Controls.Item(i).GetType() Is GetType ➥
(DreamweaverCtrls.PageBind) Then
      Page.Controls.RemoveAt(i)
    End If
  Next
End Sub

Sub Page_Load(Src As Object, E As EventArgs)
  If Not Session("SelectedDates") Is Nothing Then
    SelectedDates = Session("SelectedDates")
  Else
    SelectedDates = New System.Collections.ArrayList()
  End If

  If Not Page.IsPostBack Then
    DsRooms.DoInit()
    Me.drpRooms.DataSource = DsRooms.DefaultView
    Me.drpRooms.DataTextField = "RoomName"
    Me.drpRooms.DataValueField = "RoomID"
    Me.drpRooms.DataBind()
```

```
    If Not Request.QueryString("RoomID") Is Nothing Then
      Dim RoomID As String = Request.QueryString("RoomID")
      Dim Lst As ListItem
      For Each Lst In Me.drpRooms.Items
        If Lst.Value = RoomID Then
          Lst.Selected = true
          Exit For
        End If
      Next
    End If


    CalAvailableDates.VisibleDate = DateTime.Now
    CalAvailableDates.SelectedDate = DateTime.Now
  End If


  Me.DsBookedDays.DoInit()
  lblSelectedRoom.Text = drpRooms.SelectedItem.Text
  lblSelectedRoom.DataBind()
End Sub


Sub btnBook_Click(Src As Object, E As EventArgs)
  Dim SelectedDate As DateTime
  if SelectedDates.Count = 0 Then
    lblStatus.Text = "You did not select any dates!"
    Exit Sub
  End If
  For each SelectedDate In SelectedDates
    If IsBooked(SelectedDate) Then
      lblStatus.Text = "Some of your selected dates are already booked!"
      Exit Sub
    End If
  Next
  Response.Redirect("GetCustomerInfo.aspx?RoomID=" & ➡
Me.drpRooms.SelectedItem.Value)
End Sub


Sub btnSelectRange_Click(Src As Object, E As EventArgs)
  If SelectedDates.Count = 2 Then
    SelectedDates.Sort()
    Dim CurrentDate As DateTime = SelectedDates.Item(0)
    Do While Not CurrentDate.Equals(SelectedDates.Item(1))
      CurrentDate = CurrentDate.AddDays(1)
      If Not SelectedDates.Contains(CurrentDate) Then
        SelectedDates.Add(CurrentDate)
      End If
```

```
      Loop
        lblStatus.Text = ""
      Else
        lblStatus.Text = "To select a range 2 dates(the start and end) ➥
   must be selected!"
      End If
   End Sub


   Sub btnClear_Click(Src As Object, E As EventArgs)
      SelectedDates.Clear()
      lblStatus.Text = ""
   End Sub


   Function IsBooked(TheDate As System.DateTime) As Boolean
      Dim Dv As System.Data.DataView = Me.DsBookedDays.DefaultView
      Dv.RowFilter = "BookedDate = '" & TheDate & "'"
      Return Dv.Count > 0
   End Function


   Sub CalAvailableDates_PreRender(Src As Object, E As EventArgs)
      If Page.IsPostBack Then
        If Request.Form("__EVENTTARGET").Equals ➥
   (CalAvailableDates.ClientID) Then
          If Not Request.Form("__EVENTARGUMENT"). ➥
   SubString(0, 1).Equals("V") Then
            AddRemoveDate()
          End If
        End If
      End If
      Me.DateListBookedDays.DataSource = SelectedDates
      Me.DateListBookedDays.DataBind()
   End Sub


   Sub DateListBookedDays_ItemCreated(Src As Object, E As ➥
   System.Web.UI.WebControls.DatalistItemEventArgs)
      Dim BookedDate As DateTime = e.Item.DataItem
      Dim Lbl As Label = e.Item.FindControl("lblBookedDate")
      If IsBooked(BookedDate) Then
        Lbl.ForeColor = System.Drawing.Color.Red
      Else
        Lbl.ForeColor = System.Drawing.Color.Green
      End If
   End Sub
```

```
Sub CalAvailableDates_DayRender(sender As Object, e As ➡
System.Web.UI.WebControls.DayRenderEventArgs)
  If e.Day.Date <= DateTime.Now.AddDays(-1) Then
    e.Cell.Text = "<span style=""color:silver;"">" ➡
 & e.Day.Date.Day & "<span>"
    Exit Sub
  End If
  If IsBooked(e.Day.Date) Then
    If SelectedDates.Contains(e.Day.Date) Then
      e.Cell.BackColor = System.Drawing.Color.Red
    Else
      e.Cell.Text = e.Day.Date.Day
      e.Cell.ForeColor = System.Drawing.Color.Red
      e.Cell.BackColor = System.Drawing.Color.White
    End If
  Else
    If SelectedDates.Contains(e.Day.Date) Then
      e.Cell.BackColor = System.Drawing.Color.Green
    End If
  End If
End Sub

Sub AddRemoveDate()
  If Not SelectedDates.Contains(CalAvailableDates.SelectedDate) Then
    SelectedDates.Add(CalAvailableDates.SelectedDate)
  Else
    SelectedDates.Remove(CalAvailableDates.SelectedDate)
  End If
  SelectedDates.Sort()
  Session("SelectedDates") = SelectedDates
  lblStatus.Text = ""
End Sub
```

```
</script>
```

To help you understand the code, we will split it into individual procedures and explain each one separately. The following line declares a variable called SelectedDates that is of the type System.Collections.ArrayList:

```
Dim SelectedDates As System.Collections.ArrayList
```

You will store the user's selected dates here. This variable can be used by all the code on the page.

```
Sub Page_Init(Src As Object, E As EventArgs)
  Dim i as Integer
  For i = Page.Controls.Count-1 To 0 Step - 1
    If Page.Controls.Item(i).GetType() Is GetType(DreamweaverCtrls.PageBind) Then
      Page.Controls.RemoveAt(i)
    End If
  Next
End Sub
```

Page_Init is one of the built-in events of the Page class. Placing the event procedure into the page enables specific code to be executed when the Page_Init event is raised.

Ideally, you would like to control how and when DataBind methods are called. You may not, for example, want Page.DataBind to be called when the page loads, which is the default behavior of DreamweaverCtrls. To override this, you can remove the <MM:PageBind> tag from the page. Unfortunately, Dreamweaver automatically reinserts the tag when you edit a dataset.

This code solves the problem by programmatically removing the MM:PageBind control from the page's controls collection before it calls Page.DataBind. The code loops through the controls collection and checks the type of each control. When the code finds a control of type DreamweaverCtrls.PageBind, it recognizes it as the MM:PageBind control and removes it from the controls collection.

The code also loops the controls collection in reverse. This prevents an error from occurring when the loop reaches the last item, which has no control at this index position because the index count changes when controls are removed.

```
Sub Page_Load(Src As Object, E As EventArgs)
  If Not Session("SelectedDates") Is Nothing Then
    SelectedDates = Session("SelectedDates")
  Else
    SelectedDates = New System.Collections.ArrayList()
  End If

  If Not Page.IsPostBack Then
    DsRooms.DoInit()
    Me.drpRooms.DataSource = DsRooms.DefaultView
    Me.drpRooms.DataTextField = "RoomName"
    Me.drpRooms.DataValueField = "RoomID"
    Me.drpRooms.DataBind()

    If Not Request.QueryString("RoomID") Is Nothing Then
      Dim RoomID As String = Request.QueryString("RoomID")
      Dim Lst As ListItem
      For Each Lst In Me.drpRooms.Items
```

```
            If Lst.Value = RoomID Then
                Lst.Selected = true
                Exit For
            End If
        Next
    End If

    CalAvailableDates.VisibleDate = DateTime.Now
    CalAvailableDates.SelectedDate = DateTime.Now
    End If

    Me.DsBookedDays.DoInit()
    lblSelectedRoom.Text = drpRooms.SelectedItem.Text
    lblSelectedRoom.DataBind()
End Sub
```

The Page_Load event procedure is executed every time the page loads. In this procedure, the code first checks for a session variable called SelectedDates. If the session variable is found, the local SelectedDates variable is set to equal the value extracted from the session variable. The SelectedDates variable was declared at the beginning of the server-side code and has page scope, which allows any procedure to access or modify its value. If the session variable is not present, a new ArrayList object is created. The final result is that the SelectedDates variable will contain an ArrayList object in which you can store selected dates.

The code then checks whether the page view is the result of a postback or a fresh load. If it is the result of a postback, the code within the If block will be executed. First the DoInit method of the DsRooms dataset is called, and the dataset loads its data from the database. Then the drpRooms drop-down list has its data source set to the output of this dataset. The drop-down list's DataTextField is set to display the RoomName field value, and the DataValueField is set to use the RoomID field value. Next, the drop-down list's DataBind method is called, which fills the list. The drop-down list will retain its items on postbacks so it only needs to be filled once.

The code now checks for a query string value called RoomID. If RoomID is found, the page view is the result of a user clicking a link from RoomDetails.aspx. To select the item in the drop-down list that corresponds with the query string value as the default, store the query string value in a variable called RoomID. Next a For Each loop searches the drop-down list for the RoomID variable's value. If a matching item is found, its Selected property is set to true. Because there is a matching item, the loop is then exited using Exit For.

The code next checks whether VisibleDate and SelectedDates of the CalAvailableDates calendar are set to the current date. Then the code calls the DoInit method of the DsBookedDays dataset, which causes it to get its data from the database. The lblSelectedRoom property is set to the Text value of the drop-down list's selected item. Finally, the DataBind method of the lblSelectedRoom label is called.

```
Sub btnBook_Click(Src As Object, E As EventArgs)
  Dim SelectedDate As DateTime
  if SelectedDates.Count = 0 Then
    lblStatus.Text = "You did not select any dates!"
    Exit Sub
  End If
  For each SelectedDate In SelectedDates
    If IsBooked(SelectedDate) Then
      lblStatus.Text = "Some of your selected dates ➡
  are already booked!"
      Exit Sub
    End If
  Next
  Response.Redirect("GetCustomerInfo.aspx?RoomID=" & ➡
Me.drpRooms.SelectedItem.Value)
End Sub
```

The btnBook_Click event procedure is executed when the user clicks the btnBook button. The code within this event procedure first declares a variable called SelectedDate, which is where the current date will be stored. Next it checks if the SelectedDates variable's count equals zero; if it does, the ArrayList is empty, and the code will set the text of the lblStatus warning and then exit the btnBook_Click procedure. If the ArrayList contains at least one item, the code will loop through the list, checking that none of the selected dates are already booked. The check is performed within a function called IsBooked, which returns a Boolean value. If any of the dates are booked, the lblStatus label text is set accordingly, and the loop and the btnBook_Click procedure are exited. If all selected dates are free, Response.Redirect redirects the user to the GetCustomerInfo.aspx page, which collects user information and inserts the booking into the database. The selected room is passed to the next page by including the selected room as a URL parameter called RoomID.

```
Sub btnSelectRange_Click(Src As Object, E As EventArgs)
  If SelectedDates.Count = 2 Then
    SelectedDates.Sort()
    Dim CurrentDate As DateTime = SelectedDates.Item(0)
    Do While Not CurrentDate.Equals(SelectedDates.Item(1))
      CurrentDate = CurrentDate.AddDays(1)
      If Not SelectedDates.Contains(CurrentDate) Then
        SelectedDates.Add(CurrentDate)
      End If
    Loop
    lblStatus.Text = ""
```

```
   Else
      lblStatus.Text = "To select a range 2 ➡
   dates(the start and end) must be selected!"
   End If
End Sub
```

The `btnSelectRange_Click` event procedure is executed when the user clicks
the `btnSelectRange` button. This button provides the user with an easy method
of selecting a range of dates. The code within this procedure ensures that the
user has selected exactly two dates—if this condition is not met, the text of the
`lblStatus` label displays a warning. If the condition is met, the `Sort` method is
called to ensure that the dates are sorted in chronological order with the earli-
est first. Then the `CurrentDate` variable is created and populated with the date
value of the earlier of the two dates. The code then performs a `Do` loop that runs
until the `CurrentDate` variable is equal to the value of the later of the two dates.
For each pass through the loop, the `CurrentDate` variable is incremented by one
day, and the resulting date is added to the `SelectedDates` collection.

```
Sub btnClear_Click(Src As Object, E As EventArgs)
   SelectedDates.Clear()
   lblStatus.Text = ""
End Sub
```

The `btnClear_Click` event procedure is executed when the user clicks the
`btnClear` button. This procedure clears the selected dates by calling the `Clear`
method of the `SelectedDates` ArrayList. It also sets the `Text` attribute of the
`lblStatus` label to an empty string.

```
Function IsBooked(TheDate As System.DateTime) As Boolean
   Dim Dv As System.Data.DataView = Me.DsBookedDays.DefaultView
   Dv.RowFilter = "BookedDate = '" & TheDate & "'"
   Return Dv.Count > 0
End Function
```

The `IsBooked` function searches the `DsBookedDays` dataset for a given date and
returns a Boolean value based on whether that date is present. It does this by first
declaring a `DataView` variable called `Dv` that is set to the raw contents of the dataset's
default view, which returns all the rows in the dataset. Next the `RowFilter` attribute
of the `DataView` variable is set to a string which specifies that only rows in which the
date is equal to the passed date will be included. Finally, the function returns
a Boolean value by using the following expression:

```
Return Dv.Count > 0
```

If the filtered `DataView` variable contains any rows, the result of this expression will be true; otherwise, the result will be false.

```
Sub CalAvailableDates_PreRender(Src As Object, E As EventArgs)
  If Page.IsPostBack Then
    If Request.Form("__EVENTTARGET").Equals ➡
(CalAvailableDates.ClientID) Then
      If Not Request.Form("__EVENTARGUMENT"). ➡
SubString(0, 1).Equals("V") Then
        AddRemoveDate()
      End If
    End If
  End If
  Me.DateListBookedDays.DataSource = SelectedDates
  Me.DateListBookedDays.DataBind()
End Sub
```

The `CalAvailableDates_PreRender` procedure is attached to the `CalAvailableDates` calendar and runs when the `PreRender` event is raised. The code first checks whether the page is the result of a postback. If so, the code checks whether the `Request.Form("__EVENTTARGET")` value equals the `clientID` value of the calendar control, which indicates that the calendar control initiated the postback. The code next checks whether the first character of the `Request.Form("__EVENTARGUMENT")` value is V. If it is, the postback was caused by the user changing the visible month, so no further action is necessary. If the first character is not V, the postback was caused by the user clicking a day on the calendar control. If this is the case, the `AddRemoveDate` method is called to add or remove the selected date. Finally, the code specifies that the `SelectedDates` ArrayList is the data source of the `DateListBookedDays` datalist. The code then calls the `DataBind` method, which shows the selected dates to the user in an easy-to-understand layout.

This is done now because this is the only stage of the page's life cycle when many of the calendar control's postback variables are available. It cannot happen during `Page_Load` because the calendar's postback variables have not been initiated yet. Most server controls allow access to their postback variables much earlier, but the calendar control does not.

```
Sub DateListBookedDays_ItemCreated(Src As Object, E As ➡
System.Web.UI.WebControls.DatalistItemEventArgs)
  Dim BookedDate As DateTime = e.Item.DataItem
  Dim Lbl As Label = e.Item.FindControl("lblBookedDate")
  If IsBooked(BookedDate) Then
    Lbl.ForeColor = System.Drawing.Color.Red
  Else
    Lbl.ForeColor = System.Drawing.Color.Green
  End If
End Sub
```

The `DateListBookedDays_ItemCreated` procedure is attached to the `DateListBookedDays` datalist and runs for each item created within the datalist. The code first declares a variable called `BookedDate` and sets its value to match the element of the `SelectedDates` ArrayList displayed within the datalist. Next, an object variable of the type `Label` is created and set to use the `FindControl` method to resolve to the `lblBookedDate` label within the current datalist item. The `BookedDate` variable's value is then passed to the `IsBooked` method to return a Boolean value that indicates whether the date is booked. If the date is booked, the label's `ForeColor` attribute is set to display red text; otherwise, it displays green text. This allows the user to see instantly that some of the selected dates are booked.

```
Sub CalAvailableDates_DayRender(sender As Object, e As ➡
System.Web.UI.WebControls.DayRenderEventArgs)
  If e.Day.Date <= DateTime.Now.AddDays(-1) Then
    e.Cell.Text = "<span style=""color:silver;"">" ➡
& e.Day.Date.Day & "<span>"
    Exit Sub
  End If
  If IsBooked(e.Day.Date) Then
    If SelectedDates.Contains(e.Day.Date) Then
      e.Cell.BackColor = System.Drawing.Color.Red
    Else
      e.Cell.Text = e.Day.Date.Day
      e.Cell.ForeColor = System.Drawing.Color.Red
      e.Cell.BackColor = System.Drawing.Color.White
    End If
  Else
    If SelectedDates.Contains(e.Day.Date) Then
      e.Cell.BackColor = System.Drawing.Color.Green
    End If
  End If
End Sub
```

The `CalAvailableDates_DayRender` procedure is attached to the `CalAvailableDates` calendar control and runs when the calendar's `DayRender` event is raised. This procedure allows you to change how each day is displayed in the calendar control. The code first checks whether the date being rendered is earlier than the current date. If it is, the contents of the table cell are replaced with a `<span>` tag that causes the day to be displayed in silver text with no hyperlink. This is done by simply setting the `Cell.Text` property to the alternate HTML desired.

The code then checks whether the date is booked. If the date is booked, the code checks whether the date is in the `SelectedDates` ArrayList (that is, it is one of the selected dates). If it is, the background color of the cell is set to red, indicating that one of the selected dates is not available for the selected room.

If the date is not already booked, the code checks whether the date is one of the selected dates. If it is, the background color of the cell is set to green, indicating to the user that the room is available on the requested date.

If the date is not in the SelectedDates ArrayList, the contents of the cell are set to the date's day value, which removes the hyperlink from the text so the user cannot select it. The ForeColor attribute is set to red and the BackColor attribute is set to white to indicate to the user that the selected room is already booked on this date.

```
Sub AddRemoveDate()
  If Not SelectedDates.Contains(CalAvailableDates.SelectedDate) Then
    SelectedDates.Add(CalAvailableDates.SelectedDate)
  Else
    SelectedDates.Remove(CalAvailableDates.SelectedDate)
  End If
  SelectedDates.Sort()
  Session("SelectedDates") = SelectedDates
  lblStatus.Text = ""
End Sub
```

The AddRemoveDate method is used to add or remove the calendar control's selected date. First it checks whether the SelectedDates ArrayList already contains the calendar control's selected date. If it does, the date is removed from the ArrayList; otherwise, it is added. Then the dates in the ArrayList are sorted into chronological order using the Sort method. Finally, the updated ArrayList is stored in the SelectedDates session variable for retrieval in subsequent page views. This ensures that the updates are not lost if the user navigates to a different part of the site and then comes back to the booking section.

Creating the Final Booking Page

The final booking page collects information and saves it in the database.

Creating the Page

To create this page, follow these steps:

1. Open default.aspx, delete the contents of the table's right column, change the Text attribute of the header control to Finalize Booking, and then save the page as GetCustomerInfo.aspx.

2. Insert an HTML table with four rows and two columns into the table's right cell. In the left column of the new table, type the following text labels:

- **Row 1: FirstName**

- **Row 2: LastName**

- **Row 3: EmailAddress**

3. Insert the following asp:TextBox server controls in the right column:

- **Row 1**: txtFirstName

- **Row 2**: txtLastName

- **Row 3**: txtEmailAddress

4. Insert the following required field validators to the right of each asp:TextBox server control:

- **Row 1**: RequiredFieldValidator1

- **Row 2**: RequiredFieldValidator2

- **Row 3**: RequiredFieldValidator3

5. Set the following attributes for RequiredFieldValidator1:

- **EnableClientScript**: true

- **Display**: Dynamic

- **ErrorMessage**: Required

- **ControlToValidate**: txtFirstName

6. Set the following attributes for RequiredFieldValidator2:

- **EnableClientScript**: true

- **Display**: Dynamic

- **ErrorMessage**: Required

- **ControlToValidate**: txtLastName

7. Set the following attributes for RequiredFieldValidator3:

   - **EnableClientScript**: true

   - **Display**: Dynamic

   - **ErrorMessage**: Required

   - **ControlToValidate**: txtEmailAddress

8. Insert an asp:Button control into the right column of the bottom row, and give it the following attributes:

   - **ID**: btnOk

   - **Text**: Place Booking

   - **OnClick**: btnOk_Click

9. Insert an asp:Label control to the right of the button, and give it the following attributes:

   - **ID**: lblStatus

   - **ForeColor**: #FF0000

   The final result should look similar to Figure 11-46.

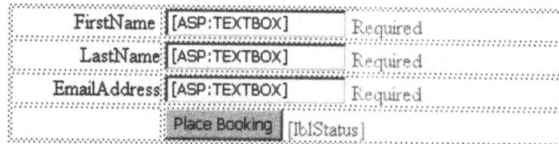

Figure 11-46. The GetCustomerInfo.aspx *page in Design view*

10. Insert a dataset into the page, and set its attributes as follows:

    - **Name**: DsCustomers

    - **Connection**: ConStr

    - **Table**: tbl_Customers

    - **Filter**: EmailAddress, =, Form Variable, txtEmailAddress

11. Leave all the other options on the DataSet dialog box set to the default values. The completed dialog box should look as shown in Figure 11-47.

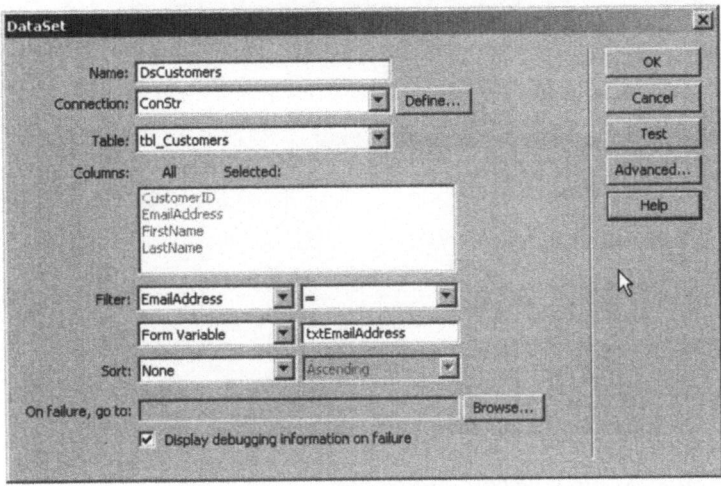

Figure 11-47. The completed DataSet dialog box for the Customers *dataset*

12. Insert an Insert Record behavior, and define its values as follows:

- **Connection**: ConStr

- **Insert into Table**: tbl_Customers

- **CustomerID**: No Value

- **EmailAddress**: Gets Value From txtEmailAddress as WChar

- **FirstName**: Gets Value From txtFirstName as WChar

- **LastName**: Gets Value From txtLastName as WChar

The completed Insert Record dialog box is shown in Figure 11-48.

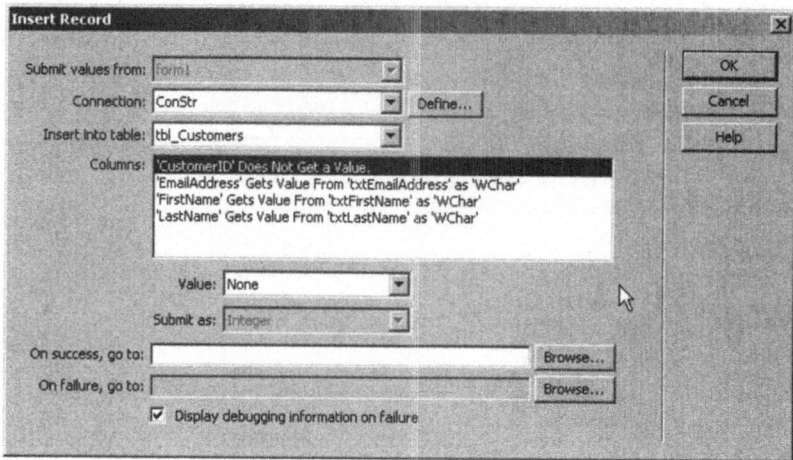

Figure 11-48. The completed Insert Record dialog box

13. Select the Insert Record behavior on the Server Behaviors tab, as shown in Figure 11-49.

Figure 11-49. The Insert Record behavior on the Server Behaviors tab

14. In the Insert Behaviors Property inspector, type **Insert1** in the ID field, and select the ManualMode check box, as shown in Figure 11-50.

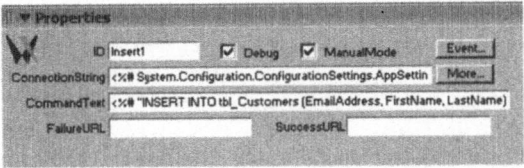

Figure 11-50. The Insert Behaviors Property inspector

15. Click the Event button, and in the Insert Event Code dialog box, select Inserted, as shown in Figure 11-51.

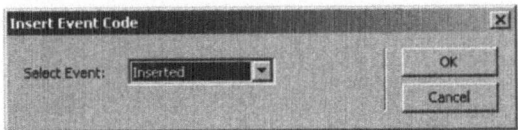

Figure 11-51. The Insert Event Code dialog box

16. Click OK to insert the following server-side code block into the document:

```
<script runat="server">
Sub Insert1_Inserted(sender As Object, e As ➡
 DreamweaverCtrls.InsertedEventArgs)
  'code here
End Sub
</script>
```

17. Replace the 'code here line with the following:

```
CustomerID = e.Identity
```

This will retrieve and store the value of the new customer record in a variable called CustomerID. You will use this value when inserting records into the tbl_Bookings table to associate those records with the parent record in tbl_Customers.

Understanding the Additional Server-Side Code

Here is the additional server-side code that is required. Again we will first show you the code in its entirety and then discuss each part in detail.

```
<script runat="server">

Dim CustomerID As String

Sub Page_Load(Src As Object, E As EventArgs)
  If Not Page.IsPostBack Then
    If Request.QueryString("RoomID") Is Nothing Then
      lblStatus.Text = "No Room Selected"
      btnOk.Visible = false
      Exit Sub
    End If
  End If
End Sub


Sub btnOk_Click(Src As Object, E As EventArgs)
  DsCustomers.DoInit()
  If DsCustomers.RecordCount > 0 Then
    CustomerID = DsCustomers.FieldValue("CustomerID")
  Else
    Insert1.DoInit()
  End If
  InsertBookedDates()
End Sub


Sub InsertBookedDates()
  Dim ObjCmd As System.Data.OleDb.OleDbCommand
  Dim SelectedDates As System.Collections.ArrayList

  If Not Session("SelectedDates") Is Nothing Then
    SelectedDates = Session("SelectedDates")
    If SelectedDates.Count = 0 Then
      lblStatus.Text = "You have not booked any dates"
      Exit Sub
    End If
  Else
    lblStatus.Text = "You have not booked any dates"
    Exit Sub
  End If

  ObjCmd = New System.Data.OleDb.OleDbCommand ➡
("INSERT INTO [tbl_Bookings]  ([Customer],[Room]) ➡
 VALUES(?,?)", DsCustomers.myConnection)
  ObjCmd.Parameters.Add("Customer", CustomerID)
  ObjCmd.Parameters.Add("Room", Request.QueryString("RoomID"))
  ObjCmd.ExecuteNonQuery()
```

```
    ObjCmd.Parameters.Clear()

    ObjCmd.CommandText = "SELECT @@Identity"
    Dim BookingID As String = ObjCmd.ExecuteScalar()

    ObjCmd.CommandText = "INSERT INTO [tbl_BookedDays] ➡
([BookingID],[BookedDate]) VALUES(?,?)"
    ObjCmd.Parameters.Add("BookingID", BookingID)
    ObjCmd.Parameters.Add("BookedDate", "")

    Dim SelectedDate As DateTime
    For each SelectedDate In SelectedDates
      ObjCmd.Parameters.Item("BookedDate").Value = SelectedDate
      ObjCmd.ExecuteNonQuery()
    Next

    Session.Remove("SelectedDates")

    Me.lblStatus.ForeColor = System.Drawing.Color.Green
    Me.lblStatus.Text = "Your Booking has been placed, Thank You."
    Me.btnOk.Visible = false
    Me.Header1.Text = "Booking placed!"

End Sub

</script>
<script runat="server">
Sub Insert1_Inserted(sender As Object, e As ➡
 DreamweaverCtrls.InsertedEventArgs)
  CustomerID = e.Identity
End Sub
</script>
```

Let's examine each part of this code to see exactly what it does. The first line is as follows:

```
Dim CustomerID As String
```

This line declares a string variable called `CustomerID` in which the `CustomerID` field value from the `tbl_Customers` database table will be stored.

```
Sub Page_Load(Src As Object, E As EventArgs)
  If Not Page.IsPostBack Then
    If Request.QueryString("RoomID") Is Nothing Then
      lblStatus.Text = "No Room Selected"
```

```
        btnOk.Visible = false
        Exit Sub
      End If
    End If
End Sub
```

Within the `Page_Load` event, the code checks the `Page.IsPostBack` property. If the page is not the result of a postback, the code checks for the `Request.QueryString("RoomID")` value. If the user arrived at the page without following the correct route, the value will be empty, so the page view is not valid. In the current example, the `lblStatus` label displays a warning to the user, and the `btnOk` button is hidden before the `Page_Load` procedure is exited.

```
Sub btnOk_Click(Src As Object, E As EventArgs)
  DsCustomers.DoInit()
  If DsCustomers.RecordCount > 0 Then
    CustomerID = DsCustomers.FieldValue("CustomerID")
  Else
    Insert1.DoInit()
  End If
  InsertBookedDates()
End Sub
```

The `btnOk_Click` procedure runs when the user clicks the `btnOk` button. The code calls the `DoInit` method of the `DsCustomers` dataset, which causes the dataset to read its data from the database. It then checks the dataset's `RecordCount` attribute to see if any records were returned. If records were returned, the `CustomerID` variable uses the dataset's `CustomerID` field value. If no records were returned, the code calls the `DoInit` method of the `Insert1` Insert Record behavior, which inserts a new record into the `tbl_Customers` table using the form field values. Finally, the `InsertBookedDates` method is called to insert the selected dates into the `tbl_Bookings` table.

```
Sub InsertBookedDates()
  Dim ObjCmd As System.Data.OleDb.OleDbCommand
  Dim SelectedDates As System.Collections.ArrayList
```

The `InsertBookedDates` method first declares two variables that it will use within the method body. The first is a `System.Data.OleDb.OleDbCommand` object called `ObjCmd` that will insert the records into the `tbl_Bookings` table. The second is a `System.Collections.ArrayList` called `SelectedDates` that will store the dates currently stored in the `SelectedDates` session variable.

```
  If Not Session("SelectedDates") Is Nothing Then
    SelectedDates = Session("SelectedDates")
```

```
    If SelectedDates.Count = O Then
      lblStatus.Text = "You have not booked any dates"
      Exit Sub
    End If
  Else
    lblStatus.Text = "You have not booked any dates"
    Exit Sub
  End If
```

The code next checks for the presence of the SelectedDates session variable. If it is not found, the lblStatus label is set to warn the user that no dates are selected, and then the InsertBookedDates method is exited. If the session variable is found, the code places the variable's value into the SelectedDates ArrayList and then checks whether the ArrayList has any items. If the ArrayList is empty, the lblStatus label is set to warn the user that no dates are selected, and then the InsertBookedDates method is exited.

```
  ObjCmd = New System.Data.OleDb.OleDbCommand ➡
("INSERT INTO [tbl_Bookings] ([Customer],[Room]) ➡
 VALUES(?,?)", DsCustomers.myConnection)
  ObjCmd.Parameters.Add("Customer", CustomerID)
  ObjCmd.Parameters.Add("Room", Request.QueryString("RoomID"))
  ObjCmd.ExecuteNonQuery()
```

Reaching this stage indicates that the user has valid dates, so the data can be inserted into the tbl_Bookings and tbl_BookedDays tables. This block of code initializes the ObjCmd variable with a new OleDbCommand object. The SQL is set to the following:

```
INSERT INTO [tbl_Bookings] ([Customer],[Room]) VALUES(?,?)
```

This code inserts values into the Customer and Room fields of the tbl_Bookings table. The runtime values that will replace the question mark characters are defined in the Parameters collection in the OleDbCommand object. The second parameter in the OleDbCommand object specifies the database connection object, in this case, the connection used by the DsCustomers dataset. This means you do not have to create and open an additional connection to the database. The OleDbCommand object has two parameters added to its collection. The first parameter, Customer, is given the value of the CustomerID variable; the second parameter, Room, is given the value of the Request.QueryString("RoomID") value. This record is inserted into the tbl_Bookings table and will store only the information that indicates which room has been booked by which customer. The dates are stored in the tbl_BookedDays table.

```
  ObjCmd.Parameters.Clear()
  ObjCmd.CommandText = "SELECT @@Identity"
  Dim BookingID As String = ObjCmd.ExecuteScalar()
```

Because the code reuses the OleDbCommand object, its parameters are cleared. Then its CommandText attribute is changed to SELECT @@Identity. Next, a string variable called BookingID is set to equal the result of calling the OleDbCommand object's ExecuteScalar method. SELECT @@Identity returns the BookingID field value of the newly inserted record. The ExecuteScalar method returns the value of the first column of the first row of the returned result set, in this case, the BookingID field value. This value is used when inserting records into the tbl_BookedDays table to ensure that each record will share the same parent record.

```
ObjCmd.CommandText = "INSERT INTO ➡
[tbl_BookedDays] ([BookingID],[BookedDate]) VALUES(?,?)"
ObjCmd.Parameters.Add("BookingID", BookingID)
ObjCmd.Parameters.Add("BookedDate", "")
```

The OleDbCommand object's CommandText attribute is changed again to prepare it to insert records into the tbl_BookedDays table. In addition, two parameters are added to its collection. The first parameter, BookingID, is given the value of the BookingID variable that holds the parent record's BookingID field value. The second parameter's value changes continually as each record is inserted, but for now the value is set to a zero-length string.

```
Dim SelectedDate As DateTime
For each SelectedDate In SelectedDates
   ObjCmd.Parameters.Item("BookedDate").Value = SelectedDate
   ObjCmd.ExecuteNonQuery()
Next
```

Next, a variable called SelectedDates is declared, and then the code enters a For Each loop that works through all the dates in the SelectedDates ArrayList. The OleDbCommand object's second parameter value for each selected date is set to the current item's date, and then the OleDbCommand object's ExecuteNonQuery method is called. This inserts a new record into the tbl_BookedDays table, which adds one record to the table for each selected date.

```
Session.Remove("SelectedDates")
```

Once all the data for the booking is stored in the database, the code removes the SelectedDates session variable.

```
Me.lblStatus.ForeColor = System.Drawing.Color.Green
Me.lblStatus.Text = "Your Booking has been placed, Thank You."
```

```
    Me.btnOk.Visible = false
    Me.Header1.Text = "Booking placed!"
End Sub
```

Finally, the `InsertBookedDates` method sets the `ForeColor` attribute of the `lblStatus` label to green and displays a message informing the user that the booking is complete. The `btnOk` button is hidden so users cannot click it a second time, and the header control's `Text` attribute also indicates that the booking is complete.

```
Sub Insert1_Inserted(sender As Object, e As DreamweaverCtrls.InsertedEventArgs)
    CustomerID = e.Identity
End Sub
```

The case study application is now complete. To convert this application to use CodeBehind, keep reading. You may be surprised by just how simple this is.

Converting the Application to Use CodeBehind

CodeBehind is a mechanism that separates the design portion of an ASP.NET page from the server-side code. This is particularly useful in multiuser environments because by separating these two sections of the page, designers and programmers can stay out of each other's way. But even if you do both the design and programming yourself, there are still benefits to using CodeBehind. For example, by compiling the code into an assembly (a DLL file), you can deploy the application in a precompiled state and keep your code hidden from prying eyes.

If you are using the sample files, you should now replace the files in your site with those in the CodeBehind directory of the sample files.

In this section, you will convert the following pages and user controls to CodeBehind.

- `Header.ascx`

- `Menu.ascx`

- `BookRoom.aspx`

- `GetCustomerInfo.aspx`

Converting the Header Control

To convert the header control, follow these steps:

1. Create a new page in Dreamweaver, delete all the contents of the page in Code view, and save the file as CodeBehind.vb.

2. Add the following three lines of code to the CodeBehind.vb file:

```
Imports System
Imports System.Web.UI
Imports System.Web.UI.WebControls
```

These three lines are used to import the namespaces you will use in your application. They are the CodeBehind equivalent to the <%@ Import Namespace="?"%> tag used with inline code.

3. Open the Header.ascx control and move the server-side script block (<script runat="server">code here</script>) into the CodeBehind file. Remove the script tags and then add the code shown in bold so the whole code block looks like the following code:

```
Public Class Header
    Inherits System.Web.UI.UserControl

    Protected WithEvents lblHeaderText As Label

    Public Property Text() As String
        Get
            Return Me.lblHeaderText.Text
        End Get
        Set(ByVal Value As String)
            Me.lblHeaderText.Text = Value
        End Set
    End Property
End Class
```

The first and last lines define a class called Header, which hosts the header control's code. The second line indicates that the Header class should inherit the existing functionality of the System.Web.UI.UserControl class. The third line declares the lblHeaderText label control on the page as a server control that supports events. This is required only for server controls that will be referenced directly within the server-side code, not for every control on the page.

4. Click the Insert/Edit Control Directive button on the WebXeL tab of the Insert bar, as shown in Figure 11-52.

Figure 11-52. The Insert/Edit Control Directive button

The Set Page Directive Attributes dialog box appears, as shown in Figure 11-53.

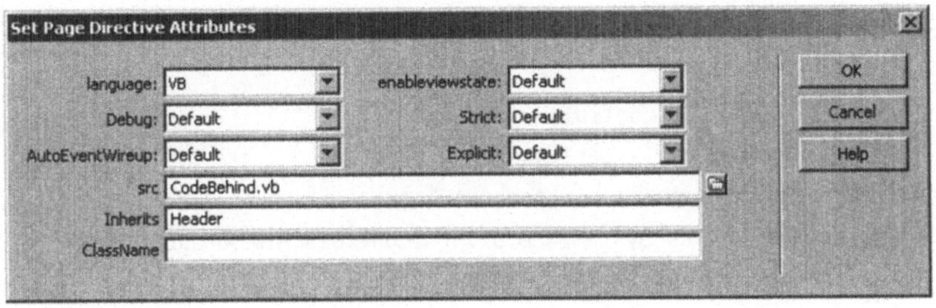

Figure 11-53. The Set Page Directive Attributes dialog box

5. In this dialog box, fill in the following attributes:

   • **src**: CodeBehind.vb

   • **Inherits**: Header

6. Click OK. The @ Control directive will change from this:

   ```
   <%@ Control Language="VB" %>
   ```

   to the following:

   ```
   <%@ Control Language="VB" src="CodeBehind.vb" inherits="Header" %>
   ```

7. Save the control.

Converting the Menu Control

To convert the Menu.ascx control, follow these steps:

1. Open the control and move the server-side script into the CodeBehind.vb file. Be sure that you place the code with modifications shown in bold at the very end of the CodeBehind.vb file.

```
Public Class Menu
  Inherits System.Web.UI.UserControl

  Sub Page_Load(Src As Object, E As EventArgs) Handles MyBase.Load
    Dim Ctl As Control
    For Each Ctl In Me.Controls
      If Ctl.GetType() Is GetType ➥
(System.Web.UI.HtmlControls.HtmlAnchor) Then
        Dim TheLink As System.Web.UI.HtmlControls.HtmlAnchor = Ctl
        Dim PageName As String = Request.Path()
        PageName = PageName.Substring(PageName.LastIndexOf("/") + 1)
        Dim LinkPage As String = TheLink.Href
        LinkPage = LinkPage.Substring(LinkPage.LastIndexOf("/") + 1)
        If LinkPage.ToLower().Equals(PageName.ToLower()) Then
          TheLink.Href = ""
          Exit For
        End If
      End If
    Next
  End Sub
End Class
```

The first, second, and last lines are used to define a class called Menu that inherits the existing functionality of System.Web.UI.UserControl and hosts the menu control's server-side code. The bold text appended to the end of the Page_Load event procedure indicates that you want to execute this procedure when the Page_Load event is raised.

2. Click the Insert/Edit Control Directive button, and fill in the following attributes:

- **src**: CodeBehind.vb

- **Inherits**: Menu

The @ Control directive will change from this:

```
<%@ Control Language="VB" %>
```

to the following:

```
<%@ Control Language="VB" src="CodeBehind.vb" inherits="Menu" %>
```

3. Save the control.

Converting the Main Booking Page

To convert the BookRoom.aspx page, follow these steps:

1. Open the BookRoom.aspx page and move all the server-side code into the CodeBehind.vb file. Remove the <script> tags and then add the code shown in bold in the following code block:

```
Public Class BookRoom
    Inherits System.Web.UI.Page

    Protected WithEvents DsRooms As DreamweaverCtrls.DataSet
    Protected WithEvents DsBookedDays As DreamweaverCtrls.DataSet
    protected WithEvents drpRooms As DropDownList
    Protected WithEvents CalAvailableDates As Calendar
    Protected WithEvents lblSelectedRoom As Label
    Protected WithEvents lblStatus As Label
    Protected WithEvents DateListBookedDays As DataList
    Protected WithEvents btnBook As Button
    Protected WithEvents btnSelectRange As Button
    Protected WithEvents btnClear As Button

    Dim SelectedDates As System.Collections.ArrayList

    Sub Page_Init(Src As Object, E As EventArgs) Handles MyBase.Init
        Dim i as Integer
        For i = Page.Controls.Count-1 To 0 Step - 1
            If Page.Controls.Item(i).GetType() Is GetType ➥
(DreamweaverCtrls.PageBind) Then
                Page.Controls.RemoveAt(i)
            End If
        Next
    End Sub
```

```
Sub Page_Load(Src As Object, E As EventArgs) Handles MyBase.Load
  If Not Session("SelectedDates") Is Nothing Then
    SelectedDates = Session("SelectedDates")
  Else
    SelectedDates = New System.Collections.ArrayList()
  End If

  If Not Page.IsPostBack Then
    DsRooms.DoInit()
    Me.drpRooms.DataSource = DsRooms.DefaultView
    Me.drpRooms.DataTextField = "RoomName"
    Me.drpRooms.DataValueField = "RoomID"
    Me.drpRooms.DataBind()

      If Not Request.QueryString("RoomID") Is Nothing Then
        Dim RoomID As String = Request.QueryString("RoomID")
        Dim Lst As ListItem
        For Each Lst In Me.drpRooms.Items
          If Lst.Value = RoomID Then
            Lst.Selected = true
            Exit For
          End If
        Next
      End If

    CalAvailableDates.VisibleDate = DateTime.Now
    CalAvailableDates.SelectedDate = DateTime.Now
  End If

  Me.DsBookedDays.DoInit()
  lblSelectedRoom.Text = drpRooms.SelectedItem.Text
  lblSelectedRoom.DataBind()

End Sub

Sub btnBook_Click(Src As Object, E As EventArgs) Handles btnBook.Click
  Dim SelectedDate As DateTime
  if SelectedDates.Count = 0 Then
    lblStatus.Text = "You did not select any dates!"
    Exit Sub
  End If
  For each SelectedDate In SelectedDates
    If IsBooked(SelectedDate) Then
```

```
          lblStatus.Text = "Some of your selected dates are already booked!"
          Exit Sub
        End If
      Next
      Response.Redirect("GetCustomerInfo.aspx?RoomID=" & ➡
Me.drpRooms.SelectedItem.Value)
    End Sub


  Sub btnSelectRange_Click(Src As Object, E As EventArgs) ➡
  Handles btnSelectRange.Click
    If SelectedDates.Count = 2 Then
      SelectedDates.Sort()
      Dim CurrentDate As DateTime = SelectedDates.Item(0)
      Do While Not CurrentDate.Equals(SelectedDates.Item(1))
        CurrentDate = CurrentDate.AddDays(1)
        If Not SelectedDates.Contains(CurrentDate) Then
          SelectedDates.Add(CurrentDate)
        End If
      Loop
      lblStatus.Text = ""
    Else
      lblStatus.Text = "To select a range 2 ➡
dates(the start and end) must be selected!"
    End If
  End Sub

  Sub btnClear_Click(Src As Object, E As EventArgs) ➡
  Handles btnClear.Click
    SelectedDates.Clear()
    lblStatus.Text = ""
  End Sub

  Function IsBooked(TheDate As System.DateTime) As Boolean
    Dim Dv As System.Data.DataView = Me.DsBookedDays.DefaultView
    Dv.RowFilter = "BookedDate = '" & TheDate & "'"
    Return Dv.Count > 0
  End Function

  Sub CalAvailableDates_PreRender(Src As Object, E As EventArgs) ➡
  Handles CalAvailableDates.PreRender
    If Page.IsPostBack Then
      If Request.Form("__EVENTTARGET").Equals ➡
```

```
        (CalAvailableDates.ClientID) Then
            If Not Request.Form("__EVENTARGUMENT").SubString ➡
(0, 1).Equals("V") Then
                AddRemoveDate()
            End If
        End If
    End If
    Me.DateListBookedDays.DataSource = SelectedDates
    Me.DateListBookedDays.DataBind()
  End Sub


Sub DateListBookedDays_ItemCreated(Src As Object, E As ➡
System.Web.UI.WebControls.DatalistItemEventArgs) ➡
Handles DateListBookedDays.ItemCreated
    Dim BookedDate As DateTime = e.Item.DataItem
    Dim Lbl As Label = e.Item.FindControl("lblBookedDate")
    If IsBooked(BookedDate) Then
      Lbl.ForeColor = System.Drawing.Color.Red
    Else
      Lbl.ForeColor = System.Drawing.Color.Green
    End If
  End Sub


  Sub CalAvailableDates_DayRender(sender As Object, e As ➡
System.Web.UI.WebControls.DayRenderEventArgs) ➡
Handles CalAvailableDates.DayRender
    If e.Day.Date <= DateTime.Now.AddDays(-1) Then
      e.Cell.Text = "<span style=""color:silver;"">" ➡
& e.Day.Date.Day & "<span>"
      Exit Sub
    End If
    If IsBooked(e.Day.Date) Then
      If SelectedDates.Contains(e.Day.Date) Then
        e.Cell.BackColor = System.Drawing.Color.Red
      Else
        e.Cell.Text = e.Day.Date.Day
        e.Cell.ForeColor = System.Drawing.Color.Red
        e.Cell.BackColor = System.Drawing.Color.White
      End If
    Else
      If SelectedDates.Contains(e.Day.Date) Then
        e.Cell.BackColor = System.Drawing.Color.Green
      End If
```

```
      End If
   End Sub

   Sub AddRemoveDate()
      If Not SelectedDates.Contains(CalAvailableDates.SelectedDate) Then
         SelectedDates.Add(CalAvailableDates.SelectedDate)
      Else
         SelectedDates.Remove(CalAvailableDates.SelectedDate)
      End If
      SelectedDates.Sort()
      Session("SelectedDates") = SelectedDates
      lblStatus.Text = ""
   End Sub

End Class
```

The class is called `BookRoom` and it inherits all the existing functionality from the `System.Web.UI.Page` class. The next few lines are the protected declarations for the server controls that you need to access. Then `Handles MyBase.Init` is added to the end of the `Page_Init` event procedure, indicating that this procedure should run when the `Page_Init` event is raised. The methods that have been attached to specific events of the page or its controls are listed in Table 11-8.

Table 11-8. The Events Attached to Each Method

Method	Event
Page_Init	Page.Init
Page_Load	Page.Load
btnBook_Click	btnBook.Click
btnSelectRange_Click	btnSelectRange.Click
btnClear_Click	btnClear.Click
CalAvailableDates PreRender	CalAvailableDates.PreRender
DateListBookedDays ItemCreated	DateListBookedDays.ItemCreated
CalAvailableDates DayRender	CalAvailableDates.DayRender

2. Click the Insert/Edit Page Directive button, and give the `BookRoom.aspx` page the following attributes:

- **src**: CodeBehind.vb

- **Inherits**: BookRoom

The `@ Page` directive will change from this:

```
<%@ Page Language="VB" %>
```

to the following:

```
<%@ Page Language="VB" src="CodeBehind.vb" inherits="BookRoom" %>
```

3. Remove the following attributes from the following tags:

- **CalAvailableDates**: OnPreRender and OnDayRender

- **DateListBookedDays**: OnItemCreated

- **btnBook**: OnClick

- **btnSelectRange**: OnClick

- **btnClear**: OnClick

4. These attributes are removed because the events are now wired to the appropriate method from the CodeBehind file using the `Handles` keyword. This ensures that as little of the behavioral attributes of the tag as possible are defined within the design portion of the page. Save the page.

Converting the Final Booking Page

To convert the `GetCustomerInfo.aspx` page, follow these steps:

1. Open the page and move its server-side code into the `CodeBehind.vb` file. Add the code shown in bold in the following code block:

```
Public Class GetCustomerInfo
  Inherits System.Web.UI.Page


  Protected WithEvents DsCustomers As DreamweaverCtrls.DataSet
  Protected WithEvents Insert1 As DreamweaverCtrls.Insert
```

```
Protected WithEvents lblStatus As Label
Protected WithEvents btnOk As Button
Protected WithEvents Header1 As Header

Dim CustomerID As String

Sub Page_Load(Src As Object, E As EventArgs) Handles MyBase.Load
  If Not Page.IsPostBack Then
    If Request.QueryString("RoomID") Is Nothing Then
      lblStatus.Text = "No Room Selected"
      btnOk.Visible = false
      Exit Sub
    End If
  End If
End Sub

Sub btnOk_Click(Src As Object, E As EventArgs) Handles btnOk.Click
  DsCustomers.DoInit()
  If DsCustomers.RecordCount > 0 Then
    CustomerID = DsCustomers.FieldValue("CustomerID")
  Else
    Insert1.DoInit()
  End If
  InsertBookedDates()
End Sub

Sub InsertBookedDates()
  Dim ObjCmd As System.Data.OleDb.OleDbCommand
  Dim SelectedDates As System.Collections.ArrayList

  If Not Session("SelectedDates") Is Nothing Then
    SelectedDates = Session("SelectedDates")
    If SelectedDates.Count = 0 Then
      lblStatus.Text = "You have not booked any dates"
      Exit Sub
    End If
  Else
    lblStatus.Text = "You have not booked any dates"
    Exit Sub
  End If

  ObjCmd = New System.Data.OleDb.OleDbCommand ➡
("INSERT INTO [tbl_Bookings] ([Customer],[Room]) ➡
 VALUES(?,?)", DsCustomers.myConnection)
```

```
        ObjCmd.Parameters.Add("Customer", CustomerID)
        ObjCmd.Parameters.Add("Room", Request.QueryString("RoomID"))
        ObjCmd.ExecuteNonQuery()

        ObjCmd.Parameters.Clear()

        ObjCmd.CommandText = "SELECT @@Identity"
        Dim BookingID As String = ObjCmd.ExecuteScalar()

        ObjCmd.CommandText = "INSERT INTO [tbl_BookedDays] ➥
    ([BookingID],[BookedDate]) VALUES(?,?)"
        ObjCmd.Parameters.Add("BookingID", BookingID)
        ObjCmd.Parameters.Add("BookedDate", "")

        Dim SelectedDate As DateTime
        For each SelectedDate In SelectedDates
          ObjCmd.Parameters.Item("BookedDate").Value = SelectedDate
          ObjCmd.ExecuteNonQuery()
        Next

        Session.Remove("SelectedDates")

        Me.lblStatus.ForeColor = System.Drawing.Color.Green
        Me.lblStatus.Text = "Your Booking has been placed, Thank You."
        Me.btnOk.Visible = false
        Me.Header1.Text = "Booking placed!"

    End Sub

    Sub Insert1_Inserted(sender As Object, e As ➥
  DreamweaverCtrls.InsertedEventArgs)  Handles Insert1.Inserted
      CustomerID = e.Identity
    End Sub
End Class
```

2. Click the **Insert/Edit Page Directive** button, and set the following attributes for the GetCustomerInfo.aspx **page:**

    • **src:** CodeBehind.vb

    • **Inherits:** GetCustomerInfo

    The @ Page directive will change from this:

```
<%@ Page Language="VB" %>
```

to the following:

```
<%@ Page Language="VB" src="CodeBehind.vb" inherits="GetCustomerInfo" %>
```

3. Remove the following attributes from the following tags:

- **btnOk**: OnClick

- **Insert1**: OnInserted

4. Save the page.

All the controls and pages have been converted to use CodeBehind. As you can see, it is not very complicated to convert inline code into CodeBehind. You simply add `WithEvents` declarations to controls and `Handles` keywords to methods that should run for specific events.

The following code block shows the `CodeBehind.vb` file in its entirety:

```
Imports System
Imports System.Web.UI
Imports System.Web.UI.WebControls

'CodeBehind Class for Header.ascx
Public Class Header
  Inherits System.Web.UI.UserControl

  Protected WithEvents lblHeaderText As Label

  Public Property Text() As String
    Get
      Return Me.lblHeaderText.Text
    End Get
    Set(ByVal Value As String)
      Me.lblHeaderText.Text = Value
    End Set
  End Property

End Class

'CodeBehind Class for Menu.ascx
Public Class Menu
  Inherits System.Web.UI.UserControl
```

```
    Sub Page_Load(Src As Object, E As EventArgs) Handles MyBase.Load
      Dim Ctl As Control
        For Each Ctl In Me.Controls
          If Ctl.GetType() Is GetType ➡
(System.Web.UI.HtmlControls.HtmlAnchor) Then
            Dim TheLink As System.Web.UI.HtmlControls.HtmlAnchor = Ctl
            Dim PageName As String = Request.Path()
            PageName = PageName.Substring(PageName.LastIndexOf("/") + 1)
            Dim LinkPage As String = TheLink.Href
            LinkPage = LinkPage.Substring(LinkPage.LastIndexOf("/") + 1)
            If LinkPage.ToLower().Equals(PageName.ToLower()) Then
              TheLink.Href = ""
              Exit For
            End If
          End If
        Next
    End Sub

End Class

'CodeBehind Class for BookRoom.aspx
Public Class BookRoom
  Inherits System.Web.UI.Page

  Protected WithEvents DsRooms As DreamweaverCtrls.DataSet
  Protected WithEvents DsBookedDays As DreamweaverCtrls.DataSet
  protected WithEvents drpRooms As DropDownList
  Protected WithEvents CalAvailableDates As Calendar
  Protected WithEvents lblSelectedRoom As Label
  Protected WithEvents lblStatus As Label
  Protected WithEvents DateListBookedDays As DataList
  Protected WithEvents btnBook As Button
  Protected WithEvents btnSelectRange As Button
  Protected WithEvents btnClear As Button

  Dim SelectedDates As System.Collections.ArrayList

  Sub Page_Init(Src As Object, E As EventArgs) Handles MyBase.Init
  Dim i as Integer
    For i = Page.Controls.Count-1 To 0 Step - 1
      If Page.Controls.Item(i).GetType() Is GetType ➡
(DreamweaverCtrls.PageBind) Then
```

```
            Page.Controls.RemoveAt(i)
          End If
      Next
  End Sub


  Sub Page_Load(Src As Object, E As EventArgs) Handles MyBase.Load

    If Not Session("SelectedDates") Is Nothing Then
      SelectedDates = Session("SelectedDates")
    Else
      SelectedDates = New System.Collections.ArrayList()
    End If

    If Not Page.IsPostBack Then
      DsRooms.DoInit()
      Me.drpRooms.DataSource = DsRooms.DefaultView
      Me.drpRooms.DataTextField = "RoomName"
      Me.drpRooms.DataValueField = "RoomID"
      Me.drpRooms.DataBind()

      If Not Request.QueryString("RoomID") Is Nothing Then
        Dim RoomID As String = Request.QueryString("RoomID")
        Dim Lst As ListItem
        For Each Lst In Me.drpRooms.Items
          If Lst.Value = RoomID Then
            Lst.Selected = true
            Exit For
          End If
        Next
      End If

      CalAvailableDates.VisibleDate = DateTime.Now
      CalAvailableDates.SelectedDate = DateTime.Now
    End If

    Me.DsBookedDays.DoInit()
    lblSelectedRoom.Text = drpRooms.SelectedItem.Text
    lblSelectedRoom.DataBind()

  End Sub
```

```
Sub btnBook_Click(Src As Object, E As EventArgs) ➥
Handles btnBook.Click
   Dim SelectedDate As DateTime
   if SelectedDates.Count = 0 Then
     lblStatus.Text = "You did not select any dates!"
     Exit Sub
   End If
   For each SelectedDate In SelectedDates
     If IsBooked(SelectedDate) Then
       lblStatus.Text = "Some of your selected dates are already booked!"
       Exit Sub
     End If
   Next
   Response.Redirect("GetCustomerInfo.aspx?RoomID=" & ➥
Me.drpRooms.SelectedItem.Value)
  End Sub


  Sub btnSelectRange_Click(Src As Object, E As EventArgs) Handles ➥
btnSelectRange.Click
   If SelectedDates.Count = 2 Then
     SelectedDates.Sort()
     Dim CurrentDate As DateTime = SelectedDates.Item(0)
     Do While Not CurrentDate.Equals(SelectedDates.Item(1))
       CurrentDate = CurrentDate.AddDays(1)
       If Not SelectedDates.Contains(CurrentDate) Then
         SelectedDates.Add(CurrentDate)
       End If
     Loop
     lblStatus.Text = ""
   Else
     lblStatus.Text = "To select a range 2 ➥
dates(the start and end) must be selected!"
   End If
  End Sub

  Sub btnClear_Click(Src As Object, E As EventArgs) ➥
Handles btnClear.Click
   SelectedDates.Clear()
   lblStatus.Text = ""
  End Sub
```

```
Function IsBooked(TheDate As System.DateTime) As Boolean
  Dim Dv As System.Data.DataView = Me.DsBookedDays.DefaultView
  Dv.RowFilter = "BookedDate = '" & TheDate & "'"
  Return Dv.Count > 0
End Function

Sub CalAvailableDates_PreRender(Src As Object, E As EventArgs) ➡
Handles CalAvailableDates.PreRender
  If Page.IsPostBack Then
    If Request.Form("__EVENTTARGET").Equals(CalAvailableDates.ClientID) Then
      If Not Request.Form("__EVENTARGUMENT").SubString(0, 1).Equals("V") Then
        AddRemoveDate()
      End If
    End If
  End If
  Me.DateListBookedDays.DataSource = SelectedDates
  Me.DateListBookedDays.DataBind()
End Sub

Sub DateListBookedDays_ItemCreated(Src As Object, E As ➡
System.Web.UI.WebControls.DatalistItemEventArgs) Handles ➡
DateListBookedDays.ItemCreated
  Dim BookedDate As DateTime = e.Item.DataItem
  Dim Lbl As Label = e.Item.FindControl("lblBookedDate")
  If IsBooked(BookedDate) Then
    Lbl.ForeColor = System.Drawing.Color.Red
  Else
    Lbl.ForeColor = System.Drawing.Color.Green
  End If
End Sub

Sub CalAvailableDates_DayRender(sender As Object, e As ➡
System.Web.UI.WebControls.DayRenderEventArgs) Handles ➡
CalAvailableDates.DayRender
  If e.Day.Date <= DateTime.Now.AddDays(-1) Then
    e.Cell.Text = "<span style=""color:silver;"">" ➡
 & e.Day.Date.Day & "<span>"
    Exit Sub
  End If
  If IsBooked(e.Day.Date) Then
    If SelectedDates.Contains(e.Day.Date) Then
      e.Cell.BackColor = System.Drawing.Color.Red
    Else
```

```
                e.Cell.Text = e.Day.Date.Day
                e.Cell.ForeColor = System.Drawing.Color.Red
                e.Cell.BackColor = System.Drawing.Color.White
            End If
        Else
            If SelectedDates.Contains(e.Day.Date) Then
                e.Cell.BackColor = System.Drawing.Color.Green
            End If
        End If
    End If
End Sub


Sub AddRemoveDate()
    If Not SelectedDates.Contains(CalAvailableDates.SelectedDate) Then
        SelectedDates.Add(CalAvailableDates.SelectedDate)
    Else
        SelectedDates.Remove(CalAvailableDates.SelectedDate)
    End If
    SelectedDates.Sort()
    Session("SelectedDates") = SelectedDates
    lblStatus.Text = ""
End Sub

End Class



'CodeBehind Class for GetCustomerInfo.aspx
Public Class GetCustomerInfo
    Inherits System.Web.UI.Page

    Protected WithEvents DsCustomers As DreamweaverCtrls.DataSet
    Protected WithEvents Insert1 As DreamweaverCtrls.Insert
    Protected WithEvents lblStatus As Label
    Protected WithEvents btnOk As Button
    Protected WithEvents Header1 As Header

    Dim CustomerID As String

    Sub Page_Load(Src As Object, E As EventArgs) Handles MyBase.Load
        If Not Page.IsPostBack Then
            If Request.QueryString("RoomID") Is Nothing Then
                lblStatus.Text = "No Room Selected"
                btnOk.Visible = false
```

```vbnet
        Exit Sub
      End If
    End If
  End Sub


  Sub btnOk_Click(Src As Object, E As EventArgs) Handles btnOk.Click
    DsCustomers.DoInit()
    If DsCustomers.RecordCount > 0 Then
      CustomerID = DsCustomers.FieldValue("CustomerID")
    Else
      Insert1.DoInit()
    End If
    InsertBookedDates()
  End Sub


  Sub InsertBookedDates()
    Dim ObjCmd As System.Data.OleDb.OleDbCommand
    Dim SelectedDates As System.Collections.ArrayList

    If Not Session("SelectedDates") Is Nothing Then
      SelectedDates = Session("SelectedDates")
      If SelectedDates.Count = 0 Then
        lblStatus.Text = "You have not booked any dates"
        Exit Sub
      End If
    Else
      lblStatus.Text = "You have not booked any dates"
      Exit Sub
    End If


    ObjCmd = New System.Data.OleDb.OleDbCommand ➥
("INSERT INTO [tbl_Bookings] ([Customer],[Room]) ➥
 VALUES(?,?)", DsCustomers.myConnection)
    ObjCmd.Parameters.Add("Customer", CustomerID)
    ObjCmd.Parameters.Add("Room", Request.QueryString("RoomID"))
    ObjCmd.ExecuteNonQuery()

    ObjCmd.Parameters.Clear()

    ObjCmd.CommandText = "SELECT @@Identity"
    Dim BookingID As String = ObjCmd.ExecuteScalar()
```

```
      ObjCmd.CommandText = "INSERT INTO ➥
  [tbl_BookedDays] ([BookingID],[BookedDate]) VALUES(?,?)"
      ObjCmd.Parameters.Add("BookingID", BookingID)
      ObjCmd.Parameters.Add("BookedDate", "")

      Dim SelectedDate As DateTime
      For each SelectedDate In SelectedDates
        ObjCmd.Parameters.Item("BookedDate").Value = SelectedDate
        ObjCmd.ExecuteNonQuery()
      Next

      Session.Remove("SelectedDates")

      Me.lblStatus.ForeColor = System.Drawing.Color.Green
      Me.lblStatus.Text = "Your Booking has been placed, Thank You."
      Me.btnOk.Visible = false
      Me.Header1.Text = "Booking placed!"

    End Sub

    Sub Insert1_Inserted(sender As Object, e As ➥
   DreamweaverCtrls.InsertedEventArgs) Handles Insert1.Inserted
      CustomerID = e.Identity
    End Sub

End Class
```

Compiling the CodeBehind File into an Assembly

You could call it a day at this point, but you might still want to go a little bit further and compile the CodeBehind file into an assembly. Doing so would enable you to pack all the server-side code into a DLL file that can be deployed into the application's bin directory. The benefits of this are as follows:

- **Better performance**: The code is already compiled, so the server does not have to compile it.

- **The code is hidden**: The code is compiled into a DLL file, so it is hidden from view. There is no need to publish the VB files to the server.

- **Simple deployment**: When the server code needs minor changes, you can simply recompile and publish the assembly (DLL) file.

To compile the CodeBehind.vb file into an assembly, you can use the Visual Basic command line compiler (vbc.exe), which is included in the .NET Framework SDK. If you have the .NET Framework redistributable, you must install the SDK version from http://www.asp.net/download-1.1.aspx?tabindex=0&tabid=1 before continuing.

1. To compile a source VB file into an assembly using the command line compiler, click the Start button on the Windows taskbar and select Run from the menu. In the Run dialog box, type **cmd**, as shown in Figure 11-54. Then click OK.

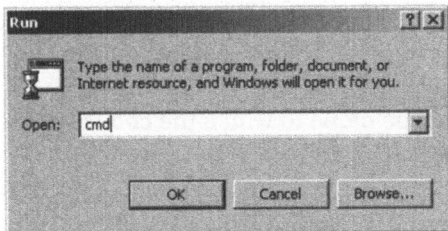

Figure 11-54. The Run dialog box

2. The command prompt window appears, in which a compiler command can be issued. By default, this window's working directory will typically be the root of the C: drive. For the purposes of this exercise, the working directory should be the case study application's root directory. Assuming you have the case study application in C:\inetpub\wwwroot\casestudy, type the following command at the command prompt:

```
cd c:\inetpub\wwwroot\casestudy
```
The command prompt window will now use the specified directory as its working directory. To compile the code, you could issue the following command:

```
vbc.exe /t:library /out: bin\ CaseStudy.dll /r:System.dll ➥
    /r:System.Web.dll /r:System.Data.dll /r:System.Drawing.dll ➥
    /r:bin\DreamweaverCtrls.dll CodeBehind.vb
```

3. Unfortunately, this is quite a complex command and it would be difficult to type it without making an error. In addition, if you made a typo or changed code that would require a recompile, you would need to type the whole command again. Instead, create a text file within the root of the case study application, place the compiler command inside this text file, and save it as Compile.bat.

4. To issue the complex compiler command, simply type the name of this
    file at the command prompt.

    ```
    Compile
    ```

    By storing the real command within a BAT (batch file), you can execute the
    command as often as you like without having to type it in at the command
    prompt each time. Now let's look at the compiler command in detail and
    find out what each part of the command does.

    The command is made up of the EXE file and a few command switches
    that control how the compilation is performed. These switches are as
    follows:

    - **/t:library**: This is the target file type name to which the code is com-
      piled. In this case, it's an assembly (DLL) file.

    - **/out: bin\CaseStudy.dll**: This is used to specify the name of the com-
      piled file. This example places the compiled assembly directly into the
      application's bin directory.

    The following switches reference other assemblies on which your code
    depends. These referenced DLL files are all standard .NET assemblies
    except DreamweaverCtrls.dll, which is supplied with Dreamweaver.

    - **/r:System.dll**: The code uses classes or methods of the System name-
      space, so this switch references System.dll.

    - **/r:System.Web.dll**: The code uses classes or methods of the System.Web
      namespace, so this switch references System.Web.dll.

    - **/r:System.Data.dll**: The code uses classes or methods of the
      System.Data namespace, so this switch references System.Data.dll.

    - **/r:System.Drawing.dll**: The code uses classes or methods of the
      System.Drawing namespace, so this switch references
      System.Drawing.dll.

    - **/r:bin\DreamweaverCtrls.dll**: This code uses classes or methods of the
      DreamweaverCtrls namespace, so this switch references
      DreamweaverCtrls.dll. Because this is not a native .NET file, you have
      to prefix the assembly name with bin\ to let the compiler know that
      DreamweaverCtrls.dll can be found in the bin directory.

The final switch passed to the compiler is the name of the source file that contains the code. You can also compile multiple source files into a single assembly by placing all the source files into the command as a comma-separated list of files like this:

```
File1.vb, File2.vb, File3.vb
```

5. To complete the process, open the four files that you converted to CodeBehind and remove the `src` attributes from the `@ Control` and `@ Page` directives. If you neglect this step, you will receive an error because the page will be compiled dynamically but it will conflict with the classes in the compiled `CaseStudy.dll` assembly. The error will be similar to the following:

```
'Header' is ambiguous
```

where `Header` is whatever file still has the `src` attribute defined.

Summary

In this chapter, you used the knowledge you gained in the previous chapters within the context of a full application. It is important to note that the case study application is not complete enough to use in a production environment; you still have to add the traditional content expected within production applications. It is also not likely to win any awards for its design elements. However, you should consider the limitations of the application a chance for you to expand your knowledge on your own time.

Migrating ASP to ASP.NET

IN THIS APPENDIX, we will demonstrate how to migrate an existing ASP web site to ASP.NET, and we will discuss a few of the important choices that you must make during the process. You can also refer to the MSDN documentation at http://msdn.microsoft.com/library/default.asp?url=/library/en-us/cpguide/ html/cpconmigratingasppagestoasp.asp for more information. If you work in a ColdFusion environment, see http://msdn.microsoft.com/library/ default.asp?url=/library/en-us/dnaspp/html/coldfusiontoaspnet.asp.

ASP.NET Improvements

The business benefits of creating a web application in ASP.NET include the following:

- **Speed**: Better caching and cache fusion in web farms make ASP.NET 3–5 times faster than ASP.

- **Compiled execution**: No explicit compile step is required to update components. ASP.NET automatically detects changes, compiles the files if needed, and readies the compiled results, without the need to restart the server.

- **Flexible caching**: Individual parts of a page, its code, and its data can be cached separately. This improves performance dramatically because repeated requests for data-driven pages no longer require you to query the database on every request.

- **Web farm session state**: ASP.NET session state allows session data to be shared across all machines in a web farm, which enables faster and more efficient caching.

- **Protection**: ASP.NET automatically detects and recovers from errors such as deadlocks and memory leaks. If an old process is tying up a significant amount of resources, ASP.NET can start a new version of the same process and dispose of the old one.

The programming benefits of creating a web application in ASP.NET include the following:

- **Programming models**: The **Web Forms** programming model is a browser-independent user interface that processes data on the web server so you do not have to create browser-specific versions. The **XML web services** programming model uses components that run on the server, typically include business logic, and are available via universal web protocols. (We do not cover XML web services in this appendix.)

    Server controls: This HTML-like style of declarative programming enables applications to be built with far less code than with classic ASP. This allows programmers to focus on the logic of page execution rather than on the HTML coding details and particularities of each browser.

- **Flexible language options**: You can work in any of over 25 .NET languages, including VB, C++, and C#.

- **Easy application deployment**: Simply copy the application to the server. Configuration is achieved via XML files, and there is no need to register any components.

- **Dynamic update of running application**: Compiled DLL files can be updated without restarting the web server.

- **Multiple device support with one set of code**: You no longer have to worry about different browser implementations. ASP.NET takes care of it all for you, no matter what browser is used.

Migration Considerations

ASP and ASP.NET applications can run simultaneously on the same server without adversely affecting each other. This is primarily because the two systems have separate processing engines: the ASP.NET processes ASPX files and ASP processes ASP files. This means that the web site can be upgraded flexibly and with no downtime. The same is true for mixing components used by ASP pages. For example, you can migrate some pages to ASP.NET while they continue to work with ADO 2.5.

It is important to remember that although your application can contain both ASP and ASP.NET pages, you cannot share state variables stored in the intrinsic Session or Application objects. You must either duplicate this information in both systems or come up with a custom solution until your application is fully migrated.

All authentication and authorization is done via XML sections in your application's web.config file. This file can specify many parameters to configure each ASP.NET application running on your server. The server is configured using the machine.config file shipped with ASP.NET. Each file directory can have its own web.config file, which sets parameters for that directory and its sub-directories. The web.config file takes effect when saved, so there is no need to restart the server.

All named subroutines and functions must be wholly contained within <script> tags. Therefore, you must replace the <% %> tags with <script language = "vb" runat = "server"> </script>. However, any code within the <%> code delim-iters is still valid and will still be executed in an ASP.NET page. For example, the following will work:

```
<script language="vb" runat="server">
    Sub RenderMe()
        Response.Write("<H3> This is HTML text being rendered. </H3>")
    End Sub
</script>


<%
    Call RenderMe()
%>
```

The Option Explicit statement is now the default, so all variables must be declared. The pages now have directives that control caching, language, and so on. Note the following attribute of the required <%@Page%> directive:

```
<%@Page aspcompat=true Language=VB%>
```

Using the aspcompat attribute will force your page to use components in an ASP-compatible fashion, for example, ADO rather than ADO.NET. Note also that the variant data type is gone (more specific types must be used), the Let and Set statements are no longer needed, and there are no default properties.

ASP.NET uses active server objects much like ASP 3.0, but with one major update: You can now include server objects with every control of a web page. In addition, you can now easily write your own server-side controls.

The Example Web Site

The case study uses a modest HTML page that contains all the elements relevant to an ASP.NET migration, including JavaScript, data access code, and a calendar. You will make the changes in a text editor rather than in Dreamweaver so you can see the details up close. We will use VB .NET in the example.

The example web site is a language school's exam reservation service. The user selects an exam subject and a date, and the page returns the number of seats available for the exam. Business rules enforced in the Access database dictate that a maximum of five students can take the exam on a certain date. The user's input is checked for completeness via JavaScript. A Cascading Style Sheet is also used to format the page. Figure A-1 shows the sample output.

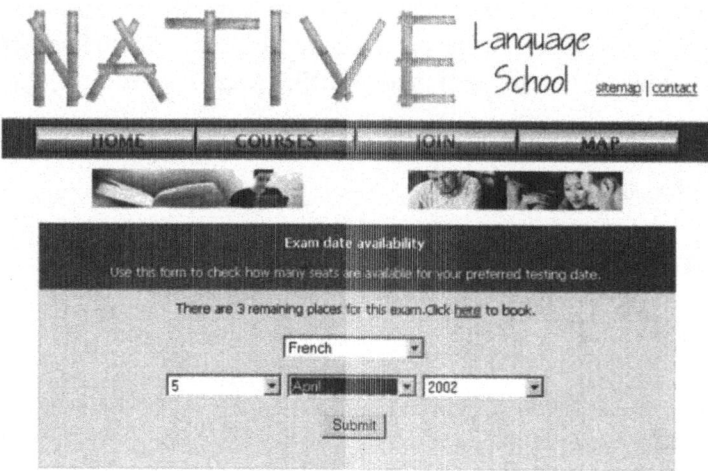

Figure A-1. The example web site

ASP to ASP.NET Web Form Controls

When you migrate an ASP page to an equivalent ASP.NET page, it is a good idea to keep the page functional so you can test the page after each change. Keep a copy of the page at each stage of the migration, and give it a version file name and number suffix to show the progression. Table A-1 is a summary of the example file's progression through the course of this appendix.

Table A-1. Example Web Site Files

File Name	Description
homeasp.asp	The original web page
homeasp0.aspx	The web page with ADO migrated to ADO.NET
homeasp1.aspx	The web page with ADO migrated to ADO.NET and a query result assigned to an asp:Label control
homeasp2.aspx	The web page with databound asp:DropDownList control and code

Table A-1. Example Web Site Files (continued)

File Name	Description
homeasp3.aspx	The web page with asp:Calendar control and handling code
homeasp4.aspx	The web page with web server validation of selected date
homeasp4upgrade.aspx	The web page with improved interface using advanced ASP.NET features
homeasp5.aspx	The completed page web server styles and links

1. Make a copy of the file homeasp.asp and name it homeasp0.aspx. Then open the file in an editor and in your browser. Ordinarily, you would start migration with simple things like images and links, but with this type of migration it is easier (and more instructive) to start with whatever error is displayed in the browser first. The .NET Framework offers help via the following directive on the top of the page:

    ```
    <%@ Page Language="vb" Debug="true" %>
    ```

2. This will enable you to put meaningful messages on the browser when there is an error. Set debug="false".

3. Open the ASPX page in your browser, as shown in Figure A-2.

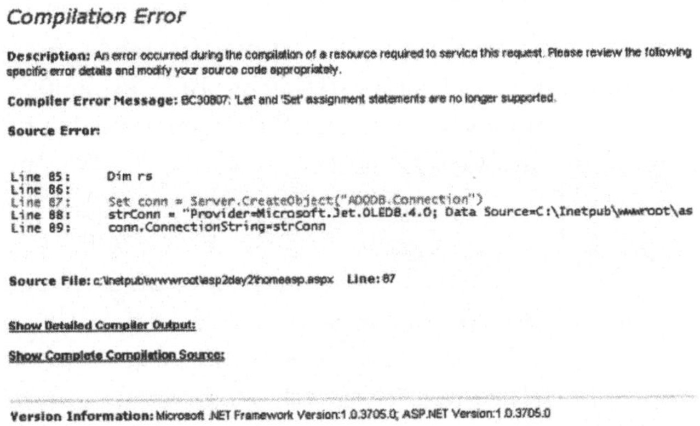

Compilation Error

Description: An error occurred during the compilation of a resource required to service this request. Please review the following specific error details and modify your source code appropriately.

Compiler Error Message: BC30807: 'Let' and 'Set' assignment statements are no longer supported.

Source Error:

```
Line 85:    Dim rs
Line 86:
Line 87:    Set conn = Server.CreateObject("ADODB.Connection")
Line 88:    strConn = "Provider=Microsoft.Jet.OLEDB.4.0; Data Source=C:\Inetpub\wwwroot\as
Line 89:    conn.ConnectionString=strConn
```

Source File: c:\inetpub\wwwroot\asp2day2\homeasp.aspx   **Line:** 87

Show Detailed Compiler Output:

Show Complete Compilation Source:

Version Information: Microsoft .NET Framework Version:1.0.3705.0; ASP.NET Version:1.0.3705.0

Figure A-2. An error caused by the syntax changes in ASP.NET

4. Add a reference pointing to the ADO.NET component, just below the <%@ Page %> directive.

    ```
    <%@ Import Namespace="System.Data" %>
    <%@ Import Namespace="System.Data.OleDb" %>
    ```

Next, you will change the data-accessing code. The easiest way to demonstrate the changes is to show the old and new code side by side. The following tables show the original ADO code in the left column and the replacement ADO.NET code in the right column. Table A-2 shows the opening declarations.

Table A-2. Comparison of ADO Code and ADO.NET Code

ADO Declarations (homeasp.asp)	**ADO.NET Declarations** (homeasp0.aspx)
`<% If Len(Request.QueryString("course"))>0`	`<script runat="server">`
`Then`	`Sub Page_Load()`
`Dim conn`	`Dim mystring as String`
`Dim strConn`	`myString = Request.QueryString("course")`
`Dim rs`	`If (myString<>Nothing) Then`
`Set conn = _`	`Dim conn As OleDbConnection`
`Server.CreateObject("ADODB.Connection")`	`Dim sqlCommand As`
`Set rs = _`	`OleDbDataAdapter`
`Server.CreateObject("ADODB.Recordset")`	`Dim strConn As String`
	`Dim rs As Dataset`
	`Dim filepath as String`
	`Dim stillFree as String`
	`Dim rr as Datarow`
	`Dim rt as Datatable`
	`Dim rc as Datacolumn`

The ADO.NET code is enclosed in `<script>` tags, it has been assigned to run within the intrinsic Page_Load subroutine, and each variable has been explicitly declared. The Set statements are also removed; their function is performed at the variable-declaration level. The code continues in Table A-3.

Table A-3. Opening a Recordset/Dataset in ADO and ADO.NET

ADO Connection	**ADO.NET Connection**
`filePath = Server.MapPath`	`filePath = Server.MapPath`
`("LanguageSchool.mdb")`	`("LanguageSchool.mdb")`
`strConn = "Provider=Microsoft.Jet.`	`strConn = "Provider=Microsoft.Jet.`
`OLEDB.4.0; Data Source=" & filepath & ";"`	`OLEDB.4.0; Data Source=" & filepath & ";"`
`conn.`	`conn.`
`ConnectionString=strConn`	`ConnectionString=strConn`
`conn.Open`	`conn.Open`

Table A-3. Opening a Recordset/Dataset in ADO and ADO.NET (continued)

ADO Connection	ADO.NET Connection
| ```
rs.Open "SELECT stillfree FROM qryResults
WHERE (Course="""" & Request.QueryString
("Course") & """ AND dateFrom=#" &
Request.QueryString("startday") & "/"
& Request.QueryString("startmonth")
& "/" & Request.QueryString("startyear")
& "#)", conn
``` | ```
sqlCommand = new OleDbDataAdapter
("SELECT stillfree FROM qryResults
WHERE (Course="""" & Request.QueryString
("Course") & """ AND dateFrom=#" &
Request.QueryString("startday") & "/" &
Request.QueryString("startmonth") & "/"
& Request.QueryString("startyear") &
"#)", conn)
rs = new DataSet()
sqlCommand.Fill(rs)
``` |

The recordset is substituted for the more powerful dataset, which can contain tables, relationships, and other schema objects. The code continues in Table A-4.

Table A-4. Displaying Results in ASP and ASP.NET

Display ASP Results	Display ASP.NET Results
| ```
If Not (rs.EOF And rs.BOF) Then
Response.
Write("There are " & rs("stillfree") &
" remaining places for this exam.")
If rs("stillfree")>0 Then
Response.Write ("Click
<a href=booking.asp>here</a> to book.")
End If
Else
Response.Write("There are 5 places
available for your selection.
Click <a href=booking.asp>here</a> to
book.")
End If
rs.Close
conn.Close
Set rs = Nothing
Set conn = Nothing
End If %>
``` | ```
For Each rt In rs.Tables
For Each rr In rt.Rows
stillFree=rr(rt.Columns ("stillfree"))
Next
Next
If (stillFree>=0) Then Response.Write
("There are " & stillFree & " remaining
places for this exam.")
If (stillFree>0) Then
Response.Write("Click
<a href=booking.asp> here</a> to book.")
End If
Else
Response.Write("There are 5 places
available for your selection. Click <a
href=booking.asp>here</a> to book.")
End If
conn.Close
rs.Dispose
conn.Dispose
End If
End Sub
</script>
``` |

The separate loop that displays the dates needs very few changes for the moment, as shown in Table A-5.

Table A-5. Displaying Dates in ASP and ASP.NET

Display ASP Dates	Display ASP.NET Dates
```<% For i=1 To 31 Response.Write("<OPTION value=""" & i & """ >" & i & "</OPTION>") Next %>```	```<% Dim i As Integer For i=1 To 31 Response.Write("<OPTION value=""" & i & """ >" & i & "</OPTION>") Next i=Nothing```

The VB .NET language enforces strict coding. A significant amount of migration work could have been avoided by simply declaring variables explicitly and using brackets in function calls. Table A-6 is a summary of some basic syntactical changes needed for migration to VB .NET.

Table A-6. Syntactical Changes Needed for Migration from ASP to ASP.NET

Error	Reason
Option Explicit statement not valid inside a procedure.	The `Option Explicit` statement needs to be defined in the `@ Page` directive using the `Explicit` attribute.
Argument lists in call statements must now be enclosed in parentheses.	Visual Basic .NET requires all subroutine calls to enclose their parameters in parentheses. Instead of `Response.Write "text"` statements, use `Response.Write ("text")`.
Let and Set statements are no longer supported on assignment statements.	The `Let` and `Set` statements have been removed from the Visual Basic language.
Date is a type, and so it is not a valid expression. A variable, constant, or procedure is expected.	In the Project Report application, the `Date()` function was used to get the current date. This is no longer supported—use `DateTime.Now` instead.
The name IsNull is not declared.	Visual Basic .NET no longer supports the `IsNull` function. Use `IsDBNull` instead.
Cast from __ComObject to String is not valid.	Visual Basic .NET no longer supports default properties, so when using classic COM components, be certain to explicitly state the properties you want to use.

Migrating Data Display Elements

If you run the ASPX page now, you will see that the Page_Load method is executed before any page elements are rendered, regardless of its location in the file. This is an important change from ASP, which executed the page from top to bottom. Consequently, the data query's result is displayed at the top of the page. Therefore, the next logical step is to display the data from the dataset at the right place.

1. Create an asp:Label control and assign the following result string:

   ```
   <asp:Label runat="server" id="message"></asp:Label>
   ```

2. To pass the result string to the label message, create a new variable and modify the Response.Write statements to assign the text message to this new variable.

   ```
   Dim lblString As String
   .
   If (stillFree <> Nothing) Then
     lblString="There are " & stillFree & " remaining places for this exam. "
     If (stillFree>0) Then
       lblString=lblString & "Click <a href=booking.asp>here</a> to book."
     End If
   Else
     lblString="There are 5 places available for this exam. "& _
   "Click <a href=booking.asp>here</a> to book."
   End If
   .
   message.Text = lblString
   ```

3. Save the changes as homeasp1.aspx and look at a sample result obtained by running it, as shown in Figure A-3.

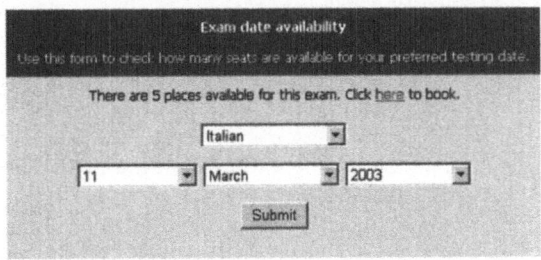

Figure A-3. The output of the ASP.NET page

Migrating Drop-Down Lists

The list of languages is static on the web page. ASP.NET makes it easy to bind data to objects so it is very convenient to improve the web site design.

Obtain the currently available exams from the database by inserting the following in the Page_Load code:

```
If (Not IsPostback) Then
    Dim coursesCommand As OleDbDataAdapter
    Dim ds As Dataset

    coursesCommand = new OleDbDataAdapter("SELECT * FROM tblCourses", conn)
    ds = new DataSet()
    coursesCommand.Fill(ds)

     bind the courses table to the course drop down list
    course.DataSource = ds
    course.DataBind()
End If
```

The (Not IsPostback) condition ensures that the database is contacted only once during the lifetime of the page to build the drop-down list. This is an important consideration in the server-centered environment of web server controls. You no longer have to update the web page whenever the database is updated. The (Not IsPostback) condition also replaced a lot of code with one element, as shown in Table A-7.

Table A-7. A Drop-Down List in ASP and ASP.NET

ASP	ASP.NET (homeasp2.aspx)
`<SELECT name="course"> <OPTION value="0" > _Select a Course_</OPTION> <OPTION value= "English">English</OPTION> <OPTION value= "French" >French</OPTION> <OPTION value= "Italian">Italian</OPTION> <OPTION value= "Spanish">Spanish</OPTION> </SELECT>`	`<asp:DropDownList runat="server" id="course" name="course" width="138px" DataTextField="Course" DataValueField="Course" > </asp:DropDownList>`

Later in this appendix, we will show you how to improve the drop-down list's functionality and take advantage of its programmability.

Migrating Date Selection Controls

Let's now look at an ASP.NET calendar control. You can use Dreamweaver to look at the ASP.NET code created automatically when a calendar control is inserted onto a page. Here is a sample listing:

```
<asp:Calendar id="examDates"
name="examDates" runat="server" Width="220px"
Height="200px" BorderWidth="1px" BackColor="White"
DayNameFormat="FirstLetter" ForeColor="#003399"
Font-Size="8pt" Font-Names="Verdana" BorderColor="#3366CC"
CellPadding="1" SelectionMode="Day"
OnSelectionChanged="SelectionChange" OnVisibleMonthChanged="MonthChange">

        <TodayDayStyle ForeColor="White" BackColor="#99CCCC"></TodayDayStyle>
        <SelectorStyle ForeColor="#336666" BackColor="#99CCCC"></SelectorStyle>
        <NextPrevStyle Font-Size="8pt" ForeColor="#CCCCFF"></NextPrevStyle>
        <SelectedDayStyle Font-Bold="True" ForeColor="#CCFF99"
BackColor="#009999">
</SelectedDayStyle>
        <DayHeaderStyle Height="1px" ForeColor="#336666" BackColor="#99CCCC">
</DayHeaderStyle>
        <TitleStyle Font-Size="10pt" Font-Bold="True" Height="25px"
BorderWidth="1px" ForeColor="#CCCCFF" BorderStyle="Solid"
BorderColor="#3366CC" BackColor="#003399"></TitleStyle>
        <WeekendDayStyle BackColor="#CCCCFF"></WeekendDayStyle>
        <OtherMonthDayStyle ForeColor="#999999"></OtherMonthDayStyle>
</asp:calendar>
```

The code just shown replaces the following three SELECT statements in the ASP code:

```
<SELECT name="startday">
..
</SELECT>
<SELECT name="startmonth">
..
</SELECT>
<SELECT name="startyear">
..
</SELECT>
```

Most of the calendar's attributes are related to style properties. That is great news for the developer because the ASP.NET engine takes care of all the data-handling intelligence. The most important elements are the following:

```
SelectionMode="Day"
OnSelectionChanged="SelectionChange"
OnVisibleMonthChanged="MonthChange"
```

SelectionMode dictates whether the user can select a day, a day and/or week, or a day and/or week and/or month. It can also be set to none to utilize the calendar as a read-only reference control. The other two attributes specify which subroutines must be run when the corresponding events occur. When the user changes the selected date, the modified version of the date is assigned to an asp:Textbox control variable via the SelectionChange subroutine. When the user navigates to another month, the variable is cleared via the MonthChange subroutine so that the context is renewed. These subroutines are inserted in between the same <script> tags as Page_Load.

```
' upon date selection run this subroutine to assign the date to a form input box
Sub SelectionChange(sender As Object, e As System.EventArgs)
    message.Text = ""
    examDate.Text = Left(examDates.SelectedDate.toString(),10)
End Sub

' upon month navigation run this subroutine to clear the date
' from the form input box
Sub MonthChange(sender As Object, e As
System.Web.UI.WebControls.MonthChangedEventArgs)
    message.Text = ""
    examDate.Text = ""
End Sub
```

The result label must be cleared because the user is entering a new navigational context. The asp:Textbox control is assigned the first ten characters of the date, formatted as DD/MM/YYYY.

```
<asp:Textbox runat="server" name="examDate" id="examDate" ></asp:Textbox>
```

Unfortunately, the form cannot be submitted as is because the JavaScript validating the values in the form still references the deleted drop-down list controls. Rather than amending the script to validate the asp:Textbox control, you can do something better. Let's look at the validator controls now.

Migrating Data Validation

The ASP.NET validator controls offer a virtually unlimited number of validation options. For example, you can force a required value, and check whether a data value matches a pattern, a range, or another control in the same page. You can also write your own function to check against a particular control. The validation controls create preset client scripts for each type of validation in browsers that enable it and server-based checks for downlevel browsers.

1. Add a required field validator that replaces the JavaScript validating function, as shown in Table A-8.

Table A-8. The Validator Control Replaces the Custom Client Script

ASP	ASP.NET (homeasp4.aspx)
```function checkSubmit() {```	```<asp:RequiredFieldValidator```
```var sDay = document.examform.startday.options```	```runat="server" id="checkdata" Text="*```
```[document.examform.startday.selectedIndex].```	```Please select a date."```
```value```	```ControlToValidate="examDate"```
```var sMonth = document.examform.```	```ErrorMessage="Please select a date." />```
```startmonth.options[document.examform.```	
```startmonth.selectedIndex].value```	
```var sYear```	
```= document.examform.startyear.options```	
```[document.examform.startyear.```	
```selectedIndex].value```	
```if ((sDay==0)||```	
```(sMonth==0)||(sYear==0)) {```	
```alert("\nPlease```	
```make sure that you have selected all```	
```date elements.\n")```	
```} else {```	
```document.examform.submit() }```	
```}```	

The ASP.NET code just shown is sent to any browser as the following HTML:

```
<script language="javascript"
src="/aspnet_client/system_web/1_0_3705_0/WebUIValidation.js"></script>
.

<input type="submit" name="_ctl0" value="Submit"
onclick="if (typeof(Page_ClientValidate) == 'function') Page_ClientValidate(); "
language="javascript" />
```

2. The browser downloads the ASP.NET file, `WebUIValidation.js`, which contains all the prepared JavaScript functions necessary for validation, including the called function `Page_ClientValidate`. You can now modify the Submit button, as shown in Table A-9.

Table A-9. The Submit Button

ASP	ASP.NET (homeasp4.aspx)
`<INPUT type="button" value="Submit" onClick="checkSubmit()" />`	`<asp:Button runat="server" Text="Submit" > </asp:Button>`

3. Run the homeasp4.aspx page in any browser. First navigate to the desired month using the calendar control, as shown in Figure A-4.

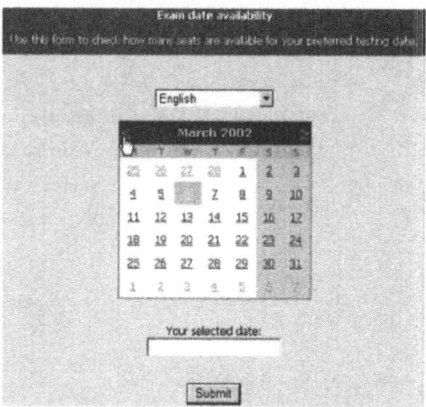

Figure A-4. Navigating via the calendar control

4. Click the desired date, and the control returns with the date indicated, as shown in Figure A-5.

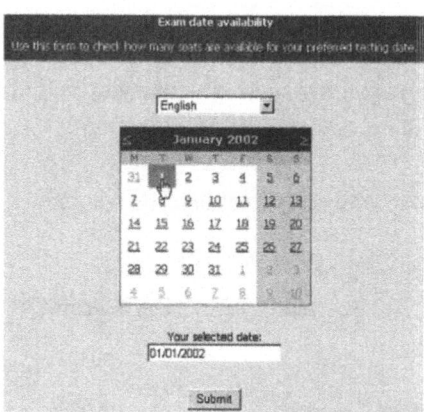

Figure A-5. Select a date by clicking it.

5. Click the Submit button to receive the results for the selection, as shown in Figure A-6.

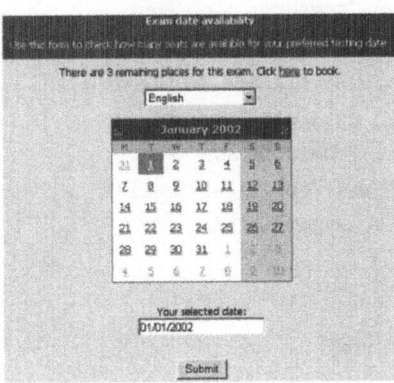

Figure A-6. Submitting the form

If you had submitted the form without a date value, you would have seen the validator control's user-side script at work, as shown in Figure A-7.

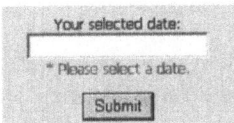

Figure A-7. Validating input migrated to ASP.NET

Migrating Hyperlinks and Images

The most significant improvements from migrating images and links are that they can be databound and easily manipulated programmatically. Migration might be appropriate if your application needs to customize a page extensively according to user selections, for example, if you need to modify a group of NavigateUrl parameters to point to an /italian/ language directory. However, migrating links and images without taking advantage of their programmable properties is counterproductive and burdens the ASP.NET engine with unnecessary work. It might be better to simply write the HTML code directly. Also remember that if you already have code within <%> delimiters, it is not essential to modify it, especially when migrating quickly is more important. For the sample web site, Table A-10 shows the changes made to the link.

Table A-10. Link Migration to ASP.NET

ASP Link	ASP.NET Link (homeasp4.aspx)
`<a href="someurl1.asp">sitemap</a>  ` `|  <a href="someurl2.asp" >contact</a>`	`<asp:Hyperlink runat="server"` `NavigateUrl="someurl1.asp" Font-` `Names="Tahoma" Font-Size="Smaller" >` `sitemap</asp:Hyperlink>  | ` `<asp:Hyperlink runat="server"` `NavigateUrl="someurl2.asp" Font-` `Names="Tahoma" Font-Size="Smaller" >` `contact</asp:Hyperlink>`

Table A-11 shows the changes made to the image.

Table A-11. Image Migration to ASP.NET

ASP Image	ASP.NET Image
`<img src="header.gif" border="0" />`	`<asp:Image runat="server"` `ImageUrl="header.gif"></asp:Image>`

Upgrading and Migrating

Strictly speaking, the ASP elements have now been fully migrated to ASP.NET controls, but the ease with which you can bind data provides a great opportunity to improve the user experience. In the first part of this appendix, you used data binding to build a drop-down list with the exam names. You could convert it into something like the list shown in Figure A-8 (`homepage4upgrade.aspx`).

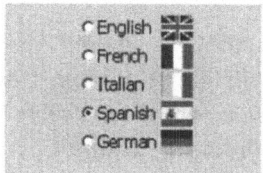

Figure A-8. Enhancing the user experience

The `tblCourses` table contains the source URL for each flag, as shown in Figure A-9.

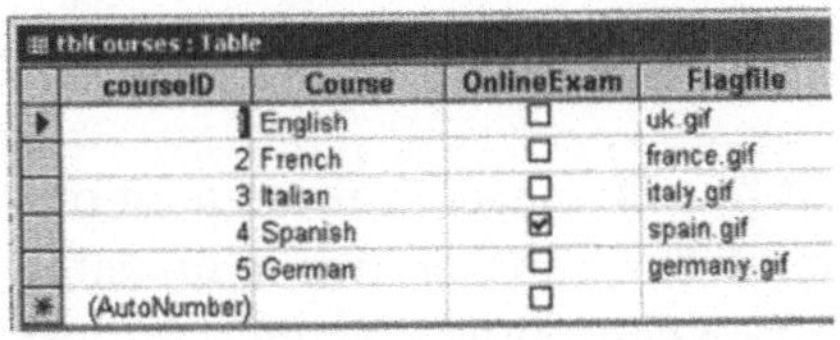

courseID	Course	OnlineExam	Flagfile
1	English	☐	uk.gif
2	French	☐	france.gif
3	Italian	☐	italy.gif
4	Spanish	☒	spain.gif
5	German	☐	germany.gif
(AutoNumber)		☐	

Figure A-9. Specifying the image URLs in the database

If you were displaying text, you could bind the dataset to an `asp:RadioButtonList` control, which automatically creates a group of radio buttons based on a data source. However, that kind of control cannot contain databound image controls. The `asp:Repeater` control allows a custom layout by repeating a specified template for each item displayed in the list. You need only evaluate the image source field for each radio button. Table A-12 shows the file before and after this upgrade.

Table A-12. The `asp:Repeater` *Control Upgrade*

ASP.NET Before Upgrade

```
<asp:DropDownList runat="server"
id="course" name="course" width="138px"
DataTextField="Course" DataValueField=
"Course" > </asp:DropDownList>
```

ASP.NET After Upgrade
(homeasp4upgrade.aspx)

```
<ASP:Repeater id="course" runat="server" >
<HeaderTemplate>
<TABLE border="0" align="center" >
</HeaderTemplate>
<ItemTemplate>
<tr><td align="left"> <INPUT
type="radio" name="course" >
<%# DataBinder.Eval(Container.DataItem,
"Course") %> </INPUT>
</td><td align="left"> <IMG src=<%#
DataBinder.Eval(Container.DataItem,
"FlagFile") %> /><br>
</td></tr> </ItemTemplate>
<FooterTemplate> </table>
</FooterTemplate></ASP:Repeater>
```

The bold areas are where each record of the bound datasets is evaluated. The modification demonstrated in this table can be used when migrating ASP code, too, especially if you have `<%=.%>` delimiters in your pages that loop through recordsets.

Appearance Properties

The ways that styles are rendered in different browsers have caused a lot of headaches for programmers. ASP.NET distinguishes between two main categories of browsers: uplevel and downlevel. **Uplevel** browsers usually support the following:

- ECMAScript (JScript, JavaScript) version 1.2

- HTML version 4.0

- The Microsoft Document Object Model (MSDOM)

- Cascading Style Sheets (CSS)

Downlevel browsers and client devices support the following:

- HTML version 3.2

The properties shown in Table A-13 render differently in uplevel and downlevel browsers.

Table A-13. Style Properties in ASP.NET

Property	Browser Rendering
AccessKey	This property works only in Microsoft Internet Explorer 4.0 or later.
BackColor	In general, only controls that render as a `<table>` tag can output a background color in HTML 3.2. This property works in controls that render in `<span>` tags.
BorderColor	This property works on downlevel browsers for the same table-based controls as `BackColor`, although the `BorderColor` attribute is not part of the HTML 3.2 standard.
BorderStyle	This property will not work on any downlevel browsers.
BorderWidth	This property works in downlevel browsers for controls that render as `<table>` or `<img>` tags, and it must be specified in pixels or it will always be rendered as either `border=1` or `border=0`.
CssClass	This property is always rendered as the `class` attribute, regardless of the browser. Most uplevel browsers recognize the `class` attribute.
Font-Size	This property works on downlevel browsers for all controls only if named font sizes are used.

Table A-13. Style Properties in ASP.NET (continued)

Property	Browser Rendering
Font-Overline	This property will not work on any downlevel browsers.
ForeColor	This property will be rendered in \<font\> tags for downlevel browsers.
Height	This property will generally not work on downlevel browsers for table-based controls.
TabIndex	This property will not work on any downlevel browsers.
ToolTip	This property will not work on any downlevel browsers.
Width	This property will generally not work on downlevel browsers for table-based controls.
GridLines	This property can only be on or off in HTML 3.2.

When the page runs, appearance properties are rendered according to the capabilities of the browser. If the browser supports Cascading Style Sheets (CSS), the appearance properties are rendered as style attributes of the HTML elements that make up the control. If the browser does not support CSS, the appearance is rendered using other HTML tags. For example, the form's heading could be written in the ASP.NET code shown in Table A-14.

Table A-14. Applying ASP.NET Control Styles

ASP	ASP.NET (homeasp5.aspx)
`<td bgcolor="#3A529C" align="center" valign="top" class="content-wht"> <b>Exam date availability</b>  Use this form to check how many seats are available for your preferred testing date. </td>`	`<asp:Label runat="server" Font-Names= "Verdana,Tahoma" ForeColor="#FFFFFF" Font-Size="Smaller" > <b>Exam date availability</b>  Use this form to check how many seats are available for your preferred testing date. </asp:Label>`

If the browser supports CSS, the HTML delivered would be as follows:

```
<span style="color:white;font-family:Verdana,Tahoma;font-size;Smaller">...</span>
```

If the browser does not support CSS, the HTML delivered would be as follows:

```
<font face="Verdana, Tahoma" color="white" size="1">..</font>
```

The original separate stylesheets become unnecessary—ASP.NET takes care of the presentation according to browser capabilities. Of course, there may be good reasons why you would want to keep the separate styles, but for the purposes of this appendix, we will avoid duplication and include the CSS styles in a common file called common.css. You can replace the JavaScript code with one stylesheet link, as shown in Table A-15.

Table A-15. Applying Styles Correctly for Each Browser

ASP	ASP.NET(homeasp5.aspx)
```if ((navigator.appName == "Microsoft Internet Explorer") && (parseInt(navigator.appVersion) >= 4)) { document.write("<link REL='stylesheet' HREF='ie.css' TYPE='text/css'>"); } else { document.write("<link REL='stylesheet' HREF='std.css' TYPE='text/css'>"); }```	```<link REL="stylesheet" HREF="common.css" TYPE="text/css">```

You can then enter a CssClass attribute to the elements you want to style.

```
CssClass="content-wht"
```

The asp:Label control then looks as follows:

```
<asp:Label runat="server"
Font-Names="Verdana,Tahoma" ForeColor="#FFFFFF"
Font-Size="Smaller" CssClass="content-wht">..</asp:Label>
```

The properties will be used to render styles in downlevel browsers and the CssClass attribute will take care of uplevel browsers.

Client Script Migration

You can specify your own client-side code but remember that ASP.NET creates its own code for the same controls. As a rule, these run separately, but they can affect the logic of your application. To specify client-side script, use the <script> tag as always, but with the runat="client" attribute.

NOTE *Even if your users have scripts disabled in their browsers, ASP.NET makes sure that validation still occurs. In this situation, the validation happens on the server rather than the browser.*

Figure A-10 shows the page tested in any browser with active scripting disabled.

Figure A-10. Client script in a browser that supports client scripting

Figure A-11 shows the page tested on WebTV, which does not allow scripting. After submitting without a date value, the server replies with a new page.

Figure A-11. Validation is performed on the server

Summary

ASP.NET and the .NET infrastructure are a big innovative leap from previous Microsoft products. However, many of you may still prefer the intuitiveness of ASP coding, especially when it comes to mingling HTML code with an If statement or a For...Next loop. The fact that ASP and ASP.NET can coexist means that ASP may be with us for a while yet as a valid application-building tool.

Index

forums.apress.com

JOIN THE APRESS FORUMS AND BE PART OF OUR COMMUNITY. You'll find discussions that cover topics of interest to IT professionals, programmers, and enthusiasts just like you. If you post a query to one of our forums, you can expect that some of the best minds in the business—especially Apress authors, who all write with *The Expert's Voice*™—will chime in to help you. Why not aim to become one of our most valuable participants (MVPs) and win cool stuff? Here's a sampling of what you'll find:

DATABASES

Data drives everything.

Share information, exchange ideas, and discuss any database programming or administration issues.

PROGRAMMING/BUSINESS

Unfortunately, it is.

Talk about the Apress line of books that cover software methodology, best practices, and how programmers interact with the "suits."

INTERNET TECHNOLOGIES AND NETWORKING

Try living without plumbing (and eventually IPv6).

Talk about networking topics including protocols, design, administration, wireless, wired, storage, backup, certifications, trends, and new technologies.

WEB DEVELOPMENT/DESIGN

Ugly doesn't cut it anymore, and CGI is absurd.

Help is in sight for your site. Find design solutions for your projects and get ideas for building an interactive Web site.

JAVA

We've come a long way from the old Oak tree.

Hang out and discuss Java in whatever flavor you choose: J2SE, J2EE, J2ME, Jakarta, and so on.

SECURITY

Lots of bad guys out there—the good guys need help.

Discuss computer and network security issues here. Just don't let anyone else know the answers!

MAC OS X

All about the Zen of OS X.

OS X is both the present and the future for Mac apps. Make suggestions, offer up ideas, or boast about your new hardware.

TECHNOLOGY IN ACTION

Cool things. Fun things.

It's after hours. It's time to play. Whether you're into LEGO® MINDSTORMS™ or turning an old PC into a DVR, this is where technology turns into fun.

OPEN SOURCE

Source code is good; understanding (open) source is better.

Discuss open source technologies and related topics such as PHP, MySQL, Linux, Perl, Apache, Python, and more.

WINDOWS

No defenestration here.

Ask questions about all aspects of Windows programming, get help on Microsoft technologies covered in Apress books, or provide feedback on any Apress Windows book.

HOW TO PARTICIPATE:
Go to the Apress Forums site at **http://forums.apress.com/**.
Click the New User link.